PRAISE FOR
A LIFE ON THE RUN

I extend my heartfelt gratitude to these many contributors of these celebrant testaments for my memoir and for me:

"Dr. John Telford's *A Life on the RUN* is a dazzling story of ardent dedication to racial equity and the best education for every student—and of a rare man in turbulent times."

—*Dr. Deborah Anthony, former director of technology,*
Rochester (Michigan) Community Schools

"*A Life on the RUN* is a spellbinding book that lays it on the line—John Telford is the champion of the underdog!"

—*Dennis Archer, Mayor of Detroit, 1994–2001, and a former*
Associate Justice of the Michigan Supreme Court

"John Telford is a living legend, and his book is *electrifying*. Dr. Telford's lifelong dedication to social equality inspires all of us who seek to make America a true democracy."

—*Prof. Joshua Bassett, director of the Wayne County Community*
College District-sponsored Institute for Social Progress

"In this evocative memoir, trailblazing educator/activist John Telford shows us in gripping personal stories the qualities of courage, imagination, and unrelenting passion he brought to his fight for equality for generations of underserved people. He demonstrates the same rigorous honesty in his writing that marked his fruitful years as a leader in education and social activism. His story is an indispensable addition to our city's rich, embattled history and a call for us to follow in the spirit of his footsteps."

—*Bill Bowles, librarian at Western International*
High School, Detroit Public Schools

"This great book is the legacy of a great teacher—a lasting (but hopefully not a *last*) legacy. Some day the misguided Madison school board will be sorry they didn't keep him as their superintendent, but the misguided and failing Detroit school board will regret even more bitterly that they didn't make him their superintendent when they had the chance to do it. John Telford has taught, coached, guided, and inspired me and countless others like me for fifty years, and he is still doing it today."

—*Reginald "Reggie" Bradford, educator;*
former quarter-mile star, Detroit Pershing High School
and the University of Michigan

"Coach Telford's life story is one of the best books I have ever read, and Coach Telford is one of the best men I have ever known."

"In his panoramic autobiography, John Telford accurately presents himself as a fierce competitor and a miraculous motivator. John first impacted my life in 1960 when I was only sixteen and he was my track coach at Detroit Southeastern High School. As a sixty-six-year-old man who still dreams the 'impossible' dream, I continue to draw inspiration and encouragement from him."

"Dr. Telford was the Barack Obama of Detroit 'back in the day.' He also was my all-time favorite teacher. The way he fought for African-American rights really stands out to me. No matter how many bad things people tried to put in his way, he kept on fighting for us. He is truly a blessing from God."

"An exemplary life for people of all colors to emulate. John Telford is an *urban legend*."

"John Telford—educator, coach, civil-rights crusader, world-class sprinter, unrelenting fighter—has truly lived a rich and productive life that continues to bear fruit. In his unabridged and extremely honest memoir, we are able to share some of his experiences. He has, without question, walked the *walk*. Better yet, he *ran* it!"

"The legendary legacy of a legendary leader."

"This explosive book is *unadulterated dynamite*—a clarion call for radical reform of urban education!"

"Telford's epic fury at the racism and classism that has condemned blacks to inferior education *burns* throughout this riveting book."

"Dr. Telford is a great teacher."

"John Telford doesn't *wait* for justice to happen—he *makes* it happen."

"Coach Telford was built for *speed*—he could outrun any of us. He looked like a white Secretariat. During the racially-charged 1960s, he provided wisdom for our lives after sports and pushed us to get college degrees. This compelling book is his proud story—and it is *our* proud story, too."

"The captivating chapter about Telford's fighter father proves the apple doesn't fall far from the tree. If they had made Telford the superintendent in Detroit any of the several times he offered to do the job, he would have uncovered the shit long before it hit the fan and an emergency financial manager had to be brought in."

"Once one of the fastest men on the planet, John Telford remains a fast and indomitable fighter for human rights. His luminous life story is in turn outraged, droll, scandalous, and *sexy*. Also, his sometimes self-deprecating and dryly ironic humor never fails to make the discerning reader smile."

"A moving, thought-provoking book. Rather than run from the problem, Dr. Telford runs to the *roar!*"

"John Telford has fought relentlessly against racism and intolerance his entire life."

"John Telford's crusades for social justice truly inspire mine."

—*Geoffrey Fieger, celebrated trial lawyer*

"Yes, I must own up to the fact that a *quarter-miler* named John Telford really *did* beat me once in a *1,000-yard* race—but he was smart enough never to race me *again* at that distance! Seriously, though—this book is far more than the memoir of an All-American athlete. It is the memoir of an All-American *man* who throughout his entire life has fought for the rights of *all* Americans."

—*Aaron Z. Gordon, Colonel, U.S. Army (retired),*
Ph.D., former world-record distance-relay runner
at the University of Michigan and former president of
OSAS (Detroit Public Schools' Organization of
School Administrators and Supervisors)

"This is the astounding story of a high-ranking administrator who retired and then actually *came back down* to a 100 percent black inner-city high school to *teach*! Dr. Telford's students at Finney were positively *hypnotized* by him. So were *other* teachers' students, when he went in and spoke to them. He pinned his students' work on boards all over his classroom, and he made that classroom their *haven*. These wild kids would get almost *eerily* quiet whenever he began to speak. He never had to raise his voice. It was a rare sight to behold—his kids would have *killed* for him. As he says in the book, he called them his 'Activist Army'—and that's exactly what they became.

"When John Telford returned to the school after a full year away to deliver a surprise address at their 2009 commencement, the entire graduating class gave him a long and loud *standing ovation* before he even started to speak."

—*Tim Gore, Detroit Finney High School teacher and*
moonlighting Detroit police officer

"Coach Telford has led a life of which *legends* are made."

—*Spencer Haywood, former Pershing High School basketball*
and track star and All-Pro forward in the NBA

"The amazing story of an amazing man who bucked a flawed system and laid his life and career on the line. John Telford inspired me and countless others. He helped me get a track scholarship to college—and I became an electrical engineer. I pray that he *never* stops running his race."

—*Ken Howse, former Michigan high school track*
and cross-country champion and a record-breaker
at the University of Illinois

"A great literary work by a great fighting educator."

—*Mrs. Connie Howse, wife of Ken Howse*

"This exciting book has *everything*—drama, humor, poetry, romance, juicy scandals, sports challenges—and above all, a lifetime of fighting for justice in inner-city schools, suburban board rooms, and down and dirty in Detroit's dangerous streets, defending the rights of the downtrodden and disenfranchised. John Telford has done it all."

—Dr. Walter Jenkins, former Detroit Miller High School and
Wayne State University track and football star, former Detroit Lion,
and retired Detroit high school principal and executive director

"John Telford made me dare to *dream*."

—Kevin Johnson (now Dr. Kevin Johnson),
a former residential director at Wolverine Human Services
who now directs Detroit's philanthropic Phoenix Friendship House

"The sensational saga of a visionary civil rights crusader. As Professor john powell writes in the *Introduction* to the book, John Telford is the only retired deputy school superintendent in America—black or white, urban or suburban—who dared to return to an inner-city high school to teach, and he was still doing it in his seventies, when we were colleagues at Finney High. This is the captivating story of his challenged boyhood, his triumphant youth, and his memorably embattled older years."

—Keith Johnson, president, Detroit Federation of Teachers

"A unique historical perspective—a lifelong mission fueled with passion to level the playing field."

—Janine Kateff, retired principal,
Long Meadow School in Rochester, Michigan

"John Telford is an icon from the past who is now being rediscovered by the masses. This book is his second coming-out party for him to take his rightful place among the giants."

—Dr. Stuart Kirschenbaum, Boxing Commissioner,
State of Michigan, 1981–92

"A great man tells his life story. John Telford is simply a civil-rights *giant*."

—Dr. John Kline, president,
Black Legends of Professional Basketball
and a former Harlem Globetrotter

"This is a *must read* for those who are working toward America becoming a more *just* society."

—Dr. Daniel Krichbaum, chief operating officer for Michigan
Governor Jennifer Granholm and a former executive director
of the National Conference for Community and Justice

"John Telford is THE champion of minority rights."

—*Richard Lobenthal, midwest director (retired),*
Anti-Defamation League

"This book is a *blockbuster*. John has valiantly battled bigotry all his life."

—*Sam Logan, publisher of the Detroit-based*
Michigan Chronicle, *the state's oldest and largest*
African-American-owned newspaper

"Dr. Telford is our Champion for Truth and Justice. His book is a blueprint any true teacher must follow."

—*Jeffrey May, Jr., motivational speaker*

"Dr. Telford always put his students first, sometimes at the risk of his own safety. He would confront hoodlums who came into the school from outside that even some *security guards* backed away from. I also saw him save some tough kids that everyone else had given up on. His life story in schools sets a sterling example for all of us to follow."

—*Anthony Merritt, senior security officer,*
Detroit Finney High School

"An insider's view of the decline of Detroit and its schools, with common-sense solutions to reverse the decline—in Detroit and throughout urban America. Educators, activists, and athletes will *love* this book."

—*Maureen Meuser, librarian at Detroit Finney High School*

"Telford's bare-knuckled prose leaves a welt above the eye of racism, arrogance, and cruelty—and it jabs the noses of inept and self-serving administrators. This fast-paced book will be appreciated by educators, activists, and anyone seeking to understand the decline of Detroit and her schools during the post-war period."

—*John Mohn, DPS custodian and philosopher*

"A fearless street fighter his entire life, John Telford has written the best memoir on Detroit I've ever read—a delightful and scandalous tale. He explicitly depicts the daily battles for respect and survival in the city's toughest schools and neighborhoods."

—*Anthony Neely, press secretary and*
publicist for two Detroit mayors

"Here is the exciting, fighting saga of one of America's top human rights pioneers. John Telford evolved from street thug to world-class track champion to heroic inner-city educator to become the clarion conscience of Rochester's suburban elite, Detroit's classist and corrupt school 'leaders,' and finally, Madison's blue-collar racists. You won't put this book down."

—*Sgt. Tom Nelson, West Bloomfield, Michigan,*
Police Department (retired); columnist;
CEO of Great Lakes Pet Supply (retired); and MENSA member

"John Telford saved my life. Now as I read the courageous story of *his* life, he inspires me once again to do great deeds for children."

—*Mike Oldham, charter school administrator,*
Academy of Warren (Michigan);
former Rose Bowl and Super Bowl player

"John Telford is the Jonathan Kozol of the high school. He is also an educationally innovative genius."

—*Greg Owens, principal (retired),*
Reuther Middle School in Rochester

(Note: Mr. Owens died at sixty-eight on July 8, 2009—just before this book went to press. He was a rare man and a loyal friend, and I shall miss him every single day that remains to me on this earth.)

"Dr. John Telford is a *rebel*, a *renegade*, and a *renaissance man*. He began his journey as a champion sprinter but found his true calling as a champion of equal education for all. This is a tough and honest account of his life and his mission to save three generations of students. You'll find tears, laughter, and inspiration in every chapter."

—*Huel Perkins, Fox 2 TV anchor, Metro Detroit*

"*A Life on the RUN* is more than just the life story of a great man. It is also great literature. In addition to everything else this amazing athlete/activist has done, he tells his spellbinding story with an eloquence and style which hauntingly evoke the eloquence and style of the recently deceased writer John Updike."

—*Robert Plumpe, defense attorney;*
board member, the Detroit-based Team for Justice

"A mentor of mentors—Dr. Telford loved his students *unconditionally*. They knew he 'had their back'—and they had *his* back, too."

—*David Points, Commander (retired), United States Navy;*
retiring teacher, Detroit Finney High School

"Throughout the years, John Telford's achievements and philosophy have had an inspirational impact on my own—as effected most recently when as a suburban school superintendent he stood steadfast in the fearsome face of racism."

*—Prof. john a. powell, who—in addition to directing the
Kirwan Institute for the Study of Race and Ethnicity at
The Ohio State University and holding the University's Chair on
Civil Rights and Civil Liberties—is a former national legal director
of the ACLU, a former professor of law at Harvard University,
and the founder and former director of the National Institute on Race and
Poverty headquartered at the University of Minnesota School of Law*

"If you care about the future of America's black children, you will *memorize* parts of this powerful book."

*—Charlie Primas, Wayne State University All-American,
former Harlem Globetrotter, and retired principal of a Detroit public
school housed at the Wayne County Juvenile Detention Facility*

"A sensational story engagingly written by a prodigious teacher, administrator, athlete—and *lover*! This captivating book is filled to the brim with Dr. Telford's passionate and often poignant personal experiences, along with his wealth of institutional knowledge and transformative insights."

—Dr. James E. Ray, superintendent (retired), Flint, Michigan Schools

"Telford is the *Superman* of Education—he fights for Truth, Justice, and the American Way. I want my children and my children's children to read this memorable profile in courage and take it to heart."

*—Marvin Rubin, former principal,
Van Hoosen Middle School, Rochester, Michigan*

"An inspiring and unique book. Telford was a great athlete and scholar—and a master teacher and administrator. Today, he remains a selfless servant for all humanity."

*—Lamont Satchel, former interim superintendent,
Detroit Public Schools*

"*A Life on the RUN* is both the chronicling of a phenomenal trailblazer's tale and an important guide for how one can exhibit an unbridled adherence to righteousness even in the face of tribulation and retribution. This book vividly reveals what most of us already know—that John lives by *love*, teaches with *heart*, speaks his *mind*, and does it all without fear of *anyone* or *anything*. If you seek to be so similarly disposed and want to know how to do it, then read this treasure of a treatise from a *true practitioner*."

*—Rev. Horace L. Sheffield III,
Detroit Association of Black Organizations*

"This book is a *masterpiece*. It is also a *must read* for anyone interested in the evolution and revolution of equality in our time. Dr. John Telford's life has been a life boldly lived on front-line duty in the ongoing fight for social justice. In this masterful memoir, he provocatively captures the essence of his engagement with the forces of progress and the forces of entrenchment—and *retrenchment*."

—*Rabbi Arnie Sleutelberg of*
Congregation Shir Tikvah, *Troy, Michigan*

"A great book!"

—*Dr. David Snead,*
former Detroit Public Schools superintendent

"While Telford dodges the label 'radical,' he is far more than a bedrock liberal."

—*Caleb Southworth, former editor,*
The Metro Times, *Detroit and Ann Arbor*

"John doesn't hesitate to fight the white *and* the black establishment when they aren't about *kids*. How many teachers, black or white, do you know whose black *and* white students—new and old—still call him every day, not only to *thank* him, but just to come and *hang out* with him? I'm proud of my African heritage, but I'm *proudest* to have John for my husband and lover. He still has those million-dollar legs—it's understandable why women chase him—but they'd better *stay away* (or else he'd better use those two swift legs of his to run *away* fast).

"John will always be the *Man*, the *Myth*, the Legend!"

—*Mrs. Gina Telford, artist, actress, activist,*
and former flight attendant

"The brave tale of a noble knight who dons armor to do battle for fairness and light in a dark world which hasn't yet recognized that 'together we *stand*, divided we *fall*'."

—*Dr, Terry Truvillion, long-time Detroit principal,*
and one of the first women to receive the
Coleman A. Young Educator of the Year Award

"John Telford's got *guts*."

—*Dr. Carl Wagner, principal, Madison High School*
Madison Heights, Michigan

"John Telford stands for what's *right*—and he's *tough*."

—*Alvin Ward, former principal, Detroit Finney High School;*
now principal, Detroit Kettering High School

"A fast life in the fast lanes of equality and justice—and also of *amour*! Anyone with a *heart* has to read this book!"

—*Sam Washington, Jr., son of the Michigan Sports Hall of Famer*

"Some call John Telford wild, a loose cannon, even *crazy*—but he *aims* his cannon straight at the perpetrators of the educational genocide of black children. And while he has fought white racists all his life, those administrators and board members whom he calls the 'elitist black *classists*' who exploit impoverished black children fear him, as well—and he gives them plenty of *reason* to fear him."

—*Tom Watkins, Michigan's state superintendent of public instruction from 2001 until 2005, now a business and education consultant in the U.S. and China*

"A legendary educational leader, activist, athlete, musician, painter, and poet has brought us his fascinating story we've all been waiting for!"

—*Dr. William Waun, general director of Secondary Education (retired), Rochester (Michigan) Community Schools*

"This resounding, bitingly fierce encomium for racial justice is also often bitingly and incredibly *funny*. It's also rich, educational, and enlightening. This book should be on *everyone's* coffee table."

—*Heaster Wheeler, director, Detroit NAACP*

"Telford is a daring Don Quixote who tackles the big issues."

—*Dan White, assistant superintendent (retired), Bloomfield Hills (Michigan) schools*

"Dr. Telford's journey illustrates his fight for justice, his passion for possibility, and his tenacious spirit to challenge the status quo and effect change in urban and suburban education. His is a story for the ages."

—*Kenyetta Wilbourn-Snapp, principal, Detroit Denby High School*

"This captivating book is a *classic*. John Telford was a great athlete, and he remains a great *integrationist*, a great *community catalyst*, and above all, a great *man*."

—*Robert E. Wollack, CEO, Wolverine Human Services, Detroit and Vassar, Michigan*

"The consummate proponent of civil rights, John Telford is an unforgiving advocate for the underdog. He will face down anyone who wields power wrongfully. What he *writes*, he *lives*."

—*Willie Wooten, department head of Language Arts (retired), Detroit Southwestern High School*

"I have an *urgent message* for any person who will *dare* to read <u>*every word*</u> of *A Life on the RUN*: I challenge you <u>*not*</u> to be intrigued and <u>*not*</u> to have your spirit moved by this book! John Telford isn't *just* a brilliant writer. He isn't *just* a gargantuan educator. He isn't *just* a former Olympic-level athlete, nor <u>*only*</u> an unrelenting defender of civil rights and children's rights. John Telford is an <u>*archangel*</u> wielding a <u>*shining sword of social justice*</u>, singlehandedly waging his holy war against the hypocrisy and horror of racism in America. Cutting through the excuses and opposition of those who maim, murder, and molest minorities, he protects those among us who are less-equipped to defend our God-given right to life and liberty in this so-called 'greatest country on earth.'

"Dr. John Telford's life story is a testament to his courage under fire and his spiritual and physical prowess, while also retaining his *humble <u>humanity</u>*. This isn't the story of a big celebrity or superstar or self-professed icon—it's the story of a *real* hero. It's also the story of a real *man*.

"I love you, Doc!"

—*Ray Wright, Detroit and Pontiac activist*
and advocate for youth

"*Wow*! I love you, too, Ray.

I now invite the righteous reader to *read righteously on*, in order to learn what these many preceding accolades are *all about*, hopefully to *become inspired*, and also to become righteously *angry*, righteously *enlightened*, and perhaps even righteously *illuminated* . . .

> —John Telford, duly designated *archangel* and *wielder* of a *shining*
> *sword of social justice*, per the hyperbolic last testifier, Ray Wright
> (—"*Because of the oppression of the weak . . ., I will now arise,*" *saith the*
> *Lord*, "*and I will protect them . . .*" – Psalms 12:5)

A Life on the RUN

Seeking and Safeguarding Social Justice

Dr. John Telford

HARMONIE PARK PRESS
Sterling Heights, Michigan

Author's Note:
In order not to hurt or embarrass anyone
(and to preclude possible lawsuits),
some names in this book have been omitted or changed.

© 2010 by Dr. John Telford
Printed and bound in the United States of America

Published by
Harmonie Park Press
Liberty Professional Center
35675 Mound Road
Sterling Heights, Michigan 48310–4727
www.harmonieparkpress.com

ISBN 0-89990-149-2 (alk. paper)
ISBN 978-089990-149-7

Library of Congress Cataloging-in-Publication Data

Telford, John, 1936-
   A life on the run : seeking and safeguarding social justice / By John Telford.
       p. cm.
   Includes index.
   ISBN 0-89990-149-2 (alk. paper)
   1. Telford, John, 1936– 2. Teachers—Michigan—Detroit—Biography. 3. School
superintendents—Michigan—Detroit—Biography. 4. Social justice—Michigan—Detroit. 5.
Public schools—Michigan—Detroit. 6. Detroit (Mich.)—Race relations. 7. Detroit
(Mich.)—Social conditions. I. Title.
   LA2317.T38T45 2010
   371.10092—dc22
   [B]
                                                              2009032073

*I dedicate this book to **Gina Telford**, the gorgeous African/Irish-American artist who took the precarious step of marrying this old maverick—her chronological elder by twenty-six tumultuous years.*

*I also dedicate it to my **teammates** alive and dead—and to the **teachers**, **administrators**, and **other insurgents** I've worked and played with who have toiled intrepidly in the trenches to enlighten the unenlightened and rally the righteous rebels.*

*I dedicate it, as well, to my **students, children,** and **grandchildren** I have lived for—and through whom I will always live. They embody my prayed-for future for an eternally strong and more egalitarian America.*

*Finally, I dedicate it to my mother, Detroit kindergarten teacher **Helen Telford** (1907–98) and to my father, **John "Scotty" Telford** (1902–87)—that Scotland-born boxer, bodyguard, union steward, coal miner, and defender of the defenseless —who was far and away the toughest true activist I ever knew, and whose ancestral Code I have done my utmost to uphold.*

"Mama, please tell us why we had to die."
"Children, that's easy—I can tell you why:
You died so the junkies can smoke their crack,
And the dope-house dealers can make their 'jack,'
And the politicians can sell their votes,
And the pimps can preen in their long fur coats,
And the crooked cops can collect their pay,
And the 'corporate cats' can run away,
And the school officials can promote their friends
While the kids don't get any books or pens,
And the drive-by shooters can perfect their aim
As the filthiest rappers get in halls of fame,
And the teenaged truants can watch TV
Or lie in the bed and catch HIV,
And the high-school dropouts can 'act the fool,'
And your sisters can be scared to walk to school . . .
And so the Lord can grant your mama the indomitable soul
To somehow staunch this tragic trauma—like a bleeding bullet hole."

CONTENTS

Contents

INTRODUCTION

Professor *JOHN A. POWELL*, *Executive Director*
Kirwan Institute for the Study of Race and Ethnicity
The Ohio State University

A Life on the RUN is a triumphant tale of teaching, fighting, loving, racing, civil-*righteous* rebellion, and raw courage. Once you start reading this spellbinding book, you won't stop. Dr. John Telford lays it on the line in exciting activist/educator style—like the exciting activist/educator he is.

An amateur boxer and world-ranked sprinter who outran Olympic champions in his youth, John Telford is the only retired deputy school superintendent in *all of America*—urban or suburban, white or black—who dared to return to teach in the inner city. He did it for *seven years* in three of the toughest high schools in the toughest town in America, and he was still doing it in his *seventies*!

Inspirationally sprinkled here and there throughout these pages are his clear and masterful solutions to the myriad social problems America faces in the twenty-first century in and out of academe.

Dr. Telford asked me to write this Introduction to what he anticipates many readers may call his "paean of self-praise"—but if this book is a *paean of self-praise*, that *praise* was *well-earned*: Dr. John Telford is nothing less than a *living legend* among human-rights activists and educators in the Detroit metropolitan area. Also, he bluntly acknowledges some rather *un*-praiseworthy amatory transgressions he committed that painfully affected his life and career. If anything, he is a bit *too* hard on himself, and perhaps a bit too *easy* on others who deserted him under fire or allowed him to *be* fired and then neglected to rehire him when they had the chance.

Telford's viscerally egalitarian philosophy and teachings helped shape mine when I was his student and runner at Detroit Southeastern High School in the early 1960s. Mine have in turn influenced *his*—as evidenced by his quoting me extensively in his *Prologue* and *Epilogue*, and elsewhere in this book.

His panoramic seventy-year saga—from his gritty Detroit boyhood to his days as a champion sprinter and his years as a caring teacher and maverick administrator—presents a captivating historic perspective of the civil-rights movement in urban and suburban schools and his key role in that movement.

In the book's title, *RUN* is actually a mere metaphor. The book is less about John Telford's *running*—or about his *romances*—than it is about his having burst out of the starting blocks nearly three quarters of a century ago to begin his long run *seeking and safeguarding social justice*.

Here follows his truly amazing story.

IN PURSUIT OF A
DREAM DEFERRED

We must <u>undermine</u> the <u>mind</u> <u>molesters</u>—and, if necessary,
<u>dismember</u> them as well.

Your venerable old author wrote the earliest version of this book's frontispiece poem, *Mama, Please Tell Us Why We Had To Die*, in 1986 when I was the
Assistant Superintendent of Schools in the far-northern Detroit suburb of
Rochester, Michigan. Nineteen eighty-six was a watershed year for children's
deaths by gunfire in Detroit, where I was born in the mid-1930s at the height
of the Great Depression, raised in the 1930s and 1940s, and publicly educated
(and exceedingly *well*-educated, I might add) in the 1940s and 1950s.

It was during the 1930s and 1940s (specifically between 1936 and 1949)
that National City Lines, a holding company sponsored and funded by General
Motors, Firestone, and Standard Oil, successfully conspired to buy out more
than one hundred electric surface transit systems in Detroit and forty-four
other cities. The company replaced them with GM buses, incidentally helping
to set the stage for George W. Bush's ruinous Iraq War half a century later and
an escalating oil crisis and plummeting stock-market crash that has pushed
much of the nation, including the 90 percent of inner-city families in Detroit
and throughout the country who are already in dire financial trouble, over
the precipice of insolvency and precipitated the government's bailout of Wall
Street. Ironically, as I write this in 2009, that series of events that began
so long ago may also have—God forbid—spelled the impending decline of
modern-day General Motors and the entire American automobile industry,

our once-formidable "Arsenal of Democracy."

How, you ask, could a criminal corporate conspiracy of so many faded decades ago possibly have helped to generate these calamities, and cause today's children in Detroit and other inner cities to die by gunfire and their bodies and minds to be molested by disintegrating families and failing schools? To discover and understand the specific answers to that question, as well as the answers to other similar questions involving similarly nefarious corporate, governmental, academic, political, and social scenarios I am going to give you, you will need to "connect the dots" as you digest this entire book.

I dedicated *Mama* to the forty-six Detroit youngsters who died in 1986 and to the many others whose minds are being molested and whose spirits are dying *every year* and *every day*—*in* and *out* of Detroit's public schools, as well as in almost every urban school in the United States of America.

This malodorous molestation of untold thousands of black children's minds, bodies, and lives—and those of brown children, too—is still being perpetrated throughout our home-grown urban ghetto bordered by Alter Road, Eight Mile Road, Telegraph Road, and that wide strait known as the Detroit River, whose swift current separates the Canadian city of Windsor from its far less clean and far more violent American sister city. This same malevolent molestation is being perpetrated in other ghettos across the land, as well as *outside* the confines of those ghettos—pervasive circumstances that I will also address in this book.

I first published *Mama* in my weekly *Telford's Telescope* column in the Detroit-based, African-American-owned *Michigan FrontPAGE* newspaper on May 10, 2002, as a topical lead-in about the then-recent shooting deaths of yet four *more* Detroit children—Cherrell Thomas, Brianna Caddell, Ajanee Pollard, and Destinee Thomas. Oftentimes we can express turbulent and bitterly ironic emotions like this *in poetry* that are far harder to articulate *in prose*. That is what some Detroit high school students did for a poetry contest in 2002 on the topic of peace that was sponsored by SOSAD (Save Our Sons and Daughters) for which I served as a judge. The top three poets were adjudged to be Sansa Sanyika of the Detroit High School of Fine and Performing Arts, Cameron Gaither of Cody High School, and James Moody of Finney High School.

Sansa wrote, "Trapped in a storm of madness, our people hunger for peace." Cameron asked, "Why am I here, the stench of death in the air?" In another poem he observed, "Police storm our blocks, pulling Glocks." James defined peace as "Love in a relation, city, state, or nation." *Peace*, he added, is "just another word . . . for *reconciliation*."

Other worthy contestants wrote, "We come from houses with no fathers, left to believe the streets are *right—schoolboy* by day, *menace* by *night*" (Aaron Peoples, Denby High); "Why is there blood on our feet instead of peace in the street?" (Raquel Bynum, Cody); "Teens today are a disaster— / There's never love or any laughter," and "Why can't there be a day without killing on the news, / Or people getting AIDS, / Or kids with bad grades?" (Monique Clay, Cody); "I don't know what's going wrong: / All these rappers with bad songs" (Sharda Perry, Cody); "Thirty percent of our males / End up in the jails" (Danyelle Howard, Cody); "The streets are just so bad, you can't go out and *play*— / Before you even know it, someone's *shot* again today" (Shakara Charley, Cody); "No peace on the street is really scary, / 'Cause you don't know *who* you're going to bury" (Valencia Washington, Cody).

Thirty-one years before I wrote the initial, shorter version of *Mama*, I was a nascent nineteen-year-old sophomore at Wayne State University running on a renowned relay team often anchored either by me or by a superb black sprinter named Cliff Hatcher—my elder by nearly three years—whose then-recent high school exploits were already legendary. Within the previous two years, Cliff and I had become as close as brothers and were so to remain for the next fifty-two—until his death.

It was the summer of 1955, the year after *Brown vs. Board of Education* had declared "separate but equal" to be inherently *unequal*, and the Mississippi murder of a black teenager from Chicago who was five years younger than me moved me to write *this* poem, which made its public debut in a little local periodical called *Nexus*:

> *Beneath a hill,*
> *In blackest chill,*
> *With peristaltic, steady drill,*
> *Blind crawlthings crawl and feed and fill*
> *On what is all of Emmett Till.*
>
> *Above the mound, the thundersounding voices cry:*
> *"He didn't die!"*

> *Though thundercries may sunder skies,*
> *No thundersound's heard underground.*
> *No lightning leaps*
> *Where Emmett sleeps.*

Twenty years later, I would add another stanza:

> *Deep thunderbolts must rend the skies*
> *Before the Movement can revive.*
> *Then lightning bolts will bend the skies*
> *As Emmett rises, re-alive!*

In perusing all of the preceding pain-filled poems or snatches of poems and pondering their poignant yet sometimes hopeful themes, we can conclude that the horrors of what has happened in America to African-Americans for the past four centuries and projected their racist residue into the most recent *half*-century can't be blamed on America's urban schools. Still, God knows I've laid plenty of *partial* blame on them in a thousand newspaper columns and many a radio and TV show throughout decades past. I did this particularly in the process of specifically targeting the most recent rapacious "leadership" of *Detroit's* failing schools as the country's most flagrant example of K-12 administrative incompetence and corruption, as U.S. Secretary of Education Arne Duncan recently noted. The unequal funding of urban vis-à-vis suburban schools which generations of state legislators have allowed to occur, plus deteriorated socio-economic conditions in urban ghettos throughout the country, bear much of the blame as well.

Nonetheless, despite the rare level of excellence attained by those very few Detroit Public School scholar/poets whose hauntingly heart-breaking verse I have excerpted in the preceding, *the following three well-documented and irrefutable facts remain*:

1. America's children of color continue to be exploited overwhelmingly by an elitist "educational" hierarchy that is dedicated to its own enrichment and aggrandizement rather than being dedicated to the children.

2. Americans of color continue to be disproportionately exploited by the dissolute white-corporate power structure whose stranglehold continues to clutch our country in an agonizing death grip that affects minorities first and worst.

3. Americans of color continue to be victimized by pervasive discrimination —both overt and covert, both racist and classist.

Traditional public K-12 education in Michigan in *general,* in the tri-county region of Wayne, Oakland, and Macomb in *particular,* and most *specifically* in the vast majority of the *public schools in Detroit, has under-educated ENTIRE GENERATIONS of its African-American and Latino students.* This is of course the case in most ghetto schools throughout America, as well.

Detroit harbors and is home to the state's largest school district in its largest city. This under-education of Detroit's public school students has had a devastatingly engrained and in fact *mind-molestful* effect on those un-told generations. It has also caused a less-recognized but similar effect on the concurrent generations of *all* Michigan children. While the ascension of Barack Obama to the American presidency is a landmark victory for racial and social justice, *a whole lot of statewide and nationwide egalitarian activism* still remains to be *activated*—particularly as that *activism* relates to black and brown children's desperate and as-yet-unmet need to become adequately educated!

I suspect that a few of you upstanding Detroiters and Michiganders and indeed, some of you Americans who dwell *beyond* the state of Michigan might be tempted to ask (and you are certainly *entitled* to ask) the following questions:

"*Whatever* in the *world* could possibly *qualify* this old John Telford dude to make such sweepingly damning statements about our *city* and our *state,* and even about our *country's* good old banks-and-Wall-Street-bailings-out, corporate-collusive political leaders—and still expect to be taken *seriously*??!!

"For pity's sake, doesn't old Telford *understand* that good old George W.'s bloody invasion of Iraq was righteous and pre-emptive and not about *oil*?

Doesn't he *know* that no black or Latino child is going hungry and homeless and undereducated in this munificent country? Doesn't he *grasp the fact* that every red-blooded American who wants a job can *get* one and *keep* one if he or she really *wants* to work? (For goodness' sake, that old Telford fellow doesn't even seem to understand that building more *prisons* is a good, *profitable* thing for America to do!)

"Also, doesn't the dummy know that actors and athletes and rappers and network news anchors and other such cerebral entertainers no longer get paid *obscene amounts of money*, and that inner-city teachers and social workers in Detroit and all across the land are no longer being *laid off*, and that these teachers and social workers are *underpaid no longer*, and that they no longer have a zillion supervisors in central offices making six-figure salaries to *mismanage their schools*—and that their class sizes are no longer ballooning *astronomically*?

"Doesn't he even realize that our cities and towns and neighborhoods and schools and churches and families are fully *racially integrated* now— all throughout Detroit's tri-county area, the state of Michigan, and the *other* forty-nine states?? Doesn't he also see that we finally have a *color-blind* and *classless society* in America? (After all, we just elected our first black president, didn't we?)

"Can't that old renegade Telford see or know or realize or understand *any* of this at *all*?? '*Mind molesters*,' indeed! That dumb Telford has *absolutely no qualifications* to say any of this, anyway, or to make all of those other far-left-wing pronouncements he's always foisting on us. The old reprobate renegade has just *got* to be *crazy*!"

Well, yes. The old reprobate renegade respectfully submits that the racial injustices in our city, state, and nation have been *more* than enough—over time— to drive all truly *just* men and women *just* a little crazy, regardless of their racial heritage. I have lived as an urban student and worked as an urban and suburban and again *urban* educator for a *lifetime*, and I will share with you the totality of that long and enlightening run that has gradually and pain-stakingly *qualified* me to say the things I am about to say about the problems involving racial and social justice in Detroit and Michigan and the rest of America in the chapters to come. I will also offer *solutions* to those problems.

John powell, my Southeastern High School student and runner and later the ACLU's national legal director (who wrote the eloquent *Introduction* to this tumultuous tome), proclaimed in a book he edited with Gavin Kearney and Vina Kay entitled *In Pursuit of a Dream Deferred* (Peter Lang Publishing, Inc., New York, 2001):

> America cannot afford to maintain two societies, white and minority, separated by race, class, and space. Nor can it afford to waste the potential of any of our children simply because they live in the forgotten parts of our urban centers. None of us can afford to turn our backs on the lawful imperative of *Brown vs. Board of Education*. We must understand *Brown* to require the integration of two societies into one not by assimilating one into the other, but by breaking down the barriers that prevent the two from enriching one another.

Yet *racist* white Americans continue to resist and reject that lawful imperative. Despite the landmark election of non-white Barack Obama to the presidency of the United States by non-white America with the overwhelming backing of *non*-racist *white* Americans, the *racist* part of white America's rank underbelly and descending intestine *remains*, spewing its excreta on black Americans. So, too, does the well-fed overbelly of bourgeois, *classist black* America likewise reject its economically lower-class black brothers and sisters and eject *its* excretory offal upon *them*!

If I've aroused your righteous outrage sufficiently for you to turn the page to Chapter One, you will learn how and why I began to care so deeply about the plight of black Americans, and I will try to answer your question regarding my qualifications to make my "sweepingly damning statements." In later chapters, I will offer you ample verification not only *for* and *of* these statements, but also for my *pronouncements-to-come* regarding the egregious *under-education* of Detroit's, Michigan's, and America's African-American youth that *remains the case today*—to the socio-economic detriment of *all* Americans. I will also offer some surprisingly simple remedies for these deeply ingrained and historic inequities that continue to endanger our democracy.

I challenge you to race beside me on tracks in America and Europe, and through the meanest streets of inner Detroit—down an unforgiving but exhilarating road where for three quarters of a century I *ran* and *fought* and ran and fought *again*, like an animal that runs and fights every day and night of its life.

That road is peopled with villains and heroes—some black and some white. Along the way, it's dotted with school districts and schools—some nearly all black and some nearly all white, some relatively affluent and many crushingly impoverished. Regardless of their social and economic circumstances, the students in these schools and school districts all *want* in some way. What most of the black students want but haven't got are healthy mental and physical growth, peace with justice, and real loving fathers in their homes.

Whether you are black or white, if you have read this far, I know you're daring and caring enough to come now and run with me down my hard but exciting road that began so long ago yet seemingly had *barely begun* before it now has neared its end. I promise that when you come and run with me, you'll never think or act in your same entire old way again.

We're on our marks. We're *set* . . . Bang!

The Celestial Starter has sent us off and running. . . .

A Life
on the RUN

Seeking and Safeguarding Social Justice

CHAPTER ONE

SIXTEENTH STREET

"The deadliest of all possible sins is the mutilation of a child's spirit."

—*Erik Erickson*

To begin, I came up on Detroit's *Sixteenth Street*, at *McGraw*.

Now, no one could ever mistake the corner of Detroit's Sixteenth Street at McGraw for your typical super-suburban crossing such as, for example, *Squirrel Road at University Drive*—nor for, say, *Long Lake Road at Cranbrook Road*, nor even *Jefferson Avenue at Fisher Road*. Obviously, Rochester Hills isn't Detroit, and the bounteous Bloomfields aren't either—nor, certainly, are the *grossly-*affluent *Grosse* Pointes. Far from it. Despite their geographic proximity to once-mighty Motown, from a socio-economic perspective, Rochester Hills and the Bloomfields and the Grosse Pointes might as well be on *Uranus*. This was certainly the case for most of the region in the 1940s, and it remains even more the case for almost all the region today.

By the late 1940s, the only white kids left in my K-8 elementary school— Estabrook, a grim, grimy nineteenth-century edifice at Linwood and McGraw in west-central Detroit—were poor southern migrants, or even poorer immigrants from Ireland, Scotland, Italy, eastern Europe, and the Scandinavian countries. They also included the children of a few lower-class, die-hard Rooseveltian Democrats like my four naturalized-American grandparents and like my mother Helen, who spoke only Danish until she was five (and who had *also* attended Estabrook), and like my father, John "Scotty" Telford, a Scotland-born ex-coal miner and prizefighter who at five foot eight and 158 pounds had been UAW president Walter Reuther's smallest and toughest bodyguard. He was fired from that job for drinking—but drunk or sober, my father remained an un-relenting champion of civil rights before anyone had ever thought to coin the term. My father and his father steadfastly protected their near-west-side Detroit neighborhood's weak and meek—white or black—and they did it with violence, if necessary. (My dad also protected his own two nubile sisters, Letty and Margaret—who didn't always *want* to be protected.)

A full seventy years before there ever were Hollywood movies called *Braveheart* or *Rob Roy*, John "Scotty" Telford and Frank Telford the Elder began to drum their ancestral homeland's ancient William Wallace Code into my hard little Telfordian head. They made me recite the Robert Burns poem that began, "Scots wha' hae wi' Wallace bled . . ." so many times that I was murmuring it as I went to sleep at night and again when I was awakening in the morning. A primary precept of that ancient Code was that women were *never* to be physically harmed, for *any* reason, *ever*—and they were to be *defended* (and if need be, *avenged*)—as were children, animals, and the elderly and infirm.

<u>*Three*</u> *relevant acts of interracial brotherhood* in my extensive store of recollec-tions about the egalitarian behaviors of my freedom-fighter father highlight what he was, and what he molded me to become. I want to share these three incidents with you because not only did they help make me the man I have been (or have *tried* to be) for the past half-century and more—they also became the ultimate inspiration for this book.

My father's <u>*first*</u> *relevant act of interracial brotherhood* that I want to tell you about occurred in the decrepit Transport Bar on McGraw. The old saloon had a cheap glass cinderblock façade and was being bought at the time at a usurious mortgage rate by an African-American man in his late thirties. He had been condemned to languish permanently in a wheelchair and diapers as a result of a factory accident that had happened when he was a co-worker of my father's on the line at the old Packard automobile plant. My father had recently been fired for drinking on that job and was therefore temporarily out of work—so he had made spur-of-the-moment plans to bring me into that little bistro one autumn day in 1941 to show me off to his paraplegic bartender buddy when I was really supposed to be in my mostly boring kindergarten class.

Initially, that kindergarten class and the company of my contemporaries had mildly amused me for maybe two or three days—but after that, I had decided it was time for me to do something new and intriguing somewhere else. When I found out that I *couldn't*—that I had to come and sit on this little oilcloth pad on the floor for much of the afternoon into the *infinite future*—a deep melancholy overwhelmed me.

Thus, it was that when I found out that my father was going to sign me out and liberate me for this wonderful afternoon, my delight was boundless. That cramped kindergarten room, I recall, smelled clingingly of Clorox, and it had a single shelf with peeling dark blue paint whereupon sat two chipped, ugly orange, dented airplanes of heavy tin for me and a motley conglomerate of other little gremlins to play with and share. It held little else of interest except for a perky student teacher named Miss Johnson and frustratingly infrequent but tantalizing opportunities to tug on Bonnie Manhart's two long, dark, bonny braids.

When I was about two, before my dad ever took me to the Transport Bar, I thought the Transport was an *airplane*, because I had a toy transport plane—so I connected the word *plane* with *transport*. My father was always telling my mother, "I'm going over to the Transport for a while"—and I wanted to see the airplane, so I kept bugging him to take me to see it, but in those earliest days he said I was too little. He didn't figure out until much later that his little son thought that the Transport *Bar* was a transport *plane*.

On that early autumn day when I was five years old, my father proudly sat me up on the Transport Bar's ebony countertop and was about to present me to the paraplegic bar owner with a flourish when two drunken white men lurched in. One of them reached out and squeezed a shapely buttock of the lissome black barmaid, who was the wife of the bar owner. Having experienced similar situations while in my father's presence and thus fully anticipating what was about to happen, I slid off the countertop and hid under a table.

From this place of retreat, I soon received a demonstrative biology/anatomy lesson in *pure impact pathology* from my fighter father: I found myself staring with more than a modicum of truly *clinical* fascination directly down into the twitching, unconscious countenance of one of the two men. He was sprawled supine on the barroom floor with his freshly flattened nose less than twelve inches from mine—my dauntless daddy had knocked him cold with a quick right cross. The other interloper—whom my father had also felled—scrambled to his feet and fled. The ancestral Code had been efficiently applied.

Clutching the separate mouthpiece from one of those old wall phones still in vogue in the 1930s and into the '40s, the rattled barmaid dialed the police, a pair of which arrived almost immediately, scooped up the one prostrate fellow remaining, and lugged him—still groggy—out the door like so much dead meat. My father leaned down with his finger over his lips (a familiar gesture from him) and, with blood bubbling from a cut inside his left ear, mumbled to me conspiratorially, "We won't tell *Mother* about this."

Even though I was only five, I remember responding, "Okay, we *won't*— but maybe you better wash that *blood* off your ear."

A few nights later, my father staggered home drunk and fell asleep in his favorite chair, setting its thick upholstery afire with a still-lit cigarette. My mother and I and my four-year-old cousin Ruth Ann awoke to a smoky house— and my mother led us down the stairs and out the back door into the yard. I ran out through the gate and down the alley and asked an old night-owl neighbor man everyone called "Uncle Joe" who was sitting smoking a pipe on his back porch to call the fire department. (We had no phone then.) He did, they came, and the fire was quickly doused—but the linoleum kitchen floor, where my father had ripped off his flaming shirt and thrown it down, had a huge charred hole in it.

The firemen took my father (under protest) to the old Providence Hospital on West Grand Boulevard at Fifteenth Street, where he stayed for a month. He was then moved across the street and a few blocks east to Henry Ford Hospital for seven *more* months of sad sobriety, enduring multiple skin grafts from his legs onto his right bicep, side, and shoulder. The bar owner's wife was one of the folks—along with several of his co-workers, black and white, as well as one recently immigrated Korean man—who donated blood to him.

He also caught pneumonia and nearly died. As he lay helpless in his hospital bed, a sadistic orderly frequently tickled the soles of his extremely ticklish feet—he later vowed that if he ever encountered that orderly again, he would do things to the orderly that the orderly wouldn't enjoy.

To digress: During the time Dad was suffering in the hospital, we had to rent out the house to a large and destructive Scottish family named Graham, who hammered multiple holes in the walls to mount pictures. My mother and I moved in with her parents a block away so I could continue to attend Estabrook. Mother taught kindergarten in two Detroit schools during the day and sold greeting cards at night, so she wasn't home much. My grandma cried a lot because the Japanese had just bombed Pearl Harbor, and her only son Jimmy—my godfather—was an army corporal stationed there at Schofield Barracks. No letters could be mailed from the Pacific Theater for many months, so throughout all those months, our family didn't know whether Uncle Jimmy was alive or dead.

One winter morning in 1942, the air raid sirens sounded. Our teachers led their bedraggled little charges out of the classrooms and took shelter with them in the windowless sections of the hallways to avoid flying shards of glass. Two scared six-year-olds—one white, the other black—whispered something to each other. Hearing them, their teacher yanked them out of line, thrust them next to a window, and ordered: "All right, Johnny Telford and Anderson Mobley—since you were noisy, now you can just stand there until the German and Japanese bombers get you." Anderson and I huddled together beneath the drafty windowsill and peered apprehensively into the stark sky, fully expecting to see enemy planes up there opening fire on us at any moment.

Back in our classroom later in the day, this teacher began to hand out the defense stamps to the children who had turned in their dimes and quarters that morning. (A dime would get you a red stamp; a quarter, a green one.) Stamp time was ordinarily a bad time for Anderson, because his grandmother was sick and he usually didn't have money for a stamp.

When the teacher got to him, she said, "Go back and sit down, Anderson— you didn't bring any money."

Anderson's expectant expression changed to one of embarrassed dismay. "Yes, ma'am, I did."

"You didn't!"

"Did *too*!"

"Anderson, you'd better confess to the class that you didn't turn in any money. Confess right *now.*"

I could contain myself no longer—to set the matter straight, I piped up, "I *saw* Anderson give you his money!"

After a few seconds of silence, the teacher snapped: "I'm *surprised* at you, Johnny. Why would you want to tell a fib to protect that lying little jigaboo?"

I winced then at the racist word which that mind-molesting teacher used in front of the entire class to describe my friend, and years later I wince still when I recall it. Already my father's egalitarian spirit had inspired mine, and I was only six.

To digress again: When I was six, I was constantly being told I was a remarkably *pretty* little boy, and older females of all racial persuasions made a considerable fuss over my long eyelashes and baby face—a fuss which I had little choice but to endure. More than once, too, a teenaged babysitter named Molly touched my private parts and had me touch hers. I should have told my mother about this, but I didn't. I was afraid that she might get angry with me for doing something I sensed was wrong. I reflect now that these surreptitious activities with Molly may also be what piqued my precociously early fascination with the eternal and labyrinthine mysteries of the feminine gender.

My father's _second_ relevant act of interracial justice and brotherhood* I want to share with you that illustrates how his core values formed mine happened during the deadly 1943 Detroit race riot, when I was seven. Three or four white men were beating a bewildered old black man in the alley that used to be just north of McGraw between Stanton and Sixteenth. The old man was already on his knees when my father got between him and the men, cursing and threatening them, and growling that they would have to go over him if they wanted to hurt the old man anymore.

The wary white men well knew my father's fistic capabilities and reluctantly backed off; thus the unwritten ancestral Code had again been fruitfully enacted. I ran out from under Danny and David Willis' back porch where I had been hiding and snatched up the old black man's broken dentures, bloody and spit-slick, from the pavement. (I also retrieved my best slingshot that Danny and David had pilfered from my backyard; it was under their porch.)

My father picked up the little old man, who was *very* old and *very* thin, and carried him down the alley to our house, with me trailing right behind with the old man's teeth. My mother washed the blood off the old man's face and fed him Campbell's tomato soup and crackers. He gummed the crackers— the damaged dentures were jaggedly cracked and couldn't be worn.

One of his attackers had urinated on him when he was down on his knees, and he himself had also urinated and moved his bowels in his trousers during the assault, so my dad had him take a bath in our old four-legged tub and lent him his robe to wear while my mother cleaned and washed his clothes.

My father drove the old man home to his house a few blocks east on

Wabash Street the next morning. Sadly, the old man died a couple of weeks later. Perhaps he had been beaten more badly than we knew.

When I was in the fifth grade, a big *sixth*-grade kid named Roger beat me up for no good reason, and I ran home crying. My dad took me back out and had me point out Roger, who ran home—with us following. Roger ran up onto his front porch and straddled the porch railing, watching us warily. "Touch my kid again," my dad said, "and I'll give you a whipping you'll never forget. Go tell your father to come out and I'll whip him, too."

A few days later, a *seventh*-grader named Frank beat me up. Again I ran home crying, and again my dad brought me back out—but when I pointed Frank out to him and he noted that the wiry seventh-grader wasn't much bigger than I was, he told me that if I didn't go and punch Frank on the eye as hard as I could, he was going to whip *me*, rather than whip Frank or Frank's father. More afraid of my father by far than I was of Frank, I approached Frank and hit him repeatedly on *both* of his eyes, with both of my fists, as hard and fast as I could. To my great surprise, Frank began to cry and beg me several times to stop hitting him on his eyes, so I hit him on his nose and his stomach instead. He never bothered me again.

The <u>third relevant egalitarian incident</u> involving my father occurred when a man came to that old house on Sixteenth Street selling cemetery lots. It was around the time of the Roger and Frank encounters, so I was about nine years old.

I heard my father ask the man if any black people were buried in the cemetery. The salesman assured him that there weren't. My father—remembering his multiple donated multi-racial transfusions for his skin grafts—announced to the salesman, "I have black blood. I'm sure you wouldn't want me to contaminate your cemetery with my black blood."

Then, in keeping with the Code, he threw the hapless salesman out the door.

CHAPTER TWO

OF FIGHTING AND
FIDDLING AND RAP

"'Twere better far to run away, and live to run another day."

—*The Cazzie Canty Credo*

Like my father, I fought a lot in those bygone 1940s days on Sixteenth Street. In adherence to his Code, I defended my sixth-grade girlfriend Bonnie Manhart, who had been my girl since kindergarten, against a rough bully named Reginald O'Bannion—more than once. I also protected her from the unwanted attentions of J. D. Jacobson, a dark-haired, Brylcreemed, good-looking boy who lived in the opulent Lee Plaza Hotel on West Grand Boulevard (now a ghostly hulk). Once I swooped down on J. D. and threw him to the ground when I spied Bonnie bending her resistant little body away from him as he pulled her braids on the school playground. Another time, J. D. jumped on me from behind when I was walking with Bonnie to choir practice at our church between Linwood Avenue and Grand River. I flipped him over my shoulder onto the sidewalk. While he was on the sidewalk, he tried to grab my foot, but the boy he was with said to him, "J. D., enough—he beat you."

Events like that still stick in my mind now, even though it happened sixty-two or sixty-three years ago. Bonnie's family moved to Sandoval, Illinois in the summer of 1947, giving me—and her—a very sad summer. She had a baby brother named Kenny and a big sister named Barbara. We wrote for three or four years, but lost touch. In 2002, I drove through Sandoval on my way to Minneapolis and tried to locate her, but no one knew who she was.

Years earlier, I had written this poem about her:

The lads I wrestled in rambunctious play
And gladsome sport of kindergarten day
Are fifty frozen winters far away.
The lasses, laughing in a long-gone May—
Pink-petticoated, pigtailed girls so gay—
For several spring-times now have ceased to say:
"Pom-pom, pull away; get on your horse and run away!"
Yet I remember twin, dark bonny braids
Whose wearer lived within my block. This maid's
Unfeeling parents, when we were in grades
Six-"B" and "A" one day
Just moved away.

One afternoon when I was about ten, my little friend Cazzie Canty, a mischievous eight-year-old African-American urchin who lived on McGraw between Sixteenth and Stanton, came to me for help. Daniel and David Willis, those two devilish boys who had stolen my best slingshot, were beating him up in the alley almost every day on his way home from school. Again in keeping with my father's Code, I told Cazzie—who was a bit chubby—that I'd hide behind a tree in a nearby backyard, and when they began to beat him up, I'd run out and take on Daniel if Cazzie would tackle the smaller David.

Things were proceeding according to plan and I was doing a workmanlike job on big Daniel when out of nowhere I suddenly got hit hard in the head from behind by small David. Turning my head (before I got hit hard in the head again from in front *and* from behind), I saw little Cazzie Canty running home down the alley. After that bruising and disappointing episode, I told little Cazzie Canty (after first cussing him out for deserting me) that he should consider taking a more varied and circuitous route home, because—ancestral Code or *no* ancestral Code—he sure wasn't going to get any more help from *me*.

*Un*like my father (but *like* little Cazzie Canty), I also, out of necessity, *ran* a lot—and not just in a ring or on a track. In that neighborhood, a boy frequently either had to *fight* or *run*—particularly if he was carrying a sissy violin case back and forth to school nearly every day, as I was. To make matters worse (that is to say, to make me an even more *inviting* target for neighborhood bullies), I had just begun to wear *glasses*. And even though I was undisputedly the fastest kid in the school—black or white, younger or older—I couldn't run too fast with the pesky violin case in my hand. (I studied the fiddle at Estabrook for six years in those golden days when the Detroit Public Schools offered lessons and K-8 schools actually had *orchestras*.) And since I therefore couldn't run really fast while encumbered with my ubiquitous fiddle in its case, I often had to stand and fight (*sans* glasses).

With such frequent *practice*, I became exceedingly adept at fighting. I also became exceedingly adept at the *fiddle*, because my unfeelingly mean mother made me *practice* it every day for an hour before she released me to go out and play baseball. Once I sneakily turned the clock forward so I could get out early to join my ball-playing buddies, but she caught me and made me practice an extra hour.

My dad's parents and his sisters Letty and Margaret and his big-time Hollywood director brother Frank loved to hear me play my fiddle over at their house on Twelfth Street on Christmas and New Year's. *Danny Boy* was one song I was never allowed to play, even though it was one of my favorites. Eight years before I was born, my dad's brother Dan had killed himself in that house at Christmas time. His Irish girlfriend's father wouldn't let her marry him because he wasn't Catholic. After his death, she never did marry. I still have a big framed, colorized picture of Dan—and a few small, black-and-white ones. He looked a lot like my dad. He was a handsome man.

When I was in the fifth grade, I went home and complained to my father that my teacher, Mrs. McGinity, had grabbed me by the hair and knocked my head against the wall. My father said, "Oh—like *this*?" and grabbed me by the hair and knocked my head against the wall. I never complained to him about Mrs. McGinity again.

When I was in the sixth grade, my teacher, Mrs. Blum, reported me for skipping school. My father beat me with his belt and belt buckle until he was out of breath and I was bleeding, and then he said, "If you ever do it again, you'd better bring a policeman home with you." I didn't do it again (in elementary school).

A couple of years later (in June of 1948 or September of 1949), I was either elected *lieutenant* or (if it was 1949) elected *captain* of the Estabrook Safety Patrol, and—feeling very full of myself sporting my freshly washed white Safety Patrol belt and the shiny silver lieutenant's (or captain's) badge pinned to it—I sauntered into Flo's candy store and soda shop on the corner

of Stanton and McGraw with three of my fellow Safety Patrol *compañeros*—
Renaldo Martinez, John Talley, and the late Earl Couch. (Earl's son, Earl Jr., is
now a Detroit cop at this writing.)

John and Earl were black, and both were already nearly six feet tall. The
proprietress—namely, the redoubtable Flo, herself—remarked to me unkindly,
"Johnny, you *know* you're not supposed to bring any big, old *black* boys in
here." She eyed John and Earl distastefully. "I'm sorry, boys, but you-all have
to leave." Then, turning back to me and making a shooing motion, she snapped,
"and you can get out and stay out *yourself*, you little spick-mick-guinea punk."

The bigoted Flo apparently (and possibly myopically) assumed I was part
Mexican or Italian, because I frequented her store with several of my friends
who were Italian—and I had brown eyes, dark hair, and a deep tan from playing
my beloved baseball from sunup to sundown. Flo also knew I was dating
Renaldo's sister, Carmen, who had agreed to be my girl after first having been
affronted by and then having magnanimously forgiven my big collie-beagle-
unknown-other-multi-mixed-mongrel mutt, "Rap" (short for "Rapscallion"), for
suddenly jumping up and humping frenetically on her leg. The day Rap chose
to do this was the day I was trying to make an initial impression on Carmen.
(I think Carmen might have intuited that the panting Rap was doing to her as
my proxy what I myself also secretly wished to do.)

On that same occasion while I was walking with Carmen, Rap further
embarrassed me by breaking free from his leash (actually, it was a piece of rope)
to dart into the alley and ravenously gobble up a big pile of dry horse manure.
One might have thought I never fed him. The manure had been dropped there
by a patient old palomino gelding that pulled the ragman's wagon.

Not too long after that, my mother was punishing me (or maybe punishing *Rap*) for some infraction or other, so she made Rap sleep out in the yard.
I didn't think that was a good idea because I was pretty sure that rather than
sleep, Rap would *howl* all night. (He usually slept with me.) I can't recall the
nature of the infraction and which of us committed it—me or Rap. The guilty
party quite possibly was Rap himself. (I know it wasn't the time he got up on
the kitchen table and ate the family roast, because that was during meat ration-
ing in World War II, and by now the war had been over for three or four years.)

It took me a long time to get to sleep that night, because predictably,
Rap did indeed howl. At the dim first light of morning, my mother heard a

single gunshot. The sound of gunfire was no longer entirely unusual in our neighborhood, so she ignored it and went back to sleep. When I went out later on that Sunday morning to untie my dog (he would have jumped the fence if I hadn't tied him), I found him shot dead on the ground. There was just a little dark red hole over his heart that hardly even bled. I strongly suspected Bus McCracken—a mean, bigoted, forty-year-old alcoholic bum who lived with his mother. Bus had a straight shot from his second-floor window into our backyard, and I knew he had a hunting rifle.

We buried Rap in the backyard. At first I cried a lot when I was by myself and pondered how I could kill Bus McCracken. I had asked my dad to beat Bus up for me, but my dad had said it wouldn't be right for him to do that because there was no proof that Bus had shot my dog—so one night I climbed over the suspected murderer's fence, borrowed a shovel from his garage, dug a deep hole in his yard, and put rosebush pickers in the hole. (I got the pickers from Mrs. Oldfield's flowery yard across the alley—she had so many flowers there that I didn't think she'd miss a few pickers.) Then I put a thin piece of cardboard over the hole and covered the cardboard with a layer of loose dirt. I hoped Bus McCracken would step in it and not his mother, because Mrs. McCracken was a nice old lady.

I never knew whether Bus fell in the hole or whether anyone else did— but I had to try to do *something* to Bus. I knew I probably would have had to go to the youth home if I had stabbed him with this well-sharpened red, white, and black swastika-decorated dagger my war-veteran Uncle Al had given me, or with the sharper of the two long nineteenth-century French bayonets Uncle Al also brought back in 1945 that Dickie Otten and my cousins Carl and Dick and I sword-fought with in the basement (until the blade of one broke off at the hilt). Even after I had put the pickers in the hole, for a while I seriously continued to consider stabbing Bus (since we didn't have a hunting rifle). Finally, I concluded that even if I did stab Bus, that wouldn't bring Rap back. Rap admittedly hadn't been the best dog in the world, but I had loved him.

Amazingly, in addition to the episode when Carmen Martinez had forgiven Rap for enthusiastically humping her leg, Carmen had actually *also* mostly overlooked the time she was walking past my house with me and my buddy Clyde Fergus Sanford when she almost stepped right smack on two rat tails, eight rat feet, and two rat heads. My three black cats had casually abandoned these twelve unsightly leftovers in the middle of the sidewalk after having made a quick, bloody meal of the entrails of their former owners. Clyde crunched one of the wide-eyed rat heads with his heel with a sickening sound that made Carmen recoil in horror and made *me* wince, as well. Carmen didn't come to my house too many times after that.

While Flo, the store owner, knew I was dating Carmen and would some-times ignorantly tease me about being in love with a "wetback," what she *didn't* know was that I was also dating Helen Hampton and Dinah Cole—both black girls—and I doubt that Flo would have approved of that at all. Flo was a Polish Catholic, so she was pulling for Nora O'Neill, Colleen Murphey, Joann Patton, and Maureen O'Mara—four Catholic (and also very *Celtic*) young ladies at Estabrook who were more interested in me than I was in them. (Ironically, Carmen was Catholic, too—but that didn't count with Flo, because Carmen was Latina.) Nora, the captain of the Service Squad, was a green-eyed blonde, and Colleen had a single brown braid that reached past her waist. Maureen was a pretty brunette, and Joann had what teens in the 1940s referred to as "nice headlights." Colleen was quiet and timid, but the other three were very loud, and they were also constantly giggling.

The tall, gangly Dinah Cole (taller than *me*), the ever-horny Helen Hampton, and the tempestuous Carmen naturally wouldn't have approved of it, either, had they become aware that I was dating them *all*. Happily for me, none of them did become aware of it at the time.

Also, I suspect that Flo—whose full first name was *Florence*—never had cared for it too much when I would breeze into her store and impertinently attempt to get her attention (and irritate her) by belting out a then-popular song that went, "Up and *down* the St. *Lawrence*, a-hollerin' *Florence!*—Florence, oh *where* can you *beee*?"

I later brought Helen with me into Flo's store without Flo uttering a single word of protest. This was probably because Flo almost immediately had begun to regret barring black folks from her store.

John, and *particularly* big Earl, could get violent when a white person called them "black boys"—and Carmen's explosive brother Renaldo's favorite expletive when angered was something that I recall sounded like "*Chinga porca.*" On the day that Flo kicked us out of her store, I greatly feared that John or Earl would explode and that Jose would utter his customary obscene expletive or do something even worse and get us into deep difficulty.

My fear was unfounded. John, Earl, and Renaldo exited the store with me quickly and quietly without smashing anything (or anyone). However, it came to pass that on the very next day, some windows in Flo's store got mysteriously shattered. While I can't say that any of us had anything to do with the shattering, I also can't say that any of us *didn't*.

Detroit's black population had doubled between 1940 and 1950, but the pool of available housing hadn't come close to keeping pace with that accelerating growth. Indeed, housing was Detroit's ticking time bomb.

In 1946—three years after the race riot when my dad had gone to the rescue of the old black man being stomped in the alley—Detroit Common Councilman Billy Rogell (a former Detroit Tiger) had remarked to my father after a game at Briggs Stadium which the Tigers had lost to Cleveland, "Scotty, we got to pick an area and move the whites the hell out of it—and move the niggers in. I want to see the niggers get a city of their own, with their own schools, and so forth. We need a *Harlem* for the niggers."

The Tigers had beaten the Chicago Cubs in the World Series the previous year, and I was Tiger-crazy and baseball-crazy. Now, after this losing game with the Indians, my father had brought his ten-year-old Tiger-crazy son with him to the Golden Lily Café, a little bar and grill near Briggs (later Tiger) Stadium. Billy Rogell—who had known my dad since his boxing days when he lived on the 6000 block of Twelfth Street—had been with us at the game. He had sat down and had some beers with my dad and helped us eat a whole rack of ribs— the ribs at the Golden Lily were great. My cousins, Carl and Dick, were with us, too—and we were wearing blue Tiger baseball hats my dad had bought us with the orange old-English "D." Carl and Dick could really *eat*. (We had already had hot dogs at the game.)

Dad checked Billy on his use of the pejorative for "Negro" and cautioned him that his three boys—my cousins and I—looked up to him and might imitate his language. We never would have, though, in a million years—we had been raised better. Also, Dad told Billy that he definitely didn't agree with him regarding his "Harlem in Detroit" idea at all—we were died-in-the-wool integrationists even then.

While Detroit's near west side was no *Harlem* by any stretch of the imagination, more and more black families were nonetheless moving onto McGraw,

Linwood, Stanton, and Sixteenth Street.

Since *still more* black families were overflowing onto Marquette Street, and since black families were now even migrating as far north as Ferry Park, the practical Flo eventually had to swallow her prejudices (at least outwardly) and allow *all* of us, black or white, to patronize her store.

Business was *business*, after all.

CHAPTER THREE

AN *UN-SCOUT-LIKE* SCOUT TROOP; A GIRL WITH A GLASS EYE

"When Irish eyes <u>aren't</u> smiling. . . ."

When I was thirteen or fourteen and already almost a man in bearing, if not yet in size (black kids and white kids alike grew up fast on Sixteenth Street), a nosy pair of elderly neighbor ladies would frequently stop me on the corner and inquire with patronizing pity, "And *how* is your *poor* mother?" Since my mother was in excellent health and bringing home a fair salary as a Detroit public-school kindergarten teacher, I never understood why these prim-and-proper old white ladies in their lacey old-white-lady hats would refer to my mother as "poor."

Perhaps, I speculated, their inquiry was in reference to my father's unfortunate turns at high-stakes poker. His gambling, which frequently cost us the month's house note and some of the food money, once resulted in his twice losing the deed to the house and twice regaining it on a single night. (My mother, thank *God*, never learned about that. I only found out because my father's buddy Mickey Ward, an Irish-Canadian who looked like a skinnier version of film star Gary Cooper because his lungs had been seared by German mustard gas in the Great War, slipped and mentioned it in my presence.)

Probably, too, those nosy ladies had observed me fighting in the street with red-haired Ralph Peterson, my best friend Dickie Otten (when we were mad at each other), Bill Proctor (who later took his stepfather's surname of Rudd), Clyde Fergus Sanford (a Scot with a hard right hand), Irish Jimmy Finnegan, Helmut Schmidt (a bully), Ronald Sutter (whom the principal appointed to succeed me as captain of the Safety Patrol when she demoted me from that elected post), the Bing brothers (I could say some interesting things about them, but if I did and they're still alive, they could sue), Elmer and Ding Raschke (one time I took them *both* on simultaneously), Malcolm Wimberley (he thought he was an airplane), Danny and David Willis (man, those two Stanton Street boys were *mean*), Jim Blackthorn (another tough Scot), Artie Peltier (got hit by a car on Sixteenth and nearly killed), Vito Maccioli, and George Moore (broke into my house one time and stole my stash of *Pirate* comics)—all frequent and (usually) well-drubbed antagonists, except for Clyde Sanford. I never could beat Clyde.

Others that I fought with only once or twice included Roosevelt Jones, Willie and Tommy "Little Tiger" Flowers (separately), Bobby Sixberry (when he visited his grandmother on the corner of Sixteenth and Marquette, where my favorite chestnut tree stood), Leonard Zoloff (I caught him kicking a puppy), big Billy Bieski (my dad made me go back and thrash him when I came home bleeding), Billy Lester (when he visited his aunt), Skip McNamara (now a Traverse City banker who lived across the street and I haven't seen for sixty years), Vito Maccioli (again—would have thought he'd learned better the first time), Eldon Laine (until he got polio—he could run pretty fast, too), or John William ("Billy") Warriner, my off-and-on friend on Sixteenth Street whose father paid to board him with a humorless lady everyone called "Nurse" Hegel, who was also nursing her ninety-year-old German-speaking mother. Most of this second group were friends more often than foes (except Leonard Zoloff and Billy Bieski).

Once, Billy Warriner and I were smoking—and inhaling—cigar-sized segments we had cut from dried hollyhock stalks under his front porch, and the nosy lady across the street spied smoke coming through the slats. She called the fire department, and they *came*. *Big* trouble.

I cleaned Irish Jimmy Finnegan's clock for him more than once and cleaned it *good* when I caught him tormenting Johnny Heath, who was retarded. Irish Jimmy also liked to taunt red-haired Tommy Duveni, who was deaf, and March Forth McGavin, who was black *and* retarded *and* deaf. Tommy and March Forth attended the school for the deaf that was on the same grounds as Estabrook School.

Two years later, I cleaned Irish Jimmy's clock one more time for good measure. This time, it was in an amateur boxing ring at a long-since-closed and abandoned venue on Woodward, downtown. I hit him exceptionally *hard*, too—right in his *Adam's apple*—because Irish Jimmy always had an insufferably cocky attitude, and he was very unkind to cats.

Those two tut-tutting, lace-collared ladies were always peering nosily out their windows, so I think they might also have witnessed two bloody fights I was goaded into on the corner of Fifteenth Street and McGraw, which was near where they lived. One fight was with a bigger boy named Glenn, that I won (*he* didn't want to fight, either). The other was with a super-sized ninth-grade dropout in the neighborhood whom I had unwisely teased and whom everyone called Big Jo, that I *didn't* win. Big Jo was a *girl*, and she had exceptionally sharp teeth and fingernails (and also a glass eye, which she liked to pop out and show to people).

Big Jo didn't just *slap*, either—she knew how to use her fists, and how to get her full weight behind her punches. My father had taught me never to hit girls, but the aggressive Big Jo gave me little choice. All of the blood that ran in that encounter with Big Jo was mine alone. The unsportsmanlike Jo didn't care where or how hard she punched, kicked, scratched, or bit. Oh, the *shame* of it all—losing a fight to a girl! (At least she was an *Irish* girl.) The Irish kids in that neighborhood were almost as tough as the Scots, but not quite. Irish kids fought for the hell of it or for pure *fun*; the Scots fought in dead earnest, like it was their *calling*.

Those two sanctimonious old white ladies who enjoyed asking me about my "poor mother" had lived in the now swiftly integrating neighborhood since perhaps as far back as the staid and ancient 1890s. Thus, one might correctly surmise that they were scandalized to see me sitting so frequently on the porches of *black* people or eating barbecue in the *backyards* of black people or simply enjoying the general *company* of black people throughout the neighborhood (particularly the *specific* company of young black *females*).

The nosy ladies undoubtedly knew I brought girls of all heritages into the house when my parents weren't home. They undoubtedly also knew that I brought my black girlfriends to the house with my liberal parents' *full approval* when my parents *were* home—and I'm sure they just couldn't fathom *that* at all.

My mama didn't seem to worry too much about what I might or might not be doing with my black (and *non*-black) girlfriends—both when she and my papa were at home and when they *weren't* at home. Actually, she *should* have been worrying *a lot*. She *did* worry constantly, however, about many of my *other* behaviors. These behaviors included my deadly accuracy with a sling-shot when targeting streetlights, rats—and one time, the seat of Billy Bieski's pants with Billy Bieski in them.

She also worried even *more* about many even *more numerous* behaviors of my daddy. Sadly, my daddy and I both gave her plenty of reasons to worry—sometimes more reasons than she even knew (thank *God*, again).

Worrying about me as she did, my mother badgered me into joining a Boy Scout troop that was housed at our church, and that incidentally was one of the few *interracial* troops in the city. While my seventh- and eighth-grade report cards were munificently adorned with a whole bunch of beautiful "E's" (for "Excellent") in my academic subjects, they had also been marred on every card-marking with ugly "U's" (for "Unsatisfactory") in a detestably corrective category called "Self-Control." I never got too many "S's" (for "Satisfactory")—I was always at one extreme or the other. This later became in many ways the story of my life.

In an episode closely related to my assorted misbehaviors that had caused my teachers to mark me "Unsatisfactory" in that detested category called "Self-Control," Estabrook principal Dorothea Hoehn had confiscated my prized Safety Patrol captain's badge. She had done this sadly and reluctantly, she told me. I had been reported to her for fighting one time too often—and this time I had fought with two other members of my own Safety Patrol (in the pugnaciously Celtic persons of one Marvin Murphy, who ordinarily was my friend, and one Mickey Carnahan, who ordinarily wasn't). As a matter of fact, Mrs. Hoehn had humiliatingly demoted me all the way back down to a patrol post on a street corner again—which lowly but essential assignment I had first achieved as a callow sixth-grader. When my mother saw that my captain's badge was missing from my white Safety Patrol belt, she obliged me to spill forth that whole shameful story, and the story did not make her happy.

Not long after Mrs. Hoehn had demoted me from the captaincy of the Safety Patrol, she punished me again for drawing little violins on the lavatory walls in the school basement with a blue ballpoint pen (a new invention at that time). I had to scrub the little violins off the walls with brown soap and a stiff brush—a laborious task—and Mr. Brinkle, the school custodian, took advantage of this opportunity to make me clean two *toilets* as well.

My mother hoped that the Boy Scouts would have a calmingly reformative influence on my questionable behavior. Unfortunately—and unknown to her—this particular Boy Scout troop just happened to be scoutmastered by a former boxing stablemate and currently insolvent boozing/gambling buddy of my father named Martin MacRaney. Scoutmaster MacRaney was perilously close to getting evicted from his bottle-strewn apartment above a liquor store on Linwood, along with his unhappy wife and children.

Thus, with Scoutmaster MacRaney's full permission and in fact *encouragement*, my fellow Scouts and I would routinely go out into the alley behind the church to settle our disagreements. Oftentimes, the flat, thudding *thwack* of fists against Afro-American or Euro-American flesh resounded repeatedly at darkening dusk in that garbage-strewn alley that stank of dead rats and a dead cat or two. In the late fall and winter, when we usually didn't fight shirtless, our uniform shirts became irremediably soiled by sweat and blood. Clearly, we weren't what you could call an exemplary troop in the proud Scouting tradition.

While I only made it to Second-Class Scout, I did manage to earn considerably more merit badges than did any of my motley fellow troopers except for big Earl Couch, who mostly stayed out of fights and achieved First-Class status.

Actually, if truth were told, I believe I may really have earned a grand total of *two* merit badges.

CHAPTER FOUR

BOXING BOY SCOUTS AND A BYE-BYE TO BOYHOOD

"As one door of happiness closes, another one opens."

—The timelessly great Helen Keller

Presently, our church—Bethel Evangelical and Reformed Lutheran Church—received a curious donation. Given our Boy Scout troop's un-Scout-like fistic inclinations, it was a curiously *fitting* donation—a *boxing ring*, old and worn, and smelling of the stale sweat of anonymous pugilists long past. The church elders purchased four pairs of spanking-new boxing gloves and set the old ring up in the huge church basement. Once the ring had been installed, Scoutmaster MacRaney decided to have us settle our petty little disagreements in the ring with the gloves, rather than out in the alley with bare knuckles anymore. This suited me fine, because I was already accustomed to boxing gloves. Starting when I was eleven, my dad had paid neighborhood boys to put on the gloves with me and try to knock me down, meanwhile forbidding me to use my fast right hand except for defensive blocking.

The church began sporadically to back a few of the older and more pugilistically capable Scouts who now were aspiring to become amateur boxers. You had to be sixteen to compete, and I was only fifteen, but my father signed a paper attesting that I was of age. With Scoutmaster MacRaney's and my father's coaching and encouragement, and suitably fitted with wraparound headgear (for sparring only), hard-rubber mouthpiece, and *very* oversized crotch cup, I was able to use my inherent hand and foot speed to represent the church's ragtag team successfully in citywide bouts while remaining ordinarily able to avoid getting hit too often or too hard. I had a near-phobic aversion to getting hit—an unbeneficial trait for any aspiring fighter, because even the fastest are going to get hit. The majority of my defeated opponents were of African or Mexican heritage, with a pugnacious pinch of Scots-Irish thrown into the mix for good measure. I eventually compiled a 16–1 record over a two-year period during which I grew from a welterweight to a middleweight. Most of the scant seven boxers I knocked out were the only ones who had managed to catch me and hurt me. My one loss was in my last bout, where a talented black boxer who was three or four years older than me broke my nose. He later turned pro and held world middleweight champion Joey Giardello to a draw.

In addition to my ex-fighter father and Mr. MacRaney (whose son Martin Jr. disappointingly couldn't fight a lick), my trainers were Mr. Gilbert Woodcock (whose red-haired violinist daughter Shirley I later abstinately dated), and Mr. Tom Briscoe— an ex-pug who became like a second father to me. Tom Briscoe served with me decades later on the board of the philanthropic (and now unfortunately defunct) Detroit Varsity Club, whereof I was the only white member.

A soon-to-become world-renowned Doctor of Divinity named Reinhold Niebuhr had confirmed my mother at that church. I was baptized there by Rev. Robert Stanger in 1936, and I was confirmed there, too, in 1949—twenty-nine years after my mother. I used to wrestle on the floor in Dr. Stanger's study with his mischievous son Dickie, who years later became a minister in Chicago. The still-occupied church building stands on the south side of West Grand Boulevard between Linwood and Grand River, next to the shell of the once-magnificent Lee Plaza Hotel, where my schoolmate J. D. Jacobson lived, and due east of the old Northwestern High School (and now due east of the *new* Northwestern High School).

Behind the altar, the old church has a huge, time-begrimed mosaic depicting a kneeling Mary Magdalene washing a beige-robed Jesus' feet with her long, orange-colored hair.

That beautiful mosaic of the sitting Jesus became one of the most memorable and inspirational icons of my early childhood. Later, it was the recurring mental image I most often invoked to stay sane during my four-and-a-half-month stint in reform school locked away from my distraught mother, whom I sorely missed. I remember smelling spring rain on grass outside a barred window of the detention facility that reminded me of the smell of rain on grass in my backyard on Sixteenth Street, and I *ached* to be back home with my mama. Attendants in that dank dungeon routinely hit me and other hapless youngsters with no degree of sadism whatever, but as a mere matter of unwritten procedure —and I was put in isolation more than once for hitting back.

I had been sentenced and sent to that terrible place for an offense I had committed on a blustery winter day in a vacant lot on Sixteenth Street at Stanley. Swiftly and impulsively, I had committed a dead-earnest act of attempted murder with the aid of a jagged little piece of brick I had snatched up in my outraged little fourteen-year-old hand (as an equalizer) and bashed it repeatedly on the left temple of a much bigger and older boy by the name of Bruno Bruder. My schoolmate Gerald Wilbur and I had just seen Bruno Bruder set fire to a stray kitten with kerosene and a lit match; therefore, I had obligatorily brought into instantaneous play the ancient ancestral Code my father and grandfather taught me—and I had applied that Code in absolute cold fury.

Some men across the street came and pulled me off the prostrate Bruno, who was bleeding badly. One man tried to hold me for the police, but I was able to twist away from him and run home. Soon a policeman came and led me out of my house in handcuffs in front of my weeping mother. When they asked me if I had tried to *kill* Bruno Bruder, I made the mistake of telling the truth, so I was charged—fairly—with attempted murder. Fortunately for me (and for Bruno), I didn't ever have to face a charge of *actual* murder, because Bruno eventually recovered consciousness—but I later learned from Gerald Wilbur that the poor little kitten unfortunately (or perhaps *fortunately*) didn't.

As my mother and uncles and aunts had done before me, including my dashingly handsome uncle Frank Telford (who teamed in track and football with the celebrated black athlete and judge-to-be Willis Ward), I enrolled at the old Northwestern High School. This was after that relatively short stint in the youth home (which to me, however, had seemed like a century). A psychologist who examined me there had attested that the potentially murderous assault incident was a one-time circumstantial episode and he didn't think I would repeat it. I might have, though, if I had seen someone torment an animal so terribly again.

After some brief and sporadic athletic forays at Northwestern, where despite my non-blackness I quickly gained a reputation for sheer, brute speed, I was expelled from the school for slapping the hands—*hard*—of an enraged assistant principal named Diekoff as he clutched my jacket collar. I also kicked him and tried to bite him to get him to let go. He had overheard me creating imaginatively scatological puns regarding his last name for the edification of my chortling buddies, who were hanging out with me in the halls. Prior to that incident, Mr. Diekoff had apparently sworn an inner oath to concern himself personally on a daily basis with my preference—*also* on a daily basis— to inhabit those halls instead of my classrooms. He must have caught me skipping classes at least twenty times, and probably more.

The pleas of Northwestern track coach Jimmy Russell to the school's principal on my behalf having fallen on unsympathetic ears (my offenses were listed as "chronic truancy" and "assault on an administrator"), I got sent to live with my father, who had found a little brick bungalow at 10776 Haverhill near Hayes on the far east side. My mother had banished him from the old frame house at 6021 Sixteenth Street several months earlier—for the umpteenth time—because of his drinking and gambling. Also, on one hot summer night he had come home drunk and yanked me out of bed and had begun to beat me—we had a telephone now and he had called the wrong number at midnight for my mother to come and get him. A boy probably about my age had answered and told him to go to hell, and he had mistakenly thought it was me. I fled from him downstairs and he chased me around the dining room table—I ran out the front door barefoot and slept in a boxcar on a railroad sidetrack down by Antoinette Street in my pajamas for the remainder of the night.

The grounds of the new McMichael Middle School now occupy the two near-west-side blocks where my boyhood house on Sixteenth Street once stood, and where the Estabrook School once stood. Sometimes when I go back now more than fifty years later and stand there looking east with the school behind me, the street looks almost the same as it did then, and I can almost see the kids who lived across the street out there playing again—but of course, now they're in their seventies, or dead.

For just a fleeting moment, though, once when I went back a few years ago, in my mind's eye I envisioned my buddy Russell "Skip" McNamara and his beautiful purebred Irish setter, Patrick, whom my scruffy mongrel mutt Rap was always happily trying to hump. Rap wasn't bi-sexual—he was *pan*-sexual. Dogs—male and female—people's legs, and sometimes even *fenceposts* weren't immune from getting mounted.

Speaking of *mounted*—Skip's hunter father had a huge deer head mounted on his living room wall. The McNamaras lived next door to little Gussie and Jeannie—a sister and brother whose last name I can't remember. Gussie's face was always grimy, and Jeannie always had dirty underpants. Gussie and Jeannie lived in a two-family flat that's also still there.

In my mind's eye, I could almost see good, old curly-haired, mean-tempered Melvin Shelton—fresh up from Nashville, Tennessee—strutting self-importantly down Sixteenth Street. Melvin's mother dragged him back outside one time after I had whipped him good for throwing a brick at Rap, and Melvin had run home. (Rap had been running toward him with a flea-ridden former rat in his mouth that he had retrieved from the alley.) Melvin's mother tugged him back across the street and made him fight me again. Reluctantly, Melvin put up his fists, with mama egging him on—"*Hit* that boy, *Mayal*-vin; hit him *hard*! Why, that boy's just a *skinny* little thing! You can *beat* him, *Mayal*-vin!"

A neighborhood audience had gathered.

I whipped good old *Mayal*-vin good, again.

CHAPTER FIVE

SOME WONDERFUL COACHES—A TEEN TRANSFORMED

"No 'meat' before the meet."

*—Cautionary double-entendre slogan that 1950s
high school track coaches taught their athletes*

In the early 1950s, there were no expressways, so to move from far west to far east or vice-versa was, to me, like moving to Yemen or somewhere equally distant. I missed all my friends, black and white, whom I had hung with since kindergarten, and one—Dickie Otten—since even *before* kindergarten.

I'd been hanging out with Dickie Otten since we were both less than two years old. In those days, we looked like two brown-eyed, brown-haired brothers. Once when we were about three or four, my mother heard us telling each other stories about Mr. Poop and Mr. Pee ("Mr. Poop and Mr. Pee were walking down the street . . ."). She washed out our mouths with soap and spanked me. I thought she should have spanked *him*, too.

Nearly seventy years later, Dickie and his wife Joann would come to dine with me and my wife Gina at our Tudor mansion on our little getaway lake in Shelby Township, Michigan (for which despite paying a whopping down payment I would have an even more whopping $2,400 monthly mortgage note, so *please spread the word today about how fascinating this book is*, and don't *loan* it to anyone, either—so they'll hopefully *buy* a copy). Gina would cook a 22-inch large-mouthed bass she had caught in the lake the same morning and serve it to Dick and Joann. Gina would also serve them steak and lobster (despite the $2,400 mortgage).

Whether for good or for ill, my poor mother was far too attracted to my wild father to stay away from him for long. Early in 1952, when I had just turned sixteen, she sold the little bit of equity we had in the house on Sixteenth Street and moved back with my father and me. She promptly joined a new church nearby and made me attend with her every Sunday. (My father—one of the most moral and righteous men I ever knew despite his drinking, gambling, and intermittent brawling—never would set foot inside a church, except for weddings and funerals.)

Some of the young church ladies who sang in the choir began to invite me to their houses when their parents weren't home. One day when my mother was washing clothes, she was appalled to find some young-church-lady lipstick on the fly area of my undershorts that I couldn't explain away. She had my father give me "The Talk"—but it didn't do much good. I was a duck-tailed, brush-topped, sometimes-bespectacled, clean-shaven and sleeker version of a young Errol Flynn. When my mother wasn't around to order me to button up, I often left my soft gabardine shirts seductively unbuttoned all the way down to my navel, and I wore my Levi's tight and low-slung. I was teenage catnip to girls then, and they to me.

This was the case with older women, too. One of my girlfriends had a married aunt who coaxed me into her bed one hot summer afternoon with remarkable ease after offering me some spiked lemonade. She had hired me to clean her basement after it had become flooded during a heavy rain.

As a matter of fact, females young and old, short and tall—regardless of race, creed, or ethnic origin—were to become my collective lifelong addiction and Achilles heel. (And for any of you psychoanalytically-inclined folks who would speculate that this preeminent predilection for the opposite sex developed due to my having been induced to touch and be touched inappropriately by a baby-sitter when I was six, or due to my father being in the hospital for eight months that same year and my teacher-mother having to move us in with her parents and moonlight selling greeting cards, or due to my girlfriend since kindergarten moving to Illinois when I was eleven, or due to any other cranial quirk in some trauma-susceptible neural pathway, let me head you off at the pass right now with this one word: *opportunities*. I offer no excuses—I became a lifelong ladies' man simply because I *could*. If they were *interested* and *interesting*—particularly if they had money—they generally got accommodated, and more were *interested* than not. Even when they weren't so *interesting*, I sometimes accommodated them anyway, because it hurt me to hurt their feelings. That's the truth.)

One of the things I most remember about that new church my mother made me join—other than its several delightfully lustful young ladies—was that some of its congregation used the vile word "nigger" casually and contemptuously. They didn't seem to realize that Jesus doesn't like to hear that word in His house, or anywhere else. To my sixteen-year-old Sixteenth Street-bred mind, this was an unthinkable word for supposedly pious adults to utter.

The overt bigotry of these churchgoing white folks confused and disillusioned me. Eventually, it caused me to stop attending church, despite my mother telling me I needed to understand that these people hadn't been raised right and their prejudices weren't their fault. Instead of quitting the church, she said, I should pity them and try to educate them. My mother was a confirmed pacifist who wanted everyone to love each other, but *I* wasn't. My notion of the best method for "educating" people like that was more in the mode of my father—a fast left hook to the jaw.

Often, too, I had observed the reverend at that church to have a long, light-greenish-grayish booger dangling from his nose. Those omnipresent, ungodly gray-greenish boogers caused me to question the reverend's true standing with God. To me, it seemed theologically illogical that God would have permitted boogers of *any* hue to hang from the hallowed nose of one of His ordained reverends if that reverend were truly reverent.

My dad got me a day-shift job paying almost two dollars an hour running one of the multiple punch presses at Keystone Metal Molding Company on Stephens Drive near Nine Mile Road in East Detroit (now Eastpointe) that manufactured small auto parts. He was a foreman there now, trying to stay mostly sober during the daytime. The little factory was owned by two rough-and-ready Scots— my dad's cousins, Jimmy and Alex Carlin. At sixteen, I had recently completed my second year of amateur boxing, and Dad suggested hopefully that I should consider boxing professionally as a supplement to my wages at Keystone, because he had a discomforting premonition that one of those girls was going to get pregnant sooner or later and I was going to need to have the means to support a family. (He himself had turned pro at sixteen. His old manager, Archie Silman, was in his eighties then, but Archie was still managing a few young fighters.) However, Mama said, "No! No more boxing! He has to get back in school."

After the man working next to me got his fingers cut off by a punch press, I decided that I agreed with Mama.

With the help of my father and his ex-manager, a former familiar of Detroit's notorious Purple Gang who still had connections downtown (and who had once sold about 150 percent of my father's boxing contract to assorted suckers), my mother was able to get my expulsion expunged and re-enroll me in Detroit Public Schools. I became a *transfer* student to the big, beautiful Denby High School, population 5,000.

That *transfer* was the move that *transformed* my life. When the Denby coaches timed me in 4.5 seconds for 40 yards (on slow *grass*, not the faster *cinders*), they took an instantaneous interest in me. They went to great lengths to keep the girls away from me and to keep me out of fights (as much as they could; one day I spotted Roger, the boy who had thrashed me at Estabrook seven years earlier and who was now a senior at cross-town Denby. My teammates guarded the gym locker room door while I quickly evened the score. That day when I got home, I wanted to brag to my father about my recognizing Roger and getting my revenge after all those years, but on second thought I decided not to, because he wanted me to fight in the *ring*, not in school).

Coach Jack Rice, a tall, muscular man with a stutter who had starred at what was then Wayne University in four sports, preached a mantra I usually tried to follow: "N-N-No 'm-meat' [girls] before the [track] m-m-meet." Coach Rice gave me the stammered pet nickname "M-M-Mustang" and took me under his protective wing, but the "M-M-Mustang" from Sixteenth Street wasn't totally tamed just yet. One day a tall, swarthy, soft-bellied kid named Carmine, who was always pushing people in the pool and hogging the basketball in gym class, cut in front of me and my new girlfriend Angie in the lunch line. I later learned that Angie had been Carmine's girl the previous year. One insulting word led to another, and Carmine—undoubtedly noting my barely-one hundred sixty-pound frame and that I was wearing glasses—challenged me to fight after school behind Midge's, a candy store across the street.

When Angie and I arrived behind Midge's at the designated time, I was wearing a jacket over a tee shirt, but no glasses. Big, beefy Carmine was already there, accompanied by three of his friends of southern European descent (as *witnesses*, not participants, and *unarmed*—this was 1952, not 2002). Big Carmine surprised me by benevolently telling me I could go home. It was, he said,

enough that I'd shown up. I thanked him and said I was going to go home.
I added that it would have been silly for us to get all bloody over something
so inconsequential as a quarrel about taking cuts in the lunch line.

"But first," I told big Carmine, "you have to apologize to Angie for taking
cuts." (I really *wasn't* going to go home, though—I had to go back into the
school for indoor track practice.) Certain that the beefy Carmine would refuse
to apologize to Angie, I slipped out of my jacket, handed it to Angie, and
loosened my shoulder muscles in anticipation.

Carmine evidently (and correctly) guessed that something was not quite
right here. After a thoughtful pause, he muttered to his former girlfriend,
"I 'pologize."

Coach Rice, who had been alerted that I was about to be involved in a
fight, got there in time to see his speedy "Mustang" from west- side Sixteenth
Street and big, soft-bellied Carmine from east-side Kelly Road peacefully and
safely shaking hands. Carmine had perceptively saved himself from being
forcibly induced to vomit in front of his friends that day.

The genuinely paternal interest those wonderful Denby coaches took in
me remained strong even after—to my dismay—the officious Mr. Diekoff *also*
got transferred from Northwestern to Denby as an assistant principal. Mr.
Diekoff got off on the wrong foot with the students, too, by beginning a speech
at an assembly in the auditorium with the words, "Here at *Northwestern* . . ."
to an immediate chorus of boos.

Luckily for me but puzzlingly *to* me, whenever Mr. Diekoff happened to
encounter me in the halls, he looked right through me and acted as though
he didn't know me or as though I didn't even *exist*. It wasn't until years later
that I figured out why: Denby principal Irving Wolf—a fine educator in most
ways—was overly eager for his school to win sports titles, and he tended to
treat his star athletes like privileged beings who virtually could do no wrong.
So, following an encounter in which my wayward fist chipped an *un*-athletic
(although much *bigger*) boy's front tooth for mischievously opening my violin
case in the lavatory (I was in the school orchestra), it was not *I* but the *other*
boy whom Mr. Diekoff suspended for three days for fighting.

Actually, that presumptuous boy *did* deserve what "Mustang's" miscreant
fist (and Mr. Diekoff) did to him, because the boy also happened to be a nasty,
natural-born bully.

CHAPTER SIX

WAYNE STATE GETS A WORLD-RANKED RUNNER

"The shortened run through summer sun on springing, warm-sand-quickened sole is swiftly, prematurely done—so win as much as can be won . . ."

—*From an introductory poem in* The Longest Dash,
Track & Field News Press, *1965, 1971*

When I graduated from Denby High School in January 1954 after having won many a race in Detroit's tough PSL (Public School League), my track coach, Ralph Green, an old Wayne University sprinter, helped me get a track scholarship to his alma mater. At Wayne, I eventually became an NCAA All-American quarter-miler in a long bygone era when there was only *one* NCAA division— the *big* division. Lorenzo Wright, a Wayne graduate and a 1948 Olympian, was also instrumental in recruiting me.

In 1954 I wouldn't have been able to accept that scholarship if I'd been a teenaged parent. Just before I was to graduate, a Denby senior I'd been dating was two weeks late with her period. She'd been accepted to (another) college, too, and we both had been scared to death until her period *thankfully* came down. This experience helped shape my philosophy regarding sex education and contraception for teens—a philosophy I made manifest when I became the Berkley School District's health and physical education director eighteen years later.

One month after graduating from high school and just turned eighteen, I won indoor 60- and 440-yard races at Central Michigan University in Mount

Pleasant wearing the green and gold of the Wayne Tartars, thus giving me the
inaccurate impression that collegiate competition was going to be a snap and
I wouldn't really need to train too hard. I never missed track practice, though,
and I eventually was to form many lifelong friendships on that Wayne team. Sadly,
most of my teammates are dead now. One who still isn't—Don Stange, who
then was a large and muscular sophomore high-hurdler—challenged me one
day at track practice in the gym in the venerable Old Main building to put on
the gloves with him. Since he outweighed me by thirty pounds, I expected that
we were just going to spar lightly with soft little pitty-pat punches. However,
I soon learned that Stange wasn't playing, and he was a *southpaw*. I had always
had trouble with southpaws (left-handed fighters). The big hurdler came out
throwing left-hand *bombs*, and he caught me and stung me with one, giving me
no choice but to retaliate with hard right crosses that landed fast and repeatedly
on his jaw. Soon I had the stunned Stange (pronounced *stang*-ee) bending down
and covering up, ripe for finishing. I backed off him then, despite my sprinter
buddy Jerry Catalina screaming at me, "Uppercut, John! Uppercut! Uppercut!"

I think this was when coach David L. Holmes, who was watching our battle
from the balcony track, realized he had something special in me. He told my
dad I had guts, and I was deliriously happy to have my fighter father hear those
words of praise from my coach.

While no one—including me—was ever able to break the 220-yard dash
record that had been set by Olympian Lorenzo Wright in 1947 on the old 22-
lap-to-the-mile balcony track in that little gym, I did break the 300-, 440-,
and 600-yard records on it. That tight-turned track wasn't really built to
accommodate athletes who could average better than ten yards per second
like Lorenzo had, and like I could. If I didn't ease off a bit on the turns in a
sprint race, I could practically fly out a window. The old, many-times-patched-
up track has since been torn down, and the gym is no longer a gym.

In my freshman year at Wayne, a comely young Miller High School honors
graduate in my four-hour-per-week geology class talked me into cutting class
with her and joining her in her apartment nearby when her roommates weren't
there. We ended up cutting so often that we got far behind in that class, and
we both withdrew from it with failing grades of "E." As a result, I nearly became
scholastically ineligible to run my sophomore year, and she lost her academic
scholarship. Even worse, my activities with the young lady—and with another

coed who drove a late model Cadillac and hung out at the Catholic Newman Club on campus, and with yet another coed in residence at an on-campus sorority house—combined to drain my strength for the quarter mile on an almost daily basis.

Thus, my workouts on the track were compromised—and to tell the truth, I wasn't really training very hard anyway. My best quarter-mile time all year was therefore a fair-to-middling 49.8 relay leg with a running start—nearly two disappointing seconds short of Coach Holmes' seasonal goal for me. Denby High School coach Jack Rice's cautionary "No 'meat' before the meet" mantra had been borne out with debilitative effect in this, my debuting intercollegiate season against competitors whom I found to be far faster than I had anticipated.

Still, I was the only freshman on the varsity mile relay team that won at the Ohio Relays in Columbus and took third-place medals at the prestigious Penn Relays in Philadelphia. I also anchored our mile relay to victory in the Bowling Green Relays at Bowling Green State University in Ohio when our regular anchor man—a veritable blur of black lightning named Cliff Hatcher—was late and missed boarding the team bus. Cliff, the Detroit PSL 440 record-holder at 48.8 seconds, a former high school All-American and my high school idol, had quickly become my mentor and best friend.

I often hung out with the twenty-one-year-old Cliff and his young first wife Jean on weekends. One day during the late spring of my freshman year, I got off a bus at Twelfth Street near Clairmount Street, where the deadly Detroit Rebellion was to begin thirteen years later. I was walking on Twelfth toward Clairmount—where Cliff and Jean were staying—when a pretty little prostitute who was near my age solicited me. She couldn't have been much older than seventeen. It bothered me that this young black girl should need to rent her body out on the street. It just didn't seem to me to be right or just for her to have to do that.

I was never into paying for feminine companionship. If anything, off and on during my life the reverse was sometimes the case. Still, not wanting to offend her, I said, "I'd love to, but I don't have any money." (This part was true.) She smiled and walked away—but she ran back between two buildings and down the alley, heading me off as I turned onto Clairmount. "I'll give you some, anyway," she said. I told her I couldn't because I was already late getting to my friends' place (which was also true). She took this as a rank rejection and hollered embarrassing cuss words at me practically all the way down Clairmount Street. Cliff and Jean thought it was funny, but I didn't.

Throughout the following track seasons, I managed to mend my amorous ways somewhat and avoid physical interactivity with girls when a big race was imminent. Resultantly, I was able to compile a series of record-breaking dual meet, conference, and state AAU championship runs at 60, 100, 220, 300, and 440 yards, culminating with a record win at 600 yards over Big Eight champion Pete Orr of Missouri and the previously unbeaten Bob Saddler of Loyola at the Michigan State Relays in Jenison Field House in East Lansing. I also won the National AAU Junior 600 in Chicago.

In 1956 I took the conference 100- and 220-yard dash titles and recorded winning times that season of 9.8 and 21.3 at those distances. I then sped a 47.7 440 in the Central Collegiate Championships at Marquette University in Milwaukee, losing the gold medal by a whisker to Pete Orr, who clocked the same time. Cliff finished fifth in that very fast eight-man final after turning in the best time in the afternoon prelims. Gastonia Finch of Iowa and Ray Wyatt of Kansas—a dangerous duo—were among the finalists.

The *Detroit Free Press* ran a university publicity shot of me in the starting blocks wearing my new Wayne State track shirt over the caption, "Tartar Triple Threat." (Wayne State athletes were called "Tartars" then—now they're the "Warriors." Also, Wayne University had become Wayne *State* University in 1955, but it took us a year to get new uniforms.) In midwestern meets, Big Ten athletes—including conference champions—had begun to ask my teammates which event I was planning to compete in and then run in events where I wasn't, because I had been beating every one of them I faced at distances ranging from 60 to 600 yards. Track fans outside of Michigan wrote to the university athletic department for autographed copies of the publicity photo. I signed several, including one for a track fan named Jeff Johnson as far away as California. I still have Jeff's letter.

After striding an eased-up 47.8 in my preliminary 400-meter heat, I tore my hamstring muscle badly in the national semifinals in California, and my 1956 season was over. The entire back of my right thigh turned black and blue; I had partially detached the muscle from the sheath, just above the knee. An orthopedic surgeon suggested that I have surgery to repair the tear, but I couldn't afford it. To this day I have a lump behind the knee where I pulled the muscle.

In 1957, with my still-sore hamstring taped (but miraculously—virtually healed), I took up where I had left off in 1956. I quickly compiled a string of wins and successfully defended my conference 220 title on a muddy track and also took the 440, which Cliff Hatcher—who had dropped out of school—had won in record time the previous year. (I didn't defend my 100 title because I was still reluctant to burst from the blocks too fast—particularly on a track that was covered with water in several places.) I also anchored Wayne State's winning 880 and mile relay teams, with Jerry Catalina and his younger brother Tim teaming with me and Ralph Carter on the mile relay. Tim Catalina had given me the nickname "the Wayne Train," but I still preferred my old nickname "Mustang," because it had been given to me by Mr. Jack Rice, my first really caring high school coach.

In the 1957 NCAA quarter mile at Austin, Texas, "the Wayne Train" chugged a fast 47.7 440 in the prelim and then beat 1956 Olympic champion Charley Jenkins of Villanova with a 47.4 in the semi twenty-five minutes later.

In the final, I outran Jenkins again with a 46.8—faster time than his Olympic win—taking the silver medal in a photo finish with Morgan State's big Bob McMurray, who also was timed in 46.8. I had broken the tape first with my neck, but McMurray's chest was an inch ahead of mine. Officials studied the photo timer for several minutes before they finally put the big Morgan State star's name up on the board in the first-place slot.

Jenkins finished a very close third in 47.1—a 440-yard time equivalent to his winning Olympic 400-meter time. He was closely followed in the star-studded field by Oklahoma's state AAU champion Gary Parr, Wisconsin's Jesse Nixon, who was the Big Ten champion, Basil Ince of Tufts University—the Eastern Intercollegiate Conference champion and a Trinidad Olympian, Southwest Conference champion John Emmett of Southern Methodist, and Harold Caffey of Indiana, the Big Ten runner-up.

I had become the first Michigan-bred sprinter to run 440 yards in less than forty-seven seconds with my sparkling 46.8, which was a scant half-second over the world record of 46.2 held by Herb McKenley of Jamaica.

The next week at the National Amateur Athletic Union (NAAU) Championships in Dayton, Ohio, Reggie Pearman of the New York Pioneer Club and I both broke the American 440-yard record on a very dusty, slow track, with times of 46.4 and 46.5. I had led into the stretch, but the big, long-striding Pearman caught me at the tape. (Our times were never ratified because there was a problem with the lane measurements.) Olympic champion Jenkins again finished third, unofficially tying his own national record of 46.7. McMurray, the NCAA and NAIA champion, finished sixth, and future Olympic champion Mike Larrabee of the Southern California Striders was seventh.

That summer of my senior year, I went undefeated at 400 meters on the United States team in Europe. California-based *Track & Field News*—the self-proclaimed "bible" of the sport—ranked me fourth in the world in the quarter mile.

I also set several more records at distances ranging from 60 to 880 yards, including still-extant 440-yard and 400-meter marks at Wayne State. At this writing fifty-two years later, I must presume that my records will stand forever unless the University, which purports to have an urban mission, does the right thing and reinstates the vaunted and comparatively inexpensive track program it eliminated in 1987. When I delivered the toast on campus at my WSU Class of 1958 Fiftieth Reunion in October of 2008, new WSU president Jay Noren told me he would be calling me to talk about restoring track, but he hasn't called yet. By the time you read this, my Detroit Track Old-Timers organization president Allan Tellis, Wayne County commissioner Keith Williams, and I will have met with him.

At one time, every single track coach in the Detroit Public School League was a former Wayne trackman!

Beginning in 1928 with John Lewis from old Northeastern, the Detroit PSL produced international sprinters Eddie Tolan from Cass Tech in the 1930s, Lorenzo Wright from old Miller in the 1940s, Willie Atterberry from old Eastern and me from Denby in the 1950s (in 1961, I was best man in Willie's wedding), Otis Davis from Miller and Henry Carr from Northwestern in the 1960s, Marshall Dill from Northern and Stan Vinson from Chadsey in the 1970s, Eliot Tabron from Murray-Wright and Deon Hogan from Kettering in the 1980s, and Darnell Hall from Pershing in the 1990s. All but me were black, and Hall in 1992 was the last PSL trackman to wear the U.S. colors abroad.

Now in the twenty-first century, the city remains a hotbed of swift black sprinters. Presently, they matriculate everywhere *except* to WSU—or more commonly, due to the NCAA's escalated admission standards, they matriculate *nowhere* except to the streets and the prisons, or to low-paying service jobs at fast-food places like McDonald's, or to the graveyard. The Detroit Track Old-Timers, a mostly black organization of 267 members that I founded with my old Detroit Track Club teammate Aaron Gordon in 1992, has tried repeatedly—but at this writing, unsuccessfully—to get the university to restore its track program. The DTOT, and I personally, see this as a civil-rights issue. Detroit NAACP director Heaster Wheeler tells me he agrees.

Accordingly, I want to re-emphasize here that despite the integral role track and athletics played in forming my core values and character, *this book's focus isn't track and athletics*. Rather, its primary focus is on my uncompromising crusade against the still-discriminatory treatment of blacks and other citizens of color in this country and against the *under-education that continues to molest the minds of non-white children* in this country.

Even though we now have achieved the election of an American president who is partially of African descent, this still-discriminatory treatment and under-education of African-Americans and other Americans of color nevertheless persists *nationwide* as we near the close of the first decade of the twenty-first century—now more than *half a century* after the 1954 United States Supreme Court ruling in *Brown vs. Board of Education* that proclaimed "separate but equal" to be inherently unequal, immoral, illegal, and unjust.

CHAPTER SEVEN

THE FAST TRACKS
OF EUROPE;
A WORLD RECORD

"We don't sponsor *Negroes*."

—Something the Detroit Athletic Club
discreetly neglected to say

Again, as I have emphasized, this book's major focus isn't track and athletics. Again, let me emphasize that its major focus is my lifelong crusade to seek and safeguard social justice. Nonetheless, in order to make manifest much of what *helped shape my personal perspectives* that led me to *launch* that lifelong crusade (aside from and in addition to the egalitarian upbringing afforded me by my freedom-loving father and grandfather), I must share <u>three</u> <u>enlightening</u> <u>racialized incidents</u> I experienced that were *relevant* to my running. These *three enlightening incidents* involved my ten black teammates on four relay teams— the first two at Wayne State University, the third on the United States national team, and the fourth with the Detroit Track Club.

<u>*First*</u> *enlightening racialized incident*: In 1956, I and my four black teammates, including my later-to-become lifelong friend and confidante Cliff Hatcher, drove with our coach from Detroit to Philadelphia nonstop and won the prestigious Penn Relays mile relay title for WSU in a huge upset, beating forty-eight college-class teams in what was hyperbolically advertised as the "College Championship of America." (Incidentally, I began a long-distance love affair that year with eighteen-year-old Margaret "Peggy" Saxton [later, Tatham], a bright, beautiful black girl from Brooklyn College whom I had met at Penn the previous year. Peggy and I saw each other for the last time fifteen years later in New York,

and I have lost touch with her.)

Another of my Penn Relays champion teammates was Ralph Williams, a handsome, well-built 9.8-second 100-yard sprinter from St. Kitts in the West Indies, who trained indifferently but played a mean guitar and sang with a Harry Belafonte-like "Down-the-way-where-the-nights-are-gay" accent that won him the hearts and bodies of many impressionable white coeds. In the process, he angered a lot of jealous, ethnocentric young white male students. Ralph's soft Caribbean accent and debonair demeanor also garnered him an imitator—a guitar-strumming impostor who affected the same accent and open silk shirt when in the company of many of the same willing young ladies (but who actually had grown up on Twelfth Street, across the street from my grandparents). I have often wondered whatever happened to Ralph Williams. I heard he became an attorney. He was a smooth dude.

My third teammate was Ralph Carter, a big, ultra-muscular and ultra-*intellectual* former Marine Corps quarter-mile star and Korean War veteran who later became a professor at Rutgers.

My fourth teammate was the explosive five foot six, 180-pound "Bullet Billy" Smith, who held the world 65-yard low hurdles record. I had gained the nickname "Train"—but if I was a train, Bullet Billy was a *locomotive*. Billy led off the 880-yard relay team that I anchored at Penn against Syracuse's 9.6-second 100-yard sprinter Jim Brown, who later set an all-time rushing record for Cleveland in the NFL and ultimately became a movie star. With Billy and *without* Ralph Carter, we won that heat going away in 1:28 flat but missed making the final by two-tenths of a second. We had won the Ohio Relays title in a record 1:27.2 in an absolute windstorm in Columbus the previous week. (Once in 1958, after I had beaten Bullet Billy in a very close 100-yard dash, I unwisely teased him about losing a 100 to a quarter-miler, and he *exploded*—insisting that I hadn't beaten him. In an attempt to convince him that I had indeed beaten him, I showed him a photo of the finish, but he said the picture had been taken from the wrong angle, and the explosive Bullet Billy exploded *again*.)

On our victorious return trip from the historic Penn Relays, coach David L. Holmes, who on such excursions was usually only able to dole out enough money for hamburgers or hot dogs for each of us from WSU's tight track budget, took us to a fancy restaurant on the Pennsylvania/Ohio border. He intended to buy us steak dinners out of his own pocket to celebrate our victory. With our empty stomachs grumbling and our mouths veritably watering in hungry anticipation, we sat and we sat and we *sat* in that restaurant for what seemed like hours without being served.

Finally, divining what was happening and tiring of being ignored by the racially discriminatory management and waiters, Coach Holmes took us back to the car. After driving many more miles into the night, we stopped at a still-open diner in a little town in Ohio where a short-order cook in a tobacco-stained apron got the rare privilege of feeding greasy hamburgers to WSU's four newly-crowned College One-Mile Relay Champions of America and their bullet-fast 880-yard relay teammate. I observed this cook to pick his nose just before he served us our Cokes with his thumbs in the glasses, but he probably meant no offense; it was apparently just his habit. Also, being extremely thirsty, I rationalized to myself that, after all, it had not been with his *thumb* but rather with his *forefinger* that he had dug in his nose so deeply. I gulped down the entire Coke and courageously ordered another with the hope that this time the cook might hold his thumb just a little higher on the glass.

Second enlightening racialized incident: In 1957, at the end of a long and arduous European track tour in which National AAU officials had scheduled us to run ourselves practically to death while allotting us the munificent amount of $2 per diem in spending money, I had lost eight pounds of pure *muscle*. I lost that muscle tissue because after a long, grueling season of training and racing I had no *fat* left to lose, and I was down to 157 pounds from my best running weight of 165. World 100-meter record holder Ira Murchison, one of three black sprinters who teamed with me in our winning U.S. 4 x 100-meter relay races during the tour, had to help me lift my heavy trophy- and medal-laden suitcase onto a train bound from Madrid to Lisbon, our last competitive stop before we were to board the plane for our long flight back home across the Atlantic. (My other two relay teammates were NCAA high-hurdles champion Elias Gilbert of Winston-Salem Teachers College and national long jump champion Ernie Shelby of the University of Kansas—and sometimes 400-meter hurdler Cliff Cushman, also of Kansas, as an alternate.)

I confided to the twenty-four-year-old Murchison, my senior by three years, that I was exceedingly ready to go home. While I had won all of my 400-meter races thus far, my new and fresh European opponents—most of them national champions—were getting faster and faster and closer and closer, and I was getting thinner and thinner and weaker and weaker.

Ira responded that he didn't care if he *ever* went home. The powerful, five foot six Olympian (who incidentally had traded wins with the equally short Bullet Billy Smith when they were stationed in the army in Germany) was being showered with attention and treated like royalty by men and women alike (*women in particular*). The team had even had a private audience with Pope Pius XII in the Vatican, and we were photographed with His Holiness—the picture appearing in several magazines both abroad and at home, including the National Amateur Athletic Association (NAAU) journal, *The Amateur Athlete*.

Ira went on to provide me with specific information regarding why he would be most happy to stay in Europe *indefinitely*. He expressly mentioned the Continental charms of some choice ladies we had encountered during our tour, and he emphasized to me that he wasn't at all ready to return to *cleaning latrines* in the dorms at Western Michigan University every week to pay the expenses his *partial* (!) track scholarship didn't cover.

Ira Murchison's words made me *think really hard*. I had encountered a twenty-six-year-old Soviet 400-meter star, Ardalion Ignatyev, whose speed had gained him a colonel's rank in the Red Army and a government-provided villa on the Black Sea, and here was America's world 100-meter record holder at 10.1 seconds—half a step faster than the immortal Jesse Owens—having to *clean other people's toilets*!?! Everything about this topsy-turvy state of affairs seemed to me to be very wrong.

Incidentally, I *did* manage to win the Portugal 400 by inches and remain undefeated—*barely*. Instead of a medal or cup, my prize was a beautiful little caravel fashioned of gold wire with the date 17–7–57 and the word *Lisboa* (Lisbon) inscribed on it. I treasure the tiny ship to this day.

That fall, I turned down an invitation to run in the Sugar Bowl track meet in New Orleans because I learned that the promoters drew the color line.

Third enlightening racialized incident: In January of 1958, after I had attained world ranking, graduated from WSU, and helped form the fledgling (and initially *penniless*) Detroit Track Club, the posh Detroit Athletic Club approached me with an offer to pay me a generous "training stipend" and cover all my expenses to invitational meets in the East and out West if I would wear its colors. A Detroit sprinter named John Owens had set a world 100-yard record of 9.8 seconds representing the DAC near the dawn of the twentieth century, but the club hadn't sponsored any runner since then.

I told the DAC's representatives that I would love to accept their offer if I could come to them as part of a package—*three black relay teammates* and me. Two of my relay teammates were former WSU speedsters Bullet Billy Smith and thirty-two-year-old Pete Petross, who later became the principal of Detroit Mumford High School. The third was future Michigan State track coach Jim Bibbs, age twenty-eight, who had tied Jesse Owens' world 60-yard mark in 1951. (Bullet Billy had held his world low-hurdles record until Olympian Hayes Jones from Pontiac, Michigan, broke it. When Billy died penniless, divorced, and on drugs at the now boarded-up Harbor Light homeless shelter in downtown Detroit in March 1990, Cliff Hatcher and I helped pay for his casket.)

The DAC people were amazed that an underpaid public servant like me would presume to set *conditions* for their offer to represent them on the track. They replied stiffly that their offer was for *me* only—so I naturally declined. What they had discreetly neglected to say, of course, was, "We don't sponsor *Negroes*"—but they hadn't really *needed* to say it.

A few short weeks after the Detroit Athletic Club turned us down, I was able to compete successfully as an individual invitee in the big indoor eastern and western meets anyway—the meet promoters paid my expenses in full. And in March of that year, running at Yost Fieldhouse in Ann Arbor in snappy red, white, and blue vests that I had designed and coach David L. Holmes had paid for, our multi-racial Detroit Track Club's 880-yard sprint relay team that the Detroit Athletic Club had discriminatorily declined to sponsor *broke the world record*. I was in bed with the flu, so former University of Detroit dashman Chuck Roehl took my place on the team that night and got himself a piece of a universal record.

After I had recovered sufficiently to rejoin the team, it would soon run even faster at the Nationals in New York.

Around that time, the draft board sent greetings. A colonel named Hull, who commanded the Presidio in California, had invited me to come and compete for him there as soon as I was inducted. I was slated to do nothing except eat, sleep, and run in Special Services for two years. Unfortunately, the army doctors downriver at the old Fort Wayne informed me that I had primary prostration of the metatarsals (flat feet) and they also detected my asthmatic wheeze, so I flunked the army physical. I called the colonel and told him my dilemma, but he said there was nothing he could do. He suggested I try the navy.

Ironically, I won the Midwest AAU 440 in record time on a muddy track in Fort Wayne, Indiana, the following weekend. I outran Mal Spence, a Jamaican Olympian competing for Arizona State (or maybe it was his twin brother Mel, also an Olympian, who was second—I never could tell those two guys apart. *Track & Field News* had dubbed them "The Gold Dust Twins").

During that track season and previous seasons, my victories were often reported in the daily newspapers, with my (and my father's) last name in headlines in big, bold letters: "Telford wins in Italy"; "Telford wins in Chicago"; "WSU's Telford flashes past record holder"; "Glory for Telford at Ohio"; Telford approaches world record," etc. One headline had my (and my father's) entire name: "John Telford takes AAU Roman holiday."

I would thrust these articles under my dad's nose like a retrieving puppy seeking approval, but he would always ignore them. He wanted me to quit running and box professionally instead. "You'll never make any money running track," he would say. "It's a total waste of time."

A day or two after I had won the Midwest AAU quarter mile, my mother sent me to make the rounds of my father's favorite saloons to find him and bring him home, because it was well past suppertime. In one watering hole where he wasn't, one of his drinking buddies clapped me on the back. "Hey, kid—congratulations for winning that race in Indiana!"

"Thanks—I guess you saw the article in the *Free Press*?"

"No, your *dad* told me about it." Those seven words were music to my ears.

That summer, I drove to Waterloo, Ontario, to compete in the North American championships, fully expecting to return to Detroit with the gold medal. I took a tall, blue-eyed blonde with me—an aspiring student-actress with long, corn-silky hair who had the lead in a Wayne State play. That night, this long-haired young lady wheedled me into intimacy.

The next day I finished second in the 440 by inches in a huge upset behind an up-and-coming teenaged prodigy from Toronto named Bill Crothers. The time, as I recall, was a shade under 49 seconds—well short of my personal best. I had met my *Waterloo* in Waterloo, thanks at least partially to my weak lapse of the previous night. Coach Rice's cautionary motto about "no 'meat' before the meet" had been borne out once more! I spoke barely a single word to this debilitating Delilah during our entire long drive back to Detroit, and I felt like throwing my silver medal out the car window. Instead, I gave it to her when we got back home, but I never dated that stage-struck temptress again—nor did I return her calls. Actually, though, my treatment of her wasn't really quite fair, because I basically had only myself to blame for losing that race.

I had just turned twenty-two. Instead of "trying the navy," as Colonel Hull had suggested, I decided to embark on a teaching and coaching career in a public high school in my hometown.

CHAPTER EIGHT

PIMPS, NYMPHS, AND A PRINCE OF SPRINTS

"For I dipt into the future, far as human eye could see."

—*Alfred, Lord Tennyson*

I had definitely (and some might say, only *semi*-sanely) decided that not only did I want to be a high school teacher—I wanted to be a high school *English* teacher in the ultra-challenging inner depths of Detroit! With this grandiose goal in mind, I enrolled in a master's degree program in English education at WSU without missing a beat after fulfilling the requirements for my Bachelor of Liberal Arts degree with a major in English. I completed student-teaching assignments at Detroit Pershing and at Denby, my alma mater, while working the night shift part-time at Keystone Metal Molding Company.

As a result of this rather busy schedule, I only ran two races indoors in 1959, winning one and losing one. I did manage to successfully defend my state AAU 440-yard title outdoors in Kalamazoo in a meet record 47.3 seconds against Western Michigan's fast-finishing John Bork, who later won the NCAA half mile, but I failed to defend my Midwest 440 title, finishing a close second to Jamaican Olympian George Kerr's near-world-record 46.3—which broke my Midwest record. Big Ten 440 champion John Brown of Iowa, the football star, was third in a personal-best 47.5.

In the Olympic year of 1960, I mounted a promising comeback indoors, beating several world-ranked runners in the eastern invitational 600-yard races, including Purdue's Canadian-born sprinter Dave Mills, who had become the quarter-miling scourge of the Midwest the previous year with a victory over

Ohio State's great sprinter/hurdler, Glenn Davis. Outdoors, after running a fast 47 flat in a late-season 440, I incurred an inflamed toe tendon. My 47 flat translated to an estimated 46.6 for the shorter Olympic distance of 400 meters, which qualified me for the nationals.

I tried to talk the DPS athletic director, one of my old high school coaches with whom I wasn't on the best of terms, into letting me take a young Northwestern High School junior named Henry Carr to the nationals with me. (Eight years earlier, a classmate I had been dating told me this coach had made improper advances toward her, and I had refused to play for him after that.) Early in that spring of 1960, at Northwestern coach Tom Hendricks' request, I had run beside Henry Carr in 220-yard speed/endurance training repetitions averaging an incredible 22 seconds, and the seventeen-year-old, six foot three sprinter later qualified for the nationals in the 200 by slicing a tenth of a second off Jesse Owens' high school 220 mark of 20.7. Henry almost lazily loped the first of these sub-22-second repetitions without even taking off his sweats while I sprinted as fast as I could to keep up with him. After taking those workouts with him, I became thoroughly convinced that this young, 198-pound rocket whom local fans dubbed "the Gray Ghost" was already the fastest furlong runner in the world.

The DPS athletic director refused to let Henry go to California with me, saying he would be ineligible for local high school competition his senior year, because Detroit PSL athletes were forbidden to compete beyond a 25-mile radius of the city. To this day, I am certain that Henry would have won the 1960 Olympic 200 meters. The following year—his senior year in high school—he would equal the world 220-yard straightaway record of 20 seconds flat, and in Tokyo in 1964, he would win the Olympic 200.

Running with two toes taped together and plagued by recurring asthma, I could manage only a 47.4 in the national 400-meter preliminaries in California and missed qualifying for the semifinals by one-tenth of a second. I was devastated. After having pulled my hamstring muscle in the 1956 NCAA semi-final, the chance I had awaited for four long years had taken only a short 47.4 seconds to slip away from me *once again*: I would have to wait four *more* long years for another chance to make the Olympic team.

For a while, I drowned my sorrows in women and whiskey, getting in a tad of trouble when I broke a mirror with a beer bottle in a bar when the bartender taunted me for getting outrun out west after all the hopeful hoopla about me in the Detroit papers. Eventually, I drowned my sorrows more healthily by immersing myself in volunteer coaching and in my teaching, which was to become my off-and-on lifetime passion. Long before I had ever decided to become an English teacher, I had taken the dashing D'Artagnan as my premier—albeit semi-*fictitious*—role model after having acquired my literary inclinations by reading every obscure work of the Afro-French author Alexandre Dumas I could get my happy little hands on that featured the heroic Gascon swordsman/Musketeer (plus nearly a dozen Dumas books that *didn't* feature him). I had also been divinely privileged, of course, to enjoy many a multicultural youthful adventure on Detroit's Sixteenth Street and later as an athlete with my African-American WSU, DTC, and U.S. teammates. Thus, it was perhaps inevitable that I would succumb to this quixotic calling—most suitable even then to pedants, saints, masochists, or madmen—and more quixotically yet, I was inevitably destined to profess it in an inner-city public high school. Only those aspiring to profess similarly in an urban junior high were (and are) more saintly—or less sane.

On my first day of formal contract teaching at predominately black Detroit Southeastern High School, my department head told me, "Here's your schedule. Here are your texts. Go *to* it!" He then walked out the door, seldom to be seen again (except whenever he wanted me to cover a sixth class or assume some additional duty, such as study hall duty, cafeteria duty, or hall-and-grounds patrol).

My seventh- and eighth-hour hall-and-grounds-patrol duties proved to be particularly challenging. School was letting out for students at those times, and members of the world's second-oldest profession sometimes circled the building in their long Cadillacs and Deuce-and-a-Quarters (Buick 225's). On days when the police were busy elsewhere—and the pimps always seemed to know when those days were—they would actually invade the school in often-successful efforts to enlist a few of our more susceptible young ladies.

An insufferably arrogant student of mine by the name of Clifford McNettles was a sort of "inside man" in that regard. The smooth-skinned Clifford looked the part—sauntering to school in an oiled pompadour, wide-brimmed lavender hat, peg-panted zoot suit, and gold chain. Many of our more impressionable and less studious nymphets, of course, absolutely adored him—and a couple of them were rumored to be already working for him.

The 187 students initially assigned to me in my five classes had many differences, but there was one thing which most of them had in common: they were illiterate writers and semi-literate readers. I found it hard to believe that these kids could have made it to high school. How, I wondered, could any of our city schools be producing illiterate *high school* students? It seemed incredible, yet there they sat—students who read aloud in halting, disjointed monotones; students who moved their lips when they read silently; students who wrote "there" indiscriminately for "their" and "they're"; students who painstakingly printed their 'n's upside-down!

One of the textbooks was a bland pacifier called *People in Literature*. It offered such un-classic stories as "Bombardier," "I Got a Name" (*sic*), and "Old Holy Joe." With apologies to Stephen Vincent Benét, who deserved more carefully considered selection at the hands of anthologizers, neither humankind's eternal questions nor our pressingly current ones were going to be answered through assigning students poetry like "The Mountain Whippoorwill" to ruminate upon: "Up in the mountains, mountains in the fog/Everything's as lazy as an old houn' dog." This was especially so then, when many black students in the Detroit Public Schools were in the clutches of an educational system that was already starting to decline, had had its way with them for over a decade, and hadn't yet taught many of them to *read*. Nearly half of Detroit's adult population is functionally illiterate today—and that disgraceful degeneration definitely didn't occur overnight.

Once, many years later when I was invited to speak to a group of school honchos in Chicago, I was last on a program whose dinner and multiplicity of windy local after-dinner testimonial speakers had taken far too much time. (Chicago, after all, *is* called the "Windy City.") I had become concerned that I might miss my flight back to Detroit, so when my turn finally came to deliver my speech, I scrapped my notes and stood up and said, "Teach them to *read*!!" Then I sat back down—and everyone got to go home, including me. (In order, however, for children to be really taught to read, their class sizes can't be thirty or more in the early elementary grades. Rather, they need to be twenty or less.)

While *trying* to teach them to read, I also had to teach *Silas Marner* to my students at Southeastern High. Some of my kids spelled their names differently every time they handed in a paper, my classes were nearly 100 percent black, and I was actually supposed to teach them that unbelievably *soporific* novel in which Anglo-Saxons are glorified (the miserly Silas saves blond Eppie, whose hair reminds him of his hoarded gold!). I decided not to even *try* to teach that book, with the racist undertones it held for my mostly black students.

At first, I couldn't figure out how I was going to be able to teach my kids Shakespeare's *Julius Caesar*, either. They adamantly didn't want to be fed any *part* of that play with its difficult late-sixteenth-century idiom, which was required fare then in the tenth grade. However, when I let them take turns lying supine on my desk with a coat covering their faces while their classmates took turns trying to recite (from memory) Mark Antony's famous "Friends, Romans, countrymen" funeral oration, they perked up and got into the play with surprisingly intense enthusiasm.

One morning, when my kids and I were enjoying a particularly dramatic and well-delivered funeral-oration performance, my department head came in and sat at the back of the classroom in the only vacant student desk. The proudly declaiming student's successful oration ended to his classmates' stamping and applauding, the bell rang, and my administrator approached me through the hubbub of scraping chairs and boisterous voices of the departing class. I tried to appear modest, but I was secretly elated that he had seen this difficult class totally engaged in a valuable learning experience.

Here, to my then-dismayed surprise, is his oral (and then *written*) assessment to me that morning of what he saw:

> Your class was too noisy this hour, Mr. Telford. Please restrict it to activities of a quieter nature. Also, I note your blackboard is not clear. There are portions of an earlier lesson on it. Always erase your board before beginning a new lesson. And never, *ever* let a student lie on your desk. Since it is improper, and moreover, *undignified*, for a teacher to *sit* on his desk while teaching—as I have incidentally observed *you* to do—it is even *more* improper for a student to *lie* across it. Further, I'd like to remind you again what I mentioned to you just last week—you must keep your window shades straighter. Uneven window shades are very *distracting* to students.

What perhaps should have been of considerably *more* concern to Southeastern's administration, faculty, support staff, parents, and students than unwashed blackboards and uneven window shades were the pregnancy and VD rates at the school. Both were attaining impressive proportions; that is to say, they were roughly in step with the accelerating national urban average. I had moved into a rather shabby apartment nearby to be close to my new job. Perhaps uncoincidentally to the school's growing numbers of students who were becoming pregnant or infected with venereal disease, I was finding audacious notes in my apartment mailbox and even under my apartment door and on my classroom desk from semi-anonymous female students that read (for example), "My pussy be [*sic*] hot for you." I intercepted a note from one female student to another during class that said, "I wonders [*sic*] what Mr. Talfore [*sic*] look [*sic*] like with his close [*sic*] off."

On more than one occasion, I was directly propositioned by female students —some were other teachers' students; a few were my own. Teachers were intermittently catching students having sex in various unsupervised areas of the school building and grounds. Some of my track athletes at the school confided to me that an unfamiliar, foul-smelling discharge was oozing from their penises and staining their pants, and it hurt to urinate—whereupon I would arrange to have them medically treated for what usually turned out to be gonorrhea. Unfortunately, a few of them kept going back and getting reinfected with the very same disease by the very same source(s)—and the source(s) herself/ themselves was/were proving exceptionally averse to any outside advisements to her/them that she/they seek medical treatment or even conceding that she/ they *needed* it.

Luckily, I was somehow able to convince big George Wesson, my fastest sprinter, to keep away from these temptations which had claimed some of his teammates. As his reward for training hard and remaining celibate (at least during track season), this veritable prince of sprints was enabled to win sixteen consecutive races ranging from 220 yards to the half-mile and go on to take the state high school 440-yard dash title in a record 49 seconds flat. George also won some memorable relay duels with old Eastern High's future Olympian Lou Scott, who was coached by 1948 Olympian Lorenzo Wright, one of my major mentors. (For any track buffs reading this torrid tome: Remember the tracks then were slow, archaic dirt-and-cinder tracks—not modern rubberized composition tracks. Also, quarter-milers in this country competed at 440 yards then—not the shorter 400 meters—and running shoes were far inferior to those worn today.)

As a result of those venereal eventualities to which some of my un-celibate athletes and other such students were increasingly falling prey, I eventually found myself assigned to yet another duty—an emergency in-house *sex-education curriculum-writing* committee. This hastily-assembled committee consisted of me, one male and one female health and physical education teacher (the female teacher didn't *look* female), two parents who were mothers of Southeastern students, and a very pretty—and very *married*—family living teacher. The family living teacher, who was only a few years older than me, had been appointed by Principal Margery Readhead to chair the committee.

Despite the family living teacher's experienced leadership capabilities and the high regard in which Miss Readhead held her, the problem with Southeastern's sex-education committee, as I saw it—and indeed with sex-education committees in general, as I *see* it—was and *is* that they tend to propose relevant curricula that cover topics that are already all too experientially familiar to most students at this age level. Such curricula should be introduced at the elementary or early middle-school level, but these are precisely the ages where parents and communities are least likely to permit their instruction. Children who haven't attained puberty are more likely to be able to deal with the subject *dispassionately* (no pun). By high school, our kids didn't need sex education information so much as they needed pregnancy-prevention and disease-prevention information.

Herpes and the deadly AIDS virus weren't around yet in the 1950s and '60s—but syphilis, the ubiquitous gonorrhea and crabs, and other unpleasant venereal phenomena definitely *were*.

Moreover, some of the diseases had grown *rampant* at Southeastern.

CHAPTER NINE

EDUCATIONAL SEX AND A "VAGINAL" TEXT

"A fond kiss, and then we sever."

—*Robert Burns*

The highly-regarded family living teacher who chaired our sex education committee just happened to possess two disturbingly bewitching baby blue eyes and a pair of tempting rosebud lips—and due to the nature of her committee's charge, those rosebud lips were dutifully and steadily spouting words like *penis*, *sexual intercourse*, and *vagina*.

And *erection*. Once when the highly-regarded family living teacher sat next to me on a sofa in the teachers' lounge where our committee usually met, an apparently accidental thigh contact nearly sent me through the ceiling. (There is more than one way to molest a mind.) When she invited me to her home one afternoon to work as a subcommittee of two on a key portion of the curriculum recommendation, the highly-regarded family living teacher made known to me her desire that I also work on *her*.

I had always believed that teachers are by nature superior beings who don't succumb to such temptations or provoke them in others. This, I had naïvely presumed, must be particularly true of *married lady* teachers. I was therefore reassured (and admittedly delighted) to discover that a highly-regarded teacher like my committee chairperson wasn't some improbably perfect icon of cold, unattainable ivory, but was in fact fashioned of the same hot, young flesh and blood that *I* was—and this discovery enabled me (at least *partially*, albeit *misguidedly*) to reconcile my abject humanness with my lofty new profession.

Lying abed afterward in the sated embrace of my highly-regarded committee chairperson, I found that my own personal regard for her had grown quite notably (and uncritically) high, too—thus, I also found myself actually composing rapturous grammatical exercise sentences using the various forms of the intransitive verb "lie," as in "recline." *Lie, lay, have lain. . . .* And now *laid* (in the *transitive* form). Several older and a few younger teachers in the men teachers' lounge were wont to speculate in my presence regarding what my highly-regarded committee chairperson looked like in the altogether. Having now become privy to this delectable knowledge, I was tempted to share it boastfully with my colleagues; but upon reflection, I felt that to keep silent was the most gentlemanly course of action for me to follow in that regard.

In a certain sense, those of us who have undertaken to teach teenagers the finer points of one of the world's most difficult languages truly become like battered boxers after only a relatively short time toiling in the classroom. I recall an old boxing stablemate of my father whose hand would shake holding his coffee cup rattling on the dish whenever he heard a bakery truck's bell. Like that poor, punch-drunk old pug, many of us teachers of English—rookies and veterans alike—just can't escape from somehow relating our every external and internal stimulus to the perpetual contemplation of our peculiar discipline, as I had done following my initial forbidden interaction with my highly-regarded committee chairperson.

Indeed, my whimsical sentences regarding the intransitive form of *lie* and the transitive form of *laid*, etc., weren't so far removed from some unintentionally similar ones I had seen in texts. My kids, of course, had practically rolled on the floor laughing the first time (and the *last* time) I had tried to use certain actual textbook sentences in my lessons. For example, I soon learned to skip a particular exercise on adjectives which began, "Let's assume you have a *box*. It could be a *white* box, a *big* box, a *black* box. . . ."

Box in those days (and perhaps still in some neo-Neanderthal circles today) being a slang pejorative for *vagina*, the writers of this particular textbook exercise might as well have included the adjective *hairy*. In fact, in another of my grammar books (a 1950s edition of *Warriner's Handbook*, as I recall), there *was* a drill sentence that—catastrophically for the poor teacher, namely, *me*— *did* verily contain a reference to a hypothetical someone named "Harry Dick." (So help me God.)

Who in the world *wrote* these textbooks? Whoever they were had to have included these abominations innocently and naïvely, hadn't they? After all, the textbooks' authors weren't diabolical monsters bent on making us poor teachers squirm and suffer—but what manner of unbelievably sheltered lives must they have led! Some of those books abounded in several absolutely *classical* Freudianisms.

Others used words like "punk," "sissy," and "trim" with their conventional (that is to say, *standard white idiomatical*) denotation. However, white teachers in black schools need to know (and some of them never *learn*) that "punk" and "sissy" mean *homosexual* in what we now call "Ebonic" slang, and "trim" means *sexual intercourse*—as in, "Tomorrow night, I'm goin' out and gettin' me some *trim*!" When these teachers use such expressions in their lessons, they wonder why their black students laugh so uproariously.

I determined that I would write to the publisher of these texts to alert them *for God's sake* not to *repeat* these monstrous errors, in order to spare future young teachers such agony as I had endured. I also decided that if I ever became an English department head or a principal or a teacher of teachers in a university, I would acquaint my young teachers with some of these idiomatic usages in order to arm them against using them in "standard English" or in any *other* version of English in their classrooms. (And later I *did*, and I did.)

I further determined that one day I, myself, would write a grammar text that wouldn't contain such embarrassing (although certainly unintentional) *double entendres*, and it would be a text that would also be better suited to address the *real* needs of my students—needs which definitely didn't include having clean blackboards and straight window shades in their classrooms.

In Mrs. D.'s Honors English class, which was down the hall from my class-room with my chronically unwashed blackboards and un-straightened window shades, there wasn't an unwashed blackboard or un-straight window shade to be seen—not *one*. There were also no students laughing uproariously at any unwittingly ribald word Mrs. D. might have uttered during her lectures on grammar, nor was there any student misbehaving in any *other* way, either—at least, not for long.

This was because Mrs. D.'s very few misbehavers—who almost without exception happened to be black—got transferred to one of my classes. I had quickly proved myself able to "handle" them, took them voluntarily at counselors' requests, and soon had a happy host of former behavior problems sitting in crowded but attentive classes of forty or more students. In one class, I had to have some students sit on the windowsills. At one point in the spring of 1961, I counted 204 students in my five classes.

All of Mrs. D.'s classes were Code "X" (Honors) classes, mostly populated by the very few white students still remaining in the school—most of them residents of a historic and exclusive all-white subdivision ironically called "*Indian Village.*" Unlike mine, her class sizes numbered less than twenty-five. Mrs. D. herself, a soft-spoken, bespectacled lady of fifty or so, had recently been named the Michigan Education Association Teacher of the Month for the entire state of Michigan. (I, myself, being a budding maverick, had joined the rival and proletarian Detroit Federation of Teachers.)

Despite Mrs. D.'s impressive award, it developed that she was experiencing considerable difficulty controlling a noisy, overwhelmingly black study hall that had been assigned to her as her obligatory duty period up on the third floor. Since she confided to me that this non-studious study hall was giving her serious nerve and intestinal problems (how *dare* it!), and she reminded me just a little bit of my father's sweet elder sister Margaret who had always been good to me, I chivalrously volunteered to take over Mrs. D.'s study hall in addition to my campus-patrol duty.

The study hall had nearly three hundred students crammed cheek-to-jowl into a huge room. This gave me a contract-violating load of five classes and two duties, plus an unpaid coaching assignment, but I didn't care—the numbers of students in my classes already far exceeded the contractual limit, anyway. My motto was, "The more the merrier." I have always been something of a ham, and my kids offered me a captive audience.

I set out, with eventual success, to keep Mrs. D.'s former study hall quiet for those few students who really wanted to study in there. Those students who wished to sleep in there I *permitted* to sleep in there. Many of them were working night jobs and attending school during the day. However, my policy of letting them sleep met with the flat disapproval of my department head. He himself taught only one class—a select twenty-student Honors class made up of seniors. He had in turn assigned this single class to a student teacher from Wayne State University whom he then generally left to his own devices, sink or swim. In fact, I benevolently arranged with his student teacher, who was floundering even with these reasonably well-behaved and mostly white students, to take some of *his* discipline problems off his hands.

The department head had no *duties*, either, except one he had evidently chosen to assume that appeared to consist mainly of giving me a hard time. I informed the department head that I would continue to allow students who chose to sleep in my study hall to do so, since I preferred that they sleep rather than disturb others who were studying.

I told the department head, "If you want my sleepers to study instead of sleep, *you* take over my study hall and make them study instead of sleep."

Thankfully, the department head left me and my study hall alone after that.

CHAPTER TEN

"WHY YOU DIDN'T *TELL* ME THAT??"

"Necessity is the mother of invention."

—*Plato, ancient Greek philosopher*

Despite Southeastern High School's many serious problems that were there even in the early 1960s, it was actually a good school with an excellent, no-nonsense principal. In order for a school to be a good school, it is unquestionably important that it have a good principal. However, would you like to know the *real secret* of *good schools*? Here's the secret—what *really* makes a school *good* is *good, dedicated, caring teachers*. This is because good, dedicated, caring *teachers* make good, dedicated, caring *students*—and even though I was just a *rookie* teacher, I was already a good, dedicated, and *exceptionally* caring one.

While teaching at Southeastern, I had begun to write stories and poems about Detroit kids and their experiences to which my students could better relate. I supplemented (and sometimes *supplanted*) the stories and poems in the school district's authorized standard anthology with those of my own that I mimeographed and handed out.

I couldn't keep enough copies in my classroom of one particular story—"The Reckoning"—that had a non-violence message my kids really needed. The boys in my classes identified intensely with the protagonist, a black teen-ager who was beaten in a fight by an older boy in a Naval Reserve uniform whom he had teased about being in the "Sea Scouts" and then got "revenge" four years later by beating him in turn when the older boy, now a man, was discharged from the navy. But the young man hardly remembered the incident, so for the teen, the "revenge" he exacted was futile. (I was the younger youth in the story. Only the race of the subjects was changed.)

I also spent part of my meager paycheck on some paperbacks of Brian Hooker's translation of French playwright Edmond Rostand's *Cyrano de Bergerac*. (My annual salary then was approximately $4,000.)

The kids loved *Cyrano*. I believe they subconsciously analogized their discriminated-against blackness with the mocked long nose of the unrequited seventeenth-century lover/swordsman. Several of them memorized the speech that went, "Was this the *nose* that launched a thousand ships...?"

A few years later in my 1968 WSU doctoral dissertation, after interacting with a dissertational sampling of students at Detroit Central and Pershing high schools and at all-white Grosse Pointe High, I proved my hypothesis that both urban and suburban students would react positively to literature curricula revamped to contain selections fostering the development of their *ethics-evaluative* powers, and that students' selection of their most-favored stories would occur along *gender* rather than *racial* lines. The black and white girls tended to choose the same stories, and the black and white boys did the same.

In these selections, I included pieces that dealt with the perennially explosive issue of racism. Both in 1968 and still in many schools today, the traditional approach to teaching literature assumed (and assumes) that literary works are like museum pieces, apart and independent from the learner, to be looked at but not touched, nor should some of their themes be accordingly examined too *closely*. This is held to be particularly so if implicative aspects of those literary works run contrary to majority mores or are perceived in some way to be too disturbing or simply not *nice*. Urban teen pregnancy and the out-of-control proliferation of venereal disease among urban teens, for example, aren't frequently examined themes in most anthologies, nor are teen muggings of the elderly, or drive-by shootings, or white racism and black classism.

Also, the similarly traditional approach in which classic and neo-classic literary works are treated like delicate museum pieces negates the awakening of *empathy* in the individual and the intensification of his/her feelings of *humanness*. Yet, these are the *very kinds of human feelings* that we as teachers have the ongoing responsibility to try to awaken and nurture in our students!

Van Cleve Morris wrote in his landmark book *Existentialism in Education*:

Examine any theme of humanistic writing—death, love, suffering, guilt, fairness, freedom—and put the student in touch with
them. Let the student ponder the meaning of his own life by
pondering the truth that on some future day it will be abruptly
cancelled from the universe with no trace remaining.

In that very same vein, the Renaissance master Hans Holbein the Younger
painted a skull in an anamorphic distortion into the foreground of a painting
which, for decades, has been on intermittent exhibit at the Detroit Institute
of Arts. After the viewer has passed the painting, the grotesquely elongated
skull assumes normal proportions and the live human figures it sits before—
viewed now at an oblique angle—become distorted in its place. Death, after
the painting has been viewed and passed by, becomes the true reality.
Consider these eleven lines of iambic pentameter:

The cosmos bides its unbeginning end.
If Bear could see or Crab could comprehend,
This microcosmic rebel might be seen
Upon one shining pebble gleaming green.
Our end is our beginning's nether twin.
Within this measured stint, <u>shall be</u> has been
And never evermore again can be.
I fancy yet I could have met, resigned,
That pre-chaotic canceling of mind—
Foreverlasting darkness undesigned—
Had here but been no existential <u>she</u>.

I wrote that poem; it is my preference that the "existential *she*" in it remain
unnamed here. The poem was chosen by poets Mark Van Doren and Norma
Millay, among other judges, to appear in *Prize Poets of 1966*, a Sharon [Connecticut]
Creative Arts Foundation-funded publication. Aptly titled *Yesterday Is Tomorrow*,
it posits (and bemoans) that our existence—but a droplet in the vast ocean of
infinity—is nearly over before it begins. Indeed, in substantive point of time,
there *is* no present. What we call "the present time" is akin to a longitudinal
line on a globe: It has no actual referential existence beyond the most infinitesimal
measure of time/space. There exists only a past and a future. Of the two, the
future is the more significant in that it can be altered for good or evil.

Like history—but even *more* than history—*literature* should be taught as a way to mold the future for the betterment of humankind. Obviously, our children *embody* the future, for better or worse. This is why I observed in my 1968 doctoral dissertation that we must anthologize into textbooks selections that awaken a social sense—what Van Cleve Morris called "the problem of 'the *Other*'." One of the most unjustly treated "*Others*" in this country has, of course, been its black citizen. I like to believe that my dissertation had some small impetus toward inducing textbook publishers to produce the texts that now deal with urban situations and to include the selections that now feature African and African-American authors.

Relevantly, in the graduate-level courses I taught at Oakland and Wayne State universities in the 1990s after I retired as the deputy superintendent of the Rochester Community Schools in 1991, I set forth an instructional process I call my "Inquiry Process." I modeled it again when I emerged from K-12 retirement to teach at predominantly black and Latino Detroit Southwestern High School in 1999 and later at 99 percent black (and ultimately *100* percent black) Detroit Finney High School for a second time between 2003 and 2008.

The Inquiry Process, as I have applied it, involves *reformulating* current secondary school (and higher education) curricula into the form of *questions* to which students are guided toward *deriving and articulating their own answers*.

Here are sample questions:

"What, if anything, seems to you to be worth dying for? How did you come to believe this? At the *present moment*, what would you most like to be able to be, or to do? Why? What would you have to know in order to be able to do it? How can "good" be distinguished from "evil"? What kind of person would you most like to be? How might you get to be this kind of person?

"What are the most important changes that have occurred in the past ten years? Twenty years? Fifty years? In the last year? In the last six months? Last month? What will be the most important changes next month? Next year? Next decade? How can you tell? What would you change if you could? How might you go about it? Of those changes which are going to occur, which would you stop if you could? Why? How?

"What are the most dangerous ideas that are popular today? Why do you think so? Where did these ideas come from?"

I included this final and most deeply engrossing question for my intrepid young students of English: "How might humankind's survival activities be different from what they are *if we didn't have* <u>language</u>?"

At Southeastern, I recall that early in the fall of 1960, I had asked my classes to ponder two questions that intrigued them but almost drove class *and* teacher insane when we tried to get our minds around them.

One question was, "What *meaning* does the word 'infinity' hold for you?"

The other question—which provoked them to ponder even *harder*—was, "What is the *meaning* of 'meaning'?"

I told my Southeastern students that they had to grapple with enigmas like this to train their brains so they could join my incipient AAAA—my All-American Activist Army—because civil rights that were supposedly universally acknowledged as belonging to all Americans were, as they pertained to non-white Americans, thus far civil *wrongs*.

Long after my initial clumsy classroom incursions into some rudimentary aspects of the Inquiry Process and my contemplative efforts to implement those aspects of it, I read a book (in the fall of 2003) entitled *Conversations with God, Book II*, that uncannily parallels the Process. In it, author Neal Walsche states:

> Right now, schools exist primarily to provide *answers*. It would be far more beneficial if their primary function were to ask *questions*. What does it mean to be honest or responsible or fair? What are the *implications*? For that matter, what does it mean that $2 + 2 = 4$? What are the *implications*? We should encourage all children to discover and create those answers for themselves.

As the historian/philosopher George Santyanna asserted, history and relevant literature must be taught as a way to enable children to learn from the past, so they can mold the future progressively and fairly. Data from a prior time or from a prior literary experience should always and only be the basis for new questions. As Walsche implies, the treasure should be in the *question*—not in the answer.

However, while all this professorially profound educational philosophy regarding the teaching of literature with my bent toward creating social activists is indeed well and good, I soon found during my days at Southeastern that literary appreciation is *one* thing, but being literately and articulately able to *write* and *speak* about literature or justice or the human condition (or about practically anything *else*) is quite *another*.

At Southeastern, the truism very soon became painfully evident to me that until my kids could be enabled to comprehend and competently *use* traditional grammatical terminology, I wouldn't be fully able to teach them to write or speak "correctly." Therefore, I *also* wouldn't be fully able to *enable* them to contemplate complex ideas clearly and articulate them coherently. I further noted—most *practically*—that thus they also wouldn't be able to learn the finer nuances of the standard "marketplace" English they were going to need to know in order to survive and prevail in the overwhelmingly white, workaday world of competitively cutthroat commercial capitalism.

So, during my second year at Southeastern, I finalized a treatise in the form of an eleven-page grammar "text" that prescribed more specifically for syntactical and dialectical deviations from "standard" English found in what decades later came to be called "Ebonics." I (Ebonically!) entitled this pioneering work of mine, "Why You Didn't *Tell* Me That??—A *'Foreign-Language'* Approach to Teaching English." As I constantly emphasized to my students in those early-1960s days, and as I was to emphasize again and again forty and fifty years later to new generations of students, the limits of their *language* would determine the limits of their *world*. This remains even more the case now as we approach the second decade of the twenty-first century, with its acceleratingly advancing technological and yet currently fragile global economy that makes urban students' mastery of marketplace English a *must* if they are to play productive roles in resuscitating that global economy and guiding it into a more enlightened and cooperatively peaceable channel.

In the 1990s, many of my educator colleagues assumed from my newspaper columns and speeches that I was at odds with University of California professor John Ogbu concerning his pedagogical support of that specifically African-American idiom now known as Ebonics. Dr. Ogbu, who died in 2002, was the native Nigerian who caused considerable controversy among blacks and many liberal whites when he recommended that Ebonics be taught in the

Oakland, California schools.

I was never at odds with Dr. Ogbu's position. I had stated in the foreword of that 1962 treatise I wrote while teaching at Southeastern:

> A dangerous byproduct of the attempt to raise the "cultural" and educational levels of those who are "different" is that in the desire to make them over, some teachers strip them of . . . individuality, and of <u>self</u>. White teachers must be continuously wary of their own . . . motives, and of any subconscious tendency they may have toward implied rejection of their Negro students through disapproval of the students' language patterns, which have a comfortable freedom of expression that traditional forms lack.

However, having written that, I went on to make this point: *"Negro students' command of standardized language skills—written and spoken—will* inexorably determine the *height of their climb* in the job hierarchy."

And it inexorably did, has, and will. Professor Ogbu actually emphasized that same point when he was consulting for Oakland, but this got lost in the media frenzy that seized singularly on his recommendation for Ebonics instruction for that California school district's predominantly African-American population. This frenzy grew particularly fierce across the country in the black press, even though Dr. Ogbu had in fact declared that he regarded the teaching of Ebonics as a merely *temporary* bridge to ensure black students' transition to the competent use of marketplace English.

The truth is, Ogbu believed that black children should be immersed in "standard" English instruction via a wide variety of methods, including their being extensively taught pertinent grammatical terminology—particularly parts of speech and sentence parts—so that, as he said, "The lingual tools they must work with have ready handles whereby they can be easily grasped."

Today, African-American students' unique learning needs still aren't being fulfilled. The main staple of urban children's education should be a K-12 language arts program specifically tailored to the culturally and regionally-induced peculiarities of their speech patterns—and you will see me persistently illustrating this point often again in this book. Unless extensive dialectically specific and prescriptive language instruction—including in-depth grounding in grammatical structure and terminology—is established and taught in Detroit and other such enclaves where there are many children of African ancestry and southern slave heritage—those children will suffer a lifetime lingual disadvantage.

My Southeastern students—most naturally being consummate *masters* of Ebonics—gave me what turned out to be invaluable advice and assistance in writing that 1962 treatise (which was then adapted for use between 1963 and 1967 in several Detroit high schools where the faculties were overwhelmingly white). For my kids, this golden opportunity for cooperative writing with their teacher also became a most effective learning experience.

CHAPTER ELEVEN

A BRIEF COMEBACK,
A FINAL RACE—
THEN *EXILE*!

"Home is where the heart is."

—*Pliny the elder, ancient Roman philosopher*

With the students already out for the summer and the staff still on duty to clean out their rooms, Principal Margery Readhead rounded a turn on the third floor a tad too quietly and happened upon her highly-regarded and highly-married sex-education committee chairperson squeezing my young, sprinter-hard rear end. She lectured us together and then separately in her office.

Despite having discovered our liaison, Miss Readhead still wanted to keep us at Southeastern. Unfortunately (or fortunately?), over her futile protest to those in power downtown, I was transferred that September to the newly-formed and 99.9 percent white Finney High School. Thus, for the next two frustrating years, I couldn't use my innovative treatise with black students, since I didn't *have* any black students (except one)—and it was pedagogically pointless to use it with white ones. (Ironically, the previous year I had turned down Principal Irving Wolf's invitation to "come home" and teach and coach at Denby, which was then also still all-white, and even though Mr. Wolf was a wonderful man and Denby was a fine institution, I had never felt completely comfortable in an all-white school. My work was with black kids.)

They had transferred me to Finney under the infamous Three-Year Plan dreamed up by typically unbrilliant downtown bureaucrats. It had been un-brilliantly designed to drag teachers who were supposedly happy teaching out on Detroit's "safe" white periphery *down*, *down*, *down* into the dire, dark depths of the "scarifying bogey-man-blackest-of-the-black" inner city. Unreflectively, no provisions had been made in the plan to accommodate committed white inner-city teachers like me who fervently wished to *remain* in the black inner city.

So off to lily-white Finney I unwillingly went, after having coached a state 440-yard dash champion and record breaker and several other All-City athletes. I left behind a top-rated young and nearly all-black track team that included many more potential champions and featured a powerful soon-to-be eleventh-grader named Johnny Saddler, whose 49.8 had been the fastest tenth-grade quarter-mile clocking in the country. Despite eventually enjoying excellent track and football success as a junior and senior, Johnny was destined never to break 50 seconds again.

That summer of 1963, before I knew I was being transferred, I made a brief comeback, winning a few local 100 and 220 races and then organizing some afternoon track meets at Southeastern. I invited everyone in the city and the suburbs to come there and run. George Wesson and I ran two 440 races, and I deliberately tied for first in both with him to keep his unbeaten record unblemished. (George's relay rival, future Olympian Lou Scott, finished third in one of them.) George and I joined hands across our ten-year gap like older/younger brothers as we crossed the finish line together. Two *memorable* moments!

I also got in some potentially bad trouble that summer when I broke the jaw of a stocky white man who had been brutally beating his white ex-girlfriend on Belle Isle, the island park in the Detroit River where I was supervising a work crew for the recreation department. She had been at the bathing beach on a blanket with a black man who had gone to get hot dogs and pop when the white guy showed up. I had backed the man up against a tree and hit him once too often and too hard while the tree was holding him upright and he was too slow to go down. The police took my statement and hers, and they conveyed the injured man and his bleeding erstwhile girlfriend across the river to the hospital.

He ended up suing me for assault. My dad got me a lawyer via his old fight manager, Archie Silman, but the lady—my star witness—disappeared back to Kentucky just before my court date, so I had to settle the case for money I felt I shouldn't have had to spend. The judge ordered me to pay the man's hospital bill, and his lawyer and mine split the fee I paid to my lawyer. (Six years later,

I returned my dad the favor—I got *him* a lawyer when he broke the jaw of a thirty-five-year-old man with his good left hand, which unfortunately was still legally classified as a deadly weapon even though he was now sixty-seven years old, had a fire-shrunken and scarred right bicep, and hadn't been inside a prize ring in more than forty years. The man had lost a pool game to him in a saloon and wouldn't pay up. The lawyer I got for my dad turned out to be a much better one than he had got for me. That lawyer—whom *I* paid—got him completely off the hook for the injured man's medical expenses. As we had in days of old, we kept my mother from learning about this little altercation.)

Across the river in Windsor late in that summer of 1963, I won the Freedom Festival quarter-mile in an eased-up 50.3 on a dusty track, nearly four seconds slower than my personal best. Then I anchored the Detroit Track Club to a record-setting win in the 440-yard relay. That relay race was to be my last-ever official race.

When I left Southeastern, I also sadly left behind many close colleagues with whom I have remained in touch and students and athletes who later became my lifelong friends. Among them was john powell, the most brilliant student I have ever taught at any level, from high school through graduate school—who nearly five decades after I taught him has now written the *Introduction* to this book.

Sadly, I also had taught and coached many Southeastern kids I would never see again. A few, I later learned, ended up in prison. Several others made their transition—including Bob Kemp, the best all-around athlete I ever coached (All-City in track, basketball, and football), who committed suicide when he was in his forties; Bob's effervescent sister Gracie, who died of alcoholism; and Lorinzo Gainer, my English student and an extremely gutsy 14.8-second 120-yard high hurdler, who once won a hurdles race wearing holey shoes with his spikes sticking up through the holes into his feet. I didn't learn until later that the soles of his track shoes had worn away, because the stoic Lorinzo never said a word to me about it.

I've often wondered whatever happened to a bright and talented Southeastern half-miler I coached named Ulysses, whom I had inherited as a student from the redoubtable Mrs. D. He never spoke much in my class, but he absorbed information like a sponge.

I once had to bail Ulysses out of jail. He'd been incarcerated for simply

riding in a car with a driver who'd been stopped for speeding and hauled off
to the hoosegow for not having a driver's license. Just before the 1962 city
track meet, one of my kids tipped me that Ulysses had been arrested again
for some minor offense. I tried to find out which precinct jail he was in, but
the white police kept moving him from jail to jail, beating him with fists and
rubber hoses, and withholding his food. By the time I got to him and was able
to have him released, he was in no condition to run the half-mile, or any other
event. (Earlier, I had arranged for him to go to the University of Detroit dental
clinic to get his teeth fixed, but his jailers had destroyed some of that dental
work.) None of this really mattered a lot to him anymore, anyway, because
the city meet was already long past. I once nearly got into a fight with another
teacher for calling Ulysses "Useless Ulysses."

In the fall of 1963, while teaching at Finney but feeling homesick for
Southeastern, I attended a Southeastern football game at the old Mack Park
where the Detroit Stars of the old Negro Baseball League used to play. There
I ran into Bill King, one of my better quarter-milers, who had graduated the
previous June. Bill, an orphan who had migrated to Detroit from the South
to be raised by his sister, asked me if I could get him into college. I immediately
called Del Russell, a now-deceased probation officer who had helped many
of my kids. Del got Bill a night job stacking boxes at Borman's Foods and also
helped me get him a half scholarship to run at Johnson C. Smith College in
Charlotte, North Carolina.

Bill's relay teammate, state 440 champion George Wesson, had already
matriculated there on a full track ride. (I later helped George get a job with
the Wayne County Sheriff's Department, where he became a detective. After
retiring, he worked in the Detroit Public Schools as a security officer—a job
I was also able to secure for him when I was a DPS executive director. He hated
that security job, though, and he recently *re*-retired and moved to Ohio.)

Bill—who resembles famous actor Sidney Poitier—was eventually destined
to run for Johnson C. Smith College on a champion Penn Relays team with future
Olympian Vince Matthews. Training on *The Longest Dash*, my best-selling track
techniques book, Vince Matthews won the Olympic 400-meter dash at Munich
and credited my book for his win in his autobiography, *My Race Be Won* (with
Neil Amdur, Charter House, New York, page 96).

Bill King became a doctor and now resides in Maryland.

One dark day in November, a Finney student named Vince came to class tardy and informed me that President John F. Kennedy had been shot. He was laughing, and I thought he was joking. Like many others, I poured my grief into a poem. Its last lines were, "What else remains for us to say? The Patriot has gone away."

Having been teacher, teammate, coach, comrade, and protector of black folks for so long, and being very much my father's son, I began at Finney to collar white students (literally) and take them to task when I caught them taunting their few bussed-in black classmates in mocking imitations of what they considered to be black dialect. I also similarly protected Finney's few East Indian kids we had, including a spunky young man named Jeat Grewal, who now owns the successful Singh Realty in West Bloomfield, Michigan.

Finney's insensitive white administrators had assigned our few African-American kids to low-paying student jobs washing the school's windows in full, embarrassing view of their white schoolmates who lived in the adjoining East Outer Drive and East English Village neighborhoods, which in the early 1960s were extremely well-to-do. Talk about *racism*—these white students' derisive behavior was a despicable display of *classism*, as well.

Around that time, I was en route to my parents' home on Haverhill Street and had just driven up the Chalmers exit ramp off I-94 with my genuine-genius girlfriend Geraldine Natalie Barclay in the car with me when a speeding car also exited, barreled past us, and crashed into a big tree. A police cruiser streaked up the ramp a few seconds later in hot pursuit.

Miraculously unscathed, four black kids sprang from the smashed car and scattered in four directions. A barefoot, big-bellied white man in an undershirt and hanging suspenders burst out of his house, brandishing a .38. He pointed the pistol at the back of a boy who was fleeing south on Chalmers (then an all-white street) and squeezed off a shot that missed.

Instructing Gerrie to keep her head down, I braked the car fast, jumped out, and chased the fleeing youth, in the meantime calling to the shooter, "Don't you dare kill that kid!" The man shouted back, "I won't, if you can catch him!" I quickly caught and collared the young man and warned him, "You've got to come back with me—that man is going to shoot you if you don't."

He complied, and it was lucky for him he did—the shooter was an off-duty Detroit cop, and the car was stolen. Presently, police in the cruiser that had been chasing the young car thieves rounded them up and hauled them to the station house—but at least all of them were still *alive*.

When the excitement was over, Gerrie—then a first-grade teacher in Warren—could only say, "John, life with you is seldom dull."

In those bad old days in Detroit, life for the *police* was seldom dull, either. During those infrequent times when it *was* rather dull for them, there were cops on the force who weren't averse to amusing themselves by using any black boy they happened to see running down the wrong street at the wrong time—car thief or not—for a casual bit of target practice.

CHAPTER TWELVE

BROTHERHOOD, BUREAUCRATS, AND BULLETIN BOARDS

"Brotherhood has nothing to do with English."

—*A Finney assistant principal*

Back at Finney the next day, I lost no time dusting off the Unit on Brotherhood that I had composed as my master's essay for my recently completed requirements for the master's degree in English education at WSU, and I proceeded to teach the Brotherhood Unit (supplementally) to my at-first-*very*-unreceptive white students.

Principal Catherine Kelly's excessive weight prevented her from being easily able to walk upstairs to my second-floor classroom, so when some irate parents called her to complain that I was teaching their offspring to "love Negroes," she ordered her assistant principal to check on it. I was summoned to the assistant principal's office and advised that brotherhood "has nothing to do with English." This advisement was thereupon echoed by my department head, who also was present (and who would have made an *excellent* Nazi). I allowed as how there must be an *echo* in the room—"Little Sir Echo," I called him, after the old song. For good measure, I made a snide crack about the assistant principal's apparent reticence to deal with me without having his "backup boy" in there as well. It wasn't a pleasant meeting.

In defiance of those two un-egalitarian gentlemen's terse advisements, I continued to teach my Brotherhood Unit. (I knew it wasn't easy to fire a tenured teacher.) Presently, a bulletin board on brotherhood I had meticulously assembled with thumb tacks and purple poster-board in my classroom got defaced with racist graffiti. These defacements included a common four-letter verb in an imperative sentence that said, "f— all niggers" and a large phallus that someone had sacrilegiously drawn on the great Jesse Owens in a magazine photo of him winning the 1936 Olympic 200. The racist pejorative was scrawled again above the picture with a jagged arrow pointing from the odious "n"-word to the legendary American champion. Indeed, the odious "n"-word might as well have been written by the assistant principal himself.

Interestingly, two of the students who became my staunch allies in my teaching of egalitarianism were a pair of exceptionally bright boys named Smith and Jennings. A nervous middle-aged teacher named Mrs. Lightbody was having a lot of trouble with Smith & Jennings. They were turning in scholarly, original, meticulously footnoted exegeses on the necrophiliac tendencies of Edgar Allan Poe and the homosexuality of Walt Whitman. Their topical term papers on the excremental discursions of Norman Mailer—in which Smith & Jennings made graphic reference to Mailer's sardonic essay matching up different consistencies of bowel matter with different personality types—most *particularly* disturbed Mrs. Lightbody, to the boys' great glee.

In the corner of their papers where the teacher's name was to appear, the smart-aleck pair would type in "Mrs. Heavybody" or "Mrs. Lightbrain." They were fast driving the poor lady *meshugah*.

At Mrs. Lightbody's request, I agreed to allow their counselors to transfer Smith & Jennings to my overloaded class that met the same hour. This was a class my department head had likened to "rows of vegetables that need a watering can—not a teacher." I duly critiqued and graded Smith & Jennings' papers on Poe, Whitman, and Mailer, gave then stiff follow-up assignments on the same topics, and kept them out of mischief and busy with their own work. I also ordered them to quit rolling their eyes theatrically when I over-simplified an instructional concept for the benefit of their new and far-less-skilled classmates, and I made them help their classmates with compositional problems involving spelling and syntax.

The assistant principal who had been charged with checking on parents' complaints that I was teaching their kids to "love Negroes" happened, ironically, to be a member of another often-persecuted minority group (he was Jewish). Even more ironically, he got promoted downtown to a position of "multicultural coordinator"—a truly remarkable assignment for him, given the Brotherhood

Unit incident. In forty-five-year retrospect, I can only look back and presume (or *hope*) that his acceptance of an appointment so out of sync with his manifest character was at least partially influenced by his having garnered some salutary information from his exposure—albeit on the "other side of the fence"—to my much-maligned Unit on Brotherhood.

Also around that time, Hobart Loomis, the new principal at Southeastern, who was the suddenly-retired and sadly cancer-stricken Margery Readhead's former assistant principal (and a retired military officer), phoned me at Finney and barked militarily, "Telford, get your *nose* out of the Nick Cheolas case immediately or I'm going to get *you*."

The Southeastern athletic director was envious of Nick, Southeastern's popular young football and track coach and my erstwhile coaching colleague. He was also unhappy that Nick sometimes balked at doing aspects of his administrative job for him. The athletic director had begun to document every time Nick was two minutes late to class, as well as continually harassing him in other ways. Varsity football tackle Ron Hunter and members of my former track team had contacted me seeking help with the problem, and I had undertaken to advise them regarding how they could be instrumental in saving Nick's job. I had also dragged Nick to see our Detroit Federation of Teachers vice president, the indefatigable Helen Bowers—a friend of my Aunt Letty—since our union's faculty representative in Nick's building was having no success advocating for him.

To the new Southeastern principal's overtly obvious threat, I responded rhetorically, "Are you *threatening* me, Mr. Loomis?"

Mr. Loomis assured me that no, his threat had not been a threat, but he would be extremely happy if I would stay out of the affair, since I didn't "have all the facts." I retorted that Mr. Cheolas was my good friend, and I intended to proffer him all the assistance I could, "facts" or not.

"You'll regret it, I promise you," the new Southeastern principal threatened again.

"Would you please say that just a little bit louder, Mr. Loomis—so my tape recorder can pick it up better?" Mr. Loomis hastily hung up. (I didn't really have a tape recorder.)

That very same day, my assistant principal at Finney summoned me to his office again, and very un-coincidentally using Mr. Loomis' very same words, he advised me that I was to get my nose out of the Nick Cheolas case immediately, it being Southeastern High School's business—not Finney's—and certainly none of *my* business. I told him the same thing that I had already told Mr. Loomis—that since Nick was my friend, I fully intended to make his business at Southeastern *my* business at Finney, and the assistant principal could go ahead and write me up for it if he wanted to.

It turned out that Coach Cheolas didn't get fired, nor did I get written up for defending him. His football team won the city championship that fall, and his mile-relay team (which had been *my* mile-relay team) won the state title in record-breaking time the following spring. These victories enabled Nick to survive and hang on to his job. Under ordinary circum-stances, victorious coaches are the *true* professional untouchables. (Just ask former Michigan State University president John DiBiaggio. Dr. DiBiaggio probably lost his presidency for trying to prevent popular head football coach George Perles from simultaneously assuming the athletic directorship at that sports-minded institution.)

I should note here, too, that Nick's black students and athletes were powerfully influential actors in his salvation. This was entirely fitting, since Nick had so often ridden to their rescue when they encountered trouble with the authorities, in and out of school. Coach Cheolas and I—along with Wayne State University track coaches David L. Holmes and later Frank McBride, DPS health and physical education director Bob Luby, Holmes' brother Carl and his Pershing colleagues Mike Haddad and later Don Gorence, then-Eastern High School basketball coach Bob Samaras, my old Northwestern coach Jimmy Russell, Mumford assistant track coach Mike Shewach, Cass Tech football coach Dick Cole, and my young former coaching assistant at Pershing (and later world-renowned self-help author) Wayne Dyer—comprised a cadre of white educators who consistently stood up for black kids in an era when to do so was far from fashionable and often even dangerous.

University of Michigan football coach Lloyd Carr, whom I was to supervise at Detroit's Butzel Junior High in 1967 and later recommend for many a coaching job, was also cut from that same cloth. So was Andy Rio, my colleague at Finney when I returned there to teach and administrate decades later in 2003.

In an interesting postscript to the Cheolas contretemps, I subsequently encountered Mr. Loomis as a fellow student in one of our graduate classes at Wayne State. (I had recently entered the university's doctoral program in curriculum and administration.) Neutral territory. To my bemusement, Mr. Loomis sought me out and absolutely *wrung* my hand. Cordial. Nonchalant. As if he hadn't done the "B" movie Mafioso bit when we had last communicated. As if we were old pals. Later, he and Nick became friends, as well—and when Nick later transferred to Finney, he coached Mr. Loomis' son on another city championship football team.

This single incident in the doctoral class proved to be more educational for me than was the entire course, which was called something like "Modern Administrative Trends in Secondary Education." The professor in that course often irritated me with his predilection for using pompous, educationese terms like "implement" for *do*, "utilize" for *use*, "replicate" for *copy*, "quantify" for *count*, "facilitate delivery" for *make sure that the subject matter damn well gets taught*, etc.

He threw around phrases like "replicate best practices" and "identify and implement objectives" and "initiate collaborative processes" and "articulate clear goals and evaluate results that impact students' competencies and performances." He dearly loved the word "efficacy" and used it with deadening frequency.

Nothing has changed much in three and a half decades. George W. Bush's Secretary of Education, Lauro Cavazos, announced in 2006 that he was going to "quantify" the "educational deficit" in our schools. Yow! My practical initiation into the phony world of some captains of higher education and the chameleon world of many K-12 administrators was progressing apace. This professor and Mr. Loomis had proved to be excellent tour guides, and I didn't like what I was learning.

I need to emphasize, though, that most of my experiences in the Wayne State University College of Education and at the new Finney High School weren't bad ones. I respected many of my WSU doctoral professors—particularly Dr. E. Brooks Smith, Dr. Earl Kelley, and Dr. William Hoth—and I came to love my Finney kids (even the misguided ones). Moreover, I was gratified to have decent youngsters at Finney who eventually adopted my democratic views despite their parents' bigotry.

In the spring of 1964, I was appointed the new high school's first-ever track and cross-country coach and got paid a modest stipend for it. While still in fair condition and able to cruise near-48-second quarter-miles at the relatively youthful competitive age of twenty-eight, I thus regretfully surrendered forever my status as a competing amateur. (I had coached at Southeastern without being paid for it.) No longer could I round up three of the city's best graduating high school quarter-milers, sign them up with my Detroit Track Club, and take them to some summer meet in Ohio or Indiana and anchor them to victory over good college runners in the mile relay, which I once did at the Northeastern AAU in Dayton in 1961—where I also won the quarter-mile for good measure.

In that summer of 1964, I felt a further pang of regret when the great Mike Larrabee—an *older* rival from California whom I had twice outrun at 400 meters—tied the world record and then won the gold medal in the Olympic 400 in Tokyo. Canadian superstar Bill Crothers, with whom I had evened the score when I narrowly defeated him in 1960 to win the quarter-mile championship of Ontario and the coveted McGill Cup, took the silver medal in the Olympic 800 behind New Zealand's Peter Snell, the world record holder. My young protégé Henry Carr of Detroit, my one-time opponent Rex Cawley of Farmington, Michigan, and my former U.S. teammate Hayes Jones of Pontiac, Michigan won the 1964 Olympic 200 meters, 400-meter hurdles, and 110-meter hurdles, respectively. It was to be the last Olympics to date where any Detroit-area track star was to win an individual title.

My Finney team of *non-black* runners surprisingly compiled a nifty 8–1–1 dual meet record in the black-dominated PSL (Public School League), and I was honored to be able to launch the high school and collegiate track and cross-country career of Ken Howse. Kenny became the only runner in the school's now forty-five-year history ever to win a state title (he won two), even though during the two years that I was Finney's track coach, the school had *no track*! We had to run all our meets on the other team's track. One time when I took my Finney kids to an all-black school nearby to compete, some young female spectators at the school almost started a riot when they insolently asked my kids, whose white track shirts sported a green "F," "Do the 'F' stand for *fuck*?" Racism sometimes runs both ways.

Back at Finney, I had pounded several hollow pipes in the ground, dropped flags in the pipes, and fashioned an oval of approximately 300 yards circling a nearby field for my fledgling little birds to fly on. Very soon Chuck Smith, Dennis Zimmer, Ron Mets, Doug Martens, Jim Starnes, Angelo Palazzolo, Andre Van Opdenbosch, Bart Lashbrooke, Doug Gardner, Eric Wickmann, and the Bellinger brothers were flying *fast*—with a little push and pull from their coach. I had no true 100-yard sprinters, but I found five football running backs who could break 53 seconds in the 440-yard dash with hard training and by running their quarters at an even pace near 26 seconds for each 220. In the 1960s, I still ran with my teams during their workouts, so any complaint that a difficult workout was "impossible" *didn't* fly, since the coach was running right beside his rookie runners.

My non-sports-minded department head resented me missing departmental meetings to coach my team at scheduled afternoon track meets. He therefore promised to see to it that I would never be promoted to a department-head position. He also ordered me to sign his departmental bulletin board as proof that I had read it. I never did sign his bulletin board, but my teaching colleague Jim Campitelle agreed to sign it for me with the understanding that he would never tell me what was on it.

In conspiracy with Jim—who incidentally was later to manage Roman Gribbs' successful one-term run for the Detroit mayoralty—I whimsically (and immaturely) *invented a student*. We christened him "Waldo Pond" in tribute to Henry David Thoreau, that champion of Yankee individualism.

"Pond comma Waldo" began to appear frequently on the absence and tardy lists despite contradictorily getting straight A's entered in the report card class rolls. We probably would have secured a scholarship to Harvard for Waldo if I hadn't finally managed to get myself transferred back to a predominately black high school to teach English and take over the track-coaching reins. The school was Pershing High at Seven Mile and Ryan Road on the north side of town, where I would also be able to use my Ebonics-specific treatise again.

After I left Finney and went to Pershing in the fall of 1965, Jim worried that my department head might miss me, so he thoughtfully kept signing my name every day to the department head's bulletin board.

CHAPTER THIRTEEN

RUNNING WITH CHAMPIONS AGAIN

"You is different from the rest. No one can push you around."

—*Anonymous Pershing student, in a*
1966 handwritten evaluation of the author

Even though Pershing had the reputation of being a wild high school, it wasn't nearly as tough as Southeastern had been. Actually, I immediately found Pershing to be like Old Home Week. Carl Holmes, the younger brother of my beloved WSU coach David L. Holmes (at whose June 1960 funeral I had been a pallbearer), had become Pershing's physical education department head and athletic director. Mr. Holmes had asked Principal Al Meyers to request my transfer from Finney to coach his track team so he could concentrate on his new administrative duties. Also, the brother of a girl I was dating at the time attended the school. I had coached against Pershing counselor Bob Samaras when he had coached at Eastern High, and he was a friend of my friend and former colleague, Nick Cheolas, whose wife's sister Toni I had dated. Bob and Nick were in a group of young men who kiddingly called themselves the "Greek Mafia." We all used to get together on Saturdays to play touch football.

In that Pershing autumn of 1965, a second incident involving an older married woman was to have an intense impact on my life three decades later. Corinna Ditta, a shapely blonde from Kentucky that I met while taking a workout with my team, bore me the only son I would ever (knowingly) sire. I was reluctant to cause trouble for her family—they had two older boys—but I was sorely tempted to claim my infant son.

I consulted a clinical psychologist for advice. He advised me that it would be best for everyone if I just tried to put my son out of my mind—but I never really could.

During my first year at Pershing, I edited Bob Samaras' two basketball-techniques books, and I later edited his poignant biography of one of his young daughters who had died of a Mediterranean blood disease. At Eastern, Bob had coached cross-country and skippered a city champion basketball team featuring future University of Michigan stars John Rowser and Moses "Bill" Yearby, and led by seven-foot Reggie Harding—who later played for the Detroit Pistons until he was fired for drug use and was murdered by a romantic rival.

I also mentored an articulate young emergency substitute in a regular position (ESRP) and made him my assistant track coach. His name was Wayne Dyer. I had coached him seven years earlier when he was a Denby high jumper in 1958 and I was a volunteer assistant to my former coach, Ralph Green. While I was at Pershing, Wayne introduced me to Lynn, who would become the first of my two wives whom I married thirty-three years apart. Lynn, a 1959 Denby graduate, was a teacher in Warren and a friend of Wayne's first wife, Judy, who had graduated with her.

Wayne Dyer was so obviously bright and so good with the kids that the Pershing counselors often used him to perform counseling duties. He also was clever with word play—an ability that would serve him well later. My friend Sam Flam, one of the counselors, wasn't amused one day when in his presence Wayne kiddingly sang the words, "*Sam*-Flam-*cisco*, open your *Golden* Gate. . . ."

I edited Wayne's doctoral dissertation, and he became a world-renowned self-help author and lecturer. He now resides in Maui, Hawaii. He mentions me kindly sometimes on late night TV when he's in town to do local fund-raisers for public television. The last time I saw him was in October of 2008 at the Denby Class of 1958 Fiftieth Reunion, where I also encountered my old flame Colorado Katie. I was also greeted by some of the other athletes I had coached, including sprinter and later Michigan State football star Larry Hudas and former city mile champion Tom Bleakley, who had become a prominent attorney. Sadly, Lennie Cercone—the 1958 city 440 champion who later starred at the University of Michigan—wasn't there. Lennie had been electrocuted in a freak accident some years earlier.

The previous day, I had been invited to deliver the banquet toast for my

WSU class of the same year, so that had been a busy, nostalgic weekend for me.

I set about using my original Detroit-based stories and poetry and my Ebonics-based grammar lessons with the students in my English classes at Pershing in the fall of 1965, since most of them were black. It developed, too, that Wayne Dyer was as much a socio-political kindred spirit to me at Pershing as Jim Campitelle had been to me at Finney. Wayne and I would often bring our English and social studies classes together and team-teach them.

Those team-teaching sessions got quite intense—particularly after Wayne and I had gone to a nearby bar during our lunch hour and come back with a few beers under our belts. Our sessions featured socio-racial, socio-political, and even sometimes socio-*sexual* topics where there were absolutely no holds barred (from a strictly professional perspective). We wouldn't have gotten away with addressing such topics at Finney in those days, but what was aired in there were things the kids at Pershing (and at Finney, too) needed to be able to discuss in a safe and educative environment.

My Pershing teams compiled a 22–0 record in 1966–67, and my 1966 Pershing mile-relay team that featured future University of Michigan All-American mile-relayist Reggie Bradford and city 440 champ Andre Broadnax sliced a full second off the state high school record that had been set by my former Southeastern runners.

In a mile-relay race for the east-side championship, Reggie lost a shoe at the baton exchange and ran the entire quarter-mile with one foot bare, bloodying it on the sharp cinders. His brand of intestinal fortitude was rare, but Andre Broadnax was even *more* gutsy. Andre *burned* to win. The day Andre won the city 440 title in school-record time with Reggie a close second, and we were carrying home a big team trophy, everyone was celebrating except Andre. He was sitting off in a corner of the bus by himself crying silently because we hadn't won the mile relay. We had broken the state record again in that event the previous day in the city semi-finals, but I had kept leadoff man John Kitchen out of the finals because he was nursing a slight leg injury, and I didn't want him to aggravate it and risk his chances of running at Eastern Michigan University the following year. I had also broken apart the rest of my state champion quartet to score points in other events, consequently diluting its speed. Thus, the remnants of our All-State relay team had finished second by inches to a good Southwestern team, despite Andre gaining nearly thirty yards on the anchor leg in a Herculean effort to make up the ground. He broke 49 seconds on the anchor and missed catching the Southwestern runner by a millisecond, but that wasn't good enough for him. I understood.

The I-75 expressway under construction wiped out Reggie Bradford's house, and he moved across town to the Mackenzie High School district, so I lost him from my 1967 relay team—but my team finished second in the state meet anyway with a totally new corps of runners, and it won the city with yet a *different* combination of athletes. (In those days, unlike today, the city meet was contested *after* the state meet.)

When Reggie graduated from Mackenzie in 1967, I picked him up at his west-side house on Normile Street, drove him to the University of Michigan, sat him down in then-track coach Don Canham's office, and talked Canham into giving this future Big Ten record-breaker a full ride.

One of my shot putters at Pershing was Spencer Haywood, who led the Pershing team to the state basketball title and later starred at the University of Detroit and in the NBA. Sprinter/football quarterback Glenn Doughty, whom I talked into choosing the University of Michigan over MSU because U-M was rebuilding its football program, later became an All-Pro wide receiver for the Baltimore Colts.

A recovered John Kitchen did indeed run at Eastern Michigan University and became a track coach at Westland John Glenn High School. My student and all-time best high jumper, Jon Lockard, starred in basketball at Michigan. Another student, Marvin Lane, became a Detroit Tiger. My hurdler and record-breaking long jumper, Dennis Baker, became the warden of the Mansfield, Ohio prison. Many years earlier, I had had to summon Dennis to my classroom at seven o'clock in the morning and lecture him when he was on Christmas break from Kentucky State, where he had gone on a track scholarship and then skipped numerous practices. Dr. William Exum, the athletic director there, had called and enlisted my help in setting Dennis straight.

One of the brightest Pershing girls, Melba Boyd, who dated my city 440 champion Andre Broadnax in high school, became a prize poet and now teaches at Wayne State.

Regrettably, some of my Pershing record breakers encountered trouble after graduating. In 1968 one of my best quarter-milers—a young man his teammates too-accurately called "Outlaw" (until I forbade it)—threatened to kill the coach

at Henry Ford Community College, where he had briefly matriculated on a track
scholarship I had arranged for him. The coach, who had refused to let him take
a trophy home that had been won by a relay team he'd anchored, called me and
appealed to me for help handling "Outlaw"—and I got the situation smoothed
over (for a while). In June 1967, I had had to make a special call to Fred Grimshaw,
a teacher who ordinarily lived up to his Dickensian name, to change "Outlaw's"
social studies grade from an "E" to the "D" that allowed him to graduate. Six
years later, Mr. Grimshaw would be murdered by intruders in the school.

Distance runner John Murray and All-City Pershing relayist Dennis Turner
were shot to death, and Turner's relay teammate Lamarr Franklin was expelled
for putting Principal Al Zack in traction after I left. (Lamarr went right around
the principal's desk after him.) A few of my Pershing stars served time in state
and federal prisons, but they are out now leading worthwhile lives, and I am
in close touch with those of them today who are still alive, as well as with all
the other Pershing kids I've named here.

In 1996 I was invited to speak at the Pershing Class of 1966 Thirtieth
Reunion. I'm still in touch with most of my athletes I saw there—including
Denny and William Ewell, George Kolb, and Joe Ezidore, whose late wife Rose
Starks-Ezidore was a parent/community liaison officer for me in 2002–03
when I served as the Detroit Public Schools' executive director of the Division
of Community Affairs. The Ewell brothers' nephew, Tim Gore, works in a
department I headed at Finney High School in my "second life" there, more
than forty years after I coached his uncles.

Pershing basketball coach Will Robinson—already a legend—eventually
became the first black coach of an NCAA Division One team and ultimately
the assistant general manager of the Detroit Pistons. Initially, Will and I clashed
when the athlete formerly called "Outlaw" refused to obey his command to
unlock the basketballs I had ordered him to lock away. I had come upon Will's
players practicing with the balls during track practice. Will was flabbergasted
that a black athlete would disobey him to follow a young white coach's directive,
but Will and I soon became cooperating allies. I conditioned many of his players
and trained them to run fast and jump high, creating champions in both sports.

Will wore a leather whistle cord around his neck that he used for whipping
his athletes on their behinds when they made the same mistake twice in practice.
One day Principal Zack stormed into the athletic office and ordered, "Robinson,

I want you to stop whipping those kids with that whistle cord!" "Okay, chief," Will replied. When the principal left, Will filled a bucket with water, dipped a shoelace in the bucket, and whipped them with *that* instead. (The kids said the wet shoelace actually hurt *more*.)

That following May, one of my long jumpers—football running back Freeman Noble—repeatedly called an official a four-syllable epithet for correctly calling a third and disqualifying foul on him in a meet against the Lorenzo Wright-coached Eastern High, which Pershing narrowly won. Uncharacteristically, I slapped Freeman to bring him to his senses. Lorenzo Wright had been Will's protégé at the old Miller High, and he mentioned the slapping incident to him. Will then took me aside and said, "John, you mustn't hit the kids." "Will," I responded, "you're right. *We* mustn't hit the kids—*we* mustn't, you and I."

He did keep on whipping them, of course. Will had his methods and I had mine—and his were successful, as were mine.

On a hot, dry Wednesday in June, 1966, Will watched me take my relay team through a grueling series of practice runs. I usually ran with them in the hardest workouts to demonstrate that a difficult workout I had prescribed was doable, but my asthma was bothering me that day, so I made them run the entire series without me. After their fourth repetition of 220 yards at a pace of 24 seconds, they were foaming at the mouth like racehorses.

Noting this, Will took Dale Hardeman by the elbow, studied him worriedly, and growled, "Telford, you're working these kids too hard." I calmly responded, "No, they're conditioned for this. We run hard today, but we'll do nothing but baton work tomorrow and Friday. On Saturday, this team is going to win the state title and break the state record."

When I got Will alone in the athletic office half an hour later, however, I was anything *but* calm. "Don't you *ever* criticize my coaching in front of my kids again," I told him heatedly.

On Saturday, my team won the state title and broke the state record. Will never second-guessed my coaching methods again.

I learned one truly memorable lesson in psychology as a motivator during the years I was coaching my Pershing, Finney, and Southeastern state champions —all of whom I told before they won those titles that I *expected* them to win those titles and that they were *going* to win those titles. It was a learned lesson which I was to invoke successfully over and over again in subsequent coaching, teaching, and administrative jobs. That one lesson is *this*: If you tell a kid he's going to win a championship, and he believes that *you* believe he's going to win the championship, he may well *over-achieve* and actually *do* it.

This psychology also obtains in the academic realm and in other worthwhile realms of endeavor as well, and it works with adults, too. If students of *any* age *believe* that their teacher believes they will achieve, they *will achieve*—and all of them without exception *can* achieve almost *anything* in the right environment with the right teacher.

A "postscript" to my days coaching at Pershing occurred when Leroy Dues, the new Pershing athletic director who had coached old Miller High to many a city track title, decided he wanted to pay himself my stipend to coach my track team. Consequently (and reluctantly), I took the English department head exam, passed it with a high score, and immediately became the language arts department head at the truly *wild* fifteen hundred student Butzel Junior High School at the corner of Van Dyke and Vernor Avenue on the east side of town.

Two weeks after I had departed for Butzel, Mr. Dues decided he wanted me to keep on coaching my team back at Pershing, after all! Excited, I appealed to my new principal—a scholarly old gentleman named Clarence Benn—and I was somehow able to talk Mr. Benn into letting me coach after school for just one more season (against the district's rules). So, I sped eagerly back crosstown from Butzel to Pershing every day at 3:45 to rejoin my close friend and assistant coach Wayne Dyer in mentoring our young speedsters for one final unbeaten season. Will had removed the athlete the kids had called "Outlaw" from his basketball team, and he had often warned me never to count on Outlaw—that he would fold under pressure.

Nevertheless, in the city championship finals I strategically put Outlaw on the ordinarily weak second leg of the mile relay—which was the last event of the meet. I told Outlaw to pour it on all the way to put the race out of reach and take the title for his team.

Outlaw did.

CHAPTER FOURTEEN

BIG BALL-HEAD JONES AND MR. NORTHRUP'S NOSE

"I will not hit Dewey in the head with a pen, I will not hit Dewey in the head with a pen . . ."

—Ronald Kelly, Butzel Junior High student,
written one hundred times

Even though I was still coaching at Pershing in 1967, I never neglected my difficult duties at Butzel for a single second. Those duties included teaching *four* challenging English classes myself, while also supervising and evaluating the English teachers and the foreign-language teachers, and supervising the teachers on cafeteria duty.

In addition, I was expected to handle the student discipline for the department and *document* infractions. My first departmental patron who sought my help with discipline was a petite young woman teacher who marched into my office with a sullen fifteen-year-old in tow.

"Mr. Telford," said she, "this young man called me a half-white bitch. I want for you to tell him that I don't think that's very nice—and I want for you to tell him that if he employs that type of vulgar, insulting language to refer to me again, I'm going to slap the little motherfucker silly."

I shifted my gaze from the young teacher to her lanky student, who towered over her—his hair in a huge natural of nearly bushel-basket size. "Has your teacher made herself clear?"

"Yes, sir."

"Good. Back to class, then."

Here, indeed, was a resourceful teacher who had used me solely as a sounding board for her to solve her own problem.

My four classes that I was assigned to teach included classes at all three junior high school grade levels—seventh, eighth, and ninth. I had never taught junior high school age kids (other than subbing), but I fell in love with mine immediately. I also began immediately—and gleefully—to pour plenty of grammatical instruction down their unwilling little throats, along with giving them a fair number of home assignments.

At first, only about nine or ten kids in each of my classes, which averaged thirty-eight students per class, handed in their homework. At the beginning of each class period, I began to admonish them reproachfully, "Only *twenty-eight* of you gave me your homework today." Actually, the number had remained at about nine, but my ruse worked: Before long, I really *did* have nearly twenty-eight papers on my desk.

Still, holdouts remained. I invited holdout Harold Stuckey to the front of the class and asked him to extend his hand, palm up. When he complied, I took a red magic marker and wrote the word "homework" on it. I then invited another holdout—Harold's good buddy Willie Spivey—to the front of the class and asked the class to find a piece of string for me. Grinning in anticipation, Harold gave me the string, and I tied it firmly around his friend Willie's finger as a reminder to Willie to bring his homework the following day. An hour or two later, at passing time in the hall, I spotted Willie and asked to see the string. He held it up—it was still firmly in place on his finger.

The next day, both Willie and Harold handed in their homework.

Forty-three years later, I still chuckle to myself when I reflect upon those incidents.

Around this time, my old friend Jim Shorter, a former University of Detroit sprinter from Pontiac whom I had once raced against at U of D Stadium (which is now a parking lot), came to visit me at Butzel. He told me about a meeting he and two of my other old track rivals—Walter Beach of Central Michigan and Jim Brown of Syracuse—had held with world heavyweight boxing champion Muhammad Ali. Jim Shorter was now a defensive back for the Washington Redskins, and Walter Beach and the legendary Jim Brown carried the ball for the Cleveland Browns. Jim's Redskin teammate Bobby Mitchell—also a former track star—the swift Gale Sayers of the Chicago Bears, and Willie Davis of the Green Bay Packers, among other black running backs, attended the meeting. So did basketball stars Bill Russell of the Boston Celtics and Kareem Abdul-Jabbar (then Lew Alcindor of UCLA). They wanted to talk Ali into joining the army, which he was refusing to do—famously saying, "I ain't got no quarrel with them Vietcong."

These influential black athletes came away from that meeting convinced that the great fighter's pacifist stand was righteous. It was the beginning of the turning of the tide of African-American sentiment in Ali's favor and against the unjust war.

On the day Jim Shorter dropped by Butzel, my teachers had sent five unruly boys and four girls to my office for disciplining, so I told them who Jim was and had him counsel them. Also, I made those five boys and four girls write why they had been sent to me. When I read today what they wrote—and the things many of my other misbehavers wrote—I chuckle now, as I chuckled then. Here follow some of those writings (*errors included*):

> A boy call me "Big Ball-Head Jones." (Dwight Jones)

> I was plaing with Robert and all the boys in my class and I hit Robert not hard [the underlining is Chavis's] and then he call me a pouch [he meant *punk*—an inner-city synonym for *homosexual*] and I said dont say it again and he hit me in the arm and all I was doing was plaing. (Chavis Jefferson)

> She [the teacher] was mad because I didnt tell what I was draw[ing]. (Willie Watkins)

> I was sent down here because I through a book at Greogry [Gregory] Because he pull up my dress so Miss Yager sent me here for that little thing. (Norita Jones)

> Yesday I was walk down the wall [hall] and Mr. Geibel come raning down the wall and he told me to come to the office and I say what for and he just kept on runing and I don't threanten him [the underlining is Joe's]. (Joe Barber, a seventeen-year-old ninth-grader)

> The reason I got sent down here was that the class was shoting rubber bands around the room. (Barbara Moses)

This girl came to my class and started hiting me so I started
hiting her back. She was realy fighting two boy and she took it
out on me but I fixed her when she came out side the two boys
and myself jumped on she and we beat her all the way to her
house, in it to. The theacher say I beat the girl up bad, but it
was the two boy and myself. (Sharon Watts)

People tell me what she be saying about me but I don't pay any
atchen to then Today she came after me and whe had it out.
(Zenia Hill)

Mr. Northups [Northrup] talk about people and tell tham who
their going to marry but when people talks about his nose he
get mad and send them to you. (Twanda Washington)

I move up two seats and [the teacher] tell me to move back so I
tell him I am cold seating by the window. He tell me to get out.
(Myron Riley)

The banished students usually entered the office clutching a Form 1029
(Student Irregularity Permit) with a hasty note scribbled by their teacher indicating the transgression. (Since "irregular" students were more *regular* that *ir*regular,
the form should probably have been labeled "Student *Regularity* Permit.")
    The notes customarily said things like:

I consider this serious. Carl King in possession of matches.
Jackie Driscoll lighting matches. Shooting forks all over the
room. He keeps make [sic] remarks about the girl who [sic] he
got pregnaunt [sic] and about bodies of other girls. Students
say he is supposed to be armed with a revolver right now.

Two notes carried by a messenger:

Could you please come down and get Darryl Anderson? I am
having a hard time. Norita is very obstreperous and will not co-
operate. Talk, talk. Laugh, laugh. Giggle, giggle. Why does she
even bother to come?

S.O.S.!

I tried various methods to prod these young exiles toward better deportment. I kept them after school. I confiscated their weapons. (A standing joke among teachers was that there should be gun racks in the locker rooms.) I had them write 100 times, e.g., "I will not cause trauch in Miss Franczek [I will not cause trouble in Ms. Franczek's class], I will not cause trauch in Miss Franczek, I will not cause trauch in . . ."; "I will not hit Dewey in the head with a pen, I will not hit Dewey. . . ." (Some ingenious students held more than one pencil in their hands at a time and endeavored to write more than one line simultaneously.)

I tried various other measures with them and with my own students. Different measures worked with different kids. If there wasn't any home phone, which frequently was the case, I wasn't the least bit hesitant to go straight to the kid's house and announce to the mother or grandmother or whomever was in charge that there was a minor matter of some unfinished homework or truancy or tardiness to be settled. It got settled that way in a hurry. With regard to my own students, such a trip usually would be prefaced by a classroom proclamation of my intent to make the visit, particularly if I was dealing with a new class early in the semester that might be inclined to test me. The next day, the word had usually spread that I had done it.

If it hadn't, I might overhear two students in a whispered exchange that went like this: "He come by your house yesterday?"

"Yeah."

"*Oh*, oh!"

And, if after a home visit or visits, a lateness-to-school problem remained chronic, I was known occasionally to park in front of the tardy kid's house at seven o'clock in the morning and honk my horn until he got dressed and came out. I usually didn't have to repeat this loud and embarrassing measure more than once. It was an extreme—but also extremely *effective*—measure which I actually only performed three times with three different students, all boys.

It's a wonder, though, that on one of those dark, cold, *early* mornings, I didn't get myself shot for raising that much racket—as my poor, howling mutt Rap had twenty years before.

CHAPTER FIFTEEN

A PEEING CONTEST—AND LIBERATING THE LIBRARY

"The library is supposed to be useable most of the day."

—Vanessa Mullins,
Butzel Junior High School student

An untried teacher only four days on the job had been informed by a boastful gaggle of her mouthier eighth-grade girls that they could make more money on the street in one day than she could make in a week of teaching. (It was later discovered that they were telling her something close to the truth—a group of them were selling sex out of a garage on Fischer Street.)

Other students were causing her other sorts of problems, as well. Overwhelmed, she led the straggling, unruly remnants of her class—minus the offending girls and boys—down to my office and announced, "Here are my keys. Here's my record book. There's what's left of my class. I quit!" She then departed, never to return.

I had to hide and lock Miss Wilma Woodhams, another young teacher, for a rather lengthy period of time in a closet in another classroom. (It was a fairly large closet that had room for a chair, and it had a functioning light bulb in it.) An irate mother of one of Miss Woodhams' students had announced in a telephone conversation with Mrs. Lockard, my secretary, that she was on her way to the school to beat up Miss Woodhams. Mrs. Lockard, who incidentally was the mother of my talented artist friend Jon Lockard and the grandmother of Jon Lockard, Jr.—my and Wayne Dyer's champion high jumper at Pershing— had cautioned me that this particular mother had a neighborhood reputation for violence. She added that this particular mother was also particularly *large*. The police didn't always come too quickly when called, so we figured a locked closet door in an empty and locked classroom could protect the teacher better than I could, and I made plans to tell the mother that Miss Woodhams had gone home ill.

Yet *another* young teacher fled to my office in tears and adamantly refused to go back to her eighth-grade classroom after three of her students had initiated a urinating contest (for height and distance) in full view of her and her class. That time the entire classroom had to be vacated because it was wintertime and the urine had splashed and sizzled copiously on a radiator. I had the offenders clean the odiferous radiator, plus two lavatories. (Try making a kid clean a lavatory in a school *today!*)

I traded one of my classes with that teacher and took over her offending class. It featured a handful of refugees from the local youth home (euphemistically titled the "Wayne County Correctional Facility")—the dismal place where I had spent eighteen nightmarish weeks seventeen years earlier, before most of my young charges at Butzel had even been born. Thankfully, this class—which included some fifteen-year-old probationers who had offenses on their records ranging from assault with a deadly weapon to solicitation and procurement—wasn't anywhere near typical.

I soon learned that two of the older, bigger boys in that class—Mickey and Ken—had bad blood between them over a girl. Previously, they had been fellow gang members and good friends, but Ken had quit the gang. One day, when I had the class in the library, Ken asked for and received a lavatory pass and left the library. Moments later, it occurred to me to look for Mickey. He was nowhere to be seen.

Leaving my class in the unhappy librarian's charge, I sprinted down the hall at a pace approaching ten yards per second and burst into the lavatory. The two boys were already circling each other purposefully with open blades. The Wayne State University College of Education doesn't offer courses in Disarmament 101 or Pacification 202, but I still managed somehow to coax the boys into simultaneously—at the count of *three*—dropping the knives, which I immediately retrieved.

I hadn't always acted in timely enough fashion in this type of situation. While in high school teaching and coaching, I had seen one of my students stabbed to death over a disagreement in the cafeteria, another stabbed and bleeding during a quarrel over dice on a stairway, and a third stabbed in the stands by a dropout over an unpaid wager on a track race. In the third incident, the young man had staggered down out of the stands, fled through a hole in the fence, and died on the sidewalk before the EMS arrived.

At Pershing, dual meets with top rivals had often drawn crowds of over a thousand, and the only security I had was my team's hefty cadre of shot putters who included Oliver Sanders and Spencer Haywood—the six-foot, nine-inch future NBA All-Pro forward. Young men half-high on cheap wine would sit in the stands and chant, "To de *wine* sto', to de *wine* sto'!", place their bets on their favorite fast quarter-milers (I had many), and sometimes refuse to pay when they lost. Student spectators would join in the chant, which ultimately morphed into an exhortative mantra for a Pershing victory.

By the time I came to Butzel Junior High School as its English department head, I had already attended several funerals of my high school students who had died violently while sticking up stores or simply being in the wrong place at the wrong time. A sick 1960s society's mind-molesting symptoms spilled over frequently into Detroit's high schools and trickled down even to Butzel Junior High, which already had multiple problems and was soon to get more.

By the fall of 1968, the country was reeling from the assassinations of Martin Luther King, Jr. and Robert F. Kennedy. Let us take a moment to hark back to what RFK said in 1968 on *Face the Nation*:

> Now we're saying we're going to fight in Vietnam so we don't have to fight in Thailand or on our west coast or so the Communists won't move over the Rockies. We say we're going to go in there and kill women and children because the Communists are 12,000 miles away and they might get to be 11,000 miles away.

When RFK was killed a few weeks later, America got Richard Nixon instead —he of the Watergate scandal and the illegal bombing of Cambodia. Thirty-six years after RFK—that soon-to-be-martyred brother of another martyr and ally of yet *another* martyr—had spoken those passionate words on *Face the Nation*, I would write in a December 31, 2004, *Michigan FrontPAGE* newspaper column headlined "Surviving George W. Bush,"

> What this country purports to stand for is again being trashed—
> this time in Iraq.

I would conclude that column with these words:

> Pray that the democracy that Bush and his handlers have im-
> periled can survive until 2008 when John Kerry or a like-minded
> leader can be elected.

Now, as I write this chapter in this book in January 2009, four years after that December 31, 2004, column appeared, we have elected that *like-minded leader* in the person of Barack H. Obama. Robert F. Kennedy is *resurrected*! Obama is hopefully going to lead and eventually effectuate the economic and spiritual recovery of Detroit and of all America.

But back then, in the fall of 1968, America definitely hadn't recovered from the fiery rebellions that had exploded all across the land, and Detroit hadn't even *begun* to recover from the devastation caused by the massive summer rebellion of 1967 which had left scores of Detroiters dead and hundreds of burnt-out houses and stores in its wake. Many of those devastated buildings were in the vicinity of Butzel Junior High School. There was also a dope pad directly across the street on Vernor Avenue. Gunshots could be heard during any day, gang fights abounded, and prostitutes sometimes plied their trade within full view of the school. Neighborhoods where buildings taken over by drug dealers had been plundered of their appliances and sometimes set afire were the very same neighborhoods where my students and I *lived*. In the fall of 1965, just before I transferred to Pershing from Finney, I had moved to 19245 Mound Road—a cheap motel-like apartment near Seven Mile Road in the Pershing district. Its single-level structure and separate front entrances conveniently offered a revolving door for my multitudinous girlfriends—married and unmarried—a veritable harem whose growing membership became obliged to make appointments for alternate evenings—and eventually, for evenings on alternate *weeks*.

In forty-year retrospect, I find it difficult to imagine how I ever could have maintained and retained such stamina and still get up at six o'clock every morning, drive to Butzel, and teach four classes every day while *administrating* there as well! I was also coaching track in the afternoon and taking doctoral courses in the evening.

In March of 1968, I wrote a hopeful poem about our town. Later, I shared it with my Butzel students. It was entitled *Blue Salt*:

> *My name is Detroit.*
> *I'm a blue-collar town.*
> *Blue salt melts my mid-March snow.*
> *Fast cars and sprinters spring from me.*
> *I father fierce fighters and funky music.*
> *Have you never seen blue salt?*
> *No complex chemistry here—*
> *Only the old color*
> *Of a new sky.*

My kids liked this defiantly upbeat poem, so I suggested that they write poetry of their own for extra credit. Many of them did.

I also asked them to address some of the school's problems in the themes they wrote in my four classes every Friday. They entitled them "Ways We Can Improve Our School," or "How To Solve School Promblems [*sic*]." Here follow some excerpts (again, exactly as they wrote them):

Arrest the dope dealers. (Centra Goode)

Get the hores off Van Dyke [street by the school]. (Centra Goode's sister Connie)

The school can be improve by putting the ceiling back in and new books, and preventing grambling [gambling] in the lab [lavatory], drafting room or in the disposal room. (Drake Gates)

I like a teacher who make you work. This is my opinion of this class, too. This is the best English class I ever been to, but for the rest of the teacher, they ant shit. (An anonymous student whose criticism of the teachers wasn't quite fair: Butzel had many excellent teachers, including a promising young teacher in my department named Lloyd Carr, for whom, as I mentioned earlier, I was later to write many a recommendation to coach football, which he ultimately did memorably at the University of Michigan.)

Get the rats and roaches out of the classrooms. (Bridget Thompson)

Teachers should not fight a student or paddle a student because some student will start talking about treacher brutalaty. (Mitchell Dunford)

They need some hall boys like last year. And it work out good their were not as much outsiders comeing in as now I was a hall gruad [guard] in the 200 House [a wing of the building] then they quiet [quit using] hall gruad. Some got paid and some got creid [credit] I got creid for being a hall gruad. (Roger Simmons)

We should have Charm as one of our classes every day. Another thing is a weapons check every week on everyone. We also should enforce our rules here and have more educational trips. (Angela Shell)

When they have dances they only have them for 1 hour. The time you get in the dance its time to go home. Another thing I don't like about this school is the boy get to wear their brogain boots and the girls can't wear their boots. The boys boots (some of them) has fur in them just like the girls do. The teachers always tell the girls the boots sweats our feet well those brogains can sweat the boys feet to. Another thing I don't like is the library teacher. We bring our books back and she put them somewhere and say we don't bring them back then we cant take out any more books and she say we have to pay for the books she lose. I don't like the rules, either. (Pam White)

Vanessa Mullins also had a problem with the librarian—a crotchety, over-weight white lady named Waldrip nearing her dotage who should have retired a few years earlier. When I complained about her to the principal, he called her "a geriatric case" and threw up his hands helplessly. Vanessa wrote:

The library is supposed to be useable most of the day, but as soon as I go in and ask can I take a book out she say I'm sorry but you have to have a pass from your teacher or you cant take a book out. I am a fast reader so about one day after I take out a book I want to go back and take out another. But if I have to go through all that fuss I just take out a book when my class go.

This was exactly what the librarian preferred that Vanessa do—or even more preferably, not take out any book at all. The librarian was more interested in book maintenance and inventory than in distribution. Students who actually wished to *use* the books were an imposition to her.

Determined to liberate the library, I encouraged my seventeen English and foreign-language teachers to sign passes there on an assembly-line basis for one week. Exactly fifteen minutes before the 3:30 p.m. daily dismissal, we flooded the library every day that week with students armed with passes to check out books. This soon forced a more liberal library policy to be instituted, and it also made the librarian my sworn enemy. She told me she was keeping a book on me, and I had better watch my step. Actually, Mrs. Waldrip's entire *career* had been one of *keeping books*—but now the books belonged to the students again.

The library had been liberated.

CHAPTER SIXTEEN

THE ORIGINAL MR. PEANUT AND A GIRL CALLED "VIETCONG"

"Your teaching made a difference in my life, and I want to extend you my grateful thanks."

—*1968 Butzel student Beverly Kindle-Walker,*
in an e-mail to the author, September 18, 2008

Angela Shell was not the only Butzel student who wanted educational trips. Brenda Wellons [now Brenda Wellons-Watkins] and Beverly Kindle [now Beverly Kindle-Walker] expressed the wish to have them, too, as did many others, so I arranged to charter buses to take English and social studies classes to the state capitol to observe the state legislature in session. The trip began inauspiciously, with a fight breaking out in my bus before it had even left the Detroit city limits. The perpetrator was pint-sized Ronald Kelly ("I will not hit Dewey in the head with a pen, I will not hit Dewey . . ."). I snatched Ronald up and sat him down next to me for the remainder of the ride with instructions to sit quietly or I would throw him out a window.

The main thing the students learned during their trip to the capitol was that the legislature can function without legislators. Virtually all were absent, including the legislator who represented the Butzel neighborhood. He was in South Korea "studying 'special educational problems affecting South Koreans'," at a then-hefty $2,000 cost to the taxpayers. *Good* thinking! He was from an impoverished district where South Koreans were such a minority that you could walk throughout the neighborhood for weeks without ever seeing one. (*South Korea was* full of South Koreans, though.) Actually, the only student of South

Korean parentage I had seen at Butzel was Chrysanthemum Brooks, a plucky
little girl with a South Korean mother and a black ex-G.I. father. Her parents
were divorced, and she lived with her mother, who worked long hours in a
Chinese restaurant on the west side.

Chrysanthemum was brought to my office one morning in January 1969
for fist-fighting with Larry Duncan, who was also brought down. Larry had
previously been in my office more than once for disciplining. I ascertained that
the fight had commenced when Larry called Chrysanthemum "Vietcong." I was
ready to read him the riot act—I accused him of being a racist and asked him
how he would like it if *he* were called names.

He responded, "But Dr. Telford" (I had completed my doctorate at WSU
the previous December), "she call *me* a name *first*. She call me *peanut-haid* !"

This revelation gave me momentary pause. I noted that Larry's close-
cropped head was indeed shaped almost perfectly like a large, unshelled
peanut. *Mr. Peanut*, himself. It was one of those moments when the urge to
laugh was nearly overwhelming, but with considerable difficulty, I remained
the stern arbitrator.

I also decided to separate Larry and Chrysanthemum by taking Larry into
one of my classes, where in one of the Friday Ideas-for-School-Improvement
themes, he then wrote (exactly as I quote him):

> Build a swimming pool get the window fix have police protection
> to prevent the outsiders from comeing in the school.

Larry Duncan—and his classmate Roger Simmons, among others—were
justifiably concerned about the outsiders. I had had more than my share of
trouble with them. Those who had become somewhat familiar with my ways
generally tried to hide from me, because I was known to have a propinquity for
slamming them up against a locker when they declined to leave or to identify
themselves upon polite request. This professionally questionable practice of
mine was becoming increasingly unwise as the outsiders grew more numerous
and dangerous.

One unseasonably warm afternoon in early March of 1969, a particularly
hostile young interloper of about twenty entered the building looking to hook
up with female students. He was invited to leave the premises by the new and

"acting" principal, a gentle lady in her sixties named Martha Sanders who felt obliged, in this instance, to assert her authority because she happened, on this relatively rare occasion, to be in the hall, and a couple of teachers and several students also happened to bear witness there at that moment. She had recently replaced the even gentler principal, Clarence Benn, whom some of the staff had fondly referred to as "Gentle Benn." He had been forced out by militant members of the community simply because they didn't want Butzel to have a white principal.

This type of black-for-white principal-replacement was being hastily effected all over the city by a still-predominately white central administration. Their appeasing stance was comparable to the preposterous cocktail party for the Black Panthers being given in New York by composer Leonard Bernstein. Unlike Bernstein, Detroit's central administration wasn't "radical-*chic*"—it was radical-*scared*. Mr. Benn had been a fine principal from whom I had learned much. He had had some health problems (cataract surgeries), and his wife had just passed away. They had transferred him to an "office boy" job downtown to join all the other ousted white principals there—some, like him, competent victims of circumstance; others perhaps not so skilled.

The young interloper whom Mrs. Sanders was trying to get to leave the premises stood over six feet, and I estimated that he weighed about 180 pounds. He probably would have left without incident, but his mere departure wasn't good enough for Mrs. Sanders. She insisted that he depart by a *designated door*. He wanted to leave by the front door; she insisted he leave by a side exit. I was standing beside her, between him and the front door, so Mrs. Sanders had given me little choice other than to tell him, while inwardly cursing her obstinacy, "You're not going out this door."

Anticipating the worst, I had removed my glasses and slipped them to a student to hold for me. The intruder sized up *my* 180 pounds, measured the width of my shoulders, and then—looking me straight in the eye—correctly concluded that there would be violence if he tried to push past me. He turned and slunk like a snarling wolf toward the side exit, spouting obscenities back at me, the school, and the world in general as he left.

The acting principal also turned and trundled back into her office, satisfied with herself. My white shirt now wet at the armpits, I returned to my duty assignment in the cafeteria just in time to observe a snub-nosed .38 fall to the floor from a girl's purse, which had been too-precariously balanced on the food tray she was carrying. The revolver discharged, taking a chunk out of the masonry at the base of the wall, then ricocheting dangerously—and pandemonium enveloped the several hundred milling, yelling students in the lunchroom.

On the floor near the place where the bullet had hit, there still lay the rank remnants of cheap Silver Satin wine mixed with other regurgitated stomach contents that a drunken student had vomited at the beginning of his lunch period that same hour. No custodian had apparently been called to clean it up. I had half-dragged, half-carried the staggering student to his counselor, who—upon being informed by the remorseful young man that he had indeed consumed an entire bottle of Silver Satin—asked one of the teachers who had a free period that hour to take him home.

So far, this definitely hadn't been my day. I confiscated the gun, which the girl had been carrying for a boy she refused to identify, and I took it with the girl to Mrs. Sanders. Hopefully, she would handle it from there.

Finally, the bell rang. I didn't feel up to ensuring that the hall was clear after the second bell, so I grabbed a six-foot, four-inch, 240-pound kid everyone called "Big Ricky" and told *him* to do it. Big Ricky was already being recruited by all the public- and private-school football powers in the area. I advised Big Ricky that I wanted to see *not a soul* in the hall after the tardy bell. It was my prep period, so I went and collapsed on the desk chair in my office.

Right after the bell, I went back out into the hall, and lo—it was entirely deserted.

There was absolutely no one there except Big Ricky.

CHAPTER SEVENTEEN

FIREBOMBS AND
TEACHER BLOOD

"Dr. Telford treat us like his own childern."

—*Butzel student Harold Stuckey,*
in a note to the witch-hunters

Having made a mental note to enlist Big Ricky's services clearing the hall on a regular basis, I returned to my office and wrote the words "Big Ricky" in the plan book on my desk. I then began to critique some of my students' "How to Improve Our School" papers.

The first paper I picked up was one written by the prolific Vendella Collins, an "A" student: "I think one way to improve our school is to stop setting things on fire, such as the lavatories."

Yes, I mused wistfully, our school would indeed be a better place if its lavatories weren't so often on fire.

"Every time someone doesn't like something," Vendella continued, "they start rumors like 'at 12:00 everyone should walk out.' At 12:00 some stupid people go to their lockers to get their hats and coats, but they don't even know why they're walking out. We can also improve the school by stopping vandalism. Some kids come on the school grounds to play after school, but others just come to break the windows and write all over the walls."

Vandalism, severe though it was, with over half of the school's windows boarded up, was a comparatively minor problem (if one can call a school problem that had cost America's taxpayers six hundred million dollars in 1967 *minor*). Vendella and her classmates, like millions of her urban contemporaries

throughout the United States, was attending public school in the midst of a
conflagration. Butzel's halls and stairways were being firebombed. The flag
was torn down and burned. Despite our now having a new African-American
principal, mass student walkouts over one grievance or another grew increasingly
frequent. Our halls were becoming as incendiary as the streets. Teachers were
being assaulted.

The bell rang for the next class period. As I was en route to a classroom
to teach my next class, I heard an unusually uproarious commotion in the hall
near my office, so I went back to investigate. A young substitute teacher who
had emigrated from the Ukraine a year or so earlier was lurching in my direction,
mumbling incoherently—his face a pulpy mass of bruises. As I put a supporting
arm around him to help him into my office, my coat sleeve on his back became
soaked with his blood. He had been stabbed through the lung. No one could,
or would, identify the assailant.

The police were called, and they bore the young man on a stretcher through
the school doors out into a shrill, milling mob to the waiting police vehicle and
thence to the hospital. The incident made the evening TV news on all three
stations. This young fellow recovered and courageously came back to Butzel
to substitute again.

Because the situation at Butzel was deemed to be out of control, a cadre
of assistant-deputy-administrative-executive-vice-superintendents and consultants and ethnic experts and other supervisory types from "downtown" and
from the region office descended like locusts upon the building, along with
some hastily recruited "community leaders," to see if they could determine what
to do. They called several evening meetings so these "leaders" could make
pompous speeches and helpfully tell us—the Butzel staff—how *we* could solve
our problem.

In their infinite wisdom, they presently decided to conduct a witch hunt
among the students—inviting them to a general after-school meeting to air their
grievances against specific members of the school's faculty and administration.

It so happened that I became an incidental beneficiary of this procedure,
since my name—along with the name of one of my young black female teachers,
Amelia Dortch—was one of the two names mentioned by the students most
often as the ones they trusted the most. Harold Stuckey wrote, "Dr. Telford
treat us like his own childern." Many others expressed similar sentiments.

Dr. Norman Fuqua, the region superintendent, relieved me of my classroom duties to back up the principal full-time in keeping the troubles from the school doors. After the gravest crisis time had passed, Dr. Fuqua had become impressed enough with my leadership ability and my way with the students to promote me to a high school department head job at the nearby Martin Luther King, Jr. Senior High School, making me the youngest high school department head in the city. When my kids at Butzel learned I was to leave, they clamored for assurance that I wasn't being sent away against my will so a black man could replace me.

As always before, it was again hard for me to leave my students. Even at Finney—my one white school—I had missed my kids when I left. But at the farewell party my Butzel students gave me, I reassured them—and reassured *myself*—that I'd be just down the street at King, and most of them would be going there when they graduated from Butzel. I invited them to come and visit me any time they wanted, and I promised I'd be back to do the same.

I was actually back sooner than I had anticipated. I was called back a day or two later to help Mrs. Sanders explain to a skeptical group of students— including Karroll Stevenson, Shirley Ivory, and Willie Spivey, who had been absent when I was transferred—that I had really been promoted and that I *wanted* to go to King. They had camped out in front of the principal's office and declined to go to class until they could talk to me personally. Karroll later sent me a picture of her to King with a letter in which she called me a "blue-eyed soul brother." (I appreciated the message even though my eyes are brown.)

During my first complete day at King, I happily returned the greetings of some of my former junior high students in the hallways, and I was delighted to find a few of them in the two multi-grade Honors English classes I had inherited from the previous department head. Ronald Kelly ("I will not hit Dewey in the head with a pen, I will not hit Dewey . . .") was now a King student. I was pleased to note that Ronald had grown considerably in size, in maturity, and in scholasticism since those "Dewey" days and since the time he had gotten into the fight on the bus to Lansing when I had threatened to open a bus window and throw him out through it if he didn't behave.

I started to teach my anti-Ebonics lessons again, although I soon found that my Honors students—particularly a very accomplished girl named Terri Tabor, whose father was a prominent local minister— didn't need the more rudimentary parts of those lessons that my Southeastern and Pershing and Butzel kids had needed so direly.

Soon after my arrival at King, student disturbances that had already begun in the school intensified. I had been imported to King from Butzel, where I had been a calming influence, in the hope that I could now similarly help the King administration put out *their* fires, as it were. Unhappily, these fires were raging flames—figurative and real—being sparked both from within and from without. This was so not only at or around King or just in Detroit, but all across the land. The fires had to run their natural course and burn themselves out. Time—and a hoped-for urban/suburban social evolution—were the only waters that could quench them.

Despite our bright hopes personified now in 2009 in President Barack Obama, these flames remain smoldering to this day, wanting but the least little spark to burst again into a raging blaze. As is the case today, in the school year 1968–69, bright young black teens in and beyond Detroit had become cynical far beyond their years—but not far beyond their *experience*—in their accurate perceptions of what was wrong, terribly wrong, with their schools. They couldn't be expected to respect what *merited* no respect, to hold *dear* what had little value.

"Ever'body walk out!" The shout blasted out of the public address speaker, startling everyone in my second-hour class. *Now, that didn't sound like Mr. Wise,* I said to myself. Roosevelt Wise, the acting principal, was in way over his head trying to stem the revolutionary tide within the building. A former amateur boxer, his main method of handling dissidents was to wrestle them to the floor wherever his authority was challenged—and it was challenged every day, all over the school. He confided to me that he was on a daily ration of tranquilizers. The troublemakers had invaded the office and taken territorial control of it again. I pondered briefly whether to go there or to stay with my class.

I decided to stay. I locked the classroom door, pulled down the window shade on the door, and calmly instructed everybody to remain seated. There was at once a chaotic rush in the hall outside and an occasional bang on the door with the call, "Walk out! Walk out!"

My entire class stayed put.

"You're really not afraid!" Cheryl Roberts, sitting tensely in the first row, whispered to me with wonder at my calmness.

Had I *been* afraid, of course, I would have tried to hide it—both out of pride and to keep my class calm. Students whose teacher is obviously frightened in a crisis can become equally frightened. But I realized with mild surprise that what Cheryl said was true. I had never considered it much, but my years in ghetto schools had instilled in me an attitude of fatalism. Also, I had always been extremely confident (maybe *too* confident) in my ability to defend myself—and besides, this school and any school like it were home to me. I also had plenty of kids who stood ever-ready to back me: My students and athletes had always been my *army*. Nor did I ever even *think* of myself as a white in a black world. Subconsciously, I actually regarded most *whites* as the aliens.

"No, Cheryl, I'm not afraid." Then in a more emphatic voice, my *teacher* voice: "Now let's take another look at James Baldwin."

My students reached for their copies of *The Fire Next Time*. Theirs was the only class in the school that didn't walk out—and they got their parents' full money's worth of taxpayer-subsidized instruction in their English class that day.

CHAPTER EIGHTEEN

RUNNING WITH A NEW TEAM!

"Faster, higher, stronger."

—*The Olympic motto translated from the Latin*

Chester Rogers, a shop teacher who later was to become principal at Martin Luther King, Jr. Senior High School, had recently assumed the track-coaching duties at the school. A former high jumper, he was a big, easy-going, amiable fellow who could use the modest stipend of a few hundred dollars, and he had a keen interest in athletics, but he knew very little about coaching runners. He came to me for help, and—delighted to be able to get back into coaching—I promptly became his unpaid assistant.

On days I had to catch up with some of my departmental responsibilities, I told Coach Rogers I would be unable to assist him, but this turned out not to work because the coach had a habit of sometimes coaching only when he felt so inclined, and whenever he happened to be golfing or at the racetrack or had simply gone home to run errands that day, his abandoned athletes sought me out.

Thus, I became the unpaid coach rather than the unpaid assistant, and Coach Rogers became the paid assistant—a rather enviable position—but I didn't care. I was back again coaching a sport I loved in the city I loved in a neighborhood where I could do the greatest good, and which in turn could do *me* the greatest good emotionally. Also, I got the added bonus of running with potential champions again and showing them by example how fast they could really move, once they broke that mental barrier.

Centra Goode, my former Butzel student who was now my office co-op (a paid student clerical aide) helped me recruit athletes for the track team. In addition, she helpfully informed me that I had a bald spot "the size of a nickel" on the back of my head—the first sign of encroaching baldness that luckily would take four more decades to make any significantly noticeable inroads. (Centra eventually matriculated at Central Michigan University in Mount Pleasant, but after that I lost touch with her.)

Another female student actively recruited trackmen for me, too. This particular young lady was reading a book entitled *The Naked Ape*, in which she had encountered the word "clitoris" and asked me what it was. I defined it for her, demonstratively likening it in dimension to the size of the tip of my little finger.

"Oh—you mean a *'spare tongue'*?"

"Yes, it's been called that—particularly by blacks."

I never knew for sure whether her curiosity was genuine or if she was just teasing me or coming on to me, to see what I would do. One line I never crossed was to involve myself romantically with any student, except for one intellectually and socially precocious Southeastern alumnus named Edith Latham whom I ran into at a party years later when she was twenty-two or so and I was maybe twenty-eight. The streetwise Edith, who had borne a son, Delano, when she was thirteen, resembled the actress Leslie Uggams. I could tell many stories about Edith, but they would fill another book.

I set about recruiting many of my swifter former Butzel students—some who a year or two earlier had demonstrated a remarkable ability to elude police in footraces down alleys, and who were now on the verge of dropping out of school. Most of them were young—sixteen or younger—and most were sophomores. If I could keep them off the street and out of the youth home, the school's track fortunes appeared sunny indeed, as did their own destinies. Their raw talent was *unreal*, better than I had ever assembled at one time to coach. Even my great athletes at Southeastern and later at Pershing—where my teams never lost—hadn't had this kind of collective potential. King was a brand-new school that had been built and dedicated a year previously as a replacement to the old Eastern High, a hundred-year-old hulk still standing nearby. As yet King had no track, and the team of the previous season hadn't won a single meet.

As I had done at Finney, I pounded steel pipes into the ground on a vacant field near the school and dropped flags on poles into the pipes, creating an elliptical "track" of about 200 yards. The kids scoured the area and removed rocks, broken glass, beer cans, wine bottles, and deceased rodents. A nearby furniture warehouse manager donated foam-rubber chips we encased in nets for pole vaulters and high jumpers to land upon. Coach Rogers had the athletes fashion boards in his carpentry class into a long-jump takeoff board, and a friend of his hauled a load of sand to the field and dumped it into a shallow pit we had dug for the long jump. Hurdles were set up in the middle of the field.

We often ran our straightaways on long stretches of sidewalk, or in the halls on cold or rainy days. Some days we would also jog across the nearby Belle Isle Bridge (MacArthur Bridge) and train on the dusty old track on Belle Isle in the Detroit River.

I ran alongside the sprinters and quarter-milers in their faster repetition workouts, exhorting them to run faster and farther, to thrust against pain, to suffer and hurt. "If it hurts, it's worth doing," I told them—and *hurt* they did, again and again. I hurt and hurt *plenty* right along with them; thus, they had no alternative but to hurt, too.

To motivate and inspire them, I confided to them that a world-ranked quarter-miler is every bit the artist in his own limited medium that Faulkner and Van Gogh were in their wider ones—and that intrinsically, his challenge is even greater, for he has not only the inescapable law of averages to thwart him, but also his own laboring lungs and sinews screaming treacherously for him to ease off in the home stretch of a hard-run race. I quoted to them from the first (1965) edition of my book *The Longest Dash*:

> A man who aspires to become an artist at any standard distance beyond 220 yards is not unlike someone seeking the most aesthetic way to be *burned at the stake*. He cannot implement his design without enduring excruciating hours of trial by fire to forge his physique into the *exotic metal* it must become for him to realize his aspirations in the crucible of top-flight competition, where the tin and the chrome-plated melt. Phonies and the faint of heart may thrive in some endeavors; none break tapes.

I also read them this passage:

> In his final forty yards when he has fought his way through the
> shadows into some bright frontier beyond fatigue, the victorious
> runner hears his own unvoiced hosanna, which he rides on his
> heartbeats like a roller coaster down into the tape as the flash-
> bulbs and screaming crowd burst inside his brain. The crushing
> fatigue is unfelt, insulated and transcended by his triumph.

And this one:

> A running contest personifies the life struggle conceived on an
> ideal, almost Platonic plane. In life, the best man man often
> loses—on the track, he nearly always wins. What could possibly
> be more *democratic*? Jesse Owens might have had the wrong
> external physical characteristics for Hitler's "super race," but
> no racist dictator on the face of the earth could deny that Jesse
> was a thoroughbred superhuman on Berlin's Olympic stadium
> track on that summer week of 1936.

These passages were from "The Mystique of the Runner," the last chapter of that first edition. My brilliant Southeastern High School student, john powell, was a scholarship student and a runner at Stanford when I was coaching at King, and he told me that this last chapter had rendered *The Longest Dash* a kind of "cult book" on the West Coast. Copies of the paperback had been passed around and underlined and quoted by runners and non-runners alike, until the books became bent and dog-eared.

My now psychologically charged-up and physically ready-to-run King team's first opponent was Pershing High—the school where I had so recently molded champions. Since my departure from Pershing, the school's track fortunes had declined a little, but the team was rebuilding under new coach Norman Young, a former city half-mile champion for Central High. Some Pershing seniors who had been sophomores when I coached them came and hugged me.

Thomas Myles, my most promising runner, outdid himself with 10-second and 50-second 100- and 440-yard performances, and he soared over 22 feet in the long jump to become a triple winner.

Going into the mile relay, the final event, we were four points behind. Victory in the relay—worth five points to the winner and none to the loser— would give King the meet by one point. (Déjà vu! This was a circumstance virtually identical to a Denby vs. Miller meet that had been won by Denby, my alma mater, in a startling upset nearly two decades before!)

The rising excitement in the crowd of a few hundred was electric. Almost half of them were King kids who had come in cars, bringing much of the team with them.

The chant began from the Pershing supporters, "To de *wine* sto'! To de *wine* sto'!" The "wine store" exhortation had now become a traditional Pershing chant at the crux of a contest, in anticipation of an imminent victory celebration. I smiled at the words, which evoked many an exultant memory (and also one *non*-exultant one—the fatal stabbing).

The King partisans responded, "*Show* time! *Show* time!"—making me think nostalgically of my best friend and old teammate Cliff Hatcher, who had always exclaimed "Show time!" when we were about to run a big-time race. Cliff often came to meets when I was coaching, but he couldn't make this one.

The starting gun sounded and the two lead-off runners got away fast and rounded the first turn together, their lifting, reaching legs a synchronized brown blur. The royal blue-and-gold of Pershing went into the lead on the backstretch, holding off the King gold-and-black in the home stretch and passing the baton to the second Pershing runner with a five-yard lead. The second quarter-mile leg ended with King ten yards behind; the third ended with us behind by twenty.

Thomas Myles took the baton for King on the final leg, and gliding into his silky-smooth overdrive, he began to whittle away at the Pershing anchorman's twenty-yard lead. On the first turn, it was down to fifteen. In the backstretch, it was still fifteen. Coming out of the last turn, it was ten; in the home stretch, five; and near the finish line, Thomas had drawn even! With a desperate, leaping lunge at the finish string, he flung his agonized gold-and-black-clad body through it in first place by inches and went head-over-heels, full-length facedown on the cinder track. The gasping and beaten Pershing runner cursed and threw down his baton.

King had won the meet by a single point.

The King crowd and team, so long without a win, went berserk. Thomas and I were hoisted to King fans' shoulders and paraded in triumph. No championship I had won as athlete or coach ever made me more delirious with joy.

Two afternoons after our upset of Pershing, the King staff was required to attend what was called a "Black Consciousness" workshop. Having attended several similar workshops in previous weeks, I decided that a) I was already more than "black conscious" enough, and b) my team, which was facing a tough and imminent test against Northern High and future Michigan State University All-American sprinter Marshall Dill, needed me at track practice more than I needed the workshop.

The next morning, a note was in my office mailbox:

> Dr. Telford, I find it most regretable [*sic*] that you, the Chairman of our Language Arts Department, thought so little of our Black Consciousness Workshop that you absented yourself from that richly benificial [*sic*] and sensitizing activity.

I am approximating the above mistakes as I recall them, because I no longer have that particular note, but it contained several errors. The note was signed by an assistant principal whose name I don't recall. It was something like "Kareem Ofumu" or "Karoom Mobutu"—which I will call him. Recently promoted from a department head job on the northwest side, where he had formerly been known by the name of "Adkins" or "Akins," this officious official sported a goatee and a dashiki. Mr. "Mobutu/Adkins" was fond of quoting the fiery black poet, Amiri Baraka, who at that writing still went by his "slave name" Leroi Jones: "We want poems like fists beating niggers out of Jocks / or *dagger* poems . . . we want poems that *kill*." That was perhaps one of the few things that this assistant principal and I had in common, because I sometimes liked to quote Leroi Jones, too.

I learned that this pseudo-militant gentleman wasn't really "*street*," though— he had actually grown up in a six-bedroom house in an upscale neighborhood that contrasted sublimely with my own Sixteenth Street origins.

There were a hundred more hypocrites like him in the school system. I was slowly becoming conscious of a galling bitterness deep within my psyche as I observed their swift climb up the administrative ladder. George Williams, a rookie department head at Butzel who was promoted there after me—and whom I had helped learn the job—had now, for example, become *principal* of *Pershing*—a job I would have given my eye-teeth to have. Mr. Mobutu/Adkins was said to be shucking and jiving the kids and the community in an effort to subvert the struggling Mr. Wise and assume the King principalship.

I stayed away from all such self-serving politicking. I resolved to just teach my kids, administer my department, and coach my team—my Activist Army whose co-captains I lost no time turning loose on Mr. "Mobutu/Adkins" regarding his note. Two or three days later—my athletes having held a persuasive conference with the gentleman—he sought me out, all slick and smiling. He knew that my co-captains were extremely influential with the student body. They were respected student leaders who in this chaotic era could capriciously make or break the career of any teacher or administrator in the building. I didn't get imposed on again about Black Consciousness workshops or any other related activity.

My Martin Luther King, Jr. Senior High School team went on to set seven varsity records and win five of their remaining six track meets. The martyred civil-rights giant would have been very proud of the runners at the school that now bore his name.

CHAPTER NINETEEN

CEREBRAL JOHNNIE THOMAS AND SOME JOLTING JOURNALS

"Dr. Telford, why is it that a black man is taught and must learn the white man's language, when [the black man] has a language himself?"

—Question posited by Johnnie Lewis Thomas II,
King High School student, April 1969

The cerebral Johnnie Thomas was already a student leader, even though he was only in the tenth grade. Now he had posed this question to me which he wrote in his classroom journal. I needed to answer it—and answer it *emphatically* —else, I was no teacher.

Meanwhile, there were two words that were beginning to trouble me more and more as time passed and I saw deserving white colleagues being bypassed for promotions while lesser-qualified blacks moved rapidly into top administrative positions. Those two words were "affirmative action." Dozens of people who had still been teachers long after I had made department head were jumping from teacher up three or four rank-classifications to principal or director in less than a year.

My aspirant young fiancée Lynn—a Warren, Michigan, elementary teacher and grade-level coordinator—had begun to plant grave concerns in my mind about the resultant long-range direction of my own career. I found this to be ambivalently troubling, because egalitarian liberal to the bone marrow that I was, I sympathized almost instinctively with affirmative action's *end result*, but was finding it increasingly difficult to live with its *means* to that end—particularly as it applied to *me*.

A black fellow-candidate for the Doctor of Education degree who had been in the doctoral program with me (he pronounced it "doctorial") had failed his Preliminary Exams twice, even though I and a study group I was part of had helped him study for them and provided him with extensive material to study. ("Preliminary" was a misnomer—the Prelims were actually the last—and a post-dissertational—hurdle a candidate had to clear before being anointed with the title of "Doctor.") Two failures of the Prelims were supposed to mean a washout, but he was mysteriously graduated from the doctoral program.

I was particularly cynical about this because the gentleman's doctoral advisor, Morrel Clute, had once threatened to short-circuit my own doctoral aspirations because I had been incisively critical (at Professor Clute's own invitation) of aspects of a summer doctoral class of his I had taken. The class had involved the teaching—not so much by the professor, but mostly by his Royal Oak lady friend (who later became his second wife)—of a group of Detroit junior high school students on closed-circuit TV in what Professor Clute optimistically but inaccurately termed a "natural classroom atmosphere."

Although the rambunctious kids rode the elevators up and down endlessly during break time and took apart the receivers in the public telephones, they didn't present truly prototypical behavioral challenges. It was hardly a typical situation at all, since they were volunteer, hand-picked students who knew their every classroom move was being watched on TV by a seminar of sixty graduate students. Unlike the Butzel Junior High School students I had worked with so recently, the seminar kids weren't about to be urinating on radiators—at least, not under circumstances like that.

Dr. Clute held a meeting with me in his office in which I began by angrily blurting out that he wouldn't have to wash me out of his "effing doctoral program," because I was going to *quit* it. When he calmed me down enough so I could listen to him, I promised not to quit—and we shook hands and agreed to drop the matter. Had he persisted, I probably would have become so disgusted with the pedagogical hoops and hypocrisies of "higher education" that I would have abandoned pursuit of the doctorate, and my life would have taken a far different course.

At the close of the 1960s, many liberals throughout the country had shifted from an espousal of total *professional* control of urban school districts to a more *community*-oriented stance—and this included more black visibility in positions of educational leadership. Many other liberals hadn't budged at all and were deeply troubled by the current thrust of their liberal former allies. Their deep distress derived from their recognition that what the black militants in any community were seeking was in diametric opposition to all that democratic liberalism stood for. The liberal commitment is to secularism, *universalism*. Liberals' commitment to the secular school continues to be supported by the American idealization of the "melting pot" mystique, of a dream of universal brotherhood in a new world where the private community will be unneeded. Insofar as the schools promote this secular ideal, they conform to the liberal tradition.

It was from this perspective that my own heartfelt philosophy derived: While the schools should seek to promote, foster, and embrace ethnically heterogeneous populations, school personnel should also be selected and advanced according to their *achieved merits* and to their allegiance to an ideal of heterogeneity as the preferred future for a democratic society. This was at direct odds with the several near-anarchical theses propounded by those who through imposition of guilt and brute intimidation were swiftly gaining control of my beloved Detroit school district, which to me—along with WSU—was the only real academic and co-curricular home I had ever known.

Over the years, the central tenet of some liberals when dealing with race has been to assert (erroneously) its *irrelevance*. A main goal of the white liberal wing of the 1960s civil-rights movement was to persuade white America to become color-blind. A corollary objective was that blacks become likewise blind to their *blackness*. This goal couldn't (and can't) be achieved, because general white unwillingness to ignore the blackness of blacks has continued to make it impossible for blacks themselves to be able to ignore their blackness. Witness the sizable number of white Americans who stated in 2008 that they wouldn't vote for Barack Obama simply because his skin was *darker* than theirs! This form of illogicality—no, *insanity*—remains pervasive in broad regions of these still racially *un*-United States. African ancestry in a democratic society should be no more or less relevant than a comparison, say, of my father's Scottish birth and ancestry to my mother's Danish ancestry, or of my brown eyes to my cousin Carl's son (and my godson) Rick's blue eyes, or indeed to *my own son* Steve's blue eyes—but neither blacks nor whites would or will just *let it be*. Hence the historic movement toward "black consciousness" which unfortunately and inevitably played a strong role in helping to engender the racial re-segregation that obtains today—a movement which played right into the hands of racist white segregationists.

In the 1960s, white liberal guilt over non-liberal white transgressions induced many *liberal* whites to support this new direction of the black community, albeit with the hope that American society would evolve toward total equality fast enough to outgrow its need for *affirmative action*.

By the early spring of 1969, I had really begun to abhor those two words. Prodded by my persistent fiancée (who incidentally was growing increasingly impatient to become my *wife*), I was on the verge of parting company with the liberal group that was willing to *wait* for society to *evolve*.

"If you stay in Detroit, you'll *never* get to be a high school principal," the ambitious Lynn told me. "A principalship in Detroit just isn't in the cards for a white man anymore."

One afternoon I left King early and went downtown to meet with my former Pershing principal, Al Meyers, who was now one of the few remaining white assistants to the Superintendent. Dr. Meyers was aware of my long-time membership in the philanthropic (and all-black) Detroit Varsity Club, and he was marginally aware of my influence with diverse elements of the black community at both the grassroots and professional levels, much of this influence having been engendered by my former prominence as an athlete and my reputation as a successful coach. He nevertheless surprised me by advising me that if I really wanted to attain my uppermost goal of becoming a high school principal, it would have to be *outside the city*—the same thing Lynn had said.

I arose the next morning as usual, and as usual, I drove to King and endeavored to teach my two classes, but my conversation with the high-ranking Dr. Meyers—a liberal Jew—had put my mind in turmoil. *Outside* the city? The city was my *home*! I was having trouble concentrating on teaching the day's lesson on *Hamlet*.

To get myself back on track, I had my kids in both classes take out their journals a bit earlier that day. The journals—personal notebooks containing each student's thoughts of the day—were a valuable linguistic learning/teaching device I had used ever since my student-teaching internship days. Whenever possible, in the final five or ten minutes of a class period I would take their journals from a locked cabinet and hand them out for the class to write whatever they chose. The grammar and spelling seldom were subject to my red pencil the way their theme papers were, and I would faithfully write a response to each student's daily entry despite the considerable time this took.

Sometimes if I didn't respond the very day an entry was made, the next day's entry would say, "Are you falling behind? You didn't respond to yesterday's entry."

This kept me on my toes.

On this particular day when I was in such uncustomary mental turmoil, the most recent entry in student Terri Tabor's journal was, "Does Gary Tyson [incidentally a talented basketball teammate of future pro star George "the Iceman" Gervin] really use profain [*sic*] language in his journal? [I wrote the response: *No*.] He won't let me read it. He says my mind is too easily influenced."

I smiled at this, and my mental turmoil immediately lessened like magic— at least, for a while.

CHAPTER TWENTY

THE JOURNALS
GROW WHIMSICAL—
AND PROFOUND

"In a world of imageless matter, perhaps color as a racial classi-
fication couldn't exist."

—*Journal entry of Cheryl Roberts,*
King High School student

I enjoyed my students' journals. I chuckled as I read and responded to them.
I soon became consistently able, at moments like these, when the students'
journal commentaries amused me, to repress Dr. Meyers' advice to leave DPS.
I don't necessarily have to be a principal to make a difference for my kids, I rational-
ized to myself. *This job is the best of all worlds—I get to teach, I get to coach, and
I get to administrate!*

At times, the kids' entries were breezily whimsical; at other times, they
became impressively and sometimes troublingly profound.

Cheryl Roberts wrote:

> If I had a chance to be anything else in this world, I'd like to be
> energy. [Teacher response {T. r.}: *In a certain scientific sense, you
> are. Everyone is.*] A law in science, I can't think which one, states
> that matter cannot be created or destroyed. I'd like to be able
> to say, hey, I created a chain reaction today, and no one can stop
> me. In a world of imageless matter, perhaps color as a racial
> classification couldn't exist." [T. r.: *Very profound thinking.*]
>
> I guess, though, that in every system, even if there was
> no black and white, there would be some *other* barrier between

people. [T. r.: *I'm afraid you're right. Jonathan Swift wrote in his book* Gulliver's Travels *about two supposedly "imaginary" countries {actually England and France} that went to war because each didn't like the way the other "broke its eggs for breakfast"—a satire on Catholic vs. Protestant ritualism.*]

As I sit here at my desk, I remember a line that you taught us in *Hamlet* that I also relate to myself: "To be, or not to be: that is the question." Sometimes I'm not sure of the answer. [T. r.: *I would rather be—and so, I hope, would you.*]

Who would believe it? I dreamed I woke up, gazed over the rooftops, and saw a round-shaped object . . . with an open hatch from which appeared a Bayer aspirin and a little green man with a message flickering between his antenna that flashed the words: "I have an Excedrin headache." I hope I have a better dream tomorrow night. [T. r.: *You watch too much TV.*]

Student unrest! Fooey! Not all, but some of the students at King are sub-adolescent. Many people follow the crowd so as not to be talked about. Me, I don't give a —dandruff who talks about me. [T. r.: *You have more courage than some others.*] I do what I see best for me. Another observation, or question: Is it wrong not to believe in God? [T. r.: *No. In a democracy, you are entitled to hold any religious belief you choose—including atheism.*]

The class period is taking a long time to be over. Maybe it's because you are absent today, Dr. Telford. The sub is a rough person. She has a medium brown complexion with false eyelashes and long black hair. Maybe it's a wig. Rusher [last name: Hunt] is pestering her. She is, and I quote, "Trying very hard to ignore you, and if you don't leave me alone, I'll send you out." Sonja, Jocelyn, and Barbara are just now coming in. The class period is nearly over. They must have heard you weren't here today.

Please don't leave us again, Dr. Telford. Rusher is still pestering the teacher. Sonja wants some sharp black and white shoes. Rusher has just walked out. Oh, oh: he's back in. This is very interesting. He is now sitting in his seat. Everyone in the class is watching Rusher to see what he'll do next. [T. r.: *It appears that Rusher was the star of the day.*]

Cheryl's journal went on for some days in a detailed exploration of other dreams. Then her subject switched to softball. (She was on King's girls' team.) She broke her right hand in a game and her next several journal entries had a very jagged appearance because they were all entered with her left hand. (My responses were equally shaky, because then I whimsically used my left hand, too.)

> What a warm day! Sonja has on a very pretty blue dress. There is a girls' gym class softball game going on in the court. One team has just struck out. The trees are very green. The wind is like a hot oven. The pitcher just made a wild throw.
>
> Martha Rogers is lazily walking down the walk. Gloria Rivers just made an out on a pop fly. Mrs. Walker [P.E. teacher] is on first base. A very distant figure is walking down the street outside the window. Five boys in a white car carefully drive away. The wind is faintly moving. A fly has just landed on the gravel rooftop below. There is a bunch of boys congregating in the parking lot. I see dice and an exchange of currency. I have a headache.
>
> Have a nice weekend. [T. r.: *I will, Cheryl, if my track team wins anything in the state meet.*]

Debra Byrd entered,

> We're messing ourselves up by continually disrupting school. Negroes now have as much opportunity as anyone else of getting ahead but we don't take advantage of it. Maybe slavery affected our minds. [T. r.: *No! You mustn't ever think that!*] We don't really seem to know what we want, and we can't change things that have been happening for centuries over a few decades.

The next day Debra replied to my brief protesting comment:

> I see you disagreed wholeheartedly with my last entry. Possibly I shouldn't say slavery affected our minds, but it *seemed* to be true, and it was only my opinion. [T. r.: *Slavery put the black man at a social and cultural disadvantage from which he's only now begin-ning to fully recover, but he's always been <u>potentially as capable as anyone</u>. Your own writing skills are a testament to that.*]

The lessons have been well-taught, although I'm still having some difficulty with *Hamlet*. I'd like to become an English teacher like you. You told us everyone in this class could and should all one day be in college, so maybe there's hope for me." [T. r.: *More than a little!*]

Johnnie Thomas, who was increasingly active in the insurrectionist student politicking on the King campus, wrote:

Dr. Telford, how can any man plan to go to the moon when there is prejudice, hunger, greed, poverty, pollution, and many other problems of the human race right here? Does he try to rid the earth of these problems and *then* go to the moon, or does he go to the moon to get away from these problems? A man is going to the moon [this was 1969], but there are rats in my sister's elementary school where she eats her lunch. It seems with the kind of technology that's been developed, there wouldn't have to be rats in my little sister's elementary school lunchroom if these "technicians" really cared about my sister and children like her as much as they care about a million-dollar hunk of machinery. [T. r.: *Yes—if we were wise, we would forget about the moon until we attend to more urgent, immediate problems. The moon will still be there when we're ready—it's not going anywhere. Less wise is our present direction—to spend a billion dollars on an Apollo program.*]

Dr. Telford, how can a man improve himself and his personality if he is considered a pest? Take, for example, Sharon Watkins— I try to be nice and playful toward her and yet she has an anti-social barrier or else she's stuck up on herself. How can I break down this barrier? [T. r.: *Be civil to her. Be nice to her. If she still doesn't respond, forget it. There are millions of others.*]

Dr. Telford, what should a person of my caliber look forward to in life? It seems that many people ask me what I plan to be but I can give them no definite answer. Just what is my hang-up? [T. r.: *First, a person of your caliber should look forward to college— definitely. Then perhaps politics, law, education, social work, the arts, business, or medicine. The world awaits you and doors are opening. I think politics might eventually be the field where you can make the greatest contribution.*]

Dr. Telford, I feel that segregation is best for black people because we need to get together.

Here was that accursed concept again! The red High-Temperature Light went on in my brain. I had to calm myself for a moment before I was able to couch my response in rational language:

> *Johnnie, this statement plays right into the hands of segregationists and white racists. It is true that black men must unite, but they must also break out of the ghetto, and also render the ghetto no longer a ghetto. Since the economy (the purse-strings) of this country is under white majority control, it is absolutely imperative that the black man strive for legal integration—open housing on a national scale. I am first, last, and always an integrationist. I wouldn't be here if I weren't. In my view, integration is the only chance for the ultimate survival of our democracy.*

New Johnnie Thomas entry:

> Dr. Telford, why is it that people believe only what they want to hear? Teachers and students do the same thing. You can tell them the truth but they only hear what they want to believe. [T. r.: *I try to hear beyond that. It isn't always easy for some people. It's easier and more comfortable to have closed minds.*]

> Dr. Telford, I'm in a mood where I just don't care what happens or what anyone says. Could you give me any examples of what are the causes and tell me how to get out of this rut? [T. r.: *There are times when I feel this way, too. I think we all do. At times like this, we have to be careful not to do or say things that might hurt someone—and that we may regret later. We don't always know why we feel like this, either. Maybe we suffered a disappointment, or a friend said something that hurt us. Worse, maybe someone we liked and admired ignored us and showed us no attention. Whatever the reason, people of your intelligence deal with situations like this philosophically. They say, "I'm not going to let this get me down. Tomorrow is another day."*]

> From where did Latin language begin? [T. r.: *Look it up—find out all you can about it, write a report, hand it in, and I'll give you extra credit.*]

Dr. Telford, I have an inner feeling but I'm afraid to express it because I would be persecuted by all of my friends because they do not expect me to feel in this sort of manner. People want me to live to their expectations but I want to be truthful about myself. [T. r.: *Truthfulness is the only way. If your friends want you to try to do, act, or be something you're really not, they aren't friends. You can't please everyone anyway, so be true to yourself. {Remember Polonius in* Hamlet?} *That way, you'll be able to face yourself in the mirror. The other way, you won't.*]

Dr. Telford, kindness can be a key to wisdom. [T. r.: *Yes, and vice versa.*]

Dr. Telford, why is it that a black man is taught and must learn the white man's language when he has a language himself—the language being different from English? [T. r.: *The black man learns it as a second language—the same way he may learn Spanish, French, etc. The more languages and dialects you can master, the wider your world becomes. It's a fact of life that so-called "white" English is the language of the mass media and of the market place—the economy— in this country, and also abroad. To become economically mobile— I'm talking about money—you need to be able to communicate with total effectiveness.*]

"Communicating with total effectiveness"—at least with their *teacher*— is indeed what Johnnie Thomas and his strong, vibrant, wonderful classmates in my two Honors English classes at King High School most definitely and eloquently did, so long ago.

CHAPTER TWENTY-ONE

A MESSIANIC MESSENGER
CALLED COCKREL

The limits of our language are the limits of our world.

When bright young Johnnie Thomas asked me in his journal why the black man must learn the white man's language, his innocently-posed question was a direct result of the benighted movement that was gaining momentum at that time among some militant but misguided blacks and some fellow-traveling hipster whites. These folks wanted to do away with "standard" English as an instructional discipline and even as a *recognized avenue of communication* for black students.

Superciliously styling themselves a "new breed of 'socio-linguists'," this group of mis-educators propounded their absurd axiom that was so destructive to blacks with such success that they had gained a large and vociferous black following throughout the country—including the officious Mr. "Mobutu/Adkins" and some teachers in my own English department at King. To exacerbate the problem, a majority of these mis-educators' misguided disciples (again, including some of my own staff) couldn't teach traditional grammar, transformational grammar, or any other form of grammar or indeed any *language* at all—including structural *Swahili*. They didn't have the foggiest notion of the difference between a phoneme and a morpheme or between a participle and a gerund.

Locally, some of the "leaders" of this movement were pompous, posturing, semi-literates who probably couldn't *spell* "participle," let alone recognize one if it popped up off the page and *bit* them. And they were *commandeering* the

Detroit Public Schools and other urban districts, grievously hampering the learn-
ing processes among marvelous young men and women like Johnnie Thomas,
Cheryl Roberts, and the other members of my two highly-motivated multi-grade
Honors English classes at King who were so willing and eager to learn.

Dialect can cause severe comprehension problems for the black student—
especially the *younger* black student—as with the child who, when asked to use
the word "so" in a sentence, comes up with, "I got a so' on my laig." Also, there
were actually some sounds in "standard" English that a number of black kids
hadn't been acculturated then to *hear* (and haven't been acculturated *now*
to hear), because those sounds don't appear in *corresponding usages* in their
dialect. The "th" blend at the end of a word is only one of many examples of
such a sound, as in "both" and "Smith," which some children pronounce "bofe"
and "Smiff."

There are black dialectical subtleties which have their own form of grammatical structure—in fact, a structure that can in some instances be even more
complex than their "standard"-English counterparts. Some uses of the infinitive
"to be," for example, sound like variations of the *same answer* to the unfamiliarized
ear—including the ears of many *middle-class* blacks; e.g., if a girl is asked where
her brother is, she might say, "He gone," or "He *be* gone," or "He *bees* gone."
Each answer dialectically has a different meaning. "He *gone*" means he has left
permanently, while "He *be* gone" means he's not present at the moment, but
he *will* be *soon*, and "He *bees* gone" means he's constantly going *off* somewhere
and may not be back any time soon.

And there are endless variations. "He *been* gone" means not only has he
left *permanently*, but it was a fairly long *time* ago that he left.

My point is this: Even though it's a fact that there is an admirably complex
structure to African-American dialect(s), that fact remains *economically* (if not
sociologically) irrelevant. As I've already said repeatedly, blacks who are to become
adept at coping and excelling in our still-white-dominated society can and should
retain their dialect(s) for appropriate moments, but they must become "bilingual."
This means they have to be given systematized *traditional* grammatical instruction
in-depth in "standard" English—as a "second language," if need be—as I asserted
previously in Chapter Ten, citing the precocious paper I had written as a relative
rookie in 1962 that was used thereafter for a far too-*brief* period of time in a
number of Detroit high schools.

One community activist who believed in my ideas regarding in-depth *traditional*-grammar instruction for black students was an eloquent young Wayne State University alumnus named Kenneth Cockrel, who had a rabidly anti-Ebonics message that was absolutely *messianic*. As a sports-minded teenager, Ken Cockrel had closely followed my running career in newspaper articles and newsreels, and as a child, he had also closely followed my track teammate Cliff Hatcher's, who became his friend. A few years later, Cliff had introduced him to me on campus in the Student Union cafeteria at the old Mackenzie Hall at Wayne State. I was taking evening and weekend courses for my doctoral degree; Cliff had remarried—this time to a sweet, supportive young teacher—and he had briefly returned to school in an abortive effort to complete his undergraduate work, and perhaps even to race again. (He had one year of track eligibility remaining.)

Ken Cockrel and I immediately felt an affinity—and he, I, Cliff, another young student who was a friend of Ken's, and my gorgeous and spunky young cousin Judy Telford, who then was an undergrad in the College of Nursing, drank coffee together (plus a surreptitious swig from Cliff's rum bottle) and held some political conversations which were enlightening to Judy, whose otherwise admirable old stepfather was (gasp!) a Republican. I later discovered that Ken was an incredible orator who maintained socialist and Marxist views remarkably similar to mine and those of my Scots-American father, my once-blacklisted Hollywood producer-director uncle Frank Telford (Judy's dad), and my beautiful aunt Letty Telford, who had been a card-carrying Communist in the 1930s and was a founder of the Detroit Federation of Teachers.

I sent Ken a copy of an article from my King student newspaper, the *Crusader*. Its headline: "Student Unrest—*Why?*"

Here is an excerpt:

> Student unrest has recently erupted at King High and other educational institutions throughout the country. Because of the tension on school campuses, students, parents, teachers, and administrators have been labeling and condemning each other. The only result of this bickering has been more noise and less action. At present, the groups involved—students, parents, teachers, and administrators—are far from either an understanding or a compromise.

(Does this ring any familiar bell now, *forty years later?*)

Upon reading this article, Ken asked me if he could come to King to speak, and I lost no time bringing him in. I had previously brought him and the prolific poet Naomi Long Madgett to speak at Butzel—and not long after Ken spoke at King, he was elected to the Detroit Common Council.

Ken Cockrel's memorable initiatives as a crusading attorney in organizing the labor coalition that battled racist police brutality puts him in the city's all-time pantheon of civil-rights leaders. Had he lived just a little longer, I believe he would have ascended to the mayoral chair in which his son who bears his name was later to sit on an interim basis. When Moms Mabley sang "Only the *good* die young" in her recording of *Abraham, Martin, & John*, she could have included Bobby Kennedy and Ken Cockrel. They were more than good—they were *great*—and they died too young.

Ken Cockrel saw right through the hypocrisy of the district's self-serving "Mobutu/Adkinses" and other *dys*educators and demagogues who were preaching that the "standard" English language should no longer be taught in the Detroit Public Schools. In the packed student assembly at King, he demonstrated his absolute command of that language in giving me eloquently golden support for what I was still propounding in my classroom (and stubbornly *trying* to propound in my department) pertaining to our students' vital and ongoing need to be taught to speak and write marketplace English. The numerous members of my departmental staff who had been listening to the demagogues instead of to me were now listening raptly to this fiery young community activist preach my gospel of traditional grammar instruction, and they were nodding their heads and smiling and jabbing their thumbs in the air and turning and pointing to me. So were some of my students.

Of all people, the soon-to-become-great Kenneth Cockrel knew that Detroit's black schoolchildren had unique instructional and curricular needs that definitely weren't being met, and the King kids and teaching staff were *hearing* him.

At every increasingly frequent opportunity that Ken Cockrel got to make a speech and get in front of a radio microphone or TV camera, he presciently warned our rapidly dwindling white Detroit and its rapidly growing white suburbs and our white Michigan and white America that very bad things were going to continue to happen and to escalate in our city, state, and nation until those unique curricular needs *were* met.

Today, a full four decades later, those needs still haven't been met in Detroit and all across urban America. This despite all the pious sound and fury that was in 1969 and still *is* forty years later in *2009* being aimed at the inner-city school—a sound and fury given a belated impetus then and now by the real and healthy fear that James Baldwin's "fire next time" will prove to be far bigger and worse than the fires *last* time.

Considering the violence I'm going to describe in later chapters—violence I dealt with on nearly a *daily* basis while working with gangs out of a police mini-station in 1998 and was a part of on an almost *hourly* basis between 2003 and 2008 at Detroit Finney High School—and considering the relevant things some of my more militant and aware Finney students have told me, "the fire *next* time" will be a real and bloody revolution in the streets of urban America that will very quickly encroach upon *suburban* America. Such a conflagration is inevitable unless something transformative is done to educate Detroit's and America's under-educated non-white masses—and unless the dynamic young Barack Obama can pull us up out of the deep economic and spiritual hole that the George W. Bush administration's criminal acts have left us to wallow in.

Believe me, this fear of a "fire next time" isn't unrealistic by any means—but many of the solutions that have been proposed thus far *are* unrealistic to the point of being ridiculous. For example, it's fine and wonderful to have "cultural enrichment" programs and field trips and community theaters and extended-day library services (all of which can be and *are* frequently and abruptly cut off at political whim), but these things should be the *dessert*—not the meat and potatoes.

The *main staples* should be: a) primary, intermediate, and secondary reading programs specifically tailored to the culturally-induced peculiarities of the inner-city child's speech patterns; b) primary, intermediate, and secondary *traditional grammar* texts which prescribe for gross irregularities of syntax and inflection that arise from "non-standard" home usages, or dialects; and c) literature anthologies with stories featuring protagonists and life situations with which inner-city children and teenagers can identify and relate.

While the social studies in both urban and suburban schools have been largely revised or supplemented to include African-Americans' contributions to American history, many of the literature texts—first-grade through twelfth—remain virtually unchanged. (That is, they remain virtually unchanged except for cosmetic touchups in which a white face with white features in a "white" environment has simply been colored brown!)

These new reading programs I'm proposing should be *massive*—because anything *less* than massive, i.e., the "compensatory" programs on the present puny and non-prescriptive scale, aren't likely to significantly improve the achievement of students who are isolated by race and social class. Also, in integrated or cross-cultural classrooms, this program would have to be modified somehow to meet the needs of students with diverse speech patterns *right in that same classroom*. (It should be noted, too, that this is a potentially touchy problem in an ethnically heterogeneous group.)

Unless these three paramount needs—these three *main staples* that I have listed here—are met, the present urban curricula will itself continue to create serious behavior problems, especially among adolescents. Illiterate youngsters whose minds are molested thus by these inadequate curricula react in one of two ways: They try to gain peer status by compensatory misbehavior that often includes *violent* behavior, or they retreat into emotional/psychological withdrawal.

One of the many reasons inner-city youngsters find it difficult to learn to read is that words *in print* and words *as they are spoken in the youngsters' homes*—as I have shown in examples here—are two *significantly different* things. God knows that the American public schools are failing to teach many children—black *and* white—to read and write adequately—but in the case of black and brown children, this *significant difference* is an absolutely crucial reason why they aren't learning (even though it is just one of *many* reasons).

I have stressed and *re*-stressed in this book that most African-American youngsters, K-12, have chronic difficulty speaking and writing "standard" English correctly and fluently because the language they learned and speak at home and to each other in the street is, in its fundamental structure and essence, almost *another language*. Indeed, an excellent (but so far as I know *untried*) supplement for my proposed Item "*b*," preceding, has been and remains—as I suggested in my paper of forty-seven years ago—a typical *foreign-language laboratory* complete with earphone sets, tape-and-playback tape recorders, and repetition-drill recordings that list and differentiate right from *wrong* pronunciation, structure, and idiom, and these lessons need to be begun in *kindergarten*, or preferably, even in *pre-school*.

As I mentioned in Chapter Ten, I had already been *doing* many of those things. I had also been suggesting them to my departmental colleagues in my beginning-teaching years at Southeastern, when I had approached the teaching of English from the standpoint of its being a virtual *foreign language*, and I had written detailed lesson plans and methodological studies relevant to this approach.

At that time, I submitted one of those methodological studies in the form of an article to the *English Journal*, a periodical with nationwide circulation. The *Journal* rejected it, but one of its junior editors was kind enough to write to me at Southeastern to inform me that this sort of material was "too limited in scope" for the magazine to consider for publication.

However, when several of the big core-cities in the country—including Detroit—went up in riotous smoke a few short years later, the *English Journal* reversed its policy and set speedily to work printing several pieces that all had that same "too limited" subject as their theme!

CHAPTER TWENTY-TWO

AN ANGRY LETTER UNSENT; ANOTHER SADLY SENT

"As a bird that wandereth from the nest, so is a man that wandereth from his place."

—*Proverbs 28:8*

Despite Ken Cockrel's wonderful words in the King assembly supporting my pedagogical stance for teaching traditional grammar to urban youth, and despite the love I held for my students and the love I knew they held for me, I had begun to experience a deepening feeling of *anomie*—of rootlessness—and of a certain racial *irrelevance*. I had coached track champions now in four Detroit high schools, and I had been a champion myself, so Tom Briscoe—my old boxing trainer and a fellow Detroit Varsity Club member—recommended me for an assistant track coaching job at Western Michigan University in Kalamazoo. (Tom had briefly matriculated at WMU on a track grant-in-aid in the 1930s.)

Head coach George Dales (who incidentally retired the following year) *wanted* me as his assistant, and I was tempted to go, but I really didn't want to move so far away from home.

When in sleep I *dreamed* of home, the home in my frequent dream was the old yellow frame house on Sixteenth Street where I had spent the first fifteen years of my life. I was thirty-three now, and the demolition of that house and my four grandparents' two houses on Sixteenth Street and Twelfth Street, plus the reduction of much of the remainder of the heartland of my boyhood to rat-infested rubble, were catalysts that were sending my troubled mind spinning aimlessly about. Sensing that my whiteness was becoming archaic in the city of my birth, I sought subconsciously for some nebulous avenue of escape.

More consciously, I had grown increasingly afraid that if I remained in Detroit, my renewed and passionate wish to be a high school principal would never be fulfilled, and what I confidently regarded as my extensive range of professional skills would never be fully used. Also, I had increasingly ambivalent feelings about "affirmative action." Blacks had been discriminated against for so long that I wondered in my secret heart whether the school district's new policy of what many of my white colleagues condemned as "reverse discrimination" really weren't justified to some degree.

However, even if this were just *partially* so, I believed then that the policy hadn't been instituted due to the mostly-white central administration's love of justice, but rather to its terrible fear of intractable black rebellion. Fear can feed upon itself in a widening spiral of attempted appeasement that leads eventually to total *capitulation*—to total abdication of all vested responsibility. The nervous and still-sizable remnants of the schools' white power structure were yielding concession after concession to militant, mobbish, black community "leaders" and neighborhood bullies, as well as to rampaging teens who—like those today—were challenging the legitimacy and very *concept* of adult authority.

The most philosophically scary of all these mobs were the teenage ones, because there could be no formal public education of those who were unwilling to be educated, and the most nihilistic among these teenagers refused to recognize the authority even of *knowledge itself*. On a not-too-decelerated scale, many of these kids could be compared to The Children in their same general age group who eight years later were to usurp from their parents, teachers, and other elders the entire leadership and control of the South African community of Soweto and organize it into a guerilla network mobilized against that apartheid community's black professional power structure, its white administrators, and the police. *Unlike* the Soweto Children, however, the militant Detroit youngsters had no coherent leadership, direction, or plan except to tear down and destroy.

In a frantic attempt to retain an un-shredded remnant of its professional (and perhaps *physical*) skin, Detroit Public Schools' crumbling white power elite found itself yielding bulwark after bulwark to the militants. Many blacks in the system who were genuinely dedicated to disciplined educational process and sound pedagogy were packing their bags and taking advantage of openings elsewhere (often in higher education) that were afforded them in part by affirmative action programs in the receiving institutions. One can imagine, then, that their white colleagues of like intellect and ability were falling all over each other in a frantic and far more difficult scramble to do likewise.

It developed that I didn't have to scramble. I learned of an opening for an assistant principal at the brand new Walled Lake Western High School, about forty miles from the city. After several days of agonizing and pondering, I applied for the job without telling anyone.

Years later, Gary Doyle, one of my Rochester principals who had been the community education director in Walled Lake at the time, told me that I almost didn't get interviewed for it. The Walled Lake interview-screeners initially presumed I was *black*, since I was from Detroit and had listed "world-ranked sprinter, WSU" on my application form under "Achievements"—and most of the world's top sprinters were black. Presently, they found out that I *wasn't* black—so, operating on the presumption that since I was a white administrator in a black high school I must be a tough disciplinarian, they interviewed me in May and promptly chose me for the job from among several more experienced applicants.

Suddenly, it was serious *decision time*. I walked around with that unsigned contract in my pocket for several days, trying to get up the nerve to take the final step of signing it and sending it back.

In the middle of a night in early June 1969, I couldn't sleep. I got out of bed and wrote an overblown and ill-advised letter to Detroit superintendent of schools Norman Drachler that went something like this:

> Dear Dr. Drachler,
>   That I must submit to you this letter of resignation is a truly tragic travesty, but you and your cadre of chicken-shit politicos downtown have finally forced my hand. If you had a modicum of courage or any sense of professional decency and justice, you would never have permitted a self-serving mob of Philistines to scare you into betraying your public trust and the democratic ideals to which I have so often heard you pay lip service in your annual state-of-the-schools address.
>   I feel extremely sorry for you, because you need desperately to retain dedicated educators like me to keep this tottering monolith of a school district from tumbling. Unfortunately, you're neither brave nor ethical enough to do what you must

do to keep me. However, I am even sorrier for the students I love and whom I nevertheless must leave—these youngsters who need me so much I nearly stayed in spite of you and your legions of wallowing, parasitic maggots who munch on the decomposing corpse of a once-proud school system.

Should I ever return—and I <u>hope</u> to return some day—it will be after you are in your grave, because the only way I can envision that the Detroit schools can be saved is by a lightning bolt from the sky, which one day soon, I pray, will flash down and annihilate you and your cowardly stooges. I earnestly consign you—and them—to the Devil.

Most sincerely,

(Dr.) John Telford
Department Head/Language Arts
Martin Luther King, Jr. Senior High School

For the remainder of the night, I stayed awake and sat and pondered, and then I pondered and agonized and pondered some more—and concluded that maybe my letter was unfair. It had finally occurred to me that Superintendent Drachler might *not* be a coward. I reflected that he was a Jew, and thus likely a social liberal. Perhaps he was bravely trying to do the right thing by placing as many blacks as he could—as fast as he could—into leadership positions in a district which was clearly becoming all-black.

I decided to give him the benefit of the doubt. Very early in the morning, I tore up that furious letter and composed another much different one:

Dear Dr. Drachler,

It is with deep and nostalgic regret that I submit my resignation. During my ten years as teacher and coach in the system, I formed many close friendships among students and faculties. I observed many of my students evolve their reading, writing, speaking, and social skills. I watched my track teams win many titles, and I secured college scholarships for scores of my students and athletes. Some have since entered law school, medical school, and other graduate schools.

After a difficult period of soul-searching, I have decided to accept an assistant principalship at the new Walled Lake Western

High School. I should like to emphasize that the city's present compensatory promotion practices were not the prime motivational factor in my decision. Among a wide range of the black community, my views on and activities within the area of human relations are well known. My appointment at King attested to this, as does the fact that the acting principal, Mr. Roosevelt Wise, has offered me the summer-school principalship there. Nor am I leaving because of the current urban ferment. I found this problem challenging, and I had confidence in my ability—and in the ability of the moderate black majority—to deal with it. At this stage in my career, the opportunity for immediate professional advancement (and to grow and develop by seeking exposure to all situations within the field of education) has simply proved to be too strong a personal temptation to resist.

I learned much in Detroit Public Schools and gave much of myself to Detroit Public Schools in return. I love my students and understand their needs. I will miss them sorely. It is my fervent hope that some day within the next few years I will be enabled to return to Detroit as a more valuable educator due to my extended experience.

Very sincerely,

(Dr.) John Telford
Language Arts Department Head
Martin Luther King High School

I mailed this second letter.

Then I signed the Walled Lake assistant principal contract, sealed it in an envelope, took a long, deep breath, and mailed *it*, too—hoping against hope that I had done the right thing.

CHAPTER TWENTY-THREE

SOME FINAL JOURNALS— AND A JOURNEY

"If all whites could get along and understand us the way you do, there would be peace in the world."

"Keep being the man that you are—we all need men like you."

—*Last journal entries of Michael Fry and David Knox, respectively, King Honors English students, June 1969*

By now, Superintendent Drachler had received my letter of resignation, but I still had unfinished business with my King students, and with my team. One Saturday morning very early in June, I piled Reggie Adams, Greg Irvin, Albert Little, and Thomas Myles into the car my runners had dubbed "The Purple Pellet"—my trusty, rusty, old purple Comet with sweat-smelly stuffing coming out of the seats—and headed for an invitational relay carnival at Pershing High, my old school. We won the featured mile relay, with Thomas Myles blazing from behind, as usual, on the anchor leg.

Pershing athletic director Leroy Dues had been promoted downtown, and Will Robinson—Pershing's legendary city and state championship basketball coach—was tapped to replace him. Will, who had been the city's first black coach (at all-black Miller High in the early 1940s), was celebrating his promotion by hosting this track meet with the able organizational assistance of Pershing football coach Don Gorence. I had volunteered to be the clerk of course. Dave Beauvais, an old WSU sprint star of the 1930s who had sent me off flying at the starting gun in many a race, was the starter. My old Denby coach, Ralph Green, was also there. He had recently become Denby's athletic director and had nominated me for the Denby Sports Hall of Fame. I was inducted at a dinner the following week.

I confided to Coach Gorence that I was leaving the Detroit system to make my professional journey out to far-suburban, near-rural Walled Lake. He shared this information with Hal Schram, a *Detroit Free Press* sportswriter covering the meet. Schram was familiar with my exploits both as an athlete and a coach, and he interviewed me on the spot.

The next day, on June 3, 1969, this headline appeared in the paper's sports section: "Inner City Loses the Good Doctor."

Here is what Mr. Schram wrote in the accompanying article, exactly as it appeared beside my picture:

> DR. JOHN TELFORD has made a difficult decision: he is leaving the Detroit Public School system and launching a new career as an assistant principal at the new Walled Lake Western High School.
>
> "In all honesty, you may say I was forced into it," says the 33-year-old department head at Martin Luther King High. "I would have stayed in the inner city, but it's evident that no one downtown (in the Detroit Board of Education offices) wanted to listen to me, so I'm going to the suburbs and a new assignment."
>
> *Who is Dr. John Telford? He's the same fellow who was named to the 1957 All-American collegiate track and field team after turning in sensational quarter-mile performances both in the U.S. and abroad for Wayne State. He was Wayne's last great track star—the final protégé of the late David L. Holmes.*
>
> Although his doctorate is in languages and art, he never turned his back on track. For ten years he worked with inner-city youngsters at Southeastern, Finney, Pershing, and King. [Note: Finney wasn't in the "inner city" at that time.] He helped more than thirty youngsters get college track scholarships and was instrumental in the development of such former state and city champions as Southeastern's George Wesson, Pershing's Andre Broadnax, and Finney's Ken Howse, who is now a Big Ten runner at Illinois.
>
> Telford took his degrees and credentials downtown [and] talked to three deputy superintendents in his efforts to land a

promise of eventual promotion to an assistant principal's job. He got little encouragement, no promises.

Then a similar job opened up at the new Walled Lake school.

"I walked around with that contract in my pocket for a week," *Telford said. "Perhaps I was hoping someone downtown would change his mind. But I didn't hear from anyone."*

"I'm not burning any bridges behind me and I'm going into the new job with considerable expectation, but I'm sorry to be leaving those fine kids at King."

"I grew up in the inner city and I've always enjoyed working with these youngsters. Now I'll have to find some way to stay in track," Telford said.

Contrary to what I had said to Hal Schram about not burning any bridges, my bridges now had *indeed* been burned—and my *britches* as well—as soon as the downtown administrators laid their angry eyes on this article. Worse still—when my *students* saw the article, some of them spontaneously marched down to the School Center Building at 5057 Woodward Avenue to protest my not being promised a promotion, and the downtown honchos had absolutely no doubt that I had sent them. (I hadn't.)

Coach Gorence, who always had been an advocate for black athletes, called me and said, "John, I don't blame you for leaving—and if you get any flack from downtown because of the Schram article, don't let it bother you. Your reputation as a champion athlete and a championship coach gives you a level of credibility and an access to the media that the rest of us can't *hope* to have. You spoke for all of us. Sure, they're going to be PO'd about the article, but you told the truth. I still haven't got the promotion I should have had, and I'll never get it because I'm white. The discrimination here is *reversed* now, but you're still young—and you've got somewhere else to go. The rest of us don't. You'd be *nuts* not to take the Walled Lake job."

My old Pershing colleague's words lightened (somewhat) my still-heavy load of guilt, because after I had read and re-read the Schram article for the third or fourth time, it had dawned on me that the article made me sound like a petulant little boy who was going to take his marbles and go home if he wasn't allowed to win the marble game. However, many white teachers and lower-level white administrators who were frozen permanently in their positions because of the district's compensatory promotion practices also called me to say that the article had struck a blow for all of them.

Unfortunately, a few of those later calls were from inept grousers I wouldn't have ever promoted myself if *I* had been superintendent, and I shrank at the disquieting thought than anyone might be mistakenly inclined to lump me with them. In the midst of my disquiet, I just happened to open and read an even more disquieting (and anonymous) letter that some racist had written to the Haverhill Street address of my father, John Telford, that he (she?) found in the phone book.

The letter began:

> Dear inner city administrator,
> I hope I am writting [*sic*] this to the right address. I read the article quoting you in the Free Press. How in the world could you ever be sorry to be leaving those dirty niggers?

This sickening letter rambled on in the same sick vein for page after page. After reading all of it, I felt that I was going to throw up. I couldn't bear to read it again or even think about it (although I did keep it).

The bright, vulnerable young students and the promising young sophomore runners I was about to leave behind to inexpert coaching and to the myriad dangers of the streets were also almost more than I could bear to think about.

But my tears didn't start to flow until I went to my English classroom and unlocked the day's journals and read them.

Cheryl Roberts had written:

> I am writing with my right hand today. It is slowly but surely beginning to heal. Dr. Telford, I have heard a rumor that you won't be teaching here next year. I hope this isn't true. But if it is true, I will be very disappointed. You have been my all-time favorite teacher—the best I ever had.

She had begun to add something else, but she had crossed it out. "Good luck," she finished. "Peace."

Debra Byrd wrote:

I regret you're leaving us, because you're a truly great teacher,
but you've taught us a lesson in non-prejudice we'll never forget.
I think this is the greatest lesson you've taught, unintentionally,
ever. Some teachers I had used to say they weren't prejudiced,
yet they doubted my learning potential and I felt belittled and
wondered "what's the use of trying . . . if the race has been won
long ago and the trend has been ground in?" You've proven me
wrong and I can humbly thank you.

Michael Fry wrote:

I would like to wish you good luck on your new job, but I don't
think you will enjoy it very much. This will be a great loss to
the public schools and especially the inner-city schools that
you have taught at. There are very few men, black or white,
that put forth the effort you did and will do to extract from your
students. I was not aware of your leaving until today. I was looking forward to having you again next semester. Due to unfortunate
circumstances, you will be leaving us. If all whites could get
along and understand us the way you do, there would be peace
in the world.

David Knox wrote:

June 4, 1969: This is probably the last journal entry I'll be writing,
since I'll be graduating and this is my last day here. [Note: My
two classes were called "phase-elective" Honors classes, so there
were graduating seniors "integrated" with younger students.
This was the only form of *integration* that existed at King, a *full
fifteen years* after *Brown vs. Board of Education!*]
    I figure school to be a tool, a tool designed to build persons'
minds. Dr. Telford, a teacher of your stature well deserves to be
called that, a teacher. You may not know it, but you helped me in
more than one way. You gave to me a much better insight into
the realm of an education, a good education. One day I wish
teachers to be of your standards. You teach not only students,
but adults as well. As the Bible says, be a catcher of men. You
teach, therefore you *catch*. I hope to see you again in my life of
the world. We all need men like you.

Veronica Donald's entry said simply, "Please stay."

When—alone in my classroom at 5:00 p.m.—I had finally finished reading them all, the tears were streaming down my face. Had I at that moment still been in possession of the signed Walled Lake contract and my letter of resignation, I would have torn both of them to tiny shreds and flung the pieces to the four winds.

CHAPTER TWENTY-FOUR

FIGHTS AT DANCES AND A PURSE IN PISS

"All <u>white folks</u> ain't bad people."

—A paraphrase of bad-boy boxer Rocky Graziano's
newly-educated remark on the Martha Raye
TV show of the 1950s: "All <u>cops</u> ain't bad people"

The single school year of 1969–70 that I was to spend at the all-white Walled Lake Western High School was notable mainly in that for me, the year was relatively *un*-notable—except for my learning (like reformed-delinquent Rocky, somewhat to my *surprise*) that I could still relate to white kids. Despite being white myself, my experiences in Detroit with racist cops and other assorted bigots who persecuted my kids had actually engendered in me a deepening (and illogical) resentment of most white people.

My rookie principal, a remarkably tall, remarkably *young* fellow (in his twenties) with the unremarkable name of Richard Smith, put me in charge of student discipline and attendance for the new, 2,400-student school that was surrounded by field and farmland. Often when I would drive back to the sprawling, single-level building from a meeting at the board office in town, I retrieved several skippers I'd caught out walking on the road to town and crammed them into my car and hauled them back to school. Most of them were from a huge trailer park in town called Walled Lake Court. I soon discovered that their youthful problems weren't at all dissimilar to those I had been obliged to deal with growing up in inner-city Detroit, where I still lived. I formed an instant affinity with these trailer park kids—especially the boys, who tended to suffer harsher discipline at the hands of the district administration and the school's principal than did the girls and the more affluent students of either gender. This marked my first encounter, as an educator, with *classism*.

More than twenty years later, a repairman fixing my ninety-one-year-old mother's telephone at her Troy, Michigan, apartment noted her name and asked if she was my mother. When she said she was, he told her I had kept him from dropping out of Walled Lake Western High School in 1970 and asked her to thank me for him. At the time, Lynn—my wife of twenty-eight years whom I still loved—was divorcing me, so the repairman's words to my mother lifted my spirits somewhat.

When misbehavers at Western were sent to me for discipline, I would often *counsel* them rather than punish them. Some had been sent for the unforgivable infraction of coming to class without a pen or pencil (not exactly like the comparatively wild Southeastern or Pershing or Butzel or King, right?). I would tell the ones who were considering dropping out and joining the army that without any educational skills they'd be sent at once to the front lines in what I assured them was an immoral war of genocide. I told them that as young lower-class Americans from blue-collar families, they needed to unite with their impoverished black and brown brothers to defy the corporate capitalists who didn't care how many of them got killed or maimed in Southeast Asia as long as these Washington and Wall Street warmongers were making fortunes over the torn and dead bodies of our soldiers (as some of them still are at this writing, forty years later).

When a few fathers who had fought in World War II or Korea got wind of the anti-war advisements I was giving their sons, they called me to complain. However, these were blue-collar guys, too, and I was able to convince many of them that there was a lot of credence to what I had to say.

I soon formed close bonds with several members of Western High School's faculty, and with the student-athletes at the school. One time at an assembly where the student body gave me a spontaneous and extended standing ovation in which most of the faculty also rose and took part, I noted a less-than-pleased expression on the face of the principal. I also happened to be the only non-central-office administrator in the school district with a doctorate, and I began to wonder whether this, too, might be threatening to my young boss.

The principal put me in charge of the Wednesday-night basketball games and the dances that followed the games, and of the gate receipts—which I would lock in the safe near midnight when the dance was over. On one game-and-dance night, I got my brand-new light-blue sport coat all bloody breaking up a fight between two very large and very drunk young men (bloody with *their* blood—not mine). I also got in a brief fistfight at that same dance with an inebriated blond kid named Carl with prominent ears whom I had politely invited to leave. Carl proved to be overly-anxious to *try* me, my having unwisely boasted earlier, as an intended warning to pugnaciously recalcitrant students, that I had been a boxer. Luckily for me, the unprovoked swing Carl took at me—which I blocked and countered with a single precisely-pinpointed punch—didn't inspire any more trials. Instead, it helped make my "rep," as it were.

As soon as Carl's head had become fairly clear and I was able to determine that he wasn't seriously hurt, I sent him home with a soberer buddy. I learned the next day that he had slept at his buddy's house overnight. That day, I declined to discipline him—figuring he had already learned a painful lesson. I was also afraid to draw any official attention to the incident, because I admittedly *had* hit him, albeit in self-defense. When Carl went home the next night—still in some pain—and complained to his mother that I had hurt his jaw, the mother called my secretary the following morning and made an appointment to meet with me. *Now* I was *really in for it*, I thought.

However, it was Carl's *father* who showed up. He had taken an hour off work and had decided to come *personally*, he said, to *thank* me!

That same Wednesday night, during the post-game dance, I gingerly fished a girl's open and plundered purse out of an un-flushed toilet bowl in the boy's lavatory, but I was unable to determine who had thrown it in, because no one was talking. By midnight, it was snowing heavily, so even though I had brought no change of clothes and my shirt was soaked with perspiration from my multiple exertions, I slept in the school in the nurse's office that night rather than try to make the long drive home to Mound Road in Detroit. The next day, I tried to maintain some distance between my aromatic self and students, staff, and visitors—to the extent that I was able.

Sleeping in the school after dances soon became my habitual *modus operandi*, and I always brought a change of clothes—or at least, a *shirt*—for game-and-dance nights. My secretary, Mrs. Barbara Nissen (whose likable but not always well-behaved son Chris was a student at the school), joked that the district should start charging me rent.

One evening at a Christmas party at Superintendent George G. Garver's home in town, the holiday cheer was flowing freely. I was coming out of an upstairs bathroom when the pretty—and pretty *tipsy*—forty-year-old wife of a senior administrator grabbed me and tongue-kissed me deeply and lingeringly and tried to push me back into the bathroom with her before I was able to pull away. This incident made me plenty uncomfortable; what I definitely didn't need was an involvement with a superior's wife—pretty or not. I was beginning to think that maybe Walled Lake wasn't the place for me.

Serendipitously, Jim Campitelle—my old Finney colleague and partner-in-crime—was now a professor at Macomb County Community College (now called *Macomb Community College*). Early that spring, Jim tipped me off that the directorship of the college's 3,400-student Division of Basic Education was vacant. I promptly applied, got interviewed, and was presently informed that I had had an excellent interview and was the number-*two* choice of the MCCC committee.

Disappointed at not being chosen for this prestigious position, but heartened at having come so close, I rebounded to apply for a posted assistant professorship several weeks later at the University of Michigan-Dearborn. (I did have some misgivings that the city of Dearborn, under Mayor Orville Hubbard, had for years been a notorious anti-black bastion.)

This time I was offered that job, and I accepted it. In May, they printed my name in the brochure for the University's summer and fall courses, and I began saying my goodbyes to my kids and colleagues at Walled Lake Western High. In my sparse spare time, I scanned the texts for the courses I was to teach and prepared relevant lesson plans and lectures. I was now eminently ready for my promising new professorial position.

Then lightning struck. MCCC officials called to offer me the directorship of the Division of Basic Education! There had been some kind of disagreement between the college people and their number-one choice for the job, and his appointment had been rescinded.

Now I was in a real and immediate dilemma. The salary they were offering me for the MCCC directorship was significantly higher than the University of Michigan-Dearborn had offered me for the assistant professorship, and the MCCC position was more prestigious by far and presented me with a much broader span of responsibility. The Division of Basic Education offered thousands of students what in essence amounted to a fifth year of high school—so to me the position was even more attractive than a high school principalship, and it paid more, too. Moreover, the reputed socially radical philosophy of the professors in that division was in absolute synchrony with my own semi-socialistic views. Also, by now Lynn had coaxed me into marrying her with no more delays or excuses, and we were anticipating starting a family (although I was nowhere near ready or willing to change any of my dissolute bachelor ways).

This is the letter I wrote to the dean of the University of Michigan-Dearborn's College of Education:

> Dear Dr. [Dennis] Papazian,
>
> It is with heartfelt and apologetic regret that I request to be released from my commitment to serve as assistant professor of education at the University of Michigan-Dearborn campus. The nature of this letter makes it difficult for me to state credibly how eagerly I had anticipated working with you and your colleagues in the preparation of prospective teachers. I have had an offer to head a division in a community college—and for professional, financial, and personal reasons, I find I cannot reject this offer. I truly hope my release will cause you a minimum of inconvenience in securing a replacement. I hope, too, that considering the circumstances and the difficult position I find myself in, you will understand and not judge me too harshly.
>
> Very Sincerely,
>
> John Telford

Thus it was that I committed a professionally unthinkable transgression. I would live to regret it.

CHAPTER TWENTY-FIVE

ANTI-WAR MARCHES AND A MODEL PROGRAM

"Compassion is not weakness, and concern for the unfortunate
is not socialism."

—*Hubert H. Humphrey (Democrat)*,
Vice President of the United States

It hasn't been without total justification or reason that often throughout my half-century career I've been called a socialist, a humanist, a Marxist, and even a Communist. In the 1930s, my Scottish grandfather, my father, and all the other activist Telfords were either *accused* of being Communists or actually *were* card-carrying members of that controversial and chameleonic political party. To them and untold others of that era, the concept of Communism—as in "commune"— offered an egalitarian, all-for-one and one-for-all proletariat ideal that was being corrupted by the Soviets and the Red Chinese into a particularly virulent form of Fascism.

Near the dawn of the twentieth century, my grandfather had organized coal miners in Maryland and had fought the mine owners' Pinkerton private police goons guerilla-style as an advance man for a descendant wing of the legendary Molly Maguires. In the 1930s, my fighter father was a union steward and a Walter Reuther bodyguard. My urbane, handsome Uncle Frank was black-listed from directing in Hollywood during the infamous McCarthy era. Also, my Aunt Letty was an early leader of the Detroit Federation of Teachers.

In this same activist mode, I soon learned that what I had heard about my professors in the MCCC Division of Basic Education was true: They proved to be spiritually kindred indeed to my Telford forebears, and thus to me. I felt that I had found a home in this activist Division of Basic Education.

My homey feeling was heightened when Dennis Zimmer, my student and athlete from Finney, walked into my office one day to tell me he was now one of our Basic Education students. Dennis would often hang around my office between classes until I shooed him to the library. I think he liked my shapely secretary, Edna (Eddie) Smith. Dennis hadn't changed—at Finney, it had been hard to separate him from shapely and amorous females, and even harder to separate shapely and amorous females from him.

Basic Education professor Jim Jacobs, for whom I felt an instant affinity, was rumored to be a member of the anarchist Weatherman organization. He wasn't—but he was still the most radical member of my staff. They followed his lead, as presently did I, in organizing and participating in an array of activities throughout the two years to follow that eventually began to embarrass and ultimately infuriate the college's conservative president, Dr. John Dimitry.

These activities included marching on the Warren Tank Arsenal (the Vietnam War was raging at its worst) and bringing in the Black Panthers and activist-actress Jane Fonda to speak. We also initiated a bus line to Detroit to bring in more black students—who included some of my former King students. Five of my former students had been killed in Vietnam—including Henry Gerstheimer, the student manager of my Finney track team. I also lost a U.S. track teammate, Cliff Cushman, whose fighter plane was shot down over Cambodia when President Richard Nixon authorized the illegal bombing of that country—a sovereign nation with which the United States was not at war.

That fall, fourteen American students met with Vietnamese students in Hanoi to plan the "People's Peace Treaty" between the peoples of the United States, South Vietnam, and North Vietnam.

Jim Jacobs was an admirer of radical author/activist Jack Scott, who allegedly had ties to the criminal Symbionese Liberation Army (SLA) that had kidnapped and brainwashed Patty Hearst. He told me he had a book by Scott that listed my leftist-philosophizing track book *The Longest Dash* in its bibliography. Jim was impressed by this, but I doubt the FBI was.

I had also repeatedly (and thus-far unsuccessfully) tried to inveigle a brilliant young Flint administrator and bold activist who had been on my staff at Butzel Junior High School in 1967 and 1968 to come to Macomb and assume a coordinative position in one of my division's four academic departments. His name was Paul Cabell. When Paul and I worked together, he had given me ideas for an article I wrote in support of cross-district interracial busing. The article had been published in Wayne State University's student newspaper, the *South End*, in October 1967.

Now, at Macomb three years later, I took some notes from that article for speeches that I began to make in churches in the city of Warren in support of busing. My divisional office was in Warren on MCCC's South Campus on Twelve Mile Road, and my professors taught most of their classes on that campus, where the college president's office was, as well.

Warren wasn't (and isn't) exactly a hot-bed of liberalism; my beloved new baby blue Mercury Montego was vandalized in the parking lot of the Moceri Arms apartment complex, where my wife and I had established residence across the street from my office. The vandals were never caught, but I always suspected they were local bigots angered by my speeches and other accordant ventures. The Warren police themselves had a code: BPIWAD. It meant "black person in Warren after dark."

President Dimitry summoned me to his office and suggested that my division and I desist from what he termed our "subversive activities." I, in turn, suggested that my division's activities were *progressive* rather than subversive, and we were doing them on our own time as citizens of a free and democratic United States of America. In retrospect, the thing that amazes me most about all this is that Dr. Dimitry didn't fire me on the spot after my conversation with him—but my division did have its supporters on the MCCC Board of Trustees. Also, one of my staff—Dennis Thompson—was the son of a respected board member.

During that spring of 1971, my wife Lynn was listening to the radio one morning while we were getting dressed for work when she heard the words, "Lorenzo Wright *was* the supervisor of Athletics in Detroit Public Schools. . . ." Lo had been at our apartment two nights before when I hosted a meeting of the board of directors of our philanthropic Detroit Varsity Club. I turned up the radio and heard the words, ". . . Supervisor Wright's wife has been arrested for his murder." I was thunderstruck. Lo was one of my life's major mentors. Several hundred of us attended his funeral. He was buried in his Olympic blazer, in a bronze coffin, in historic Elmwood Cemetery in Detroit.

Late in the fall of 1971, the MCCC secretaries went on strike. Jim Jacobs went out and stood in the cold on the secretaries' picket line with them, in violation of his Macomb County Community College Faculty Organization (MCCCFO) contractual agreement with the board. A burly vice president with the Celtic surname Blackford appeared in my office to advise his fellow Celt Telford that it was my "administrative duty" to pronounce Professor Jacobs *unfit to teach*. The college's personnel director, a disquieting individual who sported a "Herald of Truth" bumper sticker on his car, tape-recorded me regarding the Jacobs situation without my initial consent, but he didn't get what he had hoped to hear. Also, after the recorder was turned off, Mr. "Herald-of-Truth" parroted what Mr. Blackford had already advised me.

Jim asked me if I would testify in his disciplinary hearing regarding his professional dedication and competence. In the hearing, I stated for the record, "Professor Jacobs is one of the best and most dedicated educators it has ever been my privilege to supervise." (For confirmative emphasis, I immediately followed up with a written evaluation of him in which I reiterated those same observations and sentiments.)

As I was leaving the hearing room after testifying, Jim's attorney—Bernie Fieger, whose lightning-rod son Geoffrey was to become his law partner decades later and run for the governorship of Michigan—remarked to me, "Dr. Telford, I commend you. That took a lot of courage. I also suggest that you update your credentials and start sending them out, because I'm pretty sure that by trying to help me save Jim's job, you've sacrificed yours."

Jim Jacobs' job *was* saved, and he was destined, thirty-seven years later, to succeed my friend Al Lorenzo as president of the college!

I did ask Professor John Bonnell to write a letter of recommendation for me, just in case. Professor Bonnell was an embattled maverick I had recruited from the general education ranks because his teaching style and philosophy were perfect fits for my free-spirited division. Decades later they would get him in difficulty with a conservative MCCC administration—a storm he was ultimately to weather without needing to resort to my offered support.

His letter began, "If you seek a yes-man, John Telford will serve you ill. . . ."

A bright, independent-minded secretary named Eva whom Jim Jacobs had stood beside on the picket line warned me that she knew for certain that Fieger's advisement to me was sound counsel. A political liberal, Eva was disconcertingly sultry (think Elizabeth Taylor in *Cleopatra*) and sympathetic to everything that I and my professorial staff were doing educationally and politically. As secretary to the dean of General Education, Dr. Jeanne Truby—my immediate supervisor— Eva was also in a strategic position to be able to feed inside information to me and my divisional staff regarding our division's shaky standing with the college's top administration.

Eva and I were both married to apolitical people, and her hot political sympathies toward our embattled division (not to mention her hot physical appeal) tempted me into a hot romantic affair with her. Our affair would continue off and on for decades and cause the breakup of our marriages—Eva's immediate, mine long afterward. It would also cause me and people I cared about much personal pain, and it would ultimately cause me much *professional* pain as well.

President Dimitry soon got wind of this adulterous relationship, which provided him with additional ammunition against me—and thus against my division. Dr. Truby found out about the affair, too—and I was tipped off by a third administrative source that she was furious with Eva and disappointed with me (although she never once brought up the subject with either of us).

For the previous seven years, the Basic Education program at MCCC had been a nationally-celebrated college-transfer program in General Studies. We called ourselves "The Gang That Couldn't Teach *Straight*" in our promotional pamphlet, and indeed, many professors in General Education who envied us our free-wheeling pedagogical style accused us of "un-*straightening*" our students. Our program was designed to help the "academically disadvantaged" freshman student succeed in college. This pioneer program had been admired and imitated by several colleges throughout the country, including Southeastern Community College in Whiteville, North Carolina, which sent a delegation to study our operation. Basic Education introduced students to the major fields of knowledge: communications, humanities, natural science, and social science. Incorporating scheduling in which students had the same classmates and the same inter-disciplinary team of teachers, it was structured to stimulate close inter-student relationships, offer more individual attention from teachers, and stress the relationship between different academic subjects.

At the start of the 1971–72 school year—my second year in charge of the program—my division had a staff of nineteen full-time professors and no part-time teachers. This number was down from the twenty-three full-timers from the previous year. That year, I had also hired fourteen part-timers, including Dr. Jerry Divine, my successor as head of the language arts department at Butzel Junior High School, and another Ph.D. who later became a civilian deputy police chief in the Coleman Young administration and went to prison for scamming Mayor Young in the notorious investment scandal involving Krugerrands (gold South African coins).

I had also become worried about a problematic professional situation I had learned about that involved my good friend Paul Cabell, who had taught under me at Butzel with budding brilliance and now was an assistant principal at Flint Beecher High. Worrying about him as I did, I redoubled my efforts to recruit him. Only twenty-six, Paul was mature far beyond his years. Although at Butzel I was his supervisor, I had often assigned him quasi-administrative duties and turned to him for advice. This tall, light-skinned, very *caring* black man was being called *honkie* by militant black students and *nigger* by racist white ones at Flint Beecher. (Nearly forty years later, Paul's cousin Terry Cabell was to edit the columns I write for the *Michigan Chronicle*.)

Paul's having sharing this disturbing information with me made me feel extremely fearful that even this resourceful and outwardly unflappable young educator might be in over his head this time, and I had finally been able to extract an oral commitment from him to get out of Flint Beecher and come to Macomb. In what was to be our last phone conversation, he told me that he would apply to join my staff just as soon as he was able to resolve some serious racial conflicts at Beecher—a resolution which it turned out he was able to accomplish only by tragically blowing out his brains with a shotgun.

Paul's suicide had a totally shattering effect on his wife and family, on me, and on everyone else who knew him, including his students at Beecher. His loss was an immeasurable one—not only to his family, or to me, or to his students, or to the education profession, but potentially to the entire *nation*. He would have become a truly great man.

CHAPTER TWENTY-SIX

DECLINE OF
A MIGHTY DIVISION

"Other community colleges across the country have recently begun to model their own basic-education divisions after the one at Macomb."

—Charles Nathanson, writing in the
June 28, 1972 edition of the Community News

"It's time something in Macomb is being imitated!"

—MCCC Trustee Odessa Komer,
quoted by Nathanson in the same article

In the impending fall of 1972, the Division of Basic Education at Macomb County Community College was to have offered units consisting of two areas of study— either Social Studies/Communications or Natural Science/Humanities —which would have been taught by "mini-teams" of two teachers. This would have been a factor that could have restored some of my division's lost enrollment while also making it possible for part-time students to enjoy some of the Basic Education experience which had for so long been a favorite with Macomb students.

Unfortunately for the division and the students it so nobly and uniquely served, my administrative superiors' (possibly *deliberate*) "miscalculations" in the times for classes in the schedule—plus their removal of satellite classes for part-time students and teachers—rendered even some of my *full-time* professors unable to find full teaching loads drawing from even *satellite* classes by the fall of 1971.

Dean Truby (my professors called her "Dean Jeanne") had ordered me earlier to re-do our divisional schedule to conform to her extremely *reductive* specifications, which also included class times that were inconvenient for students. I suspected she was doing this at the direction of President Dimitry. I had the feeling that she would probably have followed a directive coming from his office even if it had been a *typographical error*.

Fully cognizant of what these reductive specifications would mean for my division, I refused to obey her order—so she wrote me up for insubordination and then re-did our schedule accordingly, herself. Her reworked version had given us mostly time slots at six o'clock p.m. Six o'clock was, of course, the dinner hour when most students were unwilling to take classes. "Dean Jeanne" might as well have assigned us slots at two o'clock in the morning.

Unsurprisingly, by the spring semester of 1972 there were only thirteen professors remaining in the division. My staff and I had predicted this divisional catastrophe—orally and in memoranda—when there was still time to do something about it. Either our warnings had been sincerely perceived as being overly pessimistic, or else Dr. Truby and her boss, campus dean Lyle Robertson, had colluded to destroy the college's flagship division—quite possibly at the orders of the president.

Two hundred and forty Basic Education class sections ran in 1971–72, as contrasted with three hundred and twenty-three the previous year. This decrease reversed a four-year trend of substantial and steady divisional growth. Again, this was reflective of the ill-advised divisional schedule for the fall of 1971 that had been foisted on us by Dean Truby—a schedule which was less viable for students and faculty teams than previous schedules had been. It plunged the morale of this vital division's once-vibrant professors to its lowest ebb. At the beginning of the spring semester, my entire staff dramatically took to wearing black armbands.

With the division thus evidently decimated intentionally and its team dimensions distorted, the Basic Education faculty filed a series of grievances claiming "change of working conditions." They filed these with great reluctance, in a desperate effort to restore the division's lost scope and structure—a structure that for seven years had economically enabled it to *triple its success rate with the "academically marginal" freshman students on a comparative basis with the rest of the college* in terms of credits earned by those first-year students *after two years of college!* (Basic Education was a *one-year* program.)

Campus dean Lyle Robertson and the personnel director—the "Herald-of-Truth" fellow—sat down with members of the college faculty's Divisional Affairs Committee to see if the grievances could be resolved by some compromise short of arbitration. These discussions led to further discussions between Dr. Robertson and my hand-picked divisional curriculum committee. Dr. Truby then joined some of these later meetings between her boss and my committee —so I prudently decided that if Dean Jeanne was to sit at the table, perhaps *I* had better be there, too.

The results of our meetings were encouraging. Over Dr. Truby's vehement objections, thirty-one instructional blocks of Basic Education classes got rescheduled for reasonable times—between eight o'clock in the morning and three o'clock in the afternoon—in the Fall 1972 catalog. This was one of the compromise solutions I had proposed originally to Drs. Truby and Robertson. The mini-blocks with only two instructors each were also duly scheduled in the catalog for those favorable hours. Thus, the division—at least on paper— was restored to its former dimensions, and *then* some. My staff and I breathed a long, collective sigh of relief, and we withdrew the grievances.

That which followed occurred with bewildering speed.

The campus curriculum committee and those MCCCFO members who were jealous of our success and hostile to our mission expressed concern to Dr. Truby that our division and the campus dean had overstepped our (and *his*) vested authority by having bargained what some interpreted as a "program change" in the Division of Basic Education. One MCCCFO member grieved.

Disturbed at being side-stepped, the curriculum committee summoned my division's representatives to appear before it to submit these program changes in the form of a proposal. This we did, essentially paraphrasing the compromise proposal I had initially submitted and which had been formally approved in a memorandum written by Dean Robertson—only to find on the table a contradictory memorandum from Dean Truby, Dean Robertson's *subordinate*!

Dr. Truby's memo categorically disapproved the proposal that *her own boss* had agreed to. In her memo (Item #3), she stated that initial board approval of the program at its 1965 inception had conditionally excluded students who scored below the tenth percentile on the ACT (American College Test). She was aware, however, that these students had nonetheless been part of the program from its *very beginning*—and the research done by independent researcher Marty Hogan, Ph.D., and an intra-divisional study conducted by Basic Education social science coordinator Terry Almquist, Ph.D., had found that, amazingly, first-year Basic Education students even in that sub-tenth-percentile bracket were more successful during their *second* year out in General Education than were those in the *general* General Education population who had higher ACT scores!

The committee erroneously inferred from Dr. Truby's memo that my Division was trying to change placement criteria which had been implemented successfully for the past seven years, while in fact we were merely trying to update the criteria to conform to what had *been going on in registration* for those seven years. Both Dean Robertson and Dean Truby knew that our division had always done better than the Division of General Education had done—not only with these 0–10 students, but with students with higher scores, as well. Both deans had previously agreed—one orally and one in writing—that the admissions office should continue to allow the 0–10 students to enroll in the Division of Basic Education.

The MCCCFO curriculum committee (composed primarily of non-Basic Ed professors) predictably voted down our proposal, ordering us to return to the drawing board and try again. Dean Truby's memo (which her supervisor amazingly said he hadn't *seen* prior to the committee meetings)—plus the MCCCFO committee's rejection of the proposal, as well as our series of grievances and the General Education professor's grievance countering ours—*possibly* forced Dr. Robertson into a "re-evaluation" of his agreement with me and my staff.

After all these years I still wonder whether Dr. Robertson had *already* "re-evaluated" the situation *at the president's orders*, and the two men had then dispatched Dean Truby to do their dirty work. I guess that's something we'll never know. In either case, the damage had been done.

CHAPTER TWENTY-SEVEN

THE MIGHTY DIVISION
DOOMED!

"The loss of part of me, which will remain forever. . . ."

—*Portion of a poem by Professor Dennis Thompson,*
MCCC Division of Basic Education

On June 8, 1972, Dean Lyle Robertson met with me and my divisional curriculum committee, face-to-face. At this meeting, we expected that he would
say that the mini-blocks would be scrapped and the number of regular four-
subject-area blocks might even be reduced. Instead, he announced that the
entire *program* was going to be scrapped! Only a few days earlier, he had been
assuring us that the division would roll along merrily forever.

The next morning, Dean Jeanne called all of us together and dutifully advised
us of our reassignments to other academic divisions within the college. While
she was ticking off the list of names, Basic Education professors Jim Jacobs, Art
Ritas, Sally Chalgian, John Bonnell, Phil Barrons, Dennis Choate, George Ettl,
and some of my other comrades-in-arms repeatedly rattled her throughout her
recitation by loudly humming the familiar graduation march *Pomp and Circumstance*
in mockingly bitter imitation of their being thus "graduated" from our magnificent
but nonetheless *doomed* division. One of America's foremost showpiece programs in undergraduate developmental education—this highly successful team
effort that had brought national attention to Macomb—was finally finished,
fallen victim of too many unfriendly forces within its own parent institution.

Nobody was ever able to give any good educational reason why the division
was disbanded. The anticipated Fall decline of daytime full-time students who

met the admission criteria for the program was given as one reason, but with
the proper time schedule, the program would almost certainly have attracted
660 students, and possibly twice that number. In fall 1970, twenty-eight full
blocks had been filled completely because the time schedule had been convenient
for the full-time students. The specter of incomplete teacher loads had also
apologetically been invoked as a contributing factor, but that had simply been
a self-evident, self-fulfilling prophesy. These were inadequate rationales, certainly;
but then, any rationale would have been inadequate. The program was more
than just *educationally sound*. In a truly incredible manner, it had turned scores
of young people back *on* to education who had been *tuned out* for years.

No one at MCCC could rationalize the irrational, or explain away the demise
of an experimental division whose only offense was structural—and to a lesser
extent, *philosophical*—independence. As a free-spirited, innovative alternative
to traditional curricula, the Division of Basic Education proto-typified what an
experimental program is supposed to be all about. Basic Education never should
have been forced into the mold of the other divisions. As its director, I should
instead have been assigned to report directly to the campus dean, and means
to introduce more flexibility in scheduling, teaching assignments, and teacher
class-loads should have been found.

The day after my bitter staff had hummed *Pomp and Circumstance* at our terminal
"commencement," I was walking up the stairway near my office when an administrator in the counseling department, a decent man who had a wife and many
children, happened to be descending the stairs. He put a consoling hand on my
shoulder at almost the same moment that President Dimitry appeared in the
lower doorway. Seeing Dr. Dimitry, he snatched his hand away from my shoulder
so fast it became a bluish-white blur—and I'm ashamed to say that I laughed at
him out loud as he scurried away. He did, after all, have a lot of mouths to feed.

That same day, the coordinator of one of the departments in the Division
of General Education who had long been an envious and surreptitious foe of
my Division of Basic Education walked by my office and saw me packing a few of
my affects for removal. He sneered gloatingly to me, "Telford, your radical
division needed to get thrown on the scrap heap a long time ago. They're nothing
but a bunch of Socialists."

"Meet me behind 'E' Building in five minutes," I snarled, "and I'll 'socialize'
you, you sneaky, sniveling bastard."

He didn't meet me behind "E" Building. Instead, he reported me to Dean Jeanne for threatening him, and I got written up again.

I immediately set about composing (actually, *re*-composing) my soon-to-be *de*composing division's annual report, which it was my administrative responsibility to write. I retitled it, in big, block letters: *THE MACOMB COUNTY COMMUNITY COLLEGE DIVISION OF BASIC EDUCATION'S LAST ANNUAL REPORT*. In it, I essentially told the story I have recounted in this chapter. I ended it thus:

> What finally tipped the scales toward the disbanding of the Division? Was basic education too embarrassing or threatening to someone, or <u>worse</u>—was it ultimately just too organizationally troublesome to have an interdisciplinary, block-scheduled, team-taught <u>round</u> <u>peg</u> sitting around among all the <u>individual squares</u> and have to constantly deal with the unique little nit-picking contractual and scheduling problems that arose as a result? To recognize the immensity and complexity of these problems is to be tempted to withdraw to other less frustrating endeavors.
>
> Embarrassment, threat, inconvenience, and perhaps even a slender element of political danger are a small price for an academically free institution to pay for an offering as vital and exciting as the Division of Basic Education proved itself to be, year in and year out, for its students. It is Macomb County's potential Basic Education students of the future who are almost the only real losers as a result of this proud Division's final phase-out.
>
> I say "almost" because there are some others. To quote part of a poem entitled, "On the Death of Basic Education"— written by Dennis Thompson [the Basic Ed professor whose father had been a revered board member]:
>
>> *". . . the loss of part of me*
>> *which will remain forever . . ."*

And Thompson again:

>> *"It all has vanished now.*
>> *It's null and void—*
>> *Rejected out of hand . . .*
>> <u>*CANCELLED*</u>*."*

Eddie Smith, my loyal secretary, had typed the report. After proofing it carefully, I dutifully returned the finalized document to her for her to submit copies to Dr. Dimitry, Dr. Robertson, Dr. Truby, my staff, and the MCCC Board of Trustees. Eddie sent them via the in-house mail—the college's usual means of sending internal written messages and reports. Eva miraculously was *still* Dean Truby's secretary despite her having led the secretaries' strike and her now-known affair with me, and she tipped us off that this incendiary report (unsurprisingly) wasn't ever going to see the light of day; it had been pulled at Dr. Robertson's orders. Half-expecting this news, I xeroxed more copies of it myself, drove to the U.S. Post Office, and mailed them to all of the same intended recipients.

Then, as I *also* expected—all hell broke loose. The next day, my report was quoted extensively in the community newspaper. After 2 1/2 hours of impassioned debate at a hastily called special meeting of the MCCC Board of Trustees, the badly-divided board finally voted 4–3 to support President Dimitry's recommendation to scrap the program, despite impassioned pleas from Basic Ed students, including Ed Bruley—who years later became and is now a Macomb County commissioner.

One board trustee, Bill Bowman, voted "reluctantly yes" to terminate our division. During a brief recess, Trustee Bowman told reporter Charles Nathanson that he wasn't sure he had voted correctly—a statement the reporter duly reported.

Reporter Nathanson wrote, "No one seems to question the educational effectiveness of the division. It was the plum of the college and had been attracting national attention for some time. Other community colleges had adopted it as a model—and, as Trustee [Odessa] Comer had put it, "It's time *something* in Macomb is being imitated!"

My erstwhile staff would eventually lobby the board to release President Dimitry, but his ultimate departure would come too late to do me any professional good. On the day after that fateful special board meeting, President Dimitry unceremoniously locked me out of my office and suspended me for insubordination.

CHAPTER TWENTY-EIGHT

BASKETBALL'S
BERKLEY BEARS:
RETREAT FROM ACADEME

"This is the sinner's last retreat. . . ."

—*American poet Robert Lowell,
from* Mr. Edwards and the Spider *[1946], stanza I*

Just when it appeared that *this* particular sinner's "last retreat" might be the unemployment line, a fellow member of my administrators' union disclosed to me that while the president could indeed suspend me for insubordination, he couldn't *fire* me for it without a great deal of tedious legal maneuvering, much though he undoubtedly would have loved to. My divisional directorship having thus been phased out along with my division, by contract the college had to offer me faculty status. It did so at the intermediate rank of associate professor. I accepted and was assigned a full load teaching sociology courses on the North Campus (since no English classes were available on either campus— and at the ripe old age of thirty-six, I now suddenly became the most junior member of the college faculty). Perusing the sociology texts, I noted that I already was familiar with their contents. I was raring and ready to go.

There was, however, a minor problem: If my classes didn't fill sufficiently in the coming semester or the semesters immediately to follow, as the lowest-seniority professor, I would be given only a *partial* teaching load and a *partial* salary—or even get *laid off*. Not good.

A few weeks earlier, I had attended a technology conference in New York City, where I had incidentally bid a final fond farewell to my New York off-and-on girlfriend of seventeen years, Peggy Saxton Tatham. (Peggy was the young African-American lady I had met at the Penn Relays when I was racing there in 1955.)

On the return flight, I had coincidentally been seated next to my old Pershing colleague Sam Flam, erstwhile subject of the *flam*boyant Wayne Dyer-sung "*Sam-Flam-cisco, open your Gold*en Gate. . . ." Sam Flam had confided to me that he was about to be promoted from the directorship of secondary education in the Berkley, Michigan, Community Schools to the assistant superintendency there. He was seeking a divisional director for the district's Division of Health, Physical Education & Athletics who wasn't a pure jock (or necessarily even a P.E. major, which I of course wasn't). He wanted this person to have a bent toward academics, to hold advanced degrees, to have an athletic and coaching background, and to possess the talent to be able to build Berkley's currently inferior programs into superior ones. He knew of my former status as an All-American athlete, was cognizant of my academic pedigree and motivational teaching skills, and had witnessed some of my champion Pershing teams' performances.

Also, Sam was Jewish and appreciated my egalitarian ideals. We had taken several of our doctoral courses together, too.

"You'd be *perfect* for the job," he enthused. "Are you interested?"

At the time, the Division of Basic Education at MCCC was still intact. None-theless, remembering attorney Bernard Feiger's warning words to me after I had helped save Jim Jacobs' job at the disciplinary hearing, I mused for a moment and responded that maybe I *was* interested.

To make a long story short, within two weeks of the phase-out of my MCCC division, I had jumped from one *lost* divisional directorship to a newly-*found* one in a mid-sized and well-regarded public school district, after having had what Berkley superintendent William G. Keane later called the best interview he had ever heard from any applicant. I bought a nice Tudor-style house in the Berkley district in the upscale little town of Huntington Woods, moved into it with my wife Lynn, and hired Jerome J. Catalina, my old WSU teammate and now a teacher at Van Zile School in Detroit, to coach the high school track and football teams and teach physical education. (Jerry beat out my former protégé who had taught for me at Butzel—future University of Michigan coach Lloyd Carr—for the job.)

Jerry bought a house for himself and his wife and three children two blocks from mine.

I also tried to recruit Roy Allen, a former WSU quarter-miler who was the football coach and athletic director at Detroit Northwestern High, the school of my recalcitrant boyhood, to coordinate the athletic programs at Berkley High School and its two feeder junior highs. Roy would have thus become Berkley's first black administrator, but he confided that he was about to get a similar job in Detroit. After offering the job to my predecessor, Lane Ramsdell, who declined, I gave it to Steve Rhoads, who was also Berkley's basketball coach.

We brought our high school varsity basketball team into Detroit that summer to scrimmage with the city's best black teams at the renowned Sam Washington's famous St. Cecilia gym, where ours was the only white team. This paid off big-time. For the next three basketball seasons, the Berkley Bears— led by six foot, nine-inch center and future Notre Dame and Cleveland Cavalier star Bruce Flowers—played against several Detroit teams and many more suburban teams, winning sixty-eight games while losing only four. Another star player was point guard Alan Davis, a ten-seconds-flat 100-yard sprinter who later excelled as a defensive back for Michigan State. For several weeks in 1975, our team enjoyed the number-one ranking in the state before having its undefeated streak of twenty-five games snapped almost single-handedly by sharp-shooting Highland Park guard Terry Duerod, a future University of Detroit and Piston star who scored forty-six points in the game.

The track and football teams under Catalina were successful, too, during the years when I was the district's athletic director. Catalina's track teams won back-to-back titles in the celebrated Southeastern Michigan Association, breaking many league and school records. I gave Superintendent Keane's son Dennis some advice in the state meet that helped him finish second in the two-mile and break the school record—a mark which I believe still stands. Catalina's teams also held their own in football in that conference, which included tough teams from Hazel Park, Ferndale, Royal Oak, Southfield, and Birmingham.

I generally (and uncharacteristically) tried very hard to avoid any controversy in Berkley. A little problem did arise for me initially when a now-divorced Eva, who had had too much to drink, took a day off work and came and sat in my office uninvited, waiting for me to return. My intrepid secretary, Shirley Peters, tipped me off that she was there, so I avoided the office—but the superintendent found out about it anyway. That night at about ten o'clock, the still-inebriated Eva drove her car onto my lawn just two blocks from the superintendent's house and parked there and sat.

After about an hour, my wife called the Huntington Woods police, and Sgt. John Leadford, a friend of mine, answered the call. He persuaded Eva to drive her car off the lawn, where it had left big tread marks, and go home so she could avoid arrest. Today, they would have taken her keys and impounded her car to prevent her from driving and harming someone.

I also caused a tad of short-lived commotion when I announced to the district's Staff/Parent Sex Education Committee—which I chaired wearing my health education hat—that school nurses would be empowered to issue condoms to high-school-age students on request without parental notification.

I did have to quash some male P.E. staff members' resistance to some of my ambitious adjustments to the "way things were done" in the past by offering three men who had been in-house competitors for my job quasi-administrative posts within the Division of Health, P.E. & Athletics. One—Lane Ramsdell, my predecessor in the job— turned me down, as mentioned, but the two others didn't. I gave the two newly-created junior high athletic directorships to Marty O'Dell at Anderson and Hugh "Hack" Wilson at Norup (which actually was in the city of Oak Park).

Shortly after I gave the Norup AD job to Wilson, who had been the high school football coach, he complained about the "athletic department" not having done something or other he wanted done and thought I was going to block it. "Hack," I told him, "you *are* the athletic department. Go ahead and do it!" He never complained about the athletic department after that.

I had red polo shirts with "Berkley Athletic Department" (BAD) printed on the shirts in white letters. Nearly everyone in the district—coaches and non-coaches alike—bought one. For a while my office was in a house the district owned where Director Joe Haddad and his special education department staff were quartered, and I held my physical education staff meetings in the basement. Huge, red-shirted P.E. teachers and coaches would come lumbering downstairs, and one time I let high school baseball coach Ed Nagel chair the meeting when I had other business upstairs.

Presently such a racket ensued from the basement that a special education secretary came and complained. "Dr. Telford, your coaches are misbehaving noisily and engaging in horseplay."

I went down there and told the big overgrown boys that if they ever hoped to be able to hold another meeting without me, they would have to behave.

Now I truly had my Athletic Army, albeit a bit rough around the edges. I also had my Lincolnesque Team of Rivals—*thirty-six years* before Barack Obama's—and at a time when I was still coincidentally thirty-six years old! For a while, some obstinate old principals continued to offer a bit of resistance to my initiatives, but I simply ignored them and moved my division forward with or without them.

The only other minor controversy I engendered in Berkley involved my complaining to a *Detroit Free Press* reporter and other local scribes that Berkley's athletic facilities were "abysmal." This riled a Berkley School board member sufficiently for him to urge the superintendent to "gag" me. The high school kids trained on what I had described to the reporters as a "muddy *cow path*" next to an elementary school. The reporters knew already that our high school basketball team played its games in a junior high school gymnasium that was only a little larger than the high school's tiny and outdated gym. (I told the reporters that I hesitated to call our high school's gym a "gymnasium," because the *word* was too *big*.)

Instead of becoming angry at my comments to the reporters and upset at the effect they had had on the board member, Superintendent Keane asked me to spearhead a millage campaign to get better facilities. I began by taking photos of the other Southeastern Michigan Association schools' excellent facilities and putting together a slide presentation which juxtaposed them to photos I had taken of Berkley's abysmal ones. Armed with these slides, I showed the presentation sixty-one times during the following spring and summer to community groups ranging in size from six to six *hundred*. We got a millage of $2.7 million passed that enabled us to build a new gym, pool, track, and football field.

In December 1973 my daughter Katherine was born. I set about initiating dozens of athletic teams for girls (with particular attention to girls' *track*!) After I established the girls' program, I put a dynamic young coach named Roz Warren in charge of it.

When Coordinator Rhoads later relinquished his general programmatic duties to concentrate solely on basketball, I put Mrs. Warren in charge of *all* secondary athletics—making her the first-ever woman in the *state* to supervise girls' *and* boys' programs!

CHAPTER TWENTY-NINE

BIG GEORGE AND ME— AND SLEEPING WITH PEACHES

"Coach, is there anyone you'd like to have me kill?"

—A former Pershing High School
star sprinter fresh from Vietnam

In 1974 Berkley High got a new principal, George Blaney, who had been an assistant principal at Butzel during the years immediately following my departure for King. He told me he had read the praise-filled notes my protective students had written about me during the witch hunt there, so he felt he already knew me. He also knew about my track exploits. We became instant buddies and remain so now, thirty-five years later.

The father of one of those Butzel students read in the newspaper that I was working in Berkley and called me at my office one day in 1973 to get the name of a good lawyer. His son, who never had been quite right in the head, had been sitting on top of a mailbox—and when the police told him to get off, he had refused. The cops then beat him off of the mailbox with clubs, causing a grievous injury to his already abnormal brain. I got his father a lawyer, but the father's number was later disconnected and I never found out what happened or ever heard from him again.

Around that same time, one of my Pershing runners came to me to help him beat a shoplifting rap. He had changed the price tags on some merchandise. I wrote a supportive letter to his lawyer—Hilda Gage (later a judge)—and I spoke with her, too. She was able to get him off the hook. I later told Judge Gage that he had become an exemplary professional, and she used his story from the bench as a positive example in pre-sentencing hearings.

Then another Pershing runner whom I had always had difficulty keeping out of trouble came to my office in Berkley to ask if I could find him a job. This kid had muscles on his *muscles*. He was about five foot seven inches tall and extremely powerful. He had always reminded me physically of my old teammate "Bullet Billy" Smith. Fresh from Vietnam, he asked me, "Coach, is there anyone you'd like to have me kill?" I told him there wasn't—and that he had to stop making offers like that to anyone unless he wanted them to think he was crazy.

With just a dollop of misgiving, I sent him to Del Russell, the former Wayne State tennis star who had gotten so many of my athletes jobs and helped me keep them out of trouble when he was a probation officer in Detroit. Del had since become the city's Police Athletic League director, but Mayor Coleman Young had fired him from that job and replaced him with former Detroit Piston Earl Lloyd and then with my friend and fellow Detroit Varsity Club board member Dick "Night Train" Lane, the old Detroit Lions cornerback. (When I had protested in writing about Del's firing, Mayor Young had personally written me back to say that it was interesting that only white people were interceding for Del, a light-skinned black man who sounded white when he spoke. This struck me as racist on the mayor's part.)

Del was now the security director for Borman Foods. The former athlete I sent him showed up high on weed, smelling of sweat, and in soiled clothes. Del told me never to send him anyone like that again. I had regretfully barred this young man from running in the state meet eight years earlier for skipping practice, which possibly kept him from getting a college offer. I had second-guessed myself on that decision, but too late. He was later arrested for breaking into Pershing. He still lived with his mother across the street from his old school with nothing left of value except memories of his lost track and football glory.

Inexplicably to most rational people, these three incidents made me homesick for Detroit. I felt that if I hadn't left, maybe I could have prevented more bad things like this from happening to Detroit kids. Ever since I had left my Detroit roots, I had tried intermittently to return to them. I had applied to take the DPS exams for assistant principal and principal, even though these were now positions that were beneath my current and most previous rank and salary level. Old Arthur Diekoff, my arch-nemesis of twenty years earlier when I had been a rebellious student at Northwestern High, had—for the second time—re-materialized in my life like a malevolent ghost. This time he was the only white person on my oral-interview committee for the assistant principal job, and I could tell by his demeanor that he wasn't going to vote for me. I got a letter in the mail advising me that I had passed the written interview but flunked that oral one.

I also got a letter informing me that I had flunked the principal exams. The problem was, I had never *taken* the principal exams. The competence of the top administration in Detroit Public Schools was clearly beginning to decline, even then (or else they knew I was white and decided not to interview me for any job at that level).

When we went out and drank together after work, Berkley High School Principal George Blaney and I would converse for hours about how much we missed the excitement of administrating back home in the Detroit Public Schools. George told me that before he left Butzel, black activist Frank Ditto and his paramilitary minions in camouflage with the hobnail boots and black berets were still marching into the school on occasion. George also told me that old Mrs. Blake, who had never caused me any trouble personally, was still calling the few dedicatedly remaining white staff there *racists* (which they obviously weren't, or they wouldn't have gone to teach there). George also told me that a certain King High School counselor was still frequently leading King students to march on Butzel in efforts to try to get Butzel students to walk out. I could never understand why that counselor wasn't fired.

George told me, too, about a big mama who charged into his office at Butzel clutching a butcher knife under her coat with the full intent to kill one of her son's teachers. This particular large lady was accompanied by two even larger adult sons, so George wisely turned to the large sons and pleaded, "Help me with your mother." They did, and murder was averted. I, in turn, told him about the time I had to lock Miss Wilma Woodhams in the closet to protect her from the angry mother.

One day I photographed my baby daughter Katherine sitting in her high chair draining a can of beer. Today that picture remains one of my all-time favorites. The can had actually been empty before I gave it to her, but when my mother saw the photo, she nearly had apoplexy.

Two or three years later, while shopping in a local drugstore, I was carrying my cute little Katherine in one arm, as I customarily did, when she saw a picture of a creature with a man's body and a wolf's head on the cover of a sci-fi paperback —and it scared her right out of her wits. I soon found myself telling her a hundred times that what she repeatedly referred to as the "man dog" didn't *exist*. Then she began to fear the word *exist*. She was also afraid of the big fir tree in our backyard, pictures of dinosaurs and crocodiles, the model of a seventeenth century galleon I still have, and a young fellow in a Darth Vader suit who came to entertain at a half-birthday party we gave for her one summer.

People and things she *liked* at various stages of her childhood were Kimba the white lion (star of a TV cartoon show), a tugboat named Blinky in a children's book, Michael Jackson and his *Thriller* album, Snow White and Wonder Woman (she had Snow White and Wonder Woman costumes), and unicorns. Once at the Michigan State Fair, she wanted a winged white stuffed unicorn that was nearly as big as she was, but you had to shoot fifty consecutive baskets with a regulation-size basketball to get it. I asked her if she wouldn't rather have a little blue Smurf that required only ten baskets, but *no*—she had to have the unicorn. After I had shot thirty-five consecutive baskets, I was perspiring profusely and had drawn a crowd of appreciative young black men. After a brief pause to wipe the sweat out of my eyes, I made ten more fast baskets. Then, without pausing and nearly blinded with sweat, I managed almost automatically to make the last five.

The hard-earned unicorn sits forlornly today in my now thirty-five-year-old daughter's Troy, Michigan, basement. Maybe my soon-to-be-born granddaughter Victoria will play with it some day.

In 1975 I found out that my "adopted" and later to be four-times-married cousin Ruth Ann Johnson McGee McCarty Hibbard Lowenthal—at thirty-seven, two years younger than me—was actually my *real* cousin. In 1938, my Aunt Evelyn had taken her younger sister Mary Louise to stay with relatives in Vermont until Mary Louise had the baby, and then they had returned with the baby Aunt Evelyn then raised as her own. Ruth Ann, now living in California with her fourth husband (the first three are deceased), remains as close to me as a sister. We celebrated her breaking the good news to me by hoisting a glass of champagne.

Speaking of drinking—one mid-week, mid-winter evening after departing unusually early from our offices, George Blaney and I were drinking together in the Spaghetti Company, a local bistro, as had become our weekly custom (and which would *remain* our weekly custom for the next quarter of a century). Specifically, we were drinking Black Russians—a potent concoction of vodka and Kahlua—and we were gulping them down one after another as the snow, which had started to fall as we entered, began to pelt more heavily outside and grow gradually into a good-sized snowstorm.

Congressman Jim Blanchard, who was soon to become *Governor* Jim Blanchard, was holding an election fundraising party in the establishment. George and his wife Joyce were among Jim's many friends and supporters, and I was on his Speakers' Bureau.

Spotting us at the bar, Jim came over to say hello. Having been drinking now for an hour or more, we took full and loud advantage of that golden opportunity to inform the future governor how *offended* we were that we hadn't been invited to his party. That point having thus been emphatically and indignantly driven home, we downed a few more Black Russians—this time on Blanchard's tab—before venturing out into the snow and drunkenly deciding that it was too deep for my car to be driven in it. George had snow tires, so we further drunkenly decided that I should come home with him to Sterling Heights.

En route, we got drunkenly stuck in a snow bank. Some athletes wearing letter jackets from Royal Oak Kimball High School—a school in Berkley's athletic conference, the Southeastern Michigan Association—happened to be walking by. They came over and pushed us out, whereupon I rolled down the passenger window. "Young men," I announced, pointing to George, who was in the driver's seat clutching the wheel, "*he* is the *prinz*bul of Berkley High School, and *I* am the school dissrick's *allet*ic director! We intend to *tell your prinzbul* tomorrow how you were so *wunnerful* as to come and *assiss* us!" Once we were on our weaving way again, George was able to articulate to me his concern regarding my having so ill-advisedly made it a point to tell the boys who we were, given our fairly obvious condition.

That night I slept fully clothed on the couch in the family room with Peaches, the Blaneys' golden retriever. Earlier (around ten o'clock), my wife had called George's wife, Joyce, to determine whether Joyce might know my whereabouts (although, by then, I was passed out cold on the couch and didn't hear a syllable of their conversation).

The superintendent had called, as well. He had tried with increasing impatience to reach us at our offices around four o'clock. Having failed repeatedly in those attempts, he was obliged to cancel a snowed-out "away" Berkley High School swimming meet *himself*—both his athletic director and his high school principal having been unreachable—and his athletic director having indeed been, by the time he called Joyce, un*conscious*.

In the morning, I complained of a throbbing hangover. Joyce sadistically fixed her similarly hungover husband a Bloody Mary for breakfast—and being a good hostess, she sadistically decided that I should get one, as well.

Good, solid Celts that we were, we actually *drank* them.

CHAPTER THIRTY

A BITTERSWEET GOODBYE
TO THE BEARS

"Now is the winter of our discontent."

—*William Shakespeare, from* Richard III

Berkley superintendent William G. Keane came to me one day late in 1977 and told me he was going to have to reclassify and downgrade my administrative rank and salary range factor for my job as director of the Division of Health, Physical Education, & Athletics. This meant that my salary would immediately be reduced. At the time, my wife Lynn had taken a leave from her teaching job in the Warren Consolidated Schools to stay home and raise our three-and-a-half-year-old daughter, and I had a hefty house note to pay every month, plus other expenses.

In addition, I was contributing a considerable amount of money to my philanthropic Detroit Varsity Club in inner-city Detroit, where I remained the only white man on its board of directors. I was taken aback more than a little by Dr. Keane's words. Also, I had trebled the size of the Berkley athletic programs, and our teams were winning. Moreover, we now had our state-of-the-art new Physical Education and Athletics facilities that the district had only been able to *dream* of before my persistent and well-publicized aggressions in that direction upon my arrival in Berkley. I felt a real sense of kinship with Dr. Keane (a fellow Celt), and I knew I had done an exceptional job for him, for our administrative team, and for the district.

Plaintively, I asked Dr. Keane, "Haven't I been doing a good-enough job?"

He took a deep breath. "John," he began, "please just hear me out, because this is not going to be easy for me to explain."

He took another deep breath. "You've been doing a *fine* job. You've taken the basketball kids down into Detroit to hone their skills playing in summer games and mixing sweat with a bunch of talented black players, and it's paid off superbly in the regular-season games against all athletes, both black *and* white. You were the key player in getting the millage passed for our sports complex. You've added dozens of teams to our roster—particularly girls' teams. You've founded a new statewide physical education administrative association, and you're the *treasurer* of that organization! You've hired new coaches and inspired our old ones to win games and track and swimming meets and wrestling matches all over the county, and even outside the county. You've got that All-America certificate hanging in your office along with your pictures of your city and state champions from Detroit for everyone to marvel at. It's like you've got your own personal *shrine* in there. Even our most cynical and set-in-their-ways coaches are in awe of you. We've never *won* this much before."

As he spoke, I made a note to remind him that I was also co-chairing the City of Berkley's Recreation Commission along with the city's recreation director, Robert Tooley.

Dr. Keane paused to draw a third deep breath and then plunged on: "Now the Huntington Woods parents are complaining to me that Berkley is starting to become known as a *jock district* like Ferndale or Hazel Park—and they're telling me that they aren't entirely *comfortable* with that reputation."

"Are you saying I'm getting a reduction in salary range factor because I'm doing *too* good a job? What am I supposed to do—tell my coaches to start *losing*?"

"Of *course* I'm not saying you're getting a reduction because you're doing too good a job—that would be absurd. And I just told you that I do appreciate the job you're doing. I'm simply saying that we have to cut back—and your range factor is one of the things we have to reduce."

"Bill, I don't think I should be the one to have to bite the bullet this way. The directors in the other districts in our athletic conference are all paid at least at a middle school principal's salary level, and the Birmingham director is paid more than the high school principals get. Birmingham certainly isn't a 'jock district.'"

We were both silent for a moment.

"Well," I said, breaking the awkward silence, "then put me in a principalship or assistant principalship—and do it *right away*. Right now, my family really needs to have the money."

"I *can't*. No principalships are available, nor will any *become* available in the foreseeable future. We're a relatively small district, you know—and growing smaller—and as far as I know, none of our principals will retire soon." He paused, then added with a tone of finality, "Besides, I need you too much in the job you're already in."

Need me too much, yet *demote* me? My mind reeled. Reluctantly but immediately, I sent my credentials home to Detroit (yet *again*). I also sent them to every school district—large and small—in the entire Detroit metropolitan area within a fifty-mile radius, hoping to land an administrative job again in academic education. That was where I belonged. (Actually, though, *Detroit* was where I *really* belonged.)

After this disappointing and disquieting conversation with Dr. Keane, I realized I needed to let off some steam. Even though I weighed nearly 190 pounds (my youthful sprinting weight had been between 165 and 170), I felt that I was still in pretty fair shape, so to let off a little steam and frustration, I got clocked in 10.3 for 100 yards without training—a time that was a little more than half a second slower than the best times I had clocked twenty-some years before. (For you younger readers more oriented to today's distances, a 10.3 for 100 yards is equivalent to an 11.1 for 100 meters.) My Achilles tendons were sore to the touch for a week after that impromptu run, but the 10.3 bettered the Masters (over age forty) record by a tenth of a second, so I decided to train a bit for Masters competition and have some fun.

To let off even *more* steam and frustration, I also entered a local toughman contest at the Michigan State Fairgrounds on Eight Mile Road in Detroit, where I had boxed as an amateur a quarter of a century earlier. I had to sign a waiver absolving the promoters of liability if I were to be seriously injured, but this didn't worry me. Even though I was forty-one years old now, my muscles were still hard and supple, and I reasoned that since I had run 100 yards in 10.3, I should be able to move fairly fast in a ring. I was curious to see how well I could do. I told my father about it (but not my mother), and he eagerly came to see me fight.

My preliminary-bout opponent was a short, squat, Polish fellow who was perhaps just a few years younger than me and more than forty pounds heavier than me. He was built like a beer barrel—he weighed over 230 pounds. He had a bald (or shaven) head with a tattoo on the top of it and a bushy yellowish beard which cushioned his chin from my punches. Being thus unable to put him down with head shots, I shifted my attack to his belly—a broad and inviting target. Surprisingly, though, his belly felt almost as hard as iron. My multiple poundings on his expansive midsection didn't even appear to faze him. However, I was able to bloody his nose with left jabs and fast, in-and-out rights I sneaked over his left hand, which he held very low. He was also quite slow.

He got the decision, but I felt I had won. He was constantly trying to clinch and work me over in the clinches, because he couldn't catch me to mount an effective attack. He also should have had points deducted for repeatedly trying to butt me and for flagrantly stomping on my foot in the third and final one-minute round in an attempt to render me stationary or to flatten my arch to slow me down. I did slow down and tire a bit in that round after he stepped on my foot, but I believe the judges voted for him because they thought his colorful appearance made him a good crowd-draw, so they decided to advance him even though I had landed many more punches than he had. Actually, I don't recall that he landed *any*—at least, none that *hurt*—because any time he even *tapped* me I was already back-peddling out of reach. The only wounds I suffered in those three rounds were a sore toe and a cut under my left eye when he reached up and laced me in a clinch in the last round. For an amateur, he had a full bag of dirty tricks.

My dad questioned the decision, too. In fact, he protested about it so vehemently that he nearly got himself ejected—and my buddy Cliff Hatcher, who had helped to second me in my corner, had to calm him down.

After mailing my credentials and college transcripts to school district personnel directors nearly fifty times, I was beginning to get quite discouraged. I got even more discouraged when I was admonished in an officious return letter from one of the personnel directors (in Ann Arbor) that *athletic* directors shouldn't be "wasting your time and mine" by filling out application forms for jobs in *academic* administration.

In spite of this chap's helpful words, I kept applying—and in the summer of 1977, at that relatively advanced age of forty-one, I finally landed an interview for the executive directorship of secondary education in the seventeen-thousand-student Plymouth/Canton Community School District. After two interviews there, I was chosen from a pool of more than 450 applicants for the job—which entailed my supervising and evaluating the district's nine secondary principals and directors.

I had spent five enjoyable and productive years in Berkley, and Dr. Keane had proved himself to be one of the most capable, ethical, and empathic superintendents I had ever worked for. He had also consistently proved to be one of the most courageous—as evidenced, in one instance, by his standing up as he did to the board member who had castigated me for my use of the term "abysmal" to describe the extent and condition of the district's truly abysmal health, physical education, and athletic facilities that had been there when I first came on board.

I had even written an article on global education for a *social studies journal* while I was there. I was leaving behind my old teammate and friend of twenty-plus years, Jerry Catalina, and my friends of ten years, deputy superintendent Sam Flam, who had been with me at Pershing, and a Berkley High School assistant principal, Dick Lowenthal, who had been with me at Butzel. I had also formed close friendships with George Blaney, Bill Keane, Steve Rhoads, my athletic business manager Bill Richer (who was to die of cancer that summer), and special education director Joe Haddad—whom I had beaten in Scrabble one Friday night at his elegant house in Ferndale in the first year of my five-year stint as the athletic director. Upset at losing a language-skill-oriented game to someone he perhaps considered a mere "jock," Joe had kept me (and my tired teacher wife) there until nearly midnight trying to win a rematch. I won that game, too—but it was closer.

I decided to retain my residence in Huntington Woods, so now I was faced with an hour-long drive to Plymouth/Canton every morning. That quashed any plans I had to train to run the sprints in Masters competition: I would no longer have the time. I also tried to spend as much quality time with my cute little daughter as I could, since I was away from the house for long hours every day, and even for meetings on weekends sometimes. We had a cat named Thurstine who liked to hide in secluded places, and my daughter Katherine and I would go on "cat hunts" in the house together. (When Thurstine was a tiny kitten, the pet store clerk where I bought her told me she was a male, so I had named her "Thurston"—thus, when we found out she was a female, we "feminized" her name.)

I wrote poems and read them to Katherine. One she liked was "Halloween Pussies," which I wrote for her on Halloween, 1977:

> Little black kittens with yellowish eyes
> Skitter and pit-pat and skip after flies,
> Crickets and grasshoppers, shadows and snails,
> Cute catnip mice—and their <u>very</u> <u>own</u> <u>tails</u>!

When Wayne State University inducted me into its Athletic Hall of Fame in February 1978, a photographer from the *Royal Oak Tribune* came to the Huntington Woods house. I posed with Katherine riding on her pony "Macaroni" (my right *knee*—my *left* knee was the pony "Minestrone"), and my swift-scampering little "Running Cat" (that was the Indian name I had given her) got her picture in the paper sitting on her doting daddy's knee under the alliterative caption, "Tartars' Telford Tapped." (WSU athletes were still called the *Tartars*—not the *Warriors*—when I competed for the school.)

Sometime during the early weeks that I was in Plymouth/Canton, the personnel director's frightened secretary called me urgently out of the superintendent's administrative cabinet meeting because a tall, muscular young black man was demanding to see me. It turned out to be my record-breaking Pershing quarter-miler the kids had called "Outlaw," who now was nearly thirty years old. He had a teenaged girl in tow, and he was making wild threats against former Pershing basketball coach Will Robinson, saying he was going to find Will and kill him for cutting him from the basketball team in 1966. I told him he wasn't going to do any such thing.

I also pointed out to him that he was the same age I had been when I coached him, and it was high time for him to grow up. Then I told him I had to return to my meeting, and he had to behave himself until I came back.

By the time my meeting was over, Outlaw and the girl were gone. I wasn't to see him again for many years. In fact, for quite a long time—knowing his penchant for violence and lawlessness—I feared that he was dead.

CHAPTER THIRTY-ONE

THE PERFECT ADMINISTRATOR

"For years, I've been searching for the perfect administrator. John Telford is the closest to that image I've ever met."

—*Earl Harrington, teacher,*
Plymouth Central Junior High School

For the next seven years, I made that hour-long drive to and from the Plymouth/ Canton schools—but those seven years were more than worth the drive. The first couple of weeks were tough, though—the teachers were on strike and had walked out of classes, and John Michael ("Mike") Hoben, the six foot, six-inch, 260-pound superintendent, a wounded and decorated Marine captain in the Korean War and a former Boston Celtic, immediately assigned me to the team that was negotiating with the experienced bargaining team of the teachers' union. We negotiated for ten days and nights, practically around the clock, sleeping only a few hours in a conference room some nights without going home—but we hammered out a fair contract, and I won the respect of the teachers' bargaining team.

Within the next few years, I also learned and relearned every nuance of secondary-school administration on that job, including how to thwart a bigoted school board member when this ignorant member tried to discourage me from promoting a young dynamo of diminutive physical stature named Gary Faber to a junior high school principalship. The member protested to me that Dr. Faber was "too *short*"! In the formidable presence of my very large boss, I hotly retorted that this ridiculous objection was certain evidence that the member's real problem with Dr. Faber wasn't that he was too *short* but rather that he was too *Jewish*. Dr. Hoben concurred with me (privately), and I was duly able to promote my promising young protégé. Thus professionally launched, Dr. Gary Faber went on to become a high school principal, then an assistant superintendent, and then superintendent in the West Bloomfield Schools, ultimately retiring in 2008 with myriad accolades.

I learned how to reprimand, commend, promote, demote, hire, and fire—and to do all of it with aplomb. In spite of my past penchant for simply ignoring rules I didn't agree with, I was now learning how to be the quintessential bureaucrat when circumstances so dictated. I *reprimanded* one area coordinator for referring to blacks as "burr-heads" in an administrative meeting, and I *reprimanded* a middle school principal for making public statements that challenged my Division of Secondary Education's student-scheduling formats and processes. I *hired* one particular building administrator despite some unselected internal applicants' plaintive accusations of nepotism. The administrator, Greg Owens, my friend of ten years (and now of forty-two years), was a Warren principal who was then married to my wife's Warren teaching colleague, Margot. Another building administrator I *fired*—for being too high-handed with parents and un-empathetic toward students. I fired him reluctantly, and only after giving him several chances to mend his ways, because he was very intelligent. He later became a lawyer. Happily for him, *empathy* isn't a prerequisite for admission to the bar.

I often had lunch with Tom Barry, an old World War II commando who had fought under Field Marshal Bernard Montgomery at El Alamein in North Africa. Tom's soft Scottish burr reminded me of my father's family. A custodian, Tom's job was to deliver the mail from school to school and to the board office on Harvey Street in Plymouth where my office was. When I had to stay until evening for a board meeting, I often had supper with Tom, or with Central Junior High School teacher Earl Harrington and his family. On some of those nights, I was very hungry, because I hadn't had any lunch. I had either worked right through lunch, or Human Resources supervisor Walt Bartnick had *stolen* my lunch out of the administrators' refrigerator as a joke. Joke or not, Walt would then proceed to eat both *his* lunch that his wife had fixed for him and *my* lunch that my wife had fixed for *me*. Walt—then a growing boy of respectable girth—definitely didn't need *two* lunches anywhere near as much as *I* definitely needed my *one*.

One day a senior administrator heard old World War II commando Tom Barry call me "John." He took me aside and told me I shouldn't allow custodians to call me by my first name in public, nor should I be fraternizing so often with custodians and teachers. He said that administrators fraternizing with teachers was the same as teachers fraternizing with the students and that it wasn't professional for someone of my rank to be doing this all the time.

I told him, "Teachers and students are the reason you have a *job*, sir—and our school district would have one devil of a time trying to function without custodians. Tom Barry was fighting beside American soldiers against the Nazis in North Africa when you were in short pants being chauffeured to nursery school by your mommy. I intend to continue having dinner with Tom Barry, and also with Earl Harrington. Besides, Earl's wife Joyce makes a great pot roast. You should come and sample it some time."

"No, thanks," he said—but I heard no more from him about it.

This had been my third encounter with *classism* in a school setting. I would battle it again in Detroit *big-time*, twenty-five years later.

In the fall of 1982, I took my parents to dinner at the Cadieux Café on the east side of Detroit near Finney High, where Jack Ramm and Val Maroukian, two of my old coaching colleagues from Finney, happened to be dining. They told me about this big, strong Italian kid they had at Finney who looked "more Irish than Italian" and was "incredibly fast for a white kid" but was always fighting and could never stay scholastically eligible. Even before they said the name "Steve Ditta," I knew they were talking about my son whom his married mother, Corinna—who was of English ancestry without a drop of Italian blood in her veins—had kept away from me for seventeen years. Hearing Steve's name was like having a needle stuck in my heart. Again, I had to force any thought of him out of my mind—and again, it was agonizingly hard.

Early in 1983, an economic downturn caused Superintendent Hoben to announce some probable administrative cuts in the Plymouth/Canton Community Schools that included my job and that of my elementary counterpart, Dr. Barbara Bowman. Four decades earlier, I had had a ditzy classmate at Estabrook named Malcolm Wimberley who always exited the school at dismissal time making airplane-motor noises with arms outstretched and the stupidly smitten little girls all shouting "Malcolm, Malcolm!" Now, forty years later, I had foolishly begun to believe that *I*, too, was a high-flying airplane! Indeed, in many ways I had been flying as high as the eight-year-old Malcolm had imagined *he* was flying in 1943 until that 1983 recession made Dr. Hoben worry seriously enough about the district's flagging finances to plan to eliminate my high-ranking job.

Dr. Barbara Bowman, my elementary counterpart, landed an interview in Waukegan, Illinois, and became the assistant superintendent there. I started sending out my credentials again to Detroit, Rochester, and several other large Michigan districts. (In my heart, of course, I had always really wanted to come home to Detroit.)

It turned out that I wasn't going or coming anywhere just then. More than three hundred teachers wrote or called Dr. Hoben and urged him to keep me. They also signed petitions which were published in the local newspapers. One, from the Pioneer Middle School faculty and staff, said, in part, "Telford exemplifies the type of administrator we all need."

Central Middle School teacher Earl Harrington wrote, "For years I've been searching for the perfect administrator. John Telford is the closest to that image I have met."

Many parents also wrote or called Superintendent Hoben—including a mother named Mary McGrath, whose daughter Coleen I had kept from quitting school. (She eventually graduated from the University of Michigan with honors.)

I assured the superintendent truthfully that I had nothing whatever to do with all this. I was as genuinely surprised as he was.

Detroit never called. To my Motor City hometown and to the world, I was (and evidently am *still*) a *white* man. This was a simple and irrevocable fact I had to face, regardless of whether I might sometimes have yearned to have been born black— particularly when I was racing against world-record-holder Ira Murchison in a 60-yard dash at Notre Dame and at 100 meters in Ancona, Italy, or when world record-breaking sprinter/hurdler Hayes Jones beat me at 100 yards in Birmingham, or when the great Olympian Charley Jenkins finally caught me at the finish line of a record-breaking one minute, eleven-second 600-yard invitational race in Chicago after finishing behind me three times in the quarter-mile the previous year.

A life on the *run*, indeed—but not always a *fast* enough run! These were but four of the thirty-two races I lost in a career that totaled 206 races (not counting relay races), and most of those thirty-two losses were to sprinters of African descent like Murchison, Jones, and Jenkins.

Late in 1983, President Ronald Reagan sent military assistance to Iraq in the war Saddam Hussein had begun by invading Iran—an order most civilians (including me) paid little attention to at the time. To prevent an Iraqi military collapse, the Reagan administration supplied battlefield intelligence on Iranian troop buildups to the Iraqis, sometimes through third parties such as Saudi Arabia. While political and corporate concern about this possible eventuality even before it happened was part of what had caused the economic recession that in turn had caused Superintendent Hoben to worry about the school district's revenues, this U.S. involvement with Iraq (over *oil*, naturally) was to have far graver repercussions two decades later in our country and throughout the world.

In the late spring of 1984, the Rochester Community Schools *did* contact me. They wanted me to interview for their top K-12 job in their huge Division of Instruction—and my seven formative years as an executive director in Plymouth/Canton had rendered me fully ready for that prime-time challenge. Unknown to me at the time, when Rochester Education Association president Don Healy learned I might be coming, he contacted Bill Bartlett, his counterpart in Plymouth/Canton, to get the P/C teachers' take on me. Even though those teachers didn't want to lose me, their union president assured the president of the Rochester teachers' union that I was a staunch student-and-teacher-advocate.

I interviewed in Rochester and was hired—again from an application pool of hundreds. For me, the timing was personally perfect. I had just undergone a mutually-devastating breakup from a two-year undercover (or under the *covers*) affair with a drop-dead gorgeous Detroit girl named Gina Morris, who had written me reams of impassioned poetry in which she referred to our encounters as "red-hot." (At this time, Eva and her two daughters were living in California—where Eva had temporarily moved to try to get me out of her system.)

Awaiting Gina in our Southfield trysting place on my way home to Huntington Woods from Plymouth, I would hear her wheezing old $75 rattletrap—held together with bailing wire and a prayer—as it clanked past the entrance to the E-Z Rest Motel parking lot and rolled up to the door of our cozy little hideaway.

When Gina—who despite having a two-year-old son to support had never asked me for so much as a dime—finally left me because she couldn't deal with my marriage any longer, I wrote this dark, overwrought poem, entitled *Don Juan in the Pit*:

> *Drum forth his whorish heart's fair toll*
> *Of Isabel, Marie, Nicole,*
> *Sweet Esmeralda, Carmen, Kate—*
> *Su Corazón no más. Too late.*
>
> *None who felt Juan's heartbeat fled*
> *The moonscape of his rumpled bed*
> *Save one. She sprang from that abyss*
> *To seal his Apocalypse.*

This hyperbolic, faux-Hispanic-flavored verse wasn't really about Don Juan—it was about *Sir John*. And *Gina* was the "one" in my phrase, "Save one." Despite all my efforts to resist it, she had somehow managed to burrow under both my psychic and physical defenses into my very *bone marrow*. My junior by more than a quarter of a century, the beauteous Gina Morris was destined to cross my path again—but not for eighteen more long, challenging, tumultuous years.

That summer, my cousin Carl's wild twenty-four-year-old son Carl III ("Cracker") was murdered selling drugs in Detroit, leaving behind an attractive young wife, Vickie, and two very young children—including Carl IV, who later became an excellent hockey player.

When he was younger, the handsome, devil-may-care Cracker—who like his father, his uncle Dick, and his younger brother Rick was as blond as his Viking forebears—had often sprawled on his back passed out stoned on my family room rug with his then-teenaged then-girlfriend Vickie sitting there patiently awaiting his awakening. Now Cracker had begun encroaching on the territories of two notorious dealers—White Boy Rick and Richard (Maserati Rick) Carter—and his father and I had feared he was living on borrowed time. Once in the dead of night he and his father and I had had to arm ourselves, burst into a Detroit drug house near Seven Mile Road and Van Dyke Avenue, and forcibly recover thousands of dollars of Cracker's profits which the denizens of the house had stolen from him. He had owed much of this money to suppliers, and we had assured him then that we would never do anything like this for him again. This was *emphatically* to be the *first* and *last* time. He in turn had assured us that he would never again *have* to ask for our help.

I moved into my Rochester job the same summer month that Cracker was killed and Carl lost his job; a grief-stricken Carl and his inconsolable wife Ginny moved out of Rochester to start a fresh, new life near Ginny's mother in Pearcy, Arkansas, where they opened the Busy Bee Café (and later served the best fried catfish there I have ever tasted).

With Carl's departure, I had lost one of the two closest companions of my youth, and the other—Carl's brother Dick, one year my junior—lived far away in Washington State. The family had called us "The Three Musketeers" growing up.

I had enjoyed my seven mostly wonderful years in Plymouth/Canton and made many lifelong friends. Little did I know that for the *next* seven years, I was about to experience the rare privilege and pleasure of working hand-in-glove with one of the two most dedicated and dynamic superintendents I'd ever met. I couldn't have known then, either, that I would nearly get us both fired from the top two jobs in that 98 percent white, ostensibly *Christian* district for the unpardonable act of recruiting black and Jewish administrators, banning Christmas manger scenes in the schools, and committing similar other high crimes and misdemeanors.

CHAPTER THIRTY-TWO

A ROYAL
SUPERINTENDENT—AND
LITTLE GREEN GREMLINS

"Live <u>pure</u>, speak <u>true</u>, right <u>wrong</u>, follow the <u>King</u>."

—*Alfred, Lord Tennyson, from* Idylls of the King
(based upon the Celts' misty Arthurian legends)

When I mounted my war horse and rode into Rochester to do knightly academic and egalitarian battle in the late summer of 1984, trusty lance at the ready, I admittedly wasn't *living pure*. I had continued, unlike the pure-hearted Sir Galahad of legend and lore, to ply my private *lance* in illicit ways. Still, in every *professional* regard, I *spake <u>true</u>* and was continuing to *right <u>wrong</u>* habitually and ongoingly, as my Celt father had done before me and had enjoined me always to do. Now I felt I had met the <u>*King*</u>. I was to *follow* him loyally and "have his back" for the next seven years, and indeed even beyond them.

I saw Superintendent John M. Schultz, at forty-five my junior by nearly four years, to be *kingly* in the most admirable sense. He was as un-egotistical and transparently straightforward as the day is long. I saw him as having the courage of his convictions. Moreover, he was a workaholic who was dedicated—body and soul—to running the show and running it righteously. I had found a man I believed was a rare leader I could follow without hesitation. (Also, he'd been an exceptional athlete, and he had a regal, white, genuinely *Arthurian* beard!)

Dr. Schultz had recently been promoted to superintendent from the job I was to fill, which he had occupied only for a year and a half. He was an elementary-school specialist by experience and temperament, and I was a secondary-school guy—so while he turned the entire K-12 Division of Instruction over to me to run and rarely questioned any elementary instructional decision I might make, he almost *never* questioned a *secondary* one.

An initial—and divisive—secondary-level contretemps I had to handle was quickly blooming into full flower at one of our high schools. A slim majority of the Adams High School faculty was putting heavy pressure on the superintendent to fire their principal, Ron Booth. These highbrow teachers felt that Mr. Booth was a lowbrow who favored the athletic programs, which some of them referred to contemptuously as the "toy department" of the school district.

Dr. Schultz didn't want to fire this principal, but he also didn't want to alienate the faculty—many who regarded their school as the Harvard of the West and themselves as being on a par with any Ivy League professor. Ivy Leaguers they perhaps could have aspired to be. However, I submit that most of them wouldn't have lasted a week trying to teach at Southeastern or Pershing or King, let alone trying for even a single *day* at Butzel. Also, were those paragons of professional pedagogy to have been somehow teleported in time from that year of 1984 to Detroit Finney High School between the years 2003 and 2008, I can say with *intimate* certainty that they soon would have been back in their automobiles fleeing far northward *fast*.

These esoteric souls already suspected both me and John of being Neanderthals because of our athlete backgrounds (John had played Triple-A ball for several years in the Cincinnati Reds' farm system and bore the distinction of having teamed with the celebrated Pete Rose). Thus, although I believed myself to be a more knowledgeable academician than any of them, their uneasy suspicion that I was really just another jock wasn't going to help me with them one bit regarding their issue with their principal. I was about to be charged with adjudicating that issue, and judging *him*—like it or not.

At Dr. Schultz' direction, I conducted a thorough investigation and arrived at the fair decision not to fire Mr. Booth—a decision with which my relieved superintendent concurred on the spot. Unfortunately, my decision alienated that same slight majority of the Adams faculty—alienation which in the future I would never be completely able to overcome—and they went over John's head and lobbied doggedly with the Rochester Board of Education to get them to make the superintendent *reverse* me.

Their outraged lobbying was unsuccessful. However, the heat didn't totally dissipate until Mr. Booth—perhaps wisely perceiving that discretion might be the better part of valor, or maybe just tiring of the squabbling—landed a high school principalship in Colorado, where he soon was chosen to be that state's Principal of the Year. Rochester's loss was definitely Colorado's gain.

Another early challenge I had to address came from some parents who objected to the words *globalism* and *humanism* in the school district's recently updated and revamped social studies curriculum. Except for my having shared my 1977 journal article on global education with the social studies committee, I had played a belated and minimal role in that curriculum's updating and revamping. Still, having endorsed it, I was charged with the task of convincing the Board of Education to anoint it—even though some multicultural aspects were missing that I would have preferred to see incorporated.

On August 21, 1984, in a much-anticipated, heavily-attended, and presently highly-publicized meeting for the board to rule on the social studies curriculum, I told the board and the concerned parents, "Interdependence of all of the people throughout the globe, as well as the active search for just, humanistic, and peaceful solutions, are concepts included in this curriculum—as well they should be. This revision has the *full support* of the Division of Instruction."

A concerned community member asked, "Are they teaching about these homosexual and lesbian families?"

Dr. Schultz assured the gentleman that the course did not include reference to homosexual living or familial arrangements.

After much debate, the board approved the social studies curriculum with one dissenting vote, and the concerned community members all went away—for a while.

At that time, I was on the Education Task Force of the Anti-Defamation League headed by civil-rights guru Richard Lobenthal, the League's mid-west area director. I was serving on the Michigan Board of Education's Humanities Task Force, too—and I was also involved in the *Detroit Free Press'* World of Difference program, and as a second-time advisor for similar programs with WDIV-TV Channel 4.

So, in cooperation with Reuther Middle School Social Studies Department Head Gustav DeMulder, I brought my own enhanced version of the *World of Difference* program to Reuther as a pilot program with plans to expand it to the other middle schools, eventually to the high schools, and ultimately to incorporate it into the social studies curriculum when the review time for that curricular area came around again.

Another pesky but less encompassing problem than the flap over the social studies curriculum got dropped in my lap two months later around Halloween. A fearsomely wild-eyed lady with dark makeup around her eyes that made her face look like a raccoon's led a delegation of concerned parents to my office. They had come to demand that an elementary-school library book—*Halloween ABC's*—be removed from the shelves of all the elementary schools in the district. The book featured cartoonish renderings of little green gremlins that this lady declared were "demonic."

The wild-eyed lady resembled a vampire from one of those old flickering black-and-white Bela Lugosi films. She was without makeup except for the heavy mascara, and she was very tall and thin, and pale as paste, with a remarkably leptorrhinian (elongated, aquiline) nose. She wore an ankle-length black dress with a collar buttoned to the throat, leather-laced black boots, and a wide-brimmed, conical black hat that also lent her an uncanny similarity to the bad witch in the film *Wizard of Oz* (except for the boots). Given the nature of her concern, these resemblances had to be unintentional on her part.

I recall, too, that she smelled faintly of mothballs.

Belying this extraordinary appearance was a heavy silver cross she wore suspended by a very long silver chain around her neck. Spying a small pewter rendering of Merlin the Magician holding up three crystalline balls—a statue my twelve-year-daughter Katherine had innocently given me—the fearsomely wild-eyed lady became extremely agitated and brandished her cross at it, proclaiming it to be a "demonic symbol." I hastily snatched up the little statue and slipped it out of sight into my desk drawer.

For the next hour, I tried fruitlessly to alleviate this group's concerns about the Halloween book. Failing in that, I finally told them I would refer the book to the district's Challenged-Book Review Committee.

(Speaking of my daughter—Katherine had won all her sprint races at her middle school in Rochester that season with a best 200-meter time of 26.7 seconds, but she had quit track to spend more time with some exceptionally disreputable boys. More than ten years later, I would coach some young women on *track scholarships* at the University of Detroit-Mercy who could barely run that fast. I've often wondered how fast Katherine might have run if she had stuck with it.)

The Challenged-Book Review Committee gave the harmless little *Halloween ABC's* book a clean bill of health with the concessive stipulation that it be issued only to fourth-graders and older. I told the Committee I could live with that concession, and the group of would-be censors would have to live with it, too.

So would their leader—the disturbed and disturbing black-garbed apparition with the fearsomely wild eyes—but of course I knew she couldn't. I felt more than a little sorry for her, because people like her really aren't in their right mind. I braced myself to see a lot more of her.

Surprisingly (and blessedly), I never saw her again.

CHAPTER THIRTY-THREE

AMASSING A
MIGHTIER DIVISION

"We don't have kids like that in Rochester, Dr. Telford."

—Board member opposing the proposed
establishment of an Alternative Center for
Education (ACE) for troubled teens

"You're right, Mrs. [*board member*]—they've all <u>dropped out</u>."

Superintendent John Schultz gave me an almost entirely independent hand in hiring and promoting principals and other administrators. I immediately brought two of my well-respected former Plymouth/Canton colleagues on board as principals —Janine Kateff and my trusted longtime sidekick Greg Owens.

I also tried to recruit the wise, steady George Blaney, who had risen to become the personnel director in Berkley, and the young hotshot Gary Faber, who was then the principal of West Bloomfield High School, to come and help me run my new division. They both turned me down. Big George felt he was too close to retirement (even though he's younger than me), and Dr. Faber, my former Plymouth/Canton protégé, was confidently, and it turned out *correctly*, expecting one day to attain the superintendency in his district.

I then elevated two Rochester principals, Murel Bartley and Dr. Bill Waun, to become my general directors of elementary and secondary education— titles and positions I had created to the initial chagrin of some of the principals and directors. I was aware of an incident wherein Dr. Waun, then a high school principal in Bloomfield Hills, had defied a superior's elitist order to afford a board member's daughter special parking privileges, and it had unjustly cost him his job. He therefore obviously was no yes-man, and I liked that. Waun, a tall, lanky, easygoing former Western Michigan University basketball star who was highly-regarded by most of the principals, had been my top in-house rival for my job. Thus, I was stealing another page from Lincoln's Team of Rivals strategy, as I had in Berkley—and as our dynamic young 44th president of the United States would one day do. I was, indeed, in good company— past and future!

I had tapped these two general directors to supervise and evaluate the principals and some of the directors as an integral part of their assignments— duties I had also performed when I served as the executive director of secondary education in Plymouth/Canton. Getting a new layer of instructional admini-strators who were going to be overseeing them directly didn't sit well with some of the building administrators. They debated whether to file a change-of-working-conditions grievance against me through their union, but they presently decided that this might not be the best way to get on the good side of their new bosses—and of their new bosses' new boss.

I made it a pointed priority to promote a promising young Jewish assistant principal named Marvin Rubin to the principalship of his school—Van Hoosen Middle School—after I had promoted the former principal, Dr. Jerry Freeman, to a directorship. Marv Rubin had been suspiciously rejected too many times for a principalship by internal committees. He later led his school to become a selection as a state and National Exemplary School.

The Rubin case was the first time I had encountered what appeared to be anti-Semitism in Rochester, but it wasn't to be the last. Before I could en-gage the entire conglomerate of in-house and out-house bigots in fixed battle, though, I knew that I would need to earn my knightly spurs reviewing and transforming the district's entire curricula, K-12. Also, I still regarded the social studies curriculum as a work in progress, even though I had endorsed this most recent revision.

Early in my tenure as assistant superintendent, General Director Waun came to me with a bright young middle school principal we had just promoted. The young principal wanted me to move the assistant principal she had inherited to another assignment because she felt he was "academically unaware," and I had refused.

I asked her, "What would you do if one of your teachers told you 'I'll teach these twenty-five kids you sent me, but not *these* four—or *these* three?"

She answered, "I'd tell the teacher, 'You have to teach them *all*.'"

"I rest my case," I said.

Years later, Dr. Tresa Zumsteg was an applicant for the assistant superintendency in Berkley. I think she worried that Personnel Director Blaney—who had become the elder statesman there and thus the power behind the throne—might call me to ask me whether they should select her, and of course he did.

I told George, "Choose her—she's got balls."

Dr. Zumsteg rose to become the Berkley superintendent and now is an associate superintendent in the Oakland County Intermediate School District.

In 1985, after a year on the job, I sold my house in Huntington Woods and moved to Rochester Hills with my wife and daughter. For the next five years, Rochester's workaholic superintendent and his workaholic deputy would compete with each other to see which of us could get to the office in the morning before the other, after having closed down a local bar together following a post-midnight Board of Education meeting or study session the previous day. By seven o'clock on any given weekday morning, Dr. John Schultz and I had usually already been at work for at least half an hour. We came in on weekends, too, and encouraged our staff to do likewise. We set a fast pace for the principals and assistant principals, who would make jokes that really *weren't* jokes about the two hard, *too*-hard taskmasters in the central office.

In addition to my general directors of elementary and secondary education, I surrounded myself with energetic, newly-promoted or newly-hired divisional staff. They included: Educational Technology Director Deborah Anthony, Vocational Education Director Dick Turco (now deceased), Special Education Director Cherie Simpson, Community Education Director Walt Cooper, Research Director Jerry Freeman, P.E. and Athletics Director Dick Ulrich, Pupil-Personnel Supervisor Carol Wright, Foreign Language Coordinator Margrit Bickelmann, Fine Arts Coordinator Tim Brooks, Health Education Coordinator Betty Crowder, Music Coordinator Dennis Fralick, and Gifted and Talented Education Coordinator Ro Schilke.

I also promoted four full-time, hand-picked, hard-working staff development specialists from the teaching ranks—Trish Steeby, Sally Dunlop, and Kathy

Joseph. My Staff Development specialists coordinated a teacher training program that I dubbed RISE—Rochester Instructional Skills Enhancement.

On May 16, 1987, I tremulously broke the news to my eighty-four-year-old father, in a nursing home where I had had to put him temporarily, that his beloved seventy-two-year-old brother Frank Telford, the retired Hollywood director who had discovered Lee Marvin and directed Janet Leigh, Helen Hayes, Lloyd Bridges, Dane Clark, and Tony Randall, had died in California. I promised to be back in two days with a hand-held transistor radio for him, because he was having trouble focusing on the TV set in his room.

"I don't *want* a goddamned radio," he told me. "If you bring me one, I'll just keep it turned off and won't listen to it. And anyway, I won't *be* here in two days. Can't you see I'm out of *time*?"

You've got *plenty* of time, Dad," I answered. "I'll have you out of here in a week or two after you're eating better and can walk better—but right now you need that radio. You can listen to the Tigers on it."

Two nights later, at 7:15 p.m., when I was driving home with my daughter from dinner at the Rochester Chop House, the clock mysteriously stopped in my brand new district-leased Grand Prix. I got the call from the nursing home at 7:45. I was barefoot in my undershorts, still wearing my shirt and tie. When I learned my dad had died (at 7:15), I hugged my daughter and cried, grabbed a full bottle of Dewars White Label, and still wearing only the shirt and tie and undershorts and still crying, I went out and sat on a grassy slope on the commons behind my house and drank and cried and drank some more until long after sundown. My wife arrived home from a PTA meeting at her school in Warren near midnight and came out and led me back up onto the deck and into the house, still crying and drinking, with grass stains on my undershorts and the now near-empty bottle in my hand.

A prodigious patriot had passed. Loving John "Scotty" Telford as I did, I had nearly *drained* that bottle from the land of his birth in his mighty memory. Still, I was at work at 6:30 the next morning with an aching head and heart, because my father had always been proud of my professional accomplishments—and I knew that was where he would have wanted me to be, hung over or not.

I also knew that I had better try to follow his familial Code to the *letter* now that he might decide to haunt me from on high. That unwritten Code included a clause holding other men's wives to be strictly off limits regarding amour, so I nervously vowed to myself to break things off regarding two con-nubially attached community ladies I was amorously involved with at the time. Intriguingly, the first of these two young ladies had the custom of uttering sharp little barks in bed at her ecstatic peak. The second customarily called me her "master" at *her* happiest height. Naturally, these customs—along with their almost *rueful* exclamations about how much they loved my lean body—lent further substance to my already too-substantive ego, but I nonetheless decided to try to stop seeing them.

Incidentally, I offer no apologies (on this page) for these and other pertinent amorous transgressions, nor do I seek relevant forgiveness from any adjudicate other than the Lord, one long-suffering now *ex*-wife, and the spirit of my departed father and his ancient, ancestral Code. The reader might reflect that in the circum-spect and mostly dead-serious pages preceding, no other similar situations have been described in such detail. In the pages to *come* (no pun intended), no other such situation henceforth *shall* be (save *one* in Chapter Fifty-two)—because were I to describe many more of them, it would transpose this mercurial yet essentially discreet memoir into one of quite a different and abjectly ungentlemanly genre. As many folks know, a certain amatory adventurer of legend and lore named Giacomo Jacåpo Casanova beat me and the rest of the world's furtive philanderers to the punch more than two centuries ago in that ungentlemanly genre with his timelessly torrid tome, *Histoire de ma vie*.

When I left the house on the morning after the night my father died, the clock in my new car was mysteriously *working* again—and even *more* mysteriously, it was set to the *correct time*! His still-amazed granddaughter—whom her fierce old fighter grandfather had so often baby-sat and guarded like a little treasure when she was growing up—will attest to these mysteries.

That next night, I sat down and wrote *For Scotty*—which was the first poem I had written in many a year:

> *My daddy didn't die where he was born—*
> *Larkhall, whence ancient kin rode forth on raids*
> *Or got well-bled at Culloden*
> *Or torn at bloody Bannockburn by English blades,*
> *A-gasping, gang aglie,*
> *"Dear mother, I die free!"*

No.
He croaked one drab, inconsequential day
On some gray bed in distant Michigan—
A billion heartbeats and a world away
From Highlands where the sons of warriors ran
By bright burns blue and clear,
Chasing dew-dappled deer.

I had intended to read the poem at my father's funeral—a double funeral we held for him and his younger brother—but for once in my life I couldn't speak; I was too overcome with grief. The many mourners present sang his favorite hymn (and mine)—*The Battle Hymn of the Republic*:

> *Mine eyes have seen the glory of the coming of the Lord.*
> *He is stamping out the vintage where the grapes of wrath are stored.*
> *He has loosed the fateful lightning of his terrible swift sword . . .*

For most of his eighty-four wild years on this planet, my fighter father's sword was swift and terrible, too. He asked for no quarter, and got none—but every once in a while, he *gave* it. (Don't tell anyone.) For that little "once in a while," he lives every day in my heart.

In Rochester, I had budgeted more than a hundred thousand start-up dollars for a school for needful, recalcitrant kids who for whatever reason didn't fit the "suburban image," because that was something my father would have liked to see me do, and because in his several-month absence in 1951, I had briefly become that kind of kid myself. However, to convince the board of this need proved initially difficult.

One board member protested, "We don't *have* kids like that in Rochester, Dr. Telford."

I responded, "You're right, Mrs. [board member]—they've all *dropped out*." After I said that to the board member, the board gave the program their near-unanimous blessing (a 6–1 vote) without another dissenting word.

I christened the program ACE (Alternative Center for Education), housed it in a closed and isolated elementary school, and gave its "counselor-in-charge" job to a high school assistant principal we had caught changing grades.

When we caught him, Dr. Schultz had said to me, "We could *fire* him."

"*Could* isn't necessarily *should*, John," I had replied. "He's got a special feeling for troubled kids—he just demonstrated it in the wrong way. He deserves a second chance."

John agreed.

This empathetic gentleman's second chance proved beneficial both to him and to ACE's students, who included a member of the Ciccone family— a brother of the entertainer Madonna, Adams' most famous alum.

Rochester Police officers Mark Woliung and Howard Farris, and Oakland County Sheriff's deputies Tom Parker, Paul Semann, and Susan Myszenski were all delighted that I had created this Alternative Center for Education, because ACE's existence made their work easier. They were local police personnel who reported directly to me and whose salaries the school district paid. They were also caring human beings who had a rare sensitivity for troubled youth.

Speaking of troubled youth—I felt somewhat avenged for my cousin Carl's son's 1984 drug murder when now—four years later—an old athlete I had coached who was "in the business" called me to confide that three of Cracker's killers had in turn been killed execution-style in separate hits on Detroit's east-side. I immediately called Carl and Ginny and my godson Rick and told them. Rick was Cracker's younger brother.

One of the three executed killers was Richard (Maserati Rick) Carter, who was killed in his hospital bed where he lay wounded, and was buried in a casket with chrome tires and a Mercedes grill—presumably, as *Detroit Free Press* columnist Betty DeRamus later wrote, "so he could drive in hell."

Speaking again of troubled youth—I was sitting in a fast-food restaurant in East Detroit with my long-time companion Eva one day when a group of young men in their late teens came in the door behind me. Without looking around, I said to Eva, "I have a strange feeling that my son Steve has just come in here." She had always wanted to believe that Mrs. Corinna Ditta had lied to me about my having sired her son, but when she met this young man's eyes, she exclaimed softly, "Oh, my God." I told her his name, and she went to him and confirmed under some pretext or other that he was indeed Steve Ditta, but she already *knew* the instant she saw his face.

Steve was nineteen, living on Detroit's east side, getting into street fights and other trouble—so, shortly after that restaurant encounter, his mother sent him to me for counseling with the still-in-force stipulation that I couldn't tell him I was his father. I quickly agreed to her conditions; I was overjoyed just to have some contact with my only son and to try to guide him and help him with his writing skills. I called Dorothy Savage, an old colleague at Macomb Community College, and got him enrolled there—but he didn't *stay* enrolled. Then I got my godson Rick to take him under his wing at Warren Lincoln High, where Rick was a shop teacher, and teach him drafting and robotics, but he stopped going *there*, too.

Eventually, Steve also stopped coming out to my office in Rochester to see me so often, because it was a long way from Detroit, where he lived.

Speaking yet *again* of troubled and troublesome youth—police liaison officer Mark Woliung came to me one day with a tip that I might want to keep a closer eye on my comely daughter Katherine, now sixteen. While making his rounds of the school community, Mark noted that Katherine had begun to entertain one of her classmates—a juvenile delinquent named Bud—in our house on an almost daily basis when her mother and I were at work.

Immediately, I held a confrontational conversation with Katherine—and also with the laconically surly Bud, whom the police suspected had committed several local burglaries, and in fact had badly slashed his arm on the jagged glass of a window he had broken while allegedly committing one of them. (I wasn't able to get Katherine completely away from Bud, though, until she graduated from high school and went to college. Sadly, Bud became deceased soon afterward.)

A year or two after I had gotten my police liaison department assigned to me, I had to win a brief series of semi-friendly battles with Oakland County Sheriff's Captain Gerard Carlin—a tough, by-the-book young commander of Scottish descent. Captain Carlin, who had earned his early spurs as a Detroit cop, had insisted that I review my police officers and sheriff's deputies in an *inspection line* outside my office every morning. I refused; I saw my officers more as *counselors* than as spit-and-polish handcuffers and billy-clubbers. It was as trusted confidantes and respected advocates for the kids that the officers in the Police Liaison Department functioned best—and that was how I had chosen to use them, to the resultant and everlasting benefit of the students in the Rochester Community Schools.

CHAPTER THIRTY-FOUR

THE FAMOUS (AND INFAMOUS) *TELFORD'S TELESCOPE*

"Thanks for letting me use your *Telescope* to teach my grad class.
Students were intrigued by it!"

—*Monte Clute, Avondale Schools Personnel Director*
and the late son of the late Morrel Clute,
Professor of Education, WSU

Telford's Telescope, my annual planning document for the Division of Instruction, always approached the size of a small *book*. In it, I laid out our audacious plans for the review of each subject area and other programs the superintendent and I wanted to institute or revise. Embedded in it throughout were lengthy diatribes on my philosophy of education, including this one, from page 44 of the 1990 edition, which was subtitled *A Planning Paradigm for Discovering the Year 2000*:

> The fact that the institution we call "school" is regarded as an "agent of society" does not absolve it from the responsibility to serve as an agent for progressive reconstruction. The American public school may in a certain sense be an agent of society, but it is far from being an agent of the state—and this is a fundamental difference. It is not American but Fascist political theory that would merge the will of society with the will of the government and would bestow power to the government to determine what citizens should think and say.

> All educators' responsibility to apply free-flowing thought to
> critique educational structures and to offer alternatives within
> them (or to them) after "scanning" the environment and objectively
> seeking input from many sources is essential for long-range institu-
> tional planning, as well as essential to the survival of the democratic
> state itself. It is not the function of the educational leadership
> in any democratic community to be uncritical supporters of the
> status quo. (Some cherished traditions aren't always good or
> right.) Our function is to plan freely, creatively, and courageously
> —not merely for the immediate, but for the long-term. If we do
> not fulfill our charge as educators to shape as well as anticipate
> the future, we become, in the late Sydney Harris' words, "mere
> tools of the state—or prostitutes trading our ideas for a dubious
> security, a precarious status."

I made several shorter politically and pedagogically liberal statements in the planning booklet, some in jest (poking fun at President Reagan and Vice President Quayle), others dead serious (making outraged references to our country's complicity in killing Nicaraguan peasants). I circulated copies of *Telford's Telescope* to all the central office and building administrators in the Division of Instruction, as well as to parents in leadership positions and to my counterparts in other school districts.

I published some of the reactions to the 1988 and 1989 editions in the frontispiece of the 1990 edition. Dr. Norean A. Martin, who was to become a prominent leader in several local school districts, wrote, "This is one of the most articulate, thoughtful pieces I have ever read."

My former Southeastern teaching colleague Betty Vereen, who had become the principal of Detroit Mackenzie High School, wrote, "What a fantastic journey I just experienced! Delightful, sometimes whimsical . . . I was enthralled by the brilliance. Thanks immensely for giving me a mere whiff of the excitement you still possess. I am sharing your entire document with my staff."

Betty, whose letter I cherish to this day, also wrote something in it that I did *not* put in the *Telescope*: "You left all of us Detroiters with many warm memories of a great man headed for greater things. . . . We need all of the John Telfords this world can provide."

Louis Calfin, who had been one of my two critic teachers when I had done my student teaching in Detroit decades before, wrote: "WOW! The whole *Scenario* is *formidable* (as the French would say)!"

Another complimentary respondent was Carol Klenow of the Oakland County Intermediate School District, who wrote, *"Telford's Telescope* is *great*! I am using it in my planning projections for the county."

Farmington's Mike Flanagan—then a member of the Oakland County Association of Assistant Superintendents (I was president) and now the state superintendent, wrote, "The editorials were *great*."

Rochester Schools social worker Nancy Gifford wrote, "Amazing in its comprehensiveness."

Michigan Board of Education member Dorothy Beardmore wrote, "A thought-provoking epistle."

Plymouth counselor Diane Pomish wrote, "How fortunate Rochester is to have such a scholar/philosopher in its administration!"

Rochester teacher John Houghton wrote, "I'm proud to be associated with Rochester and to know we've got *thinking* people running the place."

Capriciously, I added the four following *bogus* commentaries:

> Telford, you liberal lout! Don't you know that we administrators are supposed to do better things than write rambling prognostications in our spare time? During *my* administration, I made better use of most of *my* time—I *slept*! (Ronald Reagan)

> I agree with Reagan—and if we *do* write (or *tape*) anything, we should *erase* it. (Richard Nixon)

> What does "sociological" mean? What does "prognostication" mean? What does *anything* mean? (Dan Quayle)

> Good Lord—the fanatic has written *another* one. How in the world are we ever going to find time to *read* it? (The author's Joint Advisory Councils [my elementary, middle and high school principals and directors])

During those years, I was far too busy with my egalitarian initiatives and building my mighty division to write much poetry other than the tribute to my transitioned father, but in the August 17–23, 1988, edition of the *Metro Times*, this eighteen-year-old poem I had submitted on a whim appeared:

Sixteenth Street, 1970

My spirit in its shallow stream advanced upon Propitium.
Through back alleys,
Dark waters,
Networked black tunnels,
The Low Road flowed upon Propitium.

I sought and found foothold
In the house that was gone.
The sunshine shone again through empty rooms.
(Remember, they had never been her home;
Yet I could hear her footstep on the stairs.)

A wrecker in a painter's whites stood in an upstairs room,
     appraising a wall.
To hold him from his awful task, I cried:
"Would you please paint this scarred and peeling shelf,
Or mend this shattered toy?" "No, man," he said.
"No way."

Earlier, Dr. Greta Barclay Lipson, the elder sister of my main college girl-friend, Gerrie Barclay, had anthologized another poem of mine originally titled *Urban Renewal*. The poem appeared in *Calliope*, one of her children's poetry books published by Good Apple Press under the title *The Quadrangle: Sixteenth Street, Marquette, Linwood, and McGraw—A Sonnet of the City*. Its first lines were,

Great fragments of gray sidewalk, splintered wood,
Sharp shards of glass, and treestumps on the ground
Are monuments to memories that once stood
Where now rats, rustling through the weeds, abound.

Its last lines were:

How could they dare destroy my childhood's seeds—
The block "renewed" for only rats and weeds?

Revisiting those two poems in 1988 made me realize how much I truly missed Detroit and the bygone days with my Scottish and Danish families on Twelfth and Sixteenth Streets.

In *Sixteenth Street, 1970*, the "Low Road" was the supernatural road taken by spirits in the Scots song "Loch Lomond" ("You take the high road, and I'll take the low road, and I'll be in Scotland before ye—forr me an' me trrue love will neverr meet again, on the bonny, bonny banks of . . ."). The "her" in the second stanza could have been any number of the young ladies in my life then or much earlier. When I wrote the poem in the summer of 1970, I had been heavily involved with a Denby alumna named Katie. She ultimately moved to Colorado and married a retired World War II navy commander (her third husband). Colorado Katie lives there with him to this day.

But getting back to 1988: In December of that year, a student editor named Bryce Sandler was planning to run a huge picture of a Ku Klux Klan cross-burning that was spread across the front page of the proofs of one of Rochester's high school newspapers. The article was anti-Klan, but the photo was misleading. Secondary General Director Bill Waun and the school's principal, Richard Ickes, asked me what they should do. Even though censoring a student journalist went against my grain, I told them not to allow the picture to run. I also told them to let young Sandler know that the order came from me.

Bryce Sandler appealed my order to the Oakland County American Civil Liberties Union (ACLU) and tipped off the local newspapers. He hoped the ACLU would force me to rescind my decision and the publicity would make me back down. When reporters contacted me, I told them I was prepared to wage war with the ACLU, if necessary. (Ironically, I would eventually be receiving some badly-needed personal support from that venerable organization; also ironically, I would later serve as an ACLU board member.)

The ACLU decided not to take the case.

Meanwhile, another rights-related problem had surfaced in Rochester. In compliance with the constitutional separation of church and state, and to assuage the concerns of our few vastly outnumbered Jewish parents who had appealed to me, I had ordered the principals to remove all the Christmas manger scenes they had in their buildings. I endured a lot of flack from Christian parents for that, since a few craven elementary school principals disloyally blamed the order not on the Constitution, but on the Jewish parents—and even more specifically, on *me*. They told their protesting parents, "Hey, I don't like this any better than you do—I'm just following Telford's orders . . ."

One of those Christian parents implied that I was a "closet Jew"; another started a rumor that I was a *practicing* one.

This proved to be only the beginning of my prolonged battles with the bigots. They would eventually get their hands on copies of *Telford's Telescope* and deliberately twist many of my prognosticative planning statements in it into false and nefarious misinterpretations, in repeated attempts to get me fired.

CHAPTER THIRTY-FIVE

DEBUT OF THE DIVISIONAL OPERATIONS

"Why in the world would you want to go back and work with those niggers?"

—*A Rochester administrator*

Throughout the mid- to late 1980s, I aggressively recruited and hired black teachers and administrators from Detroit. The administrators included some of my former colleagues and a former captain of the Wayne State basketball team named Gene Seaborn, who played there for Bob Samaras, my former colleague at Pershing. They also included Dr. Eleanor White (who retired recently as Rochester's director of special education), and Carol Mims, a consultant with Wayne County's Intermediate School District (now Carol Mims-Foster, who ultimately became a principal in Las Vegas). I installed them in principalships and directorships. As yet, no other suburban school executive had dared to do that.

I also applied for vacant superintendent and assistant superintendent jobs back home in Detroit, as well as for the superintendencies in heavily black Oak Park and Southfield.

Rochester board member Julie Zboril advised me of a conversation she had had at a board workshop in Lansing with a female board member from Southfield (or maybe Oak Park—I can't remember which). This board member had told Julie, "Oh, I'd never vote for *Telford*—I hear he's *uncontrollable*." I found this to be a curious adjective for a board member to use to describe an applicant for the top job in her district.

A little earlier, a Rochester administrator—a man unfortunately in a leadership position that involved the education of *children*—inquired of me incredulously, "Why in the world would you want to go back and work with those niggers?" I reminded him that Rochester had some 250 African-American students for whose good and fair education we were legally and morally responsible. "Would you call *them* 'niggers,' too?" I asked him. "Perhaps you would like me to invite them and all of their parents together to the auditorium at one of our high schools so you can tell them what you think of them. No? Didn't think so—but if that's how you really feel, you should have the guts to tell them so."

After a further pointed discussion with this administrator that left him wondering whether he was going to keep his job, I decided that the principals, assistant principals, and some other administrators—prominently including *this* chap—definitely needed some multicultural "sensitizing." I mandated an overnight workshop at the Kingsley Inn in Birmingham and brought in high-powered consultants Monifa Jumanne of Oakland University (who, like me, was also a Rochester parent), Orion Worden, a former multicultural advisor to Vice President Hubert Humphrey, and Dick Lobenthal, the Midwest director of the Anti-Defamation League.

Years later, Lobenthal was to pronounce me the state's "foremost Caucasian casualty of the civil-rights movement." Actually, though, since I was then and am now still *alive* (at this writing), that appellation more fittingly belongs on the headstone of the martyred Viola Liuzzo.

Some of my administrators who most needed the workshop attended it grudgingly—and a few threatened to grieve me for the *overnight* mandate, but again thought better of it.

I also co-hosted and spoke before a group of administrators from sixteen surrounding school districts on the subject of multiculturalism. My co-host was Dr. Gerald Pine, the dean of Oakland University's College of Education. I accepted invitations to speak on the same topic in Romulus and Westland— racially-troubled districts that were farther away.

My reputation in Rochester for what was beginning to be seen by many as *radicalism* was accordingly spreading slowly but inexorably throughout the community and beyond. Earlier, I had written a column in the *Detroit Free Press* headlined "Ghettos, enclaves hinder equality" attacking racial segregation and affirming the need for diversity in order for America to win in the global market-place and in the morally murky waters of geopolitics.

The column began:

> As a member of the U.S. track team, I raced in Europe on victori-ous sprint relay teams, passing the baton to American athletes of African ancestry. We were not black or white—we were red, white, and blue.

I concluded that column with these words:

> We have allowed our great urban centers to become a kind of Casbah-style residential, economic, and educational Third World. . . . Like runners in a relay race, we need each other on the American team more desperately now than ever if our nation is to survive as a republic. Blacks need whites; whites need blacks; suburbanites need urbanites; Arab-Americans need Jewish-Americans; white-collar workers need blue-collar workers; Hispanics need Asian-Americans. . . . Americans will always need their diverse—and diversely talented—countrymen and women as co-workers, neighbors, classmates, friends, and family. Let's not wait any longer. Today, let us all join hands and reaffirm our red, white and blue commitment to realize a shared American dream.

Due probably to some other aggressive egalitarian proposals I had made in it, that 1987 column hadn't sat well with a few board members and a substantial segment of local readers of that newspaper. I had also made statements in the Rochester edition of the *Observer/Eccentric* newspapers and the *Rochester Clarion* indicating my intent to institute a more fully multicultural approach to the social studies and language arts curricula.

A local paper ran this headline: "Telford's dream is to foster racial understanding."

Rochester-based skinheads sprayed gunfire into my house in the middle of the night. They were caught and sent to prison. One of them died shortly after. Another—a nineteen-year-old Rochester special education student—I saved from imprisonment by writing a letter and testifying for him.

I began getting death threats and an assortment of friendly telephone calls and letters calling me "nigger-lover," "Jew-lover," "Jew," "Commie," etc., warning me to get out of Rochester. One of them called me a "black white man." I took that as a compliment, since many of my lifelong friends are black, and most of the best sprinters I had faced in national and international competition were black as well.

One letter, which was decorated with a crudely drawn American flag and signed "The Sons of Liberty," asked, "Do you have a daughter?" That was a letter I didn't like at all, and I didn't let my wife see it.

I made copies of the letters (two had swastikas on them) and turned the originals over to the Rochester Police Department via Mark Woliung, who had assumed the unofficial leadership of my on-staff police officers.

In a January 9, 1989, memo recounting the gunfire and the phone calls—including a telephoned death threat at approximately 6:30 a.m. on Christmas Day—I advised the superintendent that "I wouldn't be surprised were I to continue to be the subject of this kind of attention as my activities *progress* in this arena—and they *definitely will*."

The Christmas caller, who sounded like a white male of about forty, continued to call every Christmas morning at the same time for several years with the same threat—"Enjoy your Christmas, TELL-ford, because it will be your last one." He always said my name like that—TELL-ford.

One year, I told him I didn't think that Mary and Joseph and the baby Jesus would like what he was doing. The next year, he didn't call. When he called again the year after that, I told him, "Hey, you didn't *call* me last year. I felt *neglected*." He never called again.

Excrement was placed in my mailbox outside my house more than once. (One time there were three little turds in the mailbox that had been thoughtfully encased in a plastic baggie. No note; just three little silently expressive turds.)

I had a secret *admirer*, though, too. I got three notes in my mailbox in a feminine hand, one quoting the familiar Theodore Roosevelt quote about the "man in the arena," and sometimes leaving presents—including a tie, and a matching shirt that fit me perfectly. I wore the shirt and tie to meetings sometimes—and once a lady complimented me on the matching shirt and tie. I never found out who this secret admirer was, but I had my suspicions.

I also was obliged to confront two large and vocal elementary-school parent groups demanding to know why I was hiring *outside* (translation: *black*) principals when we had so many perfectly fine assistant principals right here in good old Rochester.

In the midst of all this, I kept my "eyes on the prize": I made sure that every subject area and support program got cyclically reviewed and revised. Dr. Joe Messana, the Oakland County Intermediate School District's assistant superintendent for instruction, declared, "Rochester's Division of Instruction under Dr. Schultz and Dr. Telford continues to be one of the most productive, cutting-edge instructional divisions in the county."

I began the cycle again. I paid special attention to the social studies curriculum, ensuring that it was to be taught on a multicultural level and that it became duly *globalized*. It featured an escalated emphasis on the American civil rights movement and on Africa, Asia, and the Middle East—where our country was unfortunately about to go to war in the Persian Gulf to protect the oil fields that were (and are) so essential to gluttonous multinational corporations' ongoing accumulation of inordinate wealth, as well as to ensuring our country's continued dependence on foreign petroleum and the acceleration of global warming.

I also ensured that every administrator was to be evaluated annually, and that tenured teachers were to be evaluated bi-annually. I instructed research director Jerry Freeman to draw up a supplementary model for teachers to evaluate their administrators (anonymously) as well, and for administrators to evaluate their supervisors—including me. I encountered fierce administrator resistance on this one, but I stuck to my guns. As a teacher, I had always arranged to have my students evaluate *me* anonymously, and one day I would do so again. Fair's *fair*, right?

During the course of these reviews and revisions, the Board of Education kept end-running the superintendent and giving me and my division little nit-picking assignments that were important to them individually but sometimes bore little significance for what the Rochester Community Schools purported to be about. The board also complained to the superintendent that I had too many of what I termed my "Divisional Operations" (D.O.'s).

These D.O.'s included one of my particular favorite projects that was beginning to make them uneasy—my Divisional Operation *Equity*. This particular D.O. was designed to "explore and develop means to foster democratic values and cross-cultural understanding." Operation *Equity* included recruiting minority administrative and instructional staff, developing lessons to foster interethnic understanding for students, and making staff sensitive to such issues. In my hiring of African-American administrators, I wasn't only trying to help black educators rise in the profession, although that was a big part of my motivation. I also wanted the thousands of white Rochester Community Schools students to see blacks in leadership positions, because that's the real world—in which Rochester is just a small, sheltered enclave on this imperiled, precious planet.

Operation *Equity* paved the way for our English as a Second Language program, our Russian-American student exchange program, our Special Education Full Inclusion Program, and many others. It also paved the way for its spin-off, "Operation *Holiday*," which was designed to limit the teaching about Christianity and augment it with exposure to other religions.

I usually undertook a whopping eighty or ninety Divisional Operations per year, most of them addressing straight academics or our co-curricular programs.

When I, in turn, complained to the superintendent about what I regarded as the board's meddling, he cautioned me that we had to keep them happy. So to fend off their concerns, and also to make them recognize the challengingly wide scope of my huge, hard-working division's commitments, I began to list in my D.O.'s every single divisional undertaking, whether large or small—and I, of course, included every extra task the board laid on me or my staff. I would also give these listed extraneous assignments the same kind of relevant names following the word "Operation" that I had given the others, e.g., "Operation *E.S.P.* (effective school planning), "Operation *Recreation*," etc. (In addition to my myriad divisional duties and enterprises, I was chairing a land-utilization planning committee that had the directors of the Rochester Community Schools' several local municipalities' recreation departments serving on it, along with members of the community who in some instances had economic interests in the outcome.)

Inevitably, these inclusions brought the total number of Divisional Operations to well over a *hundred*. Each of the D.O.'s had an action plan, complete with the *who*, *what*, *when*, and *how*—and at the bi-annual board retreats, I would deliberately subject the board to infinitely long oral reports of the progress of each D.O. I wouldn't just *read* the board my report, either—I would pause often between my typewritten sentences to *comment at length* on each D.O., as well.

Here is an excerpt from one of those *intentionally* interminable several-hundred-page reports that I inflicted upon the board:

XXXVII. <u>Tech</u>. "Develop Educational Technogy, K-12." The role
of <u>technology</u> in the instructional process has now been revisited
from the perspective of the legislated need to restructure the
district's budget—which legislation, unfortunately, I had predicted
all too accurately in Item P-15 on page 20 of the <u>Telescope</u> last
year, where I said there would be increased state attention directed
toward out-of-formula recapture. (By the way, the "P" stands
for Politics—the political "driver." [*I have a scrawled note to myself
here to add something at this point in the report in considerable detail,
but what I must have added has been lost to my memory in the twenty
years intervening.*] Although technology does call for a considerable
outlay of capital over the years to come, we need to remember
that there is much evidence to support the fact that unless we
integrate technology into the classroom, our students will not be
sufficiently prepared for the twenty-first century. Our instructional
technology goals are congruent with our proposed instructional
goals for the year 2000 in KRA's [*Key Result Areas*] #1 and 8 [*as
referenced in the Telford's Telescope booklet, KRA #1 was Student Learning and Growth; KRA #8 was Instructional Programs and Services*].
Miss Anthony [*Instructional Technology Director Deborah Anthony*]
and her committee Tri-Chairs will be meeting with some concerned
citizens, with Janet Van Damm from Oakland Schools, with the
General Directors, with me, and with others to help the committee
prepare to give us a dollar-specific and time-specific long-range
plan. . . . The issue I'm not sure we've really fully addressed
here . . . is the possibility that we may not be able to maintain
the current level of <u>human</u> investment in education and also
acquire the <u>technology</u> necessary to prepare our young people
for the century to come. I personally fear that in our snowballing
transition to an inevitably higher investment in technology, fewer
revenues will remain for essential <u>staff</u> resources. . . .

I continued interminably in the same vein on that Divisional Operation
Thirty-Seven, and I then embarked on a similarly interminable oral report regarding Divisional Operation Thirty-Eight—and thence droning on interminably
to Divisional Operation One *Hundred* and Thirty-Eight. . . .

Now the board complained even *more* about how numerous my D.O.'s had
become, so the superintendent came to me and said we had better eliminate

some of them. This was the moment I had been waiting for. I took out the list and cheerily invited him to eliminate anything he chose. I would have been *particularly* happy to be let off the hook regarding the land-utilization committee I was chairing. I knew, of course, that none of the D.O.'s would or could be eliminated—but at least now the board had a far clearer picture of the incredibly wide extent of my division's assumed tasks and responsibilities.

After Dr. Schultz had painstakingly perused all of my Divisional Operations, he said, "John, there's *nothing* here we can eliminate! They're all either essential to our programs, or else they're pet projects of board members."

"Indeed," I responded. The list remained intact.

CHAPTER THIRTY-SIX

BIGOTS BEHIND
EVERY *BUSH*
(NO PUN INTENDED)

"No bona-fide educator's time on earth is ever truly his own."

—Introductory sentence in
Telford's Telescope, *third edition*

I wrote that third edition of *Telford's Telescope* in the summer and fall of 1989 on my own time—the little time I had to myself, given the lunatic pace of my commitment of professional time, which according to a two-month time-study record I kept, averaged 72 hours per week in the office and performing other work-related tasks at home.

The sentence that <u>*followed*</u> that *introductory sentence* in the *Telescope* was:

> Since there's never any way to predict with certainty how long God or the Fates will let us continue, we must try to teach all that we can, through any medium that we can, <u>for as long as we're here</u>, in the hope that those we have taught will in turn teach—and thus <u>eternalize</u> the process.

I again expressed many other well-informed personal opinions and the similarly well-informed opinions of colleagues in that January 1990 publication, which "telescoped" the "departments" (DEPTS)—the demographic, economic, political, technological, and sociological agents that I believed would drive the future of education in Rochester and *beyond* Rochester in the twenty-first century. In doing this, I employed techniques called "Force Field" and "The Delphi Process" (a process named for the Greek oracles who resided in the ancient city of Delphi).

Delphi was a procedure in which I sought opinions of knowledgeable individuals from inside and outside the district and in some instances from outside the state. The out-of-state contributors included the respected futurist Hubert Locke, a professor at the University of Washington.

Some of those *personal opinions of my own* that I expressed in my *Telescope* very nearly shortened the length of time that *I* personally was <u>here</u> myself—the "here" being *here* surviving in my *job* in *Rochester*!

The following are samples of excerpts from the *Telescope*:

> The steel and oil and munitions magnates and their lobbyists and Congressional supporters, and the greedy Wall Street brokers would all have apoplexy if the American government diverted billions of dollars toward schools and away from unneeded and nonfunctional weapons systems in order to educate American children to compete in the twenty-first century. (When asked to explain the discredited "Star Wars," President Reagan responded with one of his characteristic classics: "My concept of the strategic defense system has been one that if and when we achieve what our goal is, and that is a weapon that is effective against incoming missiles, not a weapon system that is effective against incoming weapons, missiles." [*Pointing out the labyrinthine lingual short-comings of a Republican icon like Ronald Reagan wasn't an entirely wise move on my part, given that the overwhelming majority of my Rochester and Rochester Hills constituents were Republicans—but what an uncannily fuzzy linguistic precursor of Dan Quayle and George W. Bush he was! We can all be grateful that America has finally discovered another Robert F. Kennedy in the articulate person of Barack H. Obama.*] (Political Driver Statement Number One ["P-1"], page 16)

> Even though President George [*H. W.*] Bush . . . [*has*] declared war on drugs to the tune of a $7 billion price tag, drugs cannot be wiped out by any means that are available in a democratic government. The failure of . . . Prohibition nearly sixty [*now seventy-nine*] years ago hasn't taught us a single thing. By allowing and controlling the distribution of . . . illegal drugs, the government would save billions of tax dollars that could then be used to pay for rehabilitative and preventive programs. (Economic Driver Statement "E-7.1," page 12)

The United States presently has an annual $50 billion trade deficit with Japan [*sound familiar now, in 2009?*]. Chrysler Chairman Lee Iacocca recently complained that Japan's market is closed to Chrysler products, and this has forced plant closings in his company. [*Sound familiar today?*] (When Chrysler closed an operation in Wisconsin, it announced it was "initiating a <u>career alternative enhancement program</u>." Over 5,000 employees were "<u>enhanced</u>" out of jobs.) The corporate slogan by the year 2000 is unquestionably going to be, "Globalize or lose out." [*Again, sound familiar?*] (Economic Driver Statement "E-9.2," page 14)

The late Ayatollah Khomeini of Iran had [*the*] view that religion <u>is</u> education and religion <u>is</u> government. Our Bill of Rights, which represents abstract ideals that are oftentimes difficult to express as concrete realities, was added to our Constitution because certain rights cannot be entrusted to a hoped-for fair-mindedness in ethnocentric residential enclaves with very few minority-group members, and to the majoritarian impulses of governmental and other public officials. The <u>answer</u> to this problem is <u>better education</u> to instill an understanding of <u>what makes America unique</u>. Also, <u>celebrating</u> cultural differences rather than "tolerating" them will teach a love of diversity and validate minority feelings of dignity and self-worth; e.g., calendars representing all faiths, varied celebrations of holidays, international festivals, etc. ("P [Politics] - 19," page 21)

The Rochester Community Schools will continue aggressively to implement our Divisional Operation <u>Equity</u>. . . . Not only must American schools <u>teach</u> democracy <u>in-depth</u>—they must process and practice it. ("D [Demographics] - 2.1," page 3)

Multi-culture and secularism must be priority promulgations for educators, but they will face resistance from many <u>xenophobic, isolationist-minded residents</u> of white, Anglo-Saxon, Christian-majority communities. ("D-2," page 3)

The mounting hysteria of those "many xenophobic, isolationist-minded residents" of Rochester over these and other passages from my purple publication was nearing the boiling point. Resident parents feared that I was going to continue to flood the district with black teachers, principals, and directors.

They also feared that I intended to have the entire Rochester teaching staff use what these parents saw as my "Socialistic/Communistic" *Telescope* in every classroom in all twenty of the district's schools.

When hundreds of Rochester residents—plus some auxiliary bigots from beyond Rochester—descended on a board meeting demanding my dismissal, the frightened board banned the further circulation of *Telford's Telescope*.

At that meeting, and in numerous subsequent statements to newspaper reporters, I railed repeatedly at these residents, calling them "racists" and "bigots"—and got castigated repeatedly by the nervous board for using those words. I would then heatedly and repeatedly retort, "If it *looks* like a duck and *walks* like a duck and *talks* like a duck. . . ."

The superintendent tried to defend me, as did two of the seven board members—Democrat Keith Wittenstrom and Republican Bill Wagner. An article in the *Oakland Press* was headlined "Superintendent, Assistant targeted for firing." However, in the article, it said that I alone was the true target. Another headline read, "Two board members [Wittenstrom & Wagner] targets for recall for supporting Telford."

Another headline read, "Telford comes out fighting—recall group incensed!" Actually, by then I had begun trying to make peace and pour sand on the fire, which now was raging completely out of control.

Finally, a majority of the increasingly exasperated board decided to put a gag order on me.

I promptly called a press conference.

Then I went on former Detroit Tiger Denny McClain's radio show and fielded questions from detractors (and from supporters—I did have a few, and now their numbers were beginning to grow). The supporters included Abe Saal, a teacher at Dickenson Elementary School in the growingly multicultural Detroit enclave of Hamtramck, Michigan, who wrote to say he had heard me on the McClain show and admired my courage. Saal requested a copy of the *Telescope*, which my able secretary, Diane Stuart, sent him.

I also hosted a taped interview with TV Channel 2 in my office, and the cover of the third edition of *Telford's Telescope*—featuring a caricature of me peering into a telescope—aired in all its colorful light blue and maroon glory on the evening and late-night news. (The cartoon was penned by the talented Tim Brooks, our art coordinator.)

Neil Munro, the conservative but fair-minded editor of the *Oakland Press*, interviewed me twice on his TV show, *Oakland Perspective*. Neil titled the newspaper's ads for the show, "Dr. John Telford: On the *Benefits* of Controversy" [italics mine]—but I was finding the controversy that was exploding all over the place to be decidedly less *beneficial* by the minute, to me or to anyone—and particularly to the school district and the thousands of kids in it whom I served.

In a piece headlined "Protect the visionary or lose our freedoms" in the *Observer/Eccentric* newspapers, editor Steve Barnaby wrote:

> John Telford is rather unusual for a central office bureaucrat. Frankly, most school administrators are something less than courageous when it comes to speaking out on social issues. . . . Telford is an educator in the traditional sense. He wants individuals to think, explore, question. Telford's critics contain the echoes of a dangerous time in our history, when professors were black-balled and actors banished from the screen and stage, when publishers turned their backs on writers and government officials were accused of treason. We can't afford to go through that again. Innovators like John Telford need to be nurtured, protected from the fear-mongers. . . .

A piece in the *Rochester Clarion* by veteran columnist Charles Ferry went:

> The funny thing about all of this is that John Telford, who is currently Everyman's whipping boy, has rendered a great service to the community. He has got Everyman thinking, which is exactly what he set out to do. . . . John Telford, educator. A man who loves his country and everyone in it. Honor him; don't toss him to the wolves.

Reporter Tim Hart's article in the *Oakland Press* began:

> A group of parents [*who are trying to recall board members*] say their true target is . . . assistant superintendent John Telford. The former WSU track star turned curriculum administrator has rocked the boat once too often, parents say. Now they want him to go.

In that article, Hart quoted me:

"We're going to get burned sometimes by the very torch we carry. It comes with the territory. Educators can't hide in the weeds from controversial issues. That's not what an educator is supposed to be."

Other newspapermen or published letter-writers wrote:

Telford is an extremely rare resource among public officials—one who has consistently shown the courage to stand by his convictions regardless of the risks. (from Rochester resident Frank Mike)

Media attention has made Telford the center of controversy. His critics are calling for his job. All the while, Telford has refused to change. This reporter was impressed with Telford's honesty and guts throughout the ordeal. (Editor Ivan Helfman of the *Rochester Hills Reminder*, who was ordinarily my harsh critic)

Colorado Springs School District 11 Superintendent Ken Burnley, my old friend whom I had coached in track and I was later to work for in Detroit, wrote:

Dear John,
    Bill Banach [*the Macomb County Intermediate School District superintendent*] told me what is happening to you. [*Dr. Banach was consulting with Dr. Burnley at the time.*] Wow!! Hang tough—this too shall pass. Thinking of you, Ken

A Detroit teacher named Rhoda, an old flame from my college days, had been one of Gerrie Barclay's rivals for my attentions. (Ger had jealously dubbed her "Tobacco Rhoda" after the racy Erskine Caldwell novel *Tobacco Road*, although Rhoda didn't smoke.)
    Rhoda wrote me:

Today was the first I had ever heard about your courageous stand. I was listening to a Richard Lobenthal broadcast on WDET, and even before he said your name, I knew it was you. I admire what you have done. I just wish we could have kept close so I could have shared your hard times and dark moments.

Oakland University Professor Monifa Jumanne wrote,

> Dear John,
>   History will undoubtedly be biased in measuring the full
> impact of your work, but there are those of us who already know—
> thanks. As we said in the Sixties, "a lanta continua . . ."

College instructors in and beyond the Detroit metropolitan area wrote to tell me they were using both the current edition and the two earlier editions of the *Telescope* in their classrooms.

The third edition was beginning to get national attention and reaction— not all of it complimentary. Conservative North Carolina columnist D. L. Cuddy reviled me and my *Telescope* in an October 27, 1990, piece that ran in the *Detroit News* and elsewhere, and other writers vilified me in the *News*. Right-wing commentators, including Rush Limbaugh, took potshots at the *Telescope* over the air.

The media hadn't paid me this much attention since my maverick MCCC days—or even since the exhilarating days of my youth when I was a world-ranked runner. I have to confess that while part of me was incensed by the ignorance and unfairness of the ravenous bigots who were screaming for my scalp, another part of me was relishing all the furor I was causing.

CHAPTER THIRTY-SEVEN

A LION SURROUNDED BY JACKALS; A SKULL & CROSSBONES

"Can't anyone control that crazy assistant superintendent in the Rochester Schools?"

—*From an ironic letter in the* Detroit Free Press

I realized that I had to play up every syllable of the lavish publicity that was surrounding me for all it was worth. I knew if I didn't keep on getting what was happening to me into the light of day, the board had the votes to fire me, and it would. The board president was already putting pressure on the superintendent to do just that.

I was beginning to get very angry at people like Rush Limbaugh, D. L. Cuddy, and others who were attacking me and threatening my career. However, I again have to admit that I was also beginning to experience a fatalistic feeling of what can best be described as a paradoxical kind of *morbid revelry* in my new notoriety. I felt like a fox chased by hounds—and I loved eluding them, thumbing my nose at them meanwhile. In a letter to the *Free Press* editor, a supporter likened me to "a lone lion surrounded by jackals."

I rather fancied that—a *lion* instead of a fox. The Lion of Rochester! Roarrrr!

I had acquired an eighteenth-century-style tri-cornered patriot's hat in historic Williamsburg, Virginia, and I began sporting this democratically symbolic topper while needling my undemocratic detractors in long-winded speeches in which I instructively quoted some revolutionary words of our Founding Fathers. I did this interminably—with resonant *relish*—at board meetings, PTA meetings, and other heavily-attended gatherings throughout the district. (It's a wonder I wasn't tarred and feathered.)

Wayne State University philosophy professor Frank McBride, a former national-class miler (fifth in the 1952 Olympic Trials 1,500 meters) who had coached me in my semi-successful 1960 track comeback, wrote in another letter to the *Free Press*, "The real reason for the move to oust the assistant super-intendent is not politics but prejudice."

Eugene Paasinen, a Taylor, Michigan social studies teacher who had gone by the name Gene Pash in college, wrote to the *Free Press*:

> While I was a member of the Wayne State track team in the mid-'50s, it was my privilege to watch this man as a team leader, motivator, and nationally-ranked quarter-miler. When he spoke, our team listened. If we listened carefully, we got direction and purpose. He was like a second coach. We won because *he* was a winner. Today, John Telford is the same person. He can't run a 46-second quarter, but he's still on the *right track*.

I called Dr. McBride and thanked him. I looked Gene Pash up and thanked him, too.

To big Gene I also said, "Hey, what do you mean I can't run a 46-second quarter? Bring your stopwatch and come on out and clock me! In fact, I'll *race* you—let's run one together."

That was a spurious challenge, though: Gene had been a shot putter and discus thrower, and in shape he had weighed 225 pounds. I do recall, however, that in 1956, he did miraculously perambulate a 60-second quarter on the second leg of a dual meet relay race in Cleveland against Western Reserve University which we felt we could win going away, so we could get Gene some points toward his varsity letter. The other three runners—who included yours truly—could all break 49 seconds, and I could break 47. Even with Gene's one-minute leg, we still cruised to a clocking of about 3:25—fast enough to win. (In those days of now-archaic dirt tracks, 50 seconds flat had been regarded as the "sound barrier" for most quarter-milers.)

Another published *Free Press* letter was written by a resident of my former Huntington Woods neighborhood. She inquired ironically, "Can't anyone control that crazy assistant superintendent in the Rochester schools? The next thing you know, they'll all want to teach brotherhood and other such radical stuff out there. Seriously, though, I think John Telford should get the Nobel Peace Prize, and I hope the few board members who support him get supported by the voters."

The board was beginning to feel the pressure of this mounting accumulation of support for me, as well as getting multiple requests to have a copy of the *Telescope* (which was public information under the Freedom of Information Act). The board therefore removed the ban on the circulation of the *Telescope* with an attached letter distancing themselves from it. With sarcastic glee, I lost no time dubbing this attachment the "Skull & Crossbones"—*poison* within; *beware, beware*!

My old Southeastern student and runner john powell, who I have already mentioned uses no capital letters in his name, was now the ACLU's national legal director. He had Michigan's legal director, Howard Simon, call the president of the Rochester school board and suggest to him that if my contract wasn't renewed, the national office of the ACLU would support a lawsuit if I chose to sue.

Meanwhile, a small group of black parents headed by Professor Monifa Jumanne put their support behind me. Another even smaller group of Jewish parents headed by Dena Scher and her rabbi, Arnie Sleutelberg of Congregation *Shir Tikvah* in nearby Troy (Rochester had no synagogue) had united with a large and growing group of liberal white Christian parents calling themselves UPWARD—United Parents Working to Advance Rochester's Diversity.

UPWARD's organizers were Irene Connors (who later became a school board member and whose husband Bill was in the Rochester Rotary Club with me), parent Helen Sergott, Cecilia "Ceil" Mrock (president of the district's PTA Council), Darlene Janulis (whom I subsequently helped get elected to the school board), and Julie Zboril, who was already *on* the board and was dating my cousin, Jeff Telford.

Together, they convinced the entire board—including Roger Conley, the board president—that to renew my three-year contract was the wise and fair thing to do.

Soon, a local headline read, "Telford to stay on—Board unanimously renews contract!"

On his weekly radio show, Anti-Defamation League Director Dick Lobenthal, who had supported me in previous broadcasts, again decried the effort to fire me, proclaiming me "the administrator who is universally recognized as *THE* champion of minority rights and democratic and multicultural values." Later, Lobenthal told the *Detroit Free Press*, "Telford's only real problem is that Rochester is very resistant to minorities." He praised the board for renewing my contract.

With that signed three-year contract (including a salary raise) now in my pocket, I wrote this excerpted open letter to the community. The local *Observer/Eccentric* ran it in full on its editorial page under the headline "Telford: 'Declare peace'":

> Given the wide media coverage *Telford's Telescope* received . . ., it was perhaps inevitable that . . . people would misinterpret some firsthand or secondhand references from or to the Telescope. I want it known that:
>
> I am opposed to school-aged youngsters using intoxicative substances, legal or illegal;
>
> I am not—nor have I ever been—an affiliate of any doctrinaire organization such as the Secular Humanists;
>
> The Telescope is not being used as a text in Rochester Community Schools.

[Those were three things my attackers had accused me of thinking, being, or doing.]

> . . . My commitment to multiculturalism is intended to be inclusive of all cultures, and certainly not exclusive of the Western culture, which has played a vital role in shaping our country's institutions—including our democratic institution, which we must all be willing, if necessary, to defend with our lives. We need to remain vigilant for those in our community and beyond our community who through ignorance or design would subvert that institution. [*Too bad George W. Bush didn't read this a decade later, but I doubt it would have made any difference to his rapacious, mendacious, murderous handlers if he had.*]
>
> In recent years, aspects of my Operation Equity that have fostered interracial understanding and minority recruitment have caused both overt and covert hostilities . . . to be directed at me and

even at my family. Recently the founder of SOS (Save Our Schools) —the Board recall group—received similar threats, and I find this reprehensible. [*I had un-tactfully suggested earlier, in the heat of battle, that SOS should instead stand for "Shit On a Shingle."*]

SOS and the UPWARD and Rochester Concerned Parents groups that have supported me must now all come together and establish common ground, because divisiveness among this community's adult leaders is very bad for our children.

Wisdom is strength, and we have all become wiser through experiencing this crisis. It is time now for all of us to declare peace and get back to the cooperative and crucial business of educating our children for a multicultural, interdependent, and changing world.

The recall petitions were withdrawn. Still, my troubles—and those of the district—were far from over.

CHAPTER THIRTY-EIGHT

UNHAPPY HOLIDAYS, TRIBES, AND THE MAGIC CIRCLE

"Congratulations on the renewal of your contract. I know this
has been a trying time, but you and your work are appreciated."

—*Note from john a. powell, then the national
legal director of the American Civil Liberties Union*

Just before the furor surrounding the *Telescope* had arisen, Rochester Adams High School principal James Steeby had taken a central office position in the Auburn Hills district. I recruited Dr. Betty Hines, a highly-regarded educator in Detroit, to take his place. Throughout the previous decade, Dr. Hines had been the principal of Detroit Southwestern High School, where she had won myriad awards. She had also been a proficient and productive rookie teacher on my staff at Butzel Junior High School in 1967 and 1968.

Dr. Hines interviewed beautifully for the Adams job, was chosen, and announced to her Southwestern staff that she would be leaving to come to Rochester. She was now poised to become the first African-American principal of a large, prestigious, productive, and overwhelmingly *white* high school in the country!

Unfortunately for Dr. Hines, as well as for Adams High School and the Rochester Community Schools (but *fortunately* for Southwestern students), it was during that same week that the hundreds of raucous bigots had descended on the board meeting to try to get me fired for my multiple multicultural initiatives and my forays into *eff*ective *aff*ective education. Under resultant pressure from frightened board members, the superintendent offered Dr. Hines a salary at a figure which was far less than she was making in Detroit, so—unsurprisingly—she turned down the job.

It was partially for this reason that my general director of secondary education, Dr. Bill Waun, one year my junior at fifty-three who had become my close friend and "right hand," decided to retire. I tried to recruit Dr. Hines again—this time for Dr. Waun's job—but she understandably declined to interview.

I also took another fruitless shot at landing my sagacious buddy George Blaney or the gifted Gary Faber. I then recruited Mrs. Beverly Stone—another highly-regarded member of a minority group (she was Jewish) and an accomplished middle school principal in Bloomfield Hills—to replace him. Dr. Waun had once been a high school principal in the same district, and he recommended her highly, as did Bloomfield Hills assistant superintendents Gary Doyle, who had been one of my Rochester principals, and Dan White, who had administrated with me in Plymouth/Canton.

Thus, it was that I had unhappily begun the 1990–91 school year without secondary schools general director Bill Waun, my trusty right hand—but the cacophonous series of events that followed left me little time to miss him.

Dr. Schultz and I decided that the district's existing holiday policy (which along with *me*, was still under attack by several reactionary forces within the community) needed to be reviewed and possibly revised. We agreed that a committee should be appointed at once to review it. Such an explosive instructional issue would ordinarily have necessitated my chairing a committee like this personally, but since these "reactionary forces" perceived me to be a major part of their problem with the existing policy, the superintendent and I decided that after appointing the committee and giving it its charge to review and perhaps re-write the policy, neither of us would chair it, nor would we serve on it.

Diane Iras (now Diane *Midgeley*), our district's communications coordinator and spokesperson, told *Rochester Hills Reminder* reporter Pat Driscoll that the need for such a committee "grew out of Operation *Equity*, a program initiated by Telford." Diane was quoted further: "The purpose of Operation *Equity* was to 'foster democratic values and multicultural understanding,' according to the 1990 *Telford's Telescope*." She added that my Divisional Operation *Equity* had also led to a pilot program in multicultural education at Brewster Elementary School in Rochester Hills, and to the overnight retreat the previous April at the Kingsley Inn which "Dr. Telford designed to 'sensitize' our administrators to multiculturalism."

Acting upon my recommendation, Dr. Schultz appointed testing and research director Jerry Freeman to chair the holiday committee. At my darkest hour when even my most progressive staff had been scared to make a stand with me, Jerry had riskily dared to send me an e-mail entitled "Courage and Conviction" in which he told me, "You are making a difference, and it is a positive one." Jerry's appointment prompted Rochester parent Mark Landstrom to complain to *Reminder* editor Ivan Helfmann, "Dr. Freeman is Dr. Telford's henchman. The only worse choice for that chairmanship would have been Dr. Telford himself."

The instigative Helfmann happily quoted Mr. Landstrom's remark in the paper. Indeed, Mr. Helfmann had been a fairly constant thorn in my side for the past couple of years. He had done a two-part feature on me with the headline "Iconoclast John Telford" spread in both parts all across the front page in big black letters above my picture, which he had taken himself. In that picture, I unfortunately happened to look particularly piratical, with one eye still partially shut from a recent attack of Bell's Palsy.

In other pieces, Helfmann continued to insinuate that the district would be better off without either me *or* the superintendent, again running that picture with my squinty eye.

After Dr. Freeman's appointment as chairman of the holiday committee, I recruited a diverse assortment of membership for it, seeking a balance of divergent views. I appointed two of my most determined detractors, Clara Knaus and the vociferous Mark Landstrom, some student council members from the secondary schools, and Bob Belk—the steadfastly fair-minded principal of University Hills Elementary School, where my daughter Katherine had been a student. I also appointed the objective, cool-headed Murel Bartley, my general director of elementary education. Other key actors were parent Izzie Khapoya of West Middle School (which my daughter had attended), local Episcopalian priest Michael Link, who had staunchly defended me in the newspapers, and consultants David Harris of the Oakland Intermediate School District and Dr. Ron Kevern, a vice president at Oakland University.

When this committee didn't come up with a conclusive recommendation, The superintendent and I appointed a follow-up committee with some of the same members as the previous committee, along with some fresh membership.

The committee elected two highly-regarded Rochesterites, Beth Bock and Sally Keller, as co-chairs. Again, after giving the committee its charge, neither the superintendent nor I attended after the second meeting.

Following many lengthy sessions, the committee had strained mightily and had finally given birth to a new policy that was virtually identical to the old one that I'd endorsed and enforced. It affirmed all children in their own tradition, recognized the separation of church and state, and held the school district to be *wholly* [no pun intended] neutral in addressing religious beliefs. It stated that holiday observances should promote an educational goal and that students shouldn't be compelled to participate. The policy was backed up with fourteen (14) pages of regulations. *Mission accomplished at last!*

But no sooner had the board voted to adopt (actually re-adopt or re-*affirm*) that policy than a *new* concern brought many of the same old reactionary boo birds right back to roost at board meetings.

Sociological Driver Statement "S-16," on page 39 of the celebrated third edition of *Telford's Telescope* was, "Young children will need to find a support structure in the school often not available in the home. Full-time guidance counselors and/or social workers will become standard staff in elementary schools. *Social/emotional skills* . . . must . . . become an *integral* part of the curriculum."

Sub-statement "S-16.1" was, "As referenced in Statement "D-12.2" [on page 7], full-time social workers *are now assigned to all elementary schools in Rochester.*" (I had budgeted to do this in 1987, and by 1988 I had all of those social workers in place.)

In 1988 school social workers who included Mark Lipson—my old college girlfriend Gerrie Barclay's nephew whom I had brought to Rochester—had come to me with two new *affective* discussion processes they wanted me to anoint. They had asked me first to review and then hopefully approve these processes, which were intended to improve group dynamics and interpersonal skills in the elementary schools' classrooms.

After fully reviewing them, I gave my enthusiastic stamp of approval to the procedures—called TRIBES (Teams for Responsibility, Identity, and Belongingness in an Education System) and "Magic Circle." I was unaware that a third similar process called "Feeling Fine" and a fourth process—"Peer-Proof"—were being taught. Had I known about those third and fourth processes, I would have anointed them, too. These were *instructional* processes that required *my* approval but *not* (ordinarily) the *board's*.

The same citizens who had expressed concern over my hiring of black administrators, my order to take down the manger scenes in the schools, my sanctioning the new multiculturally-oriented social studies curriculum, my propounding the teaching of Russian in the high schools, and all my other egalitarian initiatives that had arisen out of Operation *Equity* now came forward again to protest about these *social-skills* processes I was supporting and advancing.

At this time, the superintendent was out of town, so I was the acting superintendent. Sheila Schmittel, the new board president, called a special board study session to hear the citizens' concerns, and she ordered me to have the social workers stop all of these kinds of processes until the board had a chance to review them.

I did; but then in a confidential annotated board agenda for the regular board meeting which I was required to prepare in Dr. Schultz's absence, I wrote:

> I am enclosing eight letters addressed to the Board of Education Regarding TRIBES and Magic Circle.
>
> The stated topics for the . . . study session are TRIBES and Magic Circle; however, the overriding issue at stake is the future of an aggressive Affective Education Program. The Board's decision to halt all activities associated with TRIBES and Magic Circle has been viewed by many members of the Administration and Faculty, INCLUDING ME, as a threat to our professional responsibilities for addressing the District's goals as expressed in the recently adopted Philosophy of Education; i.e., "the development of the students' capacity to utilize personal and community resources to become responsible and participating citizens."
>
> Many staff members—including a number of social workers —are presently in a state that approaches PROFESSIONAL PARALYSIS (in regard to Affective Education activities) and fearful that any technique they may use will be called into question by a small group of parents and thereby place their District reputations and perhaps even their jobs in jeopardy.
>
> The schools have always had responsibility for Affective Education even though many did not recognize this responsibility as Affective Education. Teachers and administrators have addressed

> society's needs to produce contributing citizens who can function
> with others since the earliest days of education in the United
> States. Techniques and processes used throughout our country's
> educational history have a great many similarities to those now
> coming into question. Class meetings, group discussions, and
> cooperative activities are not new or revolutionary developments.
> Good teachers and administrators have utilized these processes
> for years.

I continued in that same somewhat condescendingly instructive vein for
two more long paragraphs and then added that my divisional staff would be
putting together a presentation for the board and audience at the study session
which would serve to *re-acquaint* the board with TRIBES and Magic Circle.
(I used the word "re-acquaint" to remind the board that these programs had
been just fine with them until the *protesters* showed up again; I was becoming
extremely impatient with the board's constant kowtowing to these ubiquitous
boo-birds.)

Accordingly, I enclosed an article from *The Board* –a magazine with broad
circulation beyond Rochester—entitled "How To *Resist Censorship*," with the
annotation: "In light of recent developments in our school district and elsewhere,
I find this piece to be *most pertinent* at this time."

Under Item II—Adjournment, I expressed the wish that the meeting would
adjourn no later that 11:00 p.m.

I added,

> Should members of the Board of Education have any questions
> or concerns regarding Monday night's study session and/or other
> items of information in this week's board packet, you are encour-
> aged to contact me, the executive staff [Dr. Dan Gilmore, in charge
> of the business division, Mr. Larry Westley, executive director of
> Human Resources, and me] or Mrs. Iras, as appropriate.

I concluded this annotated agenda with, "Have a nice weekend!"

It is to be hoped that the board members *did* have a nice weekend, because
I certainly *didn't*—nor did some of my staff. Taking no chances, I summoned
involved staff members to my office and spent much of the weekend briefing
them on exactly how I wanted them to couch their presentation on TRIBES and

Magic Circle at the emergency board study session on the coming Monday night.

Thanks in part to this preparation, these intrepid professionals were destined to do a bang-up job and make me proud of them.

However, contrary to my wish as expressed in the annotated board agenda that this seven o'clock study session for Monday night last no later than eleven o'clock, it was destined to drag on well *past* eleven o'clock—and indeed, well past *midnight*.

Also and *alas*—like many previous meetings involving this kind of controversy, our big, brand-new boardroom would be packed once again with hordes of the same folks who had been calling for my dismissal—and it would prove once again to be raucously contentious.

CHAPTER THIRTY-NINE

THE GULF AND THE GOVERNOR: WAR AND *WAMPUM* WOES

"Board revives TRIBES"; "Parents mad over canceled trip to France"
> —*Two separate headlines in the* Observer/Eccentric

"Rochester schools plan for cuts totaling $5 million"
> —*Headline in the* Oakland Press

" TRIBES is back."

With that short introductory sentence, *Observer/Eccentric* reporter Brenda Dooley duly reported the board's reinstatement of that controversial instructional process after the Monday night study session. I had put special education director Cherie Simpson in charge of the TRIBES presentation. (Dr. Simpson had impressed me earlier with her courage when she stood firm with the superintendent and me in a battle with parents of non-handicapped students who were opposed to my Divisional Operation *Inclusion* that we pushed through for the handicapped students. This had afforded them *full inclusion* in regular classes, thus enabling them to receive instruction alongside the non-handicapped kids rather than be cooped away in separate classrooms.)

I opened the session by informing the board that TRIBES was a solidly *research-based* procedure. Then I introduced Dr. Simpson as the major presenter.

With efficient backup from Van Hoosen Middle School social worker Alan Must and McGregor Elementary principal Carmen Zeigler, Dr. Simpson effectively described TRIBES and how group discussion works in the "Magic Circle."

"Through TRIBES," she said, "there is a decrease in children's misbehaviors and an improvement in academic achievement. Parents will note positive changes in their child's behavior at home as well as in school."

Mr. Must interjected, "TRIBES teaches children to rely on peers to *help* them solve problems, while the teacher acts as a facilitator rather than the central authority figure. Norms for TRIBES include attentive listening and no gossip. Teachers are saying that a decrease in student *put-downs* of each other thus becomes a classroom norm." He pointed out that children can describe what happened in TRIBES but they can't attach names. He added, "If children don't want to answer, they also have the right to say 'I pass.'"

Dr. Zeigler said, "Children will carry the valuable coping techniques they learned in TRIBES with them for the rest of their lives."

In an earlier article in the *Reminder*, Pat Driscoll had written: "'After our presentation is over,' said Assistant Superintendent John Telford, '99 percent of the parents will support TRIBES.'"

Brenda Dooley's *Observer/Eccentric* article continued by quoting my summative statement: "Assistant Superintendent John Telford said [at the close of the presentation], 'I believe that now everyone has a better understanding of TRIBES.'"

Dooley duly added, "But judging by parent reaction to TRIBES, not everyone agreed with Dr. Telford. Some parents asked the Board to delay action until an evaluation process for TRIBES is established and alternative programs for children who don't participate in TRIBES can be outlined."

To the board's credit, at the close of the session, they nonetheless voted to approve TRIBES and allow the process to be taught again without giving in to the parents' requests for further delays and stalling.

Still, some parental protests regarding this issue predictably continued, rattling several principals. Their protests were particularly vehement at Long Meadow School, one of two schools where I had tangled directly with parents who were upset that I was hiring so many black principals. (The other school was Brewster.)

My loyal Plymouth/Canton import Janine Kateff was Long Meadow's principal. Janine e-mailed me, "Karen Sue Marks [her social worker] is using 'Feeling Fine' at my school. I mentioned this *five times* to you as one of many programs my social workers are using here. *Five times* I raised the question of what about the other programs like this that are being used, and now here it is again—this time brought up by Long Meadow parents at a board meeting! Another program is 'Peer Proof.' What kind of direction should I give my social worker? This seems so backward, but we'll keep smiling!"

I e-mailed her back, "I authorize you to continue this and other similar programs. We have a regulation for challenged procedures if you face a persistent challenger. Contact me or Murel [Murel Bartley, Janine's general director] if you have questions."

The parental grumbling gradually died down. Grudgingly, they had actually begun to acknowledge that the programs had value.

However, no sooner had I managed to win this *latest* war than I found myself facing community fallout regarding yet *another* decision I made. My disputed decision this time concerned a far more serious and *real* war—the war over oil in the Persian Gulf, half a world away. I issued a memo telling all the building administrators to take special care that our relatively few students of Arab or Middle Eastern heritage not be scapegoated in any way by students or staff—or indeed, by the administrators, themselves—due to this war.

Meanwhile, Americans were being warned that under the circumstances, travel abroad had become extremely dangerous. A field trip to France had been offered to all of the district's teenaged students through the Rochester Adams High School art department under the coordination of Ceil Jensen, the art department head at Adams. It had been scheduled during spring break— March 28 through April 7, 1991—with about a dozen students' parents having already paid deposits. The students would have studied French architecture, art, and culture. I, of course, recognized that this trip could be a once-in-a-lifetime, educationally beneficial experience for the kids. I *also* recognized that a trip to France unfortunately posed too great a risk to our students.

Reluctantly, I issued an order that the trip be cancelled. Dutiful reporter Brenda Dooley duly and dutifully reported, "When the issue was brought to the Board's attention, Assistant Superintendent John Telford said *he* was responsible for the decision."

This was to be the last of many times that board president Sheila Schmittel —a cool, courageous, and caring board member—would ever be asked to back a controversial move of mine. *Bless* her, she did.

On rare occasions, I found fleeting relief from the extreme stress of my job by slipping away from the board office for a short while to play my fiddle for children in an elementary school. Also, one of the many programs I had initiated was elementary string instruction—instruction from which I myself had benefited so much at Estabrook School in Detroit so long ago.

One of the traveling elementary string teachers invited me to sit in with the violins at a district-wide ensemble concert. The night I sat in and played with this group, a bright little girl who was playing her violin next to me asked, "Are you *really* that *Dr. Telford*?"

When I confessed that I was, she made an awful face and hissed, "My daddy says you're the *Devil!*" I tried to explain to her that I really *wasn't* the Devil, but she wouldn't say another word to me.

I reflect upon that brief incident to this day—nearly two decades later. How terrible that a child's trusted but benighted parent could generate such misplaced hatred in that unknowing and innocent child—and this kind of madness is still happening in multiple places throughout the land. (All hail the ascendance of Barack Obama—he has his work cut out for him.)

Immediately after our TRIBES trials and tribulations and the trip-to-France contretemps, the district's next great crisis came crashing relentlessly down upon us. The Reagan administration had consistently failed to allocate an adequate level of federal funding for K-12 education, preferring instead to fund the flawed "Star Wars" missile defense and the murder of Nicaraguan peasants. Following Reagan's lead, Governor John Engler and his Republican legislature began to hit K-12 education hard in the early months of 1991. Engler was an "outstate guy," and he was wont to push for distributing to outstate and rural districts most of the K-12 state-aid *wampum* (Native American word for *money*— an expression I often whimsically used). The tri-county region of Wayne, Oakland, and Macomb (particularly Wayne) was far down the list of Governor Engler's priorities.

Superintendent Schultz and I estimated that the governor's "recapture" plan was going to cost the Rochester schools an incredible $5.1 million from a budget of only $19 million! ("Recapture" allowed the state to take foundation money from richer districts and distribute it to poorer ones. Given my Detroit roots, I was ordinarily in total accord with this process—even though most of the rest of the Rochester community wasn't.) But this time, the state cuts had been inordinately deep all across the board. They hit *everyone*—urban, suburban, and rural. (Sound a bit familiar, today?) As I was soon to say in many of my newspaper columns, Michigan—like several other states—badly needed to consolidate its smaller municipalities and school districts or induce them to share services, in order to save millions of scarce dollars. Michigan now has 83 counties, more than 1,200 townships, nearly 500 cities and townships with fewer than 10,000 residents, more than 550 public school districts, hundreds of charter schools, and 57 intermediate school districts. That kind of duplication of bureaucracy needs to be eliminated. Given the current national and world fiscal crisis, state and federal aid must be tied to demonstrating drastic savings at all levels of government and manifesting effective use of the monies allocated.

The previous year (1990), Engler and his minions had cut $72 million from the state's K-12 coffers! Rochester's hit had been a whopping $2 million, so we were hurting already—and hurting *badly*.

Since my divisional budget accounted for more than 80 percent of the district's *entire revenue*, I called all of my fifty-plus instructional administrators together in an emergency session of my three Joint Advisory Councils and ordered them to give me recommendations for cuts from their departments and buildings. In dire desperation, Dr. Schultz and I had determined that my division's target should total a devastating $3.6 million! We would need to find a minimum of yet another million to cut from *outside* the Division of Instruction's budget.

The first cut was one I made very reluctantly—but unilaterally and immediately. I slashed 55 percent from the *athletic budget*, which this jock-worshipping community saw as *sacrosanct*. I knew that this specific cut would cause my secondary principals and athletic directors and my district athletic director all to scream bloody murder, and probably to sic the community on me (again).

There was some method to my madness. I hoped that my huge cuts in athletics might just possibly force the voters to run to the polls and give us additional operating money. I realized, though, that the disgruntled boo-birds out in the community were still very numerous, and Dr. Schultz and I both knew that even if we took this to the community for a millage vote, the bigots among the boo-birds might mobilize to vote it down just to punish the board for awarding me a three-year contract the previous year instead of firing me.

With reluctance equal to mine, Superintendent John Schultz decided to support my move to cut the athletic programs heavily, and for the same reason as mine. More than three decades earlier, John and I had both attended colleges on athletic scholarships—a God-sent opportunity that had transformed our futures—so this deep cut in the athletic budgets was an emotionally hard move for us. Also, we were all-too-cognizant of the coming fallout we would face for it. However, this financial *tsunami* was a crisis far more serious than any other that had come upon us before, so our measures to deal with it would need to be equally dire.

One further even *more* desperately dire decision I was to make in the midst of this crisis would be mine alone. No one else could help me make it—and no one else could rescind it.

CHAPTER FORTY

A FATEFUL DECISION, LAVISH PARTY, AND *LONG* SPEECH

"I believe we can maintain some further cuts at the central offices."

—*Board of Education President Sheila Schmittel*

"In his seven years as Assistant Superintendent in the Rochester Schools, John Telford turned the district on its ear."

—*Editor Caleb Southworth in a*
Metro Times *cover story, May 22–28, 1991*

After consulting with my staff, some of *their* staffs, several employees outside my division, and many community people who supported me (and even some who *didn't*), I could come up with only $3.5 million of the $3.6 million the superintendent had asked me to cut. That $3.5 million included my *athletic cuts*—I was asking the parents to pay for much of the cost for their kids to compete in sports (the infamous "pay-to-play" policy). Since I was still one hundred-thousand dollars short after peering into every nook and cranny of my divisional budget to find things to cut, the superintendent and I could thus only find $4.5 million of the *minimal* $4.6 million we knew we had to cut from the district's *total* budget. In addition to the $3.5 million my staff and I had found from within the Division of Instruction, we had managed to find and cut another *million* from non-instructional budgets, but we had cut practically to the bone.

We gave our recommendations for this total $4.5 million in cuts to the board, which in turn shared it with the public.

Once more, all hell broke loose. The athletic booster clubs were, as we had expected, particularly incensed. Kathy Hines, representing Concerned Parents for Interscholastic Athletics, asked why we were cutting the sports program so deeply and disproportionately. I responded that the school district is essentially an academic institution. Mrs. Hines asked where sports fell on the district's priority list. "The academic programs have *always* been the priority," the superintendent answered.

Sports parent Ginny Hosbach said that if she had to pay for her son to be able to play on a team, the ACE kids' parents should have to pay for their non-compliant, misbehaving offspring to attend ACE High, or else ACE should be *closed*. (The Alternative Center for Education was the only program I hadn't cut a single penny from, nor would I have, ever. ACE was my *baby*. I had founded it, funded it, and *named* it—and I felt that it was *already* under-funded.)

Again, the omnipresent *Observer/Eccentric* reporter Brenda Dooley duly reported my response to sports parent Ginny Hosbach: "'Some of the other programs offer support for kids who are less fortunate than yours,' Telford told Hosbach. 'When we don't supply this type of support, learning can suffer for *all* children.'"

Somewhere near the poignant midpoint of this stormily memorable meeting, Board President Sheila Schmittel suddenly opined out of the blue, "I believe we can maintain some further *cuts* at the *central offices*."

Hearing this, I recognized just as suddenly that the "further *cuts*" would have to be the job of Bill Waun's recent successor, Beverly Stone, my hard-working general director of secondary education, unless I could do something preventively drastic. The realization hit me like a sledgehammer. I had lured Mrs. Stone to Rochester from her union-sheltered and seniority-protected middle-school principalship in Bloomfield Hills with the now obviously foolhardy promise that her job would always be safe. Her elementary counterpart, Murel Bartley, had given up his union membership and senior status as an elementary principal when I promoted him, but his many years in the district had rendered him virtually untouchable. I, too, was of course untouchable now, after winning my multicultural wars and enjoying the total support of UPWARD and the near-total support of the new board (not to mention having that ironclad three-year contract in my pocket).

To make matters worse for Mrs. Stone (and my conscience), her husband

Howard had just been laid off as athletic director at Oak Park High School. Were Mrs. Stone to be laid off, she and her husband *would have no income.*

I felt the walls closing in on me. If I opted to retire and give my job to my general director of secondary education, it would save the district the one-hundred-thousand-plus we were spending on her salary (including benefits) that Dr. Schultz and I had been trying to find—and I was old enough to collect a pension, which my junior executive staff members weren't. However, I knew if I retired at this point, some folks would incorrectly presume that I'd been *pushed* out due to past controversies. Also, I would have liked to enjoy the fruits of my hard-won battles over the bigots for a few more years, at least.

I realized sadly that I wasn't going to be able to do that—I was left with no choice other than *to make the announcement* which inspired *Rochester Clarion* editor Craig Bryson to write, in this editorial headlined "Controversial educator forced district to question":

> Some like him, some hate him—but few doubt that outgoing Rochester School District Assistant Superintendent John Telford has been dedicated to his district—almost to a fault. . . . The 55-year-old veteran administrator announced his retirement amid the chaos resulting from the district's attempt to come to terms with the pending cuts in state funding which could reach as high as $5 million.
>
> And while district officials have not come out and said so, it seems quite likely that Telford, who is old enough to retire with a comfortable pension, volunteered to step aside so that one or more junior members of his staff would not be left hanging without a job. It is no secret that more than one member of the district's Board of Education were calling for additional budget cuts within the district's administrative staff in Telford's Division of Instruction, and the names of some of Telford's top assistants had been mentioned on more than one occasion as possible targets.

The editorial concluded:

> . . . whether or not we agree with the political positions espoused by Telford in his Telescope, we should be grateful that at least one leader in the field of education had the guts to ask us to

> think about society's significant problems—problems that can-
> not be resolved with TV-like quick fixes—but which, by their very
> nature, require complex solutions and in-depth contemplation.
> If for no other reason than this (and there are many other reasons),
> Telford's stay in the district has been a productive one.

I later learned that courageous crusader Bryson took a lot of heat for that gutsy editorial.

On May 7, my bearded mug appeared on the front page of the *Detroit Free Press* beside this quote: "I'm an *integrationist*, and I can't sit by and watch the Detroit area remain the most *segregated* in the country." The *Free Press* reporter, Margaret Trimer (now Margaret Trimer-Hartley), quoted Roger Kalisz, who had led the board recall movement: "I hate to see the guy leave. Now that I know him, I know he's brilliant."

Trimer also quoted Van Hoosen Middle School principal Marvin Rubin: "Thanks to Dr. Telford, we're on the right path—on the cutting edge. But while we've taken two steps forward, losing him takes us one step back." (Marv Rubin had written to me earlier that I would have been an abolitionist like John Brown in the 1850s.)

Two weeks later, I became the *Metro Times'* cover boy. The cover caption, "JOHN TELFORD: ROCHESTER'S MAVERICK EDUCATOR PREPARES FOR THE NEXT ROUND," was perhaps a bit misleading. The headline in the cover story (written by editor Caleb Southworth) was, "John Telford pours it on"—a reference to my quote in the article that when you're being pressured in a 46-second quarter-mile race, you've got to "pour it on." The sub-headline read, "Rochester schools administrator has resigned to protect minority administrators . . . from the budgetary axe."

The story began:

> In his seven years as Assistant Superintendent for Instruction
> for the Rochester Community Schools, John Telford turned the
> district on its ear. He pushed for integration and racial tolerance
> by "Africanizing" and "Asianizing" the curriculum. . . . He hired
> black administrators in a 98 percent white community.
>
> Now Telford, 55, is stepping down. But not because of
> the death threats. Or the bullets fired through his living room

window. Or the excrement placed in his mailbox along with the reams of hate mail. Nor is Telford a victim of the parent groups that organized to bring about his firing. His is not a casualty of the new-right idealogues that attacked him for "teaching humanism." Rather, Telford's resignation . . . is a strategic reaction to $5.1 million in state cuts his district has received.

"The cuts came abruptly, like a Pearl Harbor sneak attack," Telford says. "People kept coming to Board meetings wanting cuts that were deeper and higher. So I made a split-second decision. I said, "'If they're going to cut deeper and higher, it might as well be me.'"

(Incidentally, one of the many folks who weren't happy with my "split-second decision" was my wife Lynn, who was still teaching in Warren. I had to reassure her that my retiring didn't mean I would never earn money again.)

An *Observer/Eccentric* headline at the top of the front page blared, "Controversial educator Telford steps down." Many other papers covering my retirement also had the word "controversial" or "radical" in their headlines. How controversy and radicalism does *sell!* But the only thing that really has ever been "controversial" or "radical" about me is that I am an old-time Kennedy Democrat who stands for the things that John and Robert Kennedy and Martin Luther King, Jr. and Malcolm X would have made happen three decades earlier, had they not been murdered—and that President Barack Obama is hopefully going to make happen now.

I told Dr. Schultz, "Okay, this gives you the other one hundred grand you needed to get to that $3.6 million from my division." I also made sure that he understood that the two conditions of my retirement were that Mrs. Stone was to *get my job*, with hers being *eliminated*—and if for some reason these two things didn't happen, I promised to *un*-retire fast.

Dr. Schultz did promote Mrs. Stone to my job, and he did eliminate hers.

Mrs. Stone said in the *Rochester Hills Reminder*, "When the budget-cutting started in March, I didn't think I'd have a job. Then Dr. Telford retired, and things started swirling around me!"

My lavish retirement party that the Rochester district gave for me at Club Monte Carlo in Shelby Township was graced by more than five hundred folks, including my wife and daughter, several other members of my family that included my eighty-four-year-old mother Helen and my cousin Carl—my lifelong side-kick who had driven up from Arkansas with his wife Ginny. Old high school, college, and Detroit Track Club teammates attended, including one who flew up from Virginia.

Former Detroit TC hurdler Paul Jones and I reminisced about the time in 1960 when we were the only Detroit entries at the Ohio AAU championships. We were entered in five events—the high and low hurdles (Paul), and the 220, 440, and long jump (me). Between the two of us, we scored enough points to bring home the out-of-district team trophy. We flipped for it, and I won. (The trophy sits today in my library—I have willed it to Paul, who is two years younger than me.)

Dr. Schultz attended my retirement party, of course, and he spoke. Several superintendents and assistant superintendents from other districts also attended.

Future University of Michigan head football coach Lloyd Carr came.

Several of my past or present girlfriends were also in attendance, including Geraldine Barclay—and also including Eva. Gerrie came with her sister Greta, and Eva sat at a table with our old-time MCCC compadre, Jim Jacobs, and her brother and sister-in-law. A few other ladies from my near and far past also showed up separately and sat discreetly at rear tables.

Most of my Rochester colleagues came—including my intrepid secretary, Diane Stuart; my soon-to-be successor, Bev Stone; and Bev's general director predecessor, Dr. Bill Waun.

Dennis Anderson, my favorite Rochester custodian, came. So did my favorite custodian from Plymouth/Canton—Tom Barry, the old soldier-Scot.

Hordes of newspaper reporters also were on hand. Steve Barnaby, the editor of the *Observer/Eccentric* chain, asked me to write a column for his newspapers—an offer I enthusiastically accepted.

Many of my Pershing champions were there, including John Kitchen, who now was coaching track at John Glenn High School in Westland; NBA basketball legend Spencer Haywood; Dale Hardeman; and Reggie Bradford, who had been an All-American relayist at the University of Michigan. Southeastern's Tim Moore and Bill King (who flew in from Maryland), were in attendance.

Dr. King and Reggie Bradford spoke. They said they loved me and I had transformed their lives—and they called me a "great man." I told them I figured they were just hoping I would get them big jobs when I became governor.

Dave Berube, the president of the teachers' union, declared: "Dr. Telford has always marched to his own drummer when there wasn't even any *drum.*"

The PTA ladies had board member Keith Wittenstrom read a rhyme they had slyly written saying that I looked "neat-o in my Speedo." (We had taken a dip together in a hotel pool at some conference or other.)

My old half-miler Tim Moore had provided a six-foot, six-inch Uzi-packing chauffeur and a long, black (and bullet-proof) limo for me and my family to ride in, because we had been "tipped" that I would be assassinated at the party. This didn't seem to make sense, since I was retiring—but we decided not to take any chances. The place was crawling with plainclothes cops, including my state quarter-mile champion George Wesson, a Wayne County Sheriff's Department detective. He sat at my table with me and my family and with an even faster (by .2-second) high school quarter-miler—Cliff Hatcher, with his wife Barbara. Those two high school legends had once held the two fastest quarter-mile times in state high school history (competing twelve years apart)—and here they were, sitting together now at the same table! It was hot in there with all those people, but George couldn't take off his coat, because he had a loaded .357 magnum holstered under it.

I received gifts and certificates—one from the state legislature.

A rambunctious bunch of pretty PTA ladies, who included two board members, did a skit. I had dubbed them the "Rochettes."

In an *Oakland Press* headline that read, "Telford again bucks system on way out," reporter Dan Desmond wrote,

> Retiring Rochester schools assistant superintendent John Telford
> couldn't resist going out in a blaze of nonconformity as he blasted
> favorite targets in his retirement speech and hinted he won't
> stray far from controversy.

I told the assembled guests that the folks who for years had been trying to get me fired definitely weren't why I was stepping down. "If anything," I said, "they reinforced my need to stay until my battles were won."

Deborah Anthony, my technology director, taped the whole affair—including my fascinating retirement speech. When this book makes me universally famous, I'll donate that tape to public television for a trifling honorarium of maybe a couple million or so—or else I'll auction it off on my website to the highest bidder. (Any takers yet?)

I called on those at the packed party to—as *Clarion* editor Bryson later quoted me—"join with me in an ongoing effort to move the country toward true equality and democracy. Making this world a more humane place . . . is really our own true, worthy purpose in life—it's what gives life its *meaning*."

My speech dragged on for more than half an hour and got a bit maudlin toward the end. At one point, I held up a glass of water I was sipping from and assured my listeners, who were probably growing more than a little bit restless, "This is *water*." Because of some rather pointed remarks I'd made in the speech about local bigots, I didn't want people to think that the water might perhaps be something stronger. My old U.S. teammate Hayes Jones, the multi-world-record-breaking hurdler, later said that my remark about the glass containing only water was the one funny part of my otherwise very long, serious speech—with the accent on *long*.

I really didn't want to leave the limelight and say goodbye to all my friends. I told them that this group would never ever assemble again, and I was sadly correct: several of them are now dead.

I'm sure that near the end of my somewhat self-indulgent retirement soliloquy, the five-hundred-plus invited and uninvited guests—even including my biggest fans—were praying that I'd finish retiring just a little bit *faster*.

Holding my NCAA All-America certificate and
wearing my national team shirt, 1957.

A 1956 WSU publicity photo that appeared in meet programs
and newspapers and was mailed to fans upon request.

Outrunning Ernie Billups, Loyola's fast-finishing 440/880 star, and comebacking 1952 Olympic 400-meter champion George Rhoden of Jamaica—my high school idol—who was representing the Toronto Olympic Club, for the Michigan AAU 600-yard championship in Ann Arbor-January, 1960.

Telford's Telescope

1990 Planning Paradigm for Discovering the Year 2000

The televised cover of the third annual (1990) edition of the famous/infamous Telford's Telescope booklet. Rochester art coordinator Tim Brooks drew the cartoon, which was printed in dark maroon on light blue.

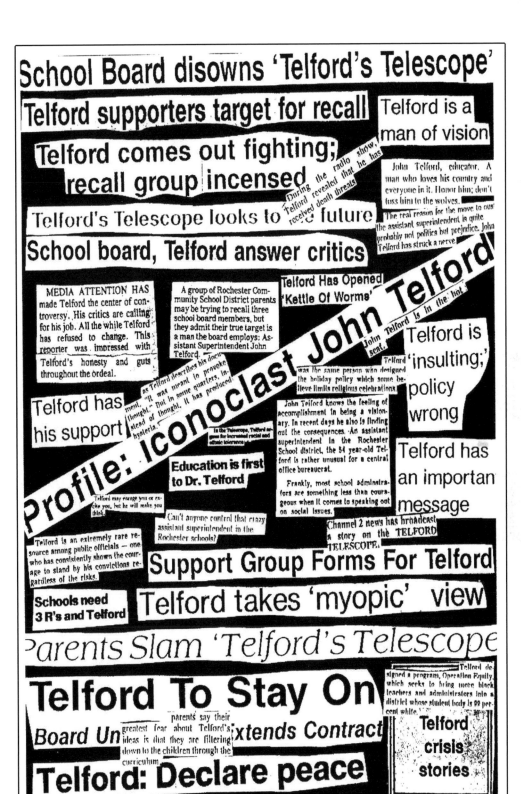

A *Michigan Chronicle* photo of the three surviving members of the 1958 Detroit Track Club sprint relay team taken at the 2008 Detroit Track Old-Timers dinner. Retired Detroit Mumford High School principal Pete Petross—who ran 100 yards in 9.6 seconds that year at the age of 32—is on my left; retired Michigan State track coach Jim Bibbs is on my right. In 1951, Bibbs tied Jesse Owens' world 60-yard record. Our fourth teammate was the late "Bullet Billy" Smith, the world record-holder for the 65-yard low hurdles. This team dropped the baton while passing the stick in the lead at the National AAU championships at New York's old Madison Square Garden and incredibly came back to finish second by a whisker in the same race. The team was generally regarded as the fastest in the country.

CHAPTER FORTY-ONE

ONE FOOT IN ONE WORLD, THE *OTHER* IN ANOTHER

"Able was I, ere I saw Elba."

—Palindrome attributed to Napoleon,
but actually penned by an unknown scribe

Like the encore-craving Emperor Napoleon, I would not yet truly retire—or *be* retired—to my "island of St. Helena" just yet. I was far from finished with schools, nor was I finished with Rochester. There were to be several Napoleonic "pre-St. Helena 'islands of Elba'" for me before I was finally to face my *ultimate* Waterloo.

I had expected to be immediately snapped up by some university and given a full-time teaching job, but I hadn't counted on having to live down my radical reputation in the conservative world of higher academe, and no full-time university job was ever offered again.

For a while, I sat at home tossing Kibbles and Bits to my cats—Whitleigh and Samantha—while my wife went off to work and my daughter went off to school. I did take my daughter to see the South African revolutionary Nelson Mandela speak at Tiger Stadium that summer—a memorable experience for both of us. I wanted to get his autograph, but we couldn't get close to him. It reminded me of the time I and a thousand others had marched with Martin Luther King, Jr., down Woodward in the summer of 1963. Even though physically and figuratively I had been marching a hundred yards behind the great later-to-be martyr, I had felt a timeless sense of oneness with him—and now I had the same spiritually timeless feeling as I listened to the great Mandela.

That fall, one of our young cleaning ladies became unhealthily fixated on me, and I imprudently succumbed to her unhealthy fixation a couple of times. (I have always suspected that she also stole a scrapbook with a black velvet cover that had several family photos in it.) Other unhealthful amorous affairs in which I was involved locally began to intensify. I soon realized that I had to get professionally busy again immediately to keep these situations from getting out of control and absorbing my entire existence—not to mention *ending* my existence at the hands of some pistol-packing husband.

Therefore, in the first few years of my "retirement," I endeavored to keep one busy foot in Oakland County as: a) a twice-defeated Rochester school board candidate (in a Republican stronghold); b) an unsuccessful county commissioner candidate from the 90 percent Republican District Eight (naturally, I was nominated by the Democrats); c) an adjunct professor of education and psychology at Oakland University; d) a board member and co-founder of MOSAIC (Michigan Organization for Social Advocacy and Intercultural Cooperation) with Dick Lobenthal and Rabbi Arnie Sleutelberg; e) a board member of the Oakland County ACLU (where I recruited my college girlfriend Gerrie Barclay and my activist associate Lobenthal for membership); f) a board member of the Oakland County Center for Open Housing (I keynoted one of their dinners); g) a board member of the Pontiac Area Urban League; h) an executive board member of the Oakland County Democrats; and i) an assistant track coach to head coach Jerry Catalina at Berkley High, where one of the sprinters I coached was Anthony Jones, the son of one of my old Pershing runners.

Regarding "a," above—In support of my two candidacies for the school board, my campaign team printed and put up signs in front of the houses and businesses of my supporters that blared the single word *TELFORD* in huge white-on-blue letters. As fast as my signs appeared, my opponents' backers made them *disappear* like magic. This time UPWARD's support for me was no longer quite enough, nor was the support of the Rochester *Observer/Eccentric* newspaper, which endorsed me fruitlessly both times.

Dr. Eleanor White, one of the African-American administrators I had hired, wrote to the black parents' organization in a letter dated June 9, 1993:

> John Telford is responsible for the employment of every African-American we have in our schools. He is a champion for human rights and is not afraid to take a stand. Vote for him on June 13.

They all did, but they and my UPWARD group were narrowly outnumbered. There were nine candidates in that run for two seats. I finished a close third.

Regarding "b"—On Thursday, November 3, 1994, at seven o'clock in the morning, I looked full into the face of hate. I was walking a Rochester neighborhood with members of my team, handing out a flyer supporting Howard Wolpe for governor and me for Oakland County commissioner in the upcoming election. Some newspapers had unhelpfully headlined me as "a lightning rod for *controversy*" (that *word* again!) and offered other similar unsupportive and copious commentary, continually using words like "controversy" and "controversial"—their favorite and frequent descriptors in articles about me.

Stopping by a small apartment complex, I was placing flyers on the landing of the outer foyer when the manager appeared and asked, "And who might *you* be?" I held up the flyer the Dems had printed with my picture.

"You're *Telford!*" His inflection was the same as if he had said, "You're *Satan!*"

A little unnerved by his vehemence, I nonetheless asked him if he'd mind placing flyers in front of the doors within.

"Not on a bet! I hate everything you stand for! I hate everything you've ever done!"

I wanted to ask, "Did you know that in the summer of 1977, I pulled an injured girl out of a burning car? [We later learned she was my wife's nineteen-year-old cousin.] Did you know that I helped your schools produce some great academic programs? Did you know I never lost a 400-meter race representing your country?"

Most of all, I wanted to ask, "What could I have ever possibly done to bring such a hate-filled expression to your face at the mere sight of me? You don't even know me."

I wondered whether the man had children, and perhaps grandchildren. The thought of him interacting with kids and contaminating them with his hatred caused me to reflect on how essential it is to teach children to listen receptively to others' views and value diverse beliefs and backgrounds. However much I had facilitated this happening in schools, I felt, was right and good. I still *believe* that today, and I would do it all *again*—the same way. As I had written in the last two sentences of the third edition of *Telford's Telescope*,

This fragile . . . pebble of a planet orbiting alone except for one
dead moon far off in solar space is the only home our children
will have (at least into the foreseeable future). We had best take
care of it—and of each other.

Regarding "c"—On January 19, 1993, one of my Oakland University grad students,
Ron Santavicca, wrote,

Dear Dr. Telford,
    Thanks for the fine example you set for me as an educator.
I worked harder in your class (CIL 580) and learned more than
in any other class that I can remember. . . . You gave us a real
purpose to learn. You rekindled my belief in myself and my
profession. The qualities you possess as an educator are not
learned from a text. They are a part of your inner fiber that has
been nurtured by your lifelong commitment to education.

Shortly after, Ron was promoted to an assistant principalship—in Clarkston,
as I recall. Other students, including Detroit teachers Rachel Tiseo and Tom Barnes
and West Bloomfield Police sergeant Tom Nelson—a former Detroit teacher
and cop who became a close friend—wrote similar commendations. I kept them
all. They were my real remuneration, and to me they were beyond price.

In addition to my unsuccessful Democratic run for county commissioner
and the other seven enterprises listed in the preceding, I wrote regular human-
rights-oriented columns for the *Observer/Eccentric* newspaper chain, the *Oakland
Press*, and the *Troy Gazette*. I was also the keynote speaker at various egalitarian
functions, including a Martin Luther King Day celebration at a Lakes-Area
Intercultural Breakfast in Walled Lake.

I delivered the commencement address at Pontiac Northern High School,
and I became a frequent civil-rights commentator on radio and television.
A WSU professor named Jack Lessenberry who at the time had a similarly liberal
column opposite mine in the *Oakland Press* has become the local media's democratic darling now, but I was the "Jack Lessenberry" of my era (or rather, I should
say, he's now the "*John Telford*" of his!).

When I served on an outdoor political debate panel in a park in Royal
Oak, I found that the numerous monster mosquitoes weren't my only irritants.

Some people in the audience who didn't like my remarks about Ross Perot's presidential candidacy and the grossly segregated metro area's need for racial integration heckled me, and a few pelted me with various objects that included overripe tomatoes that had the consistency of jelly. (Actually, though, the mosquitoes were worse—they nearly ate me alive.)

I stretched my other even busier, faster foot farther to the south in Wayne County, where I expected that I might get a more hospitable reception than I often had in Oakland. I kept my other busy foot there as: a) a founder and officer of the philanthropic Detroit Track Old-Timers (with retired U.S. Army Col. Aaron Gordon, former president of the DPS administrators union); b) an author of intermittent op-eds for the *Detroit News*, the *Michigan Chronicle*, the *Detroit Free Press*, and the *Inner City Plow*; and c) the sprint coach under head track coach Guy Murray at the University of Detroit-Mercy, where my sprinters won Midwest Collegiate Conference championships and Eric McKeon broke the school and conference 400-meter marks with a swift (and sans-steroid) 47.3.

That coaching job was perhaps the assignment I enjoyed most. I got to drive the team bus to faraway places like Tennessee, and to know some great kids who high-fived me a lot whenever they won.

I was also a presenter at the University of Michigan-Dearborn in an absolute snowstorm—where the outdoor marquee read "John Telford On Racism." The University of Michigan-Dearborn staff distributed flyers with my name and topic, but only fifty folks braved the storm to show up despite the marquee and flyers (or maybe *because* of them!).

I did some multicultural consulting again in Wayne County, too— including in Grosse Pointe, Romulus, and Westland. I unintentionally got the Westland assistant superintendent who had hired me in serious trouble when I pointed out (in the presence of board members) that the district was guilty of *de facto* segregation. There was one lone, nearly all-black middle school in that over-whelmingly white district.

The assistant superintendent later told me she never would have retained my services if she had known I had such a "red hot" reputation. Ultimately, she was demoted, and I was informed that her husband—a WSU professor of education—blamed her demotion on me. I felt very bad about that, but I still find it hard to believe that I could have been the sole cause of her demotion.

In the fall of 1993, I signed a one-year contract to head the counseling center at the Detroit Public Schools' old Trombly Adult Day High School near the corner of Harper and Van Dyke. (At that time, I could only work in any Michigan public school district for two semesters consecutively, due to pension regulations and tax laws. The school year covered half of two tax years each, so if I made less than twenty thousand dollars in each of the two tax years, I could still collect my pension.)

Before I was offered and signed the DPS contract, I had done a short, aborted stint as the deputy executive director of the Metropolitan Detroit Youth Foundation. The executive director, who had eagerly hired me, told me apologetically two weeks later that he had to *un*-hire me, because the chairman of his board wanted my job! I had already bought two expensive new suits, had business cards printed, and handed them out to some big shooters I knew who might have been able to help the failing agency, which had been plagued with alleged fiscal corruption.

This unprofessional treatment embarrassed me—so I sued, won, and ensured that my win got reported in the daily newspapers. I was fortunate to collect damages, because few others collected debts from the once-highly-respected foundation. It closed its doors soon afterward.

I had been offered that head counseling job at the Trombly Adult Day High School by DPS superintendent David Snead and Trombly principal Jim Solomon. Jim had been in the old Detroit Varsity Club with me in the early 1960s, and he had also been the basketball coach at King when I was a department head and unpaid track coach there. The Trombly job was full-time, and all the others I was doing in Oakland County—time-consuming though some of them were, what with the lesson-planning and lecture-writing, drafting columns, and attending meetings—still were only *part*-time.

I soon found, too, that the "adult" part of the title "Trombly Adult Day High School" was misleading. While we had some twenty-year-old, thirty-year-old, and even a couple of *forty*-year-old students at Trombly, most of the students there were between sixteen and nineteen. All were black, and many had dropped out or had been *kicked* out of traditional high schools—as I had likewise been kicked out of Northwestern in the days of the administrator I had once immaturely dubbed "old Dick-head Diekoff" and "old Jack-off

Diekoff" so long ago. Thus, I identified with the Trombly students far more than they knew.

In fact, I identified *totally* with my Trombly kids in a way that was bittersweetly nostalgic. I was back home in my inner-city Detroit element for the first time since my King days in 1968–69 —and I was absolutely loving it.

CHAPTER FORTY-TWO

THE ENTRANCING TRIBULATIONS OF TROMBLY

"I'm going to have to kill the assistant principal."

—*Mustaffa Benson, Black Muslim, age twenty-eight*

Each day at Trombly was a new adventure. I looked forward to getting up in the morning and going to work. There would be at least one fight to break up every day, drug deals went down outside my office window in broad daylight, and police sirens and gunfire could be frequently heard. Two bullets broke my window and lodged in a wall. We boarded up the window only to have another one similarly broken. We boarded up that one, too, and awaited the *next* onslaught.

One day a student tipped me that some young men were on their way to the school to kill big Billy Stewart, a six-foot, four-inch, 240-pound, nineteen-year-old stick of raw dynamite who had just been discharged from the Maxey Boys Training School for felonious teens. Billy had sold the men diluted drugs—an extremely unwise act in that seamy Harper/Van Dyke neighborhood. As his intended killers entered the front door, I smuggled him out the back and drove him fast down a glass-strewn alley to Van Dyke and careened onto I-94, speeding east. I dropped him off near his house in the Denby neighborhood and told him I'd arrange for him to go to night school at Denby. I also warned him never to come near Harper and Van Dyke again, day or night, or he would become an immediate corpse. "Doc," he said, "You don't have to *tell* me—I *know*. Thanks."

Another time, my fellow counselor Evelyn Petty and I spotted a student named Ramón holding hands with a new enrollee—a sweet young girl of about eighteen who had a two-year-old son in need of eye surgery. I got that girl into the counseling office in a quarter-miler-quick hurry, and we gave her the lowdown on Ramón.

"You see that row of lockers out there?" Mrs. Petty asked the girl. "Ramón has babies by almost every one of the girls whose coats are in those lockers." Indeed, the slick Ramón—who was a young-looking thirty-five—was reputed to have sired forty-four children by many, *many* young ladies. If this was true—and I have no reason to believe it wasn't—Ramon had to be Detroit's Paul Bunyan of procreating.

"Oh, Miz Petty," the sweet young girl said to Evelyn, "thanks for telling me. I won't have nothing more to *do* with Ramón."

Too late—in a few weeks the sweet young girl's sweet young belly had begun to swell sweetly and noticeably. Number forty-five was on the way.

In the middle of that school year, I took Lynn and Katherine with me on a short vacation to Cancún. We made the acquaintance of an Italian family who were sitting at our table in a nightclub, and I got to talking with the father—a stocky man with iron-gray hair who appeared to be in his fifties. I mentioned that I had raced in Italy, and he remarked that in his boyhood he had kept a scrapbook on Giovanni Scavo, the late, great Italian champion.

I told him I had beaten Scavo in the 400. "No—you couldn't have," he scoffed. "Only one man ever win a 400 race with Scavo—an American named Teleford who would have to be more than sixty now, and you look maybe forty. I watch that race at *Reunione Internazionale* track meet in Bologna as little boy," and the crowd chant '*Scavo, Scavo!*' before the race—and then they begin to chant '*Tel-ee-ford, Tel-ee-ford*' *after* it." When I showed him my driver's license and explained that my name had been spelled with an extra "e" in the meet program, he insisted on paying our entire bill.

The Scavo story had actually ended tragically: We had become immediate friends and exchanged our national team pins, and a postcard that Giovanni wrote me in excellent English arrived in the United States by slow boat two weeks after he was killed in a Fiat crash. At only nineteen, Giovanni Scavo had been the *enfant terrible* of European racing. There is no telling how fast he might ultimately have run if he hadn't been killed.

Also at midyear back at Trombly, a newly-assigned assistant principal had ordered Mrs. Evelyn Petty to close some classes that had exceeded fifty students and break them down into classes with fewer students in them. He thought she was overloading those classes, but we had advised him that Trombly had a 65 percent truancy rate on any given day, so there always was plenty of room in the classes—and the more students we enrolled, the more money the school district got from Lansing.

Evelyn ignored the order; the new AP reprimanded her in writing and sent copies of the reprimand to honchos he knew downtown to demonstrate to them how tough he was being in his new job. I wrote a response for her to the reprimand, cc'd the principal, and indicated in a separate communication that the response would also go downtown and to the daily newspapers if the AP didn't withdraw his reprimand.

He did, since the incriminatory wording of my response and my threat to circulate it as indicated had left him no other choice—but the incident understandably didn't make him my biggest fan.

When two good-sized twenty-year-old male EMI (emotionally and mentally impaired) special education students were calling each other m-f's at the top of their lungs and were about to commit mayhem upon each other, I hauled them to my office.

No sooner had I calmed them down (with extreme difficulty) when the officious AP came in and got them riled up again.

"Young man," he intoned to one of them, "*Christians* mustn't quarrel." Unfortunately, this particular young man happened not only to be a *non-*Christian—he was a very militantly-inclined member of the Black Muslims. He jumped to his feet in renewed anger, so I snapped, "Goddammit, Malik, sit *down!*" Malik sat down, and I was somehow able to calm the pair again.

After the incident, the AP put a hand on my shoulder in what I assumed was a gesture of thanks for helping him out of what could have been, for him, a most *injurious* situation. Instead, he said, "Dr. Telford, I did not appreciate your taking the name of the Lord in vain."

"Oh? All right, Mr. [assistant principal]—I'll try not to do it again."

Later, there was a note in my mailbox summoning me to his office. When I got there, the academic department head, Robert Sellers, was seated next to the assistant principal, looking uncomfortable.

The assistant principal then repeated, "Dr. Telford, I did not appreciate your taking the name of the Lord in vain."

"Is there an *echo* in here? [Shades of 1964 Finney High!] You already *told* me that." I then turned and walked out of the office.

Still later, there was yet *another* note in my mailbox: "Dr. Telford, I did not appreciate your taking the name of the Lord . . ."

That *did* it. Clutching the note, I went straight to Principal Jim Solomon, flung the note on his desk, and seethed, "If you don't get this [four-syllable curse word] off my back, I'm going to quit!"

Jim got the [four-syllable curse word] off my back.

As I drove down Van Dyke Avenue to Trombly every cold winter morning, I often saw nineteen-year-old Trombly student Vakela Benson huddled near the corner of Six Mile Road waiting for the bus, which often appeared late and erratically, and I would then pick her up and bring her to school. Soon I began to pick her up at her house, which was on a nearby street. Presently, she recruited her twenty-eight-year-old parolee brother, Mustaffa—a Black Muslim—to attend Trombly, so I then brought *him* to school sometimes, too. (Students received extra credit for anyone they successfully recruited.)

Mustaffa attended irregularly, but when he did come to school he was a model student and remained so even when the ultra-Christian assistant principal started persistently trying to get him to remove his Muslim headwear.

One day, the young man informed me sadly that he was going to have to leave school, because he didn't want to go back to prison.

"Leave school? Go back to prison?" I was perplexed. "That's not going to happen, son—let's work it out."

"I can't, Dr. Telford—if I don't leave Trombly, I'm going to have to kill the assistant principal."

I realized he *meant* it. I let him quit without another word, thus saving the assistant principal's life that day.

Mustaffa himself was later killed. In his memory, I sometimes wear a blue Muslim hat with white trim that he gave me when he left.

Former Michigan Associate Supreme Court Justice Dennis Archer was running for his first term as mayor of Detroit, so I brought him to Trombly to speak. I also supported him in my suburban newspaper columns and tried in that way to raise suburban funding for him. I was impressed with Dennis' honesty, eloquence, and vision for the city. I also helped arrange a fund-raiser for him at the Hoy Tin restaurant in the River House, where my main girlfriend

Eva owned a co-op overlooking the Detroit River and her best friend Yoonsil Cho owned the restaurant.

Other speakers I brought to Trombly included my best buddy Cliff Hatcher, who owned three menswear stores, former basketball great Spencer Haywood, Olympic hurdler and sprinter Hayes Jones, former world-record relayist Aaron Gordon, and attorney Sharon McPhail, who was running against Archer for the mayoral job.

Aaron, once a champion half-miler and miler at Detroit Miller High and the University of Michigan who was on the MOSAIC board with me and had co-founded the philanthropic Detroit Track Old-Timers with me, confessed to the students that I had won a race against him at 1,000 yards—*his* distance, not mine. I then confided to them that the only reason I had been in a race that long was because my coach had entered me in it to get me some over-distance training, and that I had retched wrenchingly and repeatedly after the race—but I had a girl stashed in the stands, and I didn't want her to see me lose. "Instead," I laughed, "she saw me *puke!*"

When Aaron and my old U.S. teammate Hayes Jones came to Trombly (on separate days), I took each of them to a little diner across the street, and then down the street to a menswear store owned by Richard Jarrett, the brother of former WSU running back Nate Jarrett. Richard gave me three sparkly, cheap rings I still like to wear. (He later killed a man and woman who were in his store taking clothes off the racks as recompense for a debt he allegedly owed. Cliff and I got him off the hook with the judge temporarily, but he eventually died in jail.)

As Hayes Jones and I—and later Aaron Gordon and I—were walking back to the school during those two separate days, they both said this same thing to me: "John, we shouldn't be out walking around down here—it's too dangerous." Both times, their words surprised me, because these were two courageous men and great former athletes who had grown up in urban ghettos—Hayes in Pontiac, Aaron in Detroit's old Black Bottom.

Still, I continued to eat at that diner and drop by Richard's place every day, because the young men in that school and on those streets trusted me now, and I was gradually instilling in them a sense of hope, pride, and civic responsibility. For the first time since I'd coached and administrated at King High a quarter of a century before, I had recruited another *Activist Army* again.

CHAPTER FORTY-THREE

WOLLACK AND WOLVERINE: A DYNAMIC DUO

"Are you Jesus?"

—*A wistful little Wolverine Human Services*
ward who had been badly beaten

I had officially retired—but as I said, I was definitely not anywhere near already to be *really* retired. Retirees are supposed to *slow down*, take it easy, and rock in rockers with a travel guide or the AARP Journal in hand. While rocking, they also should be sipping Southern Comfort or mint juleps (or *my* preferences: a braw snifter of Grand Marnier, or better yet—of fifteen-year-old Glenfiddich Special Reserve single malt Scotch mixed with a little less than half of Drambuie from the ancient Scots Isle of Skye—accompanied by a good Nicaraguan cigar grown from a Cuban seed).

I did occasionally enjoy the Glenfiddich (with and without the Drambuie) with the obligatory cigar, but instead of slowing down, I increasingly *sped up*—even if it wasn't always in the precise direction I wanted or intended.

When my year at Trombly was up, I applied for a professorship at the University of Michigan and for an academic directorship in secondary education at Oakland University, where I was already teaching part-time. Former DPS superintendent Arthur Jefferson had told me when I retired that he could get me into U-M with him full-time. College of Education dean Gerald Pine had told me the same regarding Oakland. I had also applied for professorships in other universities and for superintendencies in districts that had heavily black student populations.

Insiders whom I knew in all of those institutions told me my (partially-deserved) "radical" reputation was continuing to cause difficulty getting me hired—and in some places, even getting me *interviewed*. My incendiary newspaper columns weren't helping—particularly when I defended Arab-Americans and affirmative action and called for reparation monies to be paid to the descendants of American slaves. I had also touted the (Pontiac) Area Urban League (AUL) in one of my regular *Observer/Eccentric* columns (on Thursday, December 15, 1994) under the punning headline "Have an AUL-American Christmas," and noted cynically that Rochester had no Urban League, but needed one.

In one of my regular *Oakland Press* columns (on Sunday, March 7, 1997), headlined "Engler ready to impose mandatory diet on many," I wrote, "There's an official new game called the 'Mandatory Diet Game.' Its rules are simple: just eat for three months in any three-year period and fast for the other thirty-three months." During that month, the Family Independence Agency had begun to require childless adults under fifty-one to work twenty hours per week. The problem, as fiery activist rector Harry Cook of St. Andrew's Episcopal Church in Clawson had warned, was that many of these people had addictions and disabilities that made it nearly impossible for them to work.

In another 1997 *Oakland Press* column (on Sunday, April 6), that was head-lined "Engler most dangerous governor in state history," I accused Governor John Engler of advancing an agenda that would privatize public education, institute school prayer and a voucher system, and charter many more formerly private schools without mandating that they admit physically or mentally handicapped students or administer the MEAP test as traditional public schools are required to do. Charter schools also offered (and generally *still* offer) comparatively fewer art, music, and co-curricular programs—especially athletic programs. In every sense, John Engler would prove himself to be a veritable prince of darkness to the downtrodden and disenfranchised.

After reading these columns in the *Oakland Press*, County Executive L. Brooks Patterson wrote a letter to the *Press* defending Engler, calling me an "unmitigated fool" and referring to me sarcastically as "the eminent Sir Telford." No one had apparently informed the Republican Patterson that the knightly appellation, "Sir" is supposed to precede the *given* name—not the *surname*—of a Democratic knight such as myself. Mr. Patterson was *really* supposed to call me "Sir *John*"—not "Sir *Telford*," for goodness' sake! (Still, I did appreciate his knighting me.)

While school districts and colleges were wary of my supposed "radicalism," the ACLU and most of the Democrats weren't. I was being considered for the directorship of the Michigan ACLU. Also, some Oakland County Democrats were trying to talk me into establishing residence in nearby and heavily Democratic Pontiac so they could get me elected to Congress. I didn't tell these Dems about Eva, but she was the main reason I couldn't even *consider* that move. The Republicans would have found out about her fast, as well as about some other ladies I was still seeing regularly at the time—including the two married ones. Unfortunately, I just hadn't been willing enough to restrain myself sufficiently to be able to follow my father's familial Code in that one lone amatory category.

However, I continued to adhere to his Code *to the letter* in all of my other lifelong endeavors—and after a bit more searching, I discovered what looked like the perfect position for me. I applied and was hired for a job as the executive director of a K-12 cluster of charter schools in Detroit, Oak Park, and Southfield. More than eight hundred students in these schools were refugees from the failing Detroit public school system, and they had a long waiting list of DPS kids. While I was in philosophical opposition to the existence and even the *idea* of charter schools, I rationalized to myself that given my curricular and organizational genius (and *modesty!*), I could provide these luckless refugees with a far better education than anyone else could. This, I felt, was particularly so if the "anyone else" in question was the chronically mismanaged DPS, which wasn't far from the tail-spinning free-fall that was soon to overtake it.

I spent most of the summer of 1994 recruiting teachers, including the young lady who lived next door to me in Rochester Hills. Her husband had deserted her and their two children, and she needed a job. Let me state for the record, too, that despite her attractiveness, I didn't get romantic with her—nor did she with me. Our relationship was strictly business (also, I ordinarily didn't involve myself in that way with next-door neighbors).

To fill some vacant principalships in these schools, I recruited Reggie Bradford, my All-State quarter-miler at Pershing in 1966, the Reverend Arkles Brooks, my best quarter-miler at Southeastern in 1961, and Irving "Pete" Petross, who had run with me on that great Detroit Track Club sprint relay team in 1958. Pete had retired as principal of Mumford High School and had connections in the Detroit Public Schools' warehouse. That summer, the four of us rented a flatbed truck, hauled away thousands of discarded or never-used texts, biographies, works of fiction, and reference books—and stocked the near-empty shelves of our charter schools' libraries and classrooms with them.

In the DPS warehouse, I noted crates and crates and still *more* crates of unopened books that stretched out for what was nearly a city block. A worker confided, "They've been here for *years*—never ever used." Evidently, some DPS honchos had taken some hefty kickbacks from the companies for buying them. I didn't like this at all, and I made a mental note to write about it in my newspaper column.

I presently discovered that the president of the charter schools corporation who had hired me was *also* doing some things I didn't like—things like not paying my teachers and principals at the salary-level he had told me he would pay them and that I had in turn promised them that they would get paid. There were also rats in one of the elementary schools. I therefore accepted a job as manager of education programs at Wolverine Human Services in Detroit and brought Brooks and Bradford with me as instructional specialists.

My old mentor Petross stayed behind with his school—for a while.

I immediately took to my job at Wolverine Human Services: I loved having two of my old athletes and best friends working with me again every day. WHS was a benevolent, multi-sited, many-faceted phoenix that its visionary chief executive officer, Robert ("R. E.") Wollack, who was ten years my junior, had founded and raised from rubble and ash to fashion into a million-dollar agency with a branch in Florida and a large lockup facility in Michigan's Buena Vista Township.

Wollack and Wolverine were a dynamic duo—they were truly made for each other. Wollack ruled Wolverine nurturingly, tenderly, and *tyrannically*. Virtually all of his employees feared him, except me. I had faced and defeated Olympic champions, and he knew it. However, what *neither* of us knew then was that we had a lot more in common than we thought: For one thing, we had both been incarcerated—although this wasn't something one would put on a resumé; for another, we both had very healthy egos—and neither of us backed down from anything or anyone. We were both also blunt and frank to a fault.

Wollack—a certified social worker—surrounded himself with a few loyal men who had "done time" with him, and he also liked to recruit athletes. I had brought him three—two of us ex-All-Americans, and one (glory be!) a *Michigan* man! Wollack was a U-M grad and a rabid fan of Michigan athletics. In fact, the WHS logo was a huge inverted maize-colored block "M," which formed the "W," on a blue background—U-M's colors.

Wollack knew I had received a medal in my hand from a pope and rubbed elbows with many "captains and kings." He knew, too, that I had managed budgets and divisions that dwarfed his, and I was a retiree who had embarked upon my life's "second season." My hefty (and hard-earned) pension freed me of concerns about getting or holding any job, and my doctorate afforded me lavish latitude in choosing *where* I would work, with *whom*, and *for* whom.

I had chosen *him*. I admired this man and his mission to help the helpless and house the homeless—and I had his back 100 percent.

He likewise had mine. One day I interviewed and decided to hire a former Rose Bowl and Super Bowl player named Mike Oldham who I noted had leadership potential but had fallen on hard times. I knew that Mr. Wollack would be delighted to land this rare prize. Mike had been a star wide receiver at Michigan, teaming with my Pershing sprinter, Glenn Doughty. At U-M, they had lived in a celebrated athletes' residence they dubbed the "Den of the Mellow Men." Another Wolverine Human Services staffer—tight end Paul Seal, a future NFL star who had hurdled at Pershing—had stayed there, too.

Meanwhile, residents whose cases would break the hardest heart continued to pour into the Wolverine Shelter. A little seven-year-old black boy who had been beaten literally out of his wits by his mother's boyfriend asked me hopefully, "Are you Jesus?" I had a beard and shoulder-length brown hair then (as I do now, although the hair is turning somewhat grayer)—and I was wearing a loose, white, collarless shirt that day.

"No," I told him gently, "I'm not Jesus—but I can still be your friend."

A thirteen-year-old inmate at Wolverine's lockup on Alter Road had been toting a .38 caliber revolver and selling drugs worth thousands of dollars on the street. He had a baby by a twenty-six-year-old woman.

The crackhead mother of a smart, handsome fifteen-year-old at Wolverine's St. Jude's Residential Center had sold her son to a Detroit drug dealer for drugs. The dealer had in turn sold the boy's services performing oral sex to female drug buyers—black and white—and the boy described those experiences in graphic detail in his compositional themes at our in-house school.

This point in *time* for these three youngsters was—to borrow a Shakespearean phrase—"*out of joint*" (to put it mildly). The magnificent WHS was giving food, shelter, and succor to hundreds of other youthful sufferers of similar circumstances.

The same day that the little seven-year-old asked me if I was Jesus, I had retrieved my unregistered .38 from a friend who'd been having problems with his daughter's abusive ex-lover. I was driving home late from a dinner meeting I had attended with Mr. Wollack and his administrative staff at a local Mexican restaurant. The loaded gun was beside me under an *Oakland Press* newspaper. (I had a column that I had written about Wolverine in it.) Suddenly, a man materialized out of some tall weeds by the expressway ramp with his hand in his pocket, ordered me out of my car, and demanded that I give him the keys. I was parked at a light with the window down, just before I was to enter the westbound freeway at Chalmers Avenue. I grabbed my gun, cocked it, and pointed it at his nose. "I'd rather not," I said—and he faded fast into the dusk.

The next day that car—a beautiful robin's-egg blue nineteen-foot Cadillac Brougham D'Elegance—got hit-and-run hard in the parking lot at St. Jude's. I had it fixed, but it never ran quite right after that.

In that summer of 1996, my wife and I took our daughter Katherine on a whirlwind tour of Venice, Florence, and Rome to get her away from a slick gigolo from Mississippi named Brad, whom she had met at Panama City Beach while vacationing in Florida with her Michigan State sorority. The unemployed Brad had migrated up to East Lansing on an unlicensed motorcycle and was lolling around in my daughter's off-campus East Lansing apartment paid for with my money. He was also drinking Southern Comfort that my daughter had purchased for him with my money. (He had the gall to offer me a glass.)

Eventually, we starved Brad out by paying Katherine's rent directly to her landlord and allotting her just enough food money for one person—*her*. First, though, they both got very thin—but ultimately Brad had to either ride his motorcycle back home to Mississippi or get a job, because the one older female client he had been able to find in East Lansing wasn't giving him enough side money to help support his lifestyle. He was wearing expensive clothing from Abercrombie & Fitch that Katherine had bought for him—also, of course, with my money. *Thank God*, the underfed Brad chose to go back home.

This Italian tour was the first time I had been to the historic peninsula since touring with the U.S. Team there four decades earlier, when a Roman fortune teller had told me I would return to Rome during the Olympic Games. Since *Track & Field News* had named me an early favorite for the 400-meter gold medal in the upcoming 1960 Olympics in that city, I believed the fortune teller was naturally referring to the Rome Olympics. Ironically, it turned out that (if her predictive skill was bona fide) she must have been referring to the 1996 *Barcelona* Olympics—I was in *Rome* while they were being held in *Spain*.

We met a talented young sculptor from Royal Oak, Michigan, named Robert Landry in the Rome subway. He was in Italy studying the painting and sculpture of the great Italian masters. It so happened that Robert held the Royal Oak high school record for the mile run, as well as the record for that distance at Western Michigan University—with an impressive time of four minutes, nine seconds at WMU.

When we got back home to Michigan, Katherine began to date Robert, as well as some other new young fellows, and the shadily enterprising Brad blessedly became a permanent part of her past.

Back at Wolverine, I arranged to have former Rose Bowl and Super Bowl player Mike Oldham teach a sample lesson at the Wolverine shelter on Dickerson Street. While observing the lesson, I immediately perceived Mike's empathy for these kids, and I became even more convinced that he would be a wonderful teacher for the poor little beaten boy at the shelter and the other neglected or abandoned boys there.

When the director of the shelter, which was one of Wolverine's four local residential centers, decided that he didn't *want* Mike to be his instructional specialist, our mutual immediate supervisor ordered me not to hire him. In a previous evaluation of me, this supervisor had written that I was a "charismatic leader."

He apparently wasn't sufficiently impressed with my judgment of charismatic leadership potential in *others* to let me hire Mike despite the shelter director's unfounded objections, so I went over his head to R. E. Wollack. My supervisor was informing colleagues that Mike would never work for WHS at the very moment Mr. Wollack was offering the former University of Michigan Rose Bowl and Washington Redskins Super Bowl player a contract.

When my supervisor found out that I had gotten the CEO to hire Mike, he was embarrassed and angry. He began to assign time-consuming busy-work tasks to my staff—including my close compadres Brooks and Bradford—as a way of getting at *me*.

I didn't want to trouble Wollack or Wolverine with this kind of petty and destructive dissension within our managerial ranks, and I didn't want my staff to suffer unjustly, so I decided it was time for me to go.

I resigned from the education manager job and confidently bought myself another Cadillac the same day.

CHAPTER FORTY-FOUR

A RIGHTS-AGENCY DECIMATED; A LIFE-ALTERING ERROR

"May you live in *interesting* times."

—*Old Chinese proverb (and curse)*

I had made many friends at Wolverine, including CEO Wollack and his two top lieutenants—Jeff Ferguson and Pete Walsh, nursing coordinator Elacey Buchanan, community liaison officer Charles Dukes, residential directors Norbert Akins and Kevin Johnson (whom I had encouraged to get his doctorate), Eddie Carr (whose son Oba was a world welterweight boxing contender), and former super middleweight boxer Muhammad Alif. I also had to bid a sad goodbye to all of my instructional and DPS liaison staff, including public-schools liaison Linda Watkins; social studies teacher Mark Biolchino; the lockup's art instructor, Brenda Davis; and former Detroit and Pontiac principal David Badger—an old Western Michigan University long jumper I had hired as an instructional specialist.

Wollack later appointed me to the Wolverine Human Services advisory board. This pleased me enormously, since I believed so fervently in the agency's crucial mission.

The director who didn't want me to hire Mike to be his instructional specialist became Mike's staunchest supporter, because Mike proved himself to be a gifted and versatile teacher.

Mike's recurring drinking problem resurfaced, though, just after I left. I helped him get sober by literally commanding him to pour all his liquor down the sink, and I found a new job for him—and also for Brooks and Bradford—teaching in the charter school at the Wayne County Juvenile Detention Facility.

Previously, I had kept Mike sober and got him job interviews and driven him to them while his car was impounded. I had also driven him to the car pound and given him money to reclaim his car.

Bewildered, Mike had asked, "Why are you helping me like this?"

"Because right now you need it," I had answered.

Mike, who has written a testimonial blurb for this book, is now a sober and respected charter-school administrator in Warren.

Having once been a budding Boy Scout, I did another good deed later that year at Onassis Coney Island in downtown Detroit. An indigent black man was sitting at the counter making a meal of ketchup and some little doughy, round dumplings in cellophane he had picked up from a small dish on the counter when the owner told him to get out. I asked the man what he wanted to eat. "A chili dog," he said. I ordered two for him. It was cold outside and he had no coat, so as I was leaving, I gave him my overcoat. When I got home that night and Lynn asked me why I wasn't wearing my overcoat, I told her I had left it in a restaurant—which was technically the truth.

Meanwhile, MOSAIC—the organization I had co-founded with Dick Lobenthal, Rabbi Arnie Sleutelberg, feminist Carol King, the Skillman Foundation's Dave Fukazawa, and State Representative Maxine Berman—had also performed some memorable *mitzvahs*, and we were getting a lot of positive newspaper and television attention. These *mitzvahs* included getting a rapacious and criminally neglectful Royal Oak landlord to rectify his transgressions against an indigent black lady—a Pershing alumna two years older than me named Alberta Withers with whom I had coincidentally had a romantic interlude nearly forty years earlier.

However, there was a growing problem on our executive board. When Lobenthal and I brought Dr. Henry Messer and another leader of the Triangle Foundation onto the board, every single one of our black board members protested.

I had been Triangle's education chair for a brief time and had come to believe strongly in gay rights after I learned that gays' sexual proclivities are genetic—something they cannot help. Dick Lobenthal, Bishop Thomas Gumbleton, and I had authorized Triangle to list our names on its stationery letterhead as members of its advisory board along with other human-rights activists, both gay and straight. Now, in addition to calling me a "radical Commie," etc., some of my reactionary foes began to call me "queer," as well! Inveterate womanizer that I was, I found this amusing, but Professor Monifa Jumanne did not.

Monifa knew that I didn't have a gay bone in my body. She had been my close compadre ever since she'd rallied Rochester's black parents to my defense when the bigots came after me, and I asked her if Triangle could use her name on its list along with mine and Lobenthal's. "John," she replied, "*No way*—their lifestyle goes against my religion. I can't even stay on the *MOSAIC board* if the Triangle people are going to be part of it."

Professor Jumanne's sentiments were shared by Rev. Arkles Brooks and Col. Aaron Gordon (incidentally a Korean War veteran who had once nearly been court-martialed for forcibly integrating a segregated Officers Club). Despite my best efforts to talk them into staying, all three of them resigned from the board, to my dismay. North Oakland County NAACP director Bill Nabers and Dr. Norman McCrae, DPS' director of social studies, subsequently resigned, too, for other reasons. The executive board of the agency I had co-founded to fight for African-American rights now no longer had any African-Americans on it! Our board also lost co-founder Arnie Sleutelberg. The young rabbi's Congregation *Shir Tikvah*, which had once given me a certificate "for stamping out prejudice and bigotry," was keeping him too busy to donate any more time to MOSAIC. Thus the agency was in effect decimated, although Lobenthal and I managed to keep it alive a little longer.

Around this time, my thirty-seven-year-old godson Rick Boudro, a former All-State wrestler at Utica High and the son of my first cousin and lifelong friend Carl who still lived in Arkansas, was having marital troubles and was staying with us in my house in Rochester Hills. As I mentioned, a few years earlier Rick's older brother Cracker had been slain in Detroit by rival drug dealers and his body tossed in a dumpster in mid-July. Carl and I had both tried many times to get Cracker to change his lifestyle, and when I told my father that one of my cousin Carl's two sons had been murdered, he had asked laconically, "Was it the *good* one or the *bad* one? The *bad* one?—*good*."

Rick—the "*good* one" (and the only *remaining* one)—was sitting with me in my family room when I made one of my infrequent calls to say hello to my thirty-one-year-old son, Steven. Steve still didn't know he was my son. The reader may recall that Steve's married mother, Corinna, had let me into his life to counsel him when he was a troubled nineteen-year-old on the condition that I wouldn't tell him he was my son as long as her husband who had raised him was alive. In the course of our brief phone conversation, Steve casually mentioned to me that his father had passed away nearly a year earlier.

Rick was listening with great interest to every word. As soon as I hung up the phone, Rick asked, "Well, are you going to call him back and tell him?"

"No, I'm going to *meet* him and tell him. If his mother won't do it with me, I'll do it alone."

I did do it alone, and we hugged. A blood test proved our father-son kinship, and Steve changed his name to Telford.

However, while Steve now had found a new father, I soon discovered that I never could really replace the old one, because Steve and I had perforce spent a world of time apart during his crucial formative years. My lovely wife Lynn didn't take well, either, to the prospect of suddenly having an uneducated *bastard* (*her* word) son of mine hanging around, even though I had told her about Steve before I married her.

Also, while Lynn had known about my relationship with Eva for years, she picked this time to ask me, "Is Eva always going to be a part of our lives?" I answered unwisely that I didn't think it would be right for me to abandon Eva now that she was old and overweight, after so many years of her devotion to me. This turned out to be a response that very shortly would inexorably seal my fate and that of my family.

Can a man love more than one woman simultaneously? Yes, he can—but if he *acts* on all of his feelings, this ends up hurting the women deeply, and if he's sensitive to *their* feelings, it hurts *him* as well. Sadly, too, philandering is all too easy for married men to rationalize. They need only point to prominent Americans—both historic and contemporary—such as Franklin Roosevelt, Dwight Eisenhower, the three Kennedy brothers, Bill Clinton, presidential hopefuls Gary Hart and John Edwards, Martin Luther King, Jr., Joe Louis, Sugar Ray Robinson, Muhammad Ali, film stars Gary Cooper and Peter Lawford, Elvis Presley, basketball stars Kobe Bryant and Earvin "Magic" Johnson, preacher Jimmy Swaggart, North Carolina governor Mark Sanford and former New York governor Elliott Spitzer, former Detroit mayor Kwame Kilpatrick, plus a zillion other actors, entertainers, and politicians, *ad infinitum*. However, this certainly doesn't make it *right*. If truth were told, at least half of my own friends and colleagues over the years also would qualify for this list—but the best thing a man can do for his children is to marry their mother before they're born, *stay* married to her *after* they're born, wear his wedding ring at all times, and always remain faithful to her.

Lynn and I were having problems with our very beautiful and very headstrong twenty-three-year-old daughter, Katherine, too. After running through a string of ne'er-do-well boyfriends and a few good ones who included Patrick Butler, a Rochester attorney I had taken a liking to, and Robert Landry, the teacher/sculptor who had particularly impressed me, Katherine had become engaged to a man from a wealthy Republican family—a handsome, chauvinistic young Irish-Italian who I feared would hurt her emotionally. (More than a decade later, this gentleman would mature and evolve to become a town councilman in Shelby Township, Michigan.)

As I had done every week for the past twenty-four years, I came home late one evening after drinking too much with my old Berkley buddy George Blaney (we usually put away a bottle of Chardonnay apiece). The date was October 28, 1997. I was planning to host a party for an Oakland University class I was teaching, and since Lynn would be unable to host it, I asked my dauntless daughter to do the honors for me.

"Well, I don't *know*—I'll have to check my *calendar*," Katherine replied flippantly. This adult daughter of mine was eating and sleeping under her parents' roof virtually free of charge, still attending college at our expense, running up credit cards, getting speeding tickets (including one where she was clocked at 97 mph on I-75), and driving the second car we had bought her after she had totaled my silver Lincoln and her mother's white Chrysler Fifth Avenue— but she'd have to *check her calendar* to do her father this single small favor!

The sour taste of indignation was rising in my throat along with the tart taste of the residue of too much wine. I was indignant not just about her obvious reluctance to host the party, but also about all the other things she had done to worry and upset us over the years.

"Check your *calendar*? *Check your calendar*? Did I *actually* hear you say you'll have to *check your calendar*?"

"*Yes*, Dad," she snapped with curt impatience. "You *heard* me right."

Impulsively, I got up and slapped her. She fled upstairs—and I ran up right after her and yelled, "I'm not paying for any *wedding*, either!" I fanned a couple more slaps past her face to scare her, intentionally missing her by about an inch—and her mother threatened to call the police. I told her mother to go ahead and call them.

My daughter screamed at me, "You *never* wanted him to marry me!"

"Damn straight. Your considerate fiancé wouldn't even take my ninety-year-old mother home from our house the night I asked him to—remember that time when I was throwing up? My cousin Jeff ended up taking her and going far out of his way to do it. And your fiancé was driving right by her apartment with you to go to some nebulous late-night party that then never even *took place*."

I fanned at her face again and huffed, "Not only *that*—your fiancé made *racial jokes* when I had Muhammad Alif and the two Golden Gloves champs over to watch Eddie Carr's son fight on TV for the welterweight title—and your fiancé sat there bragging to all those talented fighters about what a great *boxer* he'd been, when as far as I know he never ever boxed a *round*. Muhammad had been a *pro*—and those two tough kids of his stayed polite for my sake, but I was so embarrassed I wanted to fall through the floor!"

I was nearly sixty-two years old, and now my blood pressure was soaring into the stratosphere. "I think you're *crazy* to even *consider* marrying him!"

At this point, Katherine started hitting and scratching me—and since I wouldn't *really* hit her, I retreated back downstairs and sat down sadly at the kitchen table. That was where the Oakland County Sheriff's deputies found me sitting when they came.

CHAPTER FORTY-FIVE

THREE CARLOADS OF COPS; THREE PAIN-FILLED POEMS

"If my *father* can't walk me down the aisle, *no one* will."

—*Katherine Telford*

Three carloads of Oakland County Sheriff's deputies had arrived fast, red flashers whirling surreally in the gathering dusk. *Three squad cars* to arrest one old, sixty-one-year-old man!?! The sergeant in command was apologetic, even deferential: "You're going to have to come with us, Dr. Telford—and we're going to have to cuff you."

How, I wondered, could this young sergeant know I was <u>Dr.</u> Telford?

They led me out in handcuffs in front of all the neighbors, with my daughter crying upstairs. I learned later from my godson Rick that when they took a statement from Katherine, she had begged them not to arrest me, but my wife said, "No—go ahead and *take* him."

I was photographed and fingerprinted, and I spent the next three nights—which included a weekend—in the Oakland County Jail in a large gymnasium packed with hundreds of prisoners and one cold, seatless porcelain toilet stool in the middle of the gym. (I noted that even though Oakland County is over-whelmingly white, about two-thirds of the prisoners were black.)

How the once-mighty had fallen! I felt then how the fallen and jailed Detroit Mayor Kwame Kilpatrick must feel now, as I write this chapter. Kwame had once told his mentor, Charlie Primas, "I *like* that little white guy (me), even though I know he didn't vote for me." Well, I still like that big *black* guy, too—and I hated to watch him self-destruct. Also, I did vote for him in his first run for mayor. (The second time, I voted for former mayor Dennis Archer's deputy, Freman Hendrix.)

On that fateful late October day in 1997, *I* was the one who self-destructed. The rim and sides of that single cold toilet bowl in the Oakland County jail were slimy with excrement. We stood in line to use it—or to make a phone call. During the night, I got in a brief scuffle over a pallet to lie on. There weren't enough pallets for everyone, and someone had tried to snatch mine out from under me. As I lay on my musty, well-worn pallet, I listened sleeplessly to loud singing or moaning or crazed cackling and cursing all through the night. After my scuffle, two scrawny, scared white teenagers I had befriended kept very close to me.

When I was finally able to call home the next morning, my daughter answered, "Hello?"

"Get me *out* of here!"

Katherine handed the phone to her mother. "I'm divorcing you," my wife of twenty-eight years said flatly, and hung up. The altercation with Katherine hadn't been her real reason for divorcing me, but it had given her a rare window of opportunity. My ongoing and seemingly never-to-end relationship with Eva was her real reason, and she suspected correctly that there were and had been other women as well.

Katherine hadn't known about Eva, but now her mother told her, and her mother also told all of her friends and mine.

I didn't want Lynn to divorce me, but I richly deserved it.

Past midnight of my next night in the Oakland County Jail, I stepped on and stumbled over a sleeping man's ankle on my way to the toilet. Wakened so rudely, he sprang up without a word and hit me hard in the chest, cracking cartilage in my lower sternum. I split a knuckle in my left hand putting him down (I had already hurt my *right* hand in the previous scuffle). For a suspenseful moment, the man reared back up in the dim light from a solitary deputy's plexiglass cage nearby, and then thankfully sank back down. The ruckus had stirred the seated deputy from his doze, and he admonished us sleepily, "*Quiet down* out there." Then he immediately went back to sleep—but *I* didn't. My injured chest hurt, and both of my aching hands had begun to swell.

The next morning, the two teenagers—both in for car theft—continued to tag along after me like a pair of puppies. Where I walked, *they* walked.

When I stopped, *they* stopped. On Monday morning, the last day I was there, one of them got released. Then *I* was released. As I was leaving, the look of fear on the face of the boy left behind still haunts me, because that dangerous, stinking, overcrowded Oakland County jail was no place for a kid.

A deputy who knew me dropped me off at my lavish home in the Hills. Lynn had already changed the locks, so I couldn't get in the house, but my Cadillac was still in the driveway. I drove it downtown to Eva's place overlooking the river and moved in with her until I found a one-bedroom furnished apartment in Royal Oak. Its name was a clever pun—*Suite* Life.

However, life wasn't so *sweet* for me just then. Lynn had taken out a PPO (personal protection order) on me in her and my daughter's names, so I couldn't contact either of them. This was searing and stabbing my very entrails, because despite everything that had happened and all the serious mistakes I had made, I still loved them.

To make matters worse, my mug shot had appeared in the *Oakland Press* and elsewhere, in living color. I was still somewhat inebriated when the picture was taken, and my dark-bearded Celtic countenance staring stonily at the camera resembled that of an IRA bomber caught blowing up the Brits. Sigrid Grace of the Oakland Democrats told me she had inside information that Sheriff's Captain McCabe had informed Oakland County Executive L. Brooks Patterson that they had caught a "big-fish Dem" and asked him what they should do with me. The order had then come down from the Republican Patterson to release my mug shot to the media—an order that sealed my sad fate.

Oakland University reluctantly let me finish teaching the term. Lynn had me served with divorce papers and the personal protection order right in my classroom while I was teaching my class. The University declined to rehire me the next semester. Also, the *Oakland Press* unceremoniously terminated my column. Soon afterward, the *Observer/Eccentric* newspapers followed suit.

When my daughter got married, I attended the wedding but wasn't allowed to walk her down the aisle, wear a tuxedo, or be photographed with the wedding party. I was also barred from attending the $28,000 reception which Lynn paid for from our savings—coincidentally a thousand dollars for every year we had been married. Lynn had recently had a breast-reduction procedure, so she gleefully announced to my friends George and Joyce Blaney and others at the reception, "I got rid of my boobs and my husband at the same time!"

Lynn had wanted the husband of a friend of hers to walk Katherine down the aisle, but my daughter had said, "If my *father* can't walk me down the aisle, *no one* will."

Katherine walked down the aisle alone. I was sorely tempted to jump up out of my pew and join her, but I didn't want to do anything to upset her or cause an unclassy commotion at her classy wedding. As I watched my little girl—all grown up now—walk down the aisle, my heart went out to her, and I felt tears on my cheeks. I remembered all the PTA meetings and piano recitals and ballet performances and school plays (Katherine had had the starring role in *James and the Giant Peach*, at West Middle School in Rochester, and I had had my tech director, Deborah Anthony, videotape it).

I also remembered the times she had gotten in trouble in school— including the time she beat up an older boy who had pulled her long brown locks at Burton Elementary School in Huntington Woods, and her fistfights in Rochester with big middle school girls envious of her tapered allure who sorrowfully learned that despite her willowy look, she could throw a tooth-loosening right cross. I was right there after every single incident, negotiating on her behalf.

I remembered, too, her cute little kindergartener tantrum after she repeatedly and compulsively counted her 101 black marbles that were in her little 101 Black Marbles Bag, and *one* marble, marble no. 101, repeatedly turned up missing—and I remembered her suspending her tantrum to listen to me when I told her that if she would just listen for a moment, I had a solution to her problem. Then, being unable to produce the lost 101st black marble, when I told her my solution was for her to be happy that she still had a full *100* black marbles, she resumed her tantrum.

I remembered our "cat hunts" chasing our elusive tabby Thurstine all throughout our Huntington Woods house, and all of our long daughter-and-daddy walks and picnics in nearby Oak Park Park—and us giving the bones from our half-eaten ribs to a hungry and soon very happy stray dog that befriended us in the park. Nostalgically, I recalled visits to Major Magic's All-Star Pizza Review, and to the many movies, and to the Children's Zoo on Belle Isle, and to the Detroit Zoo in Royal Oak that backed up to Huntington Woods, nearly in our backyard.

I recalled the half-birthday parties her mother and I gave for her every June, when I would line up the boys in the little corner park by our house and have them race her—and she would always win. (In one of the later years, two boys refused to run, saying: "We're not running against *her* again.")

I remembered her asking her daddy if she was in trouble for crushing the flower in the paper cup that belonged to the little girl visiting next door and me answering, "Yes, you definitely are in trouble"—but still reading her the *Goodnight, Moon* book that night, plus the picture books about "where the wild things are" and about naughty *Pierre* who didn't *care* and was eaten by a lion.

Now *I* was a lonely, old, lost lion—and I was eating away my lonely, old, humiliatingly humbled, lost-lion heart.

Rochester school board member Julie Zboril, who was deeply disappointed in me, told me: "I have lost my only hero." I protested, "But, Julie—Katherine totally *deserved* that slap. Some day in the distant future she may actually mature and come to realize that I was a pretty fair father." Upon reflection, though, I figured that it probably wasn't so much my slapping Katherine that had bothered Julie the most. Learning about *Eva* was what had undoubtedly bothered Julie the most. When that part of my less-than-admirable private life came to light, I had damaged the one thing of greatest value to me—my good name. (*Proverbs 22:1: A good name is rather to be chosen than great riches. . . .*)

In November 1998, my ninety-one-year-old mother dropped down on her bathroom floor and died of a failing body and a broken heart. If I had had any lingering doubts before, I was now absolutely certain that the God of my forefathers was punishing me for scorning His seventh commandment throughout my twenty-eight-year marriage and thus violating the pertinent edict in the unwritten ancestral Code that had been handed down to me by those ancient Caledonian progenitors for a full thirty-five generations.

Helen Telford was the saintliest, most loving soul I have ever known. It was and is a rare honor and blessing to have been and to *be* her son. My doctor had told me I would die if I stopped taking my thyroid medicine, so after my mother passed, I stopped taking the medicine—but I didn't die. Instead, I lost hair and had a mini-stroke which caused me to drag one leg a bit when I walked. Eva and my old buddy Chuck Roehl, the former star sprinter from the University of Detroit, got me to Chuck's doctor, Dominick Cusumano, pronto—and Dr. Cusumano put me on stronger medication.

However, I took it only sporadically. I didn't feel much like living, but I really didn't want to die, either. More than once, I found myself calling the suicide prevention center in Royal Oak at two o'clock in the morning. I missed my family and my six-year-old cats—my mischievous calico Whitleigh and her ditzy black sister, Samantha—who had slept with me every night. I mused morbidly and incessantly about my parents and other relatives and friends lost forever in what Shakespeare called *death's dateless night*, and about Dan Telford—my tall, handsome uncle who had killed himself over a girl at twenty-eight, and whom I had never known except as a solemn image in old photographs. I was approaching my 62nd birthday, but I wasn't at all certain that I would still be alive by then. My glory days of defeating Olympic champions were long behind me, and reflecting upon those golden days in this gray time of despair brought nostalgia no longer, but only bitterness.

In his 2008 book *Lincoln: The Biography of a Writer*, Fred Kaplan cites a poignant early poem that Abraham Lincoln once penned about a mortally wounded animal he had seen brought to bay in a hunt. It was highlighted by these chilling closing lines:

> *But leaden death is at his heart;*
> *Vain all the strength he plies—*
> *And spouting blood from every part,*
> *He reels, and sinks, and dies.*

In 1865, the Great Emancipator in turn famously became the mortally wounded animal he had so eloquently described, thus proving himself to also be a great *poet*—and 137 years later, I was perilously close to becoming that dying animal, too (if not as great a poet). I scribbled these two poems of my own during that sad Christmas season of 1997, in the deadest hours of the night:

> *Mr. Sandman's Sick*
> *Between gray dusk and dawn exist*
> *Alone, those nightless, nowhere wisps*
> *Of subjugated sometime which,*
> *Arrived upon, into—can twist*
> *The torque of my sub-consciousness*
> *Until it surfaces. Corpse-kissed,*
> *I wrest away my face. My wrist*
> *Is pinioned by a phantom fist*

Whose undead flesh my other wrist
Escapes. My sweating hand uplifts
The dripping bed-sheet, winding its
Loose folds around my widened lids;
And there I—with convulsive fits
Of flexion in my captive wrist—
Stare up with but half-hidden head:
A leering, lurking mask of mist
Above, agrin, looms by my bed.

And:

Requiem for a Quarter-miler
I defeated the best
At a pace lightning-fast
For one wondrous spring
And two summers.
In my final home stretch,
I just couldn't outlast
That ultimate king
Of all runners.

One of my two poems was nightmarish; the other was moribund—and it also was semi-suicidal. A decade later, I would change the pronouns from the first person to the second person in both poems and use them in inner-city English classes to teach *iambic tetrameter* (in the first poem), *alliteration* (in both), and *personification* in the second poem: the "king of all runners" is of course Death. My Detroit students in the first decade of the twenty-first century would later tell me they loved those two poems. They would find the first poem to be deliciously scary, and they would note that the other poem had haunting overtones of their own vulnerability to sudden demise—a salubrious specter that stalks them in their violence-ridden, narcotics-infested neighborhoods every minute of every day.

I also wrote a *third* poem with suicidal overtones during one of those interminable, sleepless nights in that late December of 1997. I had drunk nearly a fifth of Johnny Walker Red before I wrote it, but I was still able to pen some decent iambic tetrameter from the depth of my despair:

Johnny Walker Red
I bear the universal weight
Of infinite blind skies.
How is it that I hesitate
To claw behind my eyes?
I feel the untold cosmos squeeze;
I lie burnt-out in bed.
These great ungodly galaxies
That haunt me in my head
Were better dead.

That third poem I *never* taught, ever.

CHAPTER FORTY-SIX

AN *UN*-FOND FAREWELL
TO OAKLAND COUNTY

"Unless we finally tackle the tough task of desegregating Detroit,
the toxic effects of residential segregation will continue to poison
the aspirations of us all."

—*May 9, 1999* Detroit Free Press *column co-authored
with native Detroiter john powell, then the
Executive Director of the National Institute on Race
and Poverty at the University of Minnesota Law School*

To avoid killing myself in Royal Oak, I moved in with Eva at the River House in Detroit for several weeks. Eventually, I bought my own place on the eleventh floor two doors from her, overlooking the magnificent river—which actually is a strait connecting Lake Erie and Lake St. Clair. (*Detroit* is taken from two French words that mean, "of the strait.")

I will always be grateful to Eva, because even though my long relationship with her finally ended my twenty-eight-year marriage, it also probably saved my life when she took me in. Despite what judgmental people may say about the "other woman," there are always three sides to every such triangle. Eva was and *is* a good person—and she loved me. I loved her, too, and I loved her family. My non-judgmental mother had loved them, as well. With my assistance and counsel, Eva had earned bachelor's and master's degrees and had become a Wayne County social worker serving children with AIDS. I admired her tremendously for that—but due to what I felt was her chronically excessive drinking, and admittedly due also to my restlessly roving eye, our relationship couldn't stand the test of total togetherness.

Case in point: One steamy August night, Eva and I had been drinking for about eight hours in a humid Hamtramck bar with her hard-drinking Hamtramck girlfriends (whom I unkindly referred to as "whales") and with some of their equally hefty and hard-drinking husbands. Having become extremely tired (and extremely drunk), I asked Eva to drive me back to the River House or give me the keys so I could drive myself, because we had gone there in her car, and it was now past one o'clock in the morning. While she doesn't remember it this way, my recollection is that she refused—and kept drinking.

Although I was wearing only shorts, sandals, and a tank top, I drunkenly decided to walk the several miles home to the river. After I had meandered south on Mt. Elliott Street for about a mile, four young black men sitting drinking wine in a junk-strewn vacant lot got up and started walking purposefully toward me. "Oh, oh," I thought, becoming instantly less drunk. A taxicab suddenly materialized miraculously out of the darkness like some vehicular specter. "Taxi!" I yelled frantically, but it kept on going.

I kicked off my sandals and got ready to do some serious barefoot, middle-of-the-night street-sprinting, when the ghostlike vehicle braked abruptly about forty-five feet ahead. I lumbered to that God-sent cab as fast as I could, stumbled inside, and—still barefoot—mumbled to the driver, "Th' River House!"

We sped safely away.

After four or five more roller-coaster years like this of trying to make a life together despite Eva's drinking and my off-and-on womanizing, Eva and I eventually broke up. This was deeply painful for both of us, because we had been together for a very long time.

I had now been virtually destroyed both personally and professionally in Oakland County. Old friends, colleagues, and even some protégés and family members continued to shun me—many of them following the lead of their wives, who had been friends with mine. Ironically, I was privy to extramarital affairs that some of them—men and women alike—had had or were having, so I felt that some of this *shunning* was rather hypocritical.

Gradually, I "regrouped" and set about re-establishing myself in the county and city of my birth and youth, which I had always regarded as my real home. Detroiters are generally more forgiving of various forms of transgression than are many more judgmental and uptight suburbanites, and mine they would definitely have only winked at or shrugged off entirely—while laughing out loud at my tight-butt-conservative suburban "judges."

The Right Reverend Edwin Rowe, a white-bearded Denby alum and fiery activist several years younger than me to whom I confessed my whole sad story, quoted the Apostle Paul, who said we should forget those things that are behind. The Reverend also told me, "Life isn't about surviving your storm, John; it's about learning how to *dance* in it!"—good secular advice from a man of the cloth.

Reverend Rowe hired me to direct his PEACE-for-Youth programs at the huge and historic Central United Methodist Church on downtown Woodward Avenue, and I began joyfully to *dance* in my storm. I, in turn, recruited the great motivator Reggie Bradford, my ex-Pershing sprint star, to be my deputy director, and he hired nineteen-year-old ex-PSL sprint star Mario Dewberry, from Detroit's Redford High, to be his part-time assistant.

Reggie, Mario, and I quickly organized multiple activities for some forlorn teenaged boys and girls from local homeless shelters, from residential agencies like Wolverine, and from off the streets. These activities included our tutoring them, feeding them, praying with them, teaching them Kingian non-violence, providing them with materials to do crafts, playing plenty of basketball and volleyball with them, and bringing in guest speakers—who included a firmly on-the-wagon Mike Oldham—to inspire them. Mike showed them his Super Bowl ring, which put them in absolute awe of him. Soon, *they* were joyfully dancing in *their* storms, too!

Reggie also managed the church's huge parking lot, which was just across the street from the Fox Theater (he and his son Bradford Bradford are still managing it eleven years later as I write this chapter).

After several months directing PEACE-for-Youth, I left those superb programs in Reggie's competent directorial hands to take over the HUD-sponsored executive directorship of Detroit SNAP (Safe Neighborhoods Action Plan). While administering SNAP, I co-authored a May 5, 1999, column in the *Detroit Free Press* with john powell outlining how to produce safer schools and neighborhoods. The luminous powell was then directing the National Institute on Race and Poverty at the University of Minnesota Law School and using me off and on as a consultant.

Here are excerpts from that powell/Telford column of ten years ago, which was headlined, "Race problems stand in way of true growth":

Many of the most persistent problems of metro Detroit will go uncorrected unless we address the issue of <u>racial segregation</u>. Residential segregation is closely tied to economic segregation and the phenomenon known as "concentrated poverty"—where more than 40 percent of the people in a given census tract are living on incomes below the poverty standard.

In Detroit, the number of impoverished residents rose from 55,913 in 1970 to 418,947 in 1990—and 79.5 percent of them are black. . . . Such conditions engender teenage childbearing and truancy, welfare dependency, the proliferation of AIDS, prostitution, violence, drug abuse, infant mortality, inferior schools and housing, higher insurance rates, and . . . profiteering by those who exploit the people trapped in this economic quarantine.

Using data from a 1977 study by the U.S. Department of Housing and Urban Development [*HUD*], George Galster of Wayne State University found that white discrimination sets the pattern of racial residential change. His findings confirm that skin color is the organizing determinant of urban housing markets. Race dominates all other factors that impact upon where, and with whom, Americans live. It is crucial to understand how this pattern of impoverishment devastated Detroit. Black renters and buyers had less money [than whites] to start with, and their efforts to keep up their neighborhoods were hindered by discrimination by banks and insurance companies. HUD must establish permanent testing teams of black and white home-seekers to catch real estate agents who discriminate. Throughout our tri-county area, there has to be an affirmative effort to create access for minorities to housing that is close to jobs and other opportunities.

In addition, federal officials should routinely scrutinize banks' lending data to spot suspiciously high rejection rates. Hate crimes against blacks who integrate and against whites who support them should be prosecuted at the federal level as civil rights violations. Tax incentives to re-integrate inner-city Detroit and other urban centers should be offered to businesses, residential developers, landlords, and individual home buyers.

Unless we finally tackle the tough task of <u>desegregating Detroit</u>, the toxic effects of residential segregation will continue to poison the aspirations of us all.

That column could have been written *today*.

In 1999 the state had taken over the faltering Detroit Public Schools and removed the sitting school board. As a voting Detroiter, I felt that this takeover disenfranchised me and my fellow voters, and I said so in a *Telford's Telescope* column in the *Inner City Plow*—a local quarterly. Governor Engler had also told Detroit Mayor Dennis Archer that he wanted him to appoint a new "reform" board, and the governor had named the newly-retired CEO of my three-time alma mater, former Wayne State University President David Adamany, as interim superintendent of schools.

Mayor Archer was well-acquainted with my background in education. He had already read an earlier *Free Press* column I had written on March 9 on how to improve DPS, and when he read the powell/Telford column, he asked me if I wanted to serve on his task force to reform the Detroit Public Schools.

I quickly said *yes*.

CHAPTER FORTY-SEVEN

BACK TO THE FUTURE!

"Do you know there's a teacher up there teaching diagramming?"

—*Joyce Moore, Supervisor of Language Arts,*
Detroit Public Schools

Working out of my small office in a Detroit Police mini-station on Chene on the city's gritty east side, I continued to help nearby residents with landlord problems and other problems, including plumbing problems. At the Pasadena Apartments on East Jefferson, a tenant's toilet was leaking into another tenant's bathtub on the immediate lower floor. I went over there and had some fruitful conversations with the manager. I was sponsoring a Neighborhood Watch operation out of my office, as well. (I would have liked to arm those volunteers, issuing guns to them and checking them back in when they came off patrol.) I was also striving mightily—with some slight success—to educate, rehabilitate, and reform two extremely dangerous east side youth gangs. The gangs were selling drugs, stealing cars, and shooting, stomping, or stabbing non-gang members and each other indiscriminately over embossed leather coats, girls, and Nike gym shoes. Some of their little sisters were skipping school and trading sex for drugs—lolling around stoned and naked in nearby dope-houses all day.

Senior citizens in the neighborhood were afraid to come out of their houses. Local gang-affiliated children, like the thirteen-year-old father who had been in enforced residence at Wolverine Human Services, were mugging senior citizens and also packaging and peddling drugs, often toting loaded pistols in potato chip bags.

In September I left Detroit SNAP in the overworked but capable hands of my imposingly tall, tough executive assistant, Pat Richardson, to return to DPS under a special legislative bill allowing retirees like me to teach and still draw our pensions. I was slated to teach English and journalism and coach track at Southwestern High School. Hallelujah! Now I had *really* come full circle!

Several principals had wanted me, including Osborn High School's Stan Allen—a star high jumper in 1963 under coach Lorenzo Wright at old Eastern High—and Freddie Williams at Trombly, the scruffy adult high school where I had counseled five years before.

I chose Dr. Betty Hines at Southwestern because she had worked for me in the 1960s and I had come close to working with her again when she almost came to Rochester as principal at Adams High School. She also chose *me*. I thus became the only retired deputy superintendent in America—urban or suburban, black or white—who actually dared to come back and teach again in a regular, full-time position in a tough inner-city high school (or *any* high school), and I did it at the advanced age of *sixty-four*.

I knew that I would have to establish my reputation with the tough kids at Southwestern immediately. One day in September, Thomas Chastain— a football lineman and the varsity team captain—walked into my class five minutes late. I asked him to come to my desk so I could have a word or two with him. Ignoring my request, Tom sauntered to his seat.

Saying nothing, I took attendance and then brought the class to the library, where there was a guest presenter for the English classes. When I had my kids all seated and quieted down, I asked Tom to come with me into the library's annex hall. I asked another teacher—Avery Jackson, Jr.—to slip away with me, too, as a witness.

When the three of us were in the isolated little hall, I handed Avery my glasses, and pointing to my chin, I said to Tom, "Okay—take your shot." The big lineman was nonplussed, as I'd hoped he would be.

"Don't wanna hit you, Dr. T."

"Come on, take your shot! You think you're so big you can just keep walking away from me when I tell you to come to my desk? Take your *shot!*"

"Don't wanna."

"Well, do you want to do what I tell you to do?"

"Yeh."

"If I tell you to jump three times in the air, will you do it?"

Hesitation. "Yeh."

"Then go back in there and sit down."

When I told Dr. Hines about this, she said, "You *didn't*."

"Yes, Betty, I did—but you know what? I'm not having any more trouble with him now, and he's even rounding up the dawdlers for me and herding them into class before the bell."

My department head Willie Wooten and I had hit it off immediately when he saw I was controlling the discipline for my entire second-floor wing and he therefore rarely needed to come upstairs. In turn, he let me teach the in-depth traditional grammar my kids needed desperately, even though it was no longer in the curriculum. I dusted off the paper I had written and first used at Southeastern in 1962, and I was able to use it again now across town at Southwestern in 1999, thirty-seven years later.

By March, my kids' writing skills had markedly improved. One day, a supervisor from downtown named Joyce Moore walked by my classroom and saw my tenth-graders diagramming compound-complex sentences (taking the sentences apart and analyzing their components) on the blackboard. Horrified, she went straight to Department Head Wooten and Principal Hines. "Do you know there's a teacher up there teaching *diagramming*? That's not part of the approved curriculum!"

"Yes, we know what he's doing. It's our experimental program in traditional grammar. His students' *writing* is improving *measurably*—by leaps and bounds—and he's sharing some of his methods and concepts with the other teachers."

My varsity athletes' *sprint times* on the track were also improving *measurably* —and their *long-jumping* and *high-jumping* marks were also improving by "leaps and bounds." Sergio Ramirez' *distance-running* records were becoming more and more impressive, too. Sergio was an irrepressible tenth-grader from Texas who had won several 5,000-meter cross-country races and had approached ten minutes in the two-mile run (actually 3,200 meters) on the track. This was impressive time for Detroit's PSL (Public School League), which had always been far better known for its sprinters. He was also raising just a teeny bit of hell in every class except mine.

In the spring of the year 2000, I taught a poem about my late-career losses in and historic discouragement with my competitive running to Sergio and my other runners, of whom I had several in my classes. I had written this never-published poem thirty-eight winters earlier (in 1962) after barely winning one last state AAU title indoors at Ann Arbor in comparatively slow time, and then losing a big invitational 600-yard race at the Milwaukee Journal Games in even *slower* time. My students liked the poem, which provoked a lot of class discussion about what was most important in life, and which also enabled me to demonstrate a little bit to them about internal rhyme. The poem was entitled *Pyrite*:

> *Blue ribbons have purpled; my day's dying fast.*
> *Too long have I hurtled in chase of my past.*
> *Ten trophies have tarnished. My medals are mould*
> *The tone of old varnish. They're only fool's gold.*
> *Old rivals quit training, abandon the track,*
> *Yet I—muscles straining—pursue a new pack.*
> *I lose now more often, more now than past years—*
> *Whose passing can soften voluminous cheers.*
> *Tomorrow has passed, and next week sneaks apace—*
> *Far time I unfastened my feet from the chase.*

In 1962 I had been teaching and coaching at Southeastern and had begun doctoral studies in night school, so I hadn't had time to train adequately for those long-ago races in Ann Arbor and Milwaukee. I stressed to my Southwestern athletes how important conditioning is for them to be able to perform well.

I never had trouble with *Sergio's* conditioning, though—he consistently covered far more mileage in training than I asked of him. Bright though he was, however, I was having *plenty* of trouble keeping him scholastically eligible and off the suspension list for misbehavior.

Then, out of the blue, Sergio came to me with a far more serious problem that had nothing to do with his in-school behavior.

"Coach," he said, "I got to queet the team."

"*What?!* You *can't* quit—you're outrunning *everybody!*"

"Coach, I got to join a gang."

"A *gang?* Are you *loco?* You're not joining any gang!"

"Coach, you no onnerstan'. Eef I no join, they say they going to hurt my *mother*."

Now I understood. I paid an immediate visit to a southwest side community activist and former gang member I'd met at an anti-gang conference in the Coleman A. Young (City-County) Building downtown when I was directing Detroit SNAP. He arranged for me to meet—hat in hand—with the gang leader, a muscular, tattooed Mexican-American of about twenty-five or thirty who had lucrative transactional drug connections with Chicago's Latin Counts. His wasn't just a *gang*—it was a *business* and an autocratic but semi-benevolent form of neighborhood *government* whereof this astute gentleman was the *absolute governor*. He governed several city blocks in southwest Detroit, day and night.

We negotiated with mutual respect: the gang leader saw that I was trying to *help* Sergio, and he granted him permission to run.

Four years later, as DPS' executive director of community affairs, I would be seated on a dais between Detroit's promising new young mayor, Kwame Kilpatrick, and his new chief of police, Jerry Oliver, in a community forum in the auditorium at King High, where I had coached track thirty-four years earlier. I would then tell the mayor and the chief of police about this local drug lord who was still controlling entire city blocks in southwest Detroit. I would also tell them about the drive-by shooting perpetrated by that same Mexican gang, which had halted Southwestern's 1999 homecoming game and forced us to herd all the kids back into the school to safety.

Chief Oliver would tell me then, "I'll look into it."

I doubt that he ever did.

CHAPTER FORTY-EIGHT

TWO TEENS WHO
WERE *MEN*—
FOUR DECADES APART

"Telford not only taught students—he nourished them."

—Detroit Southwestern High School
honor student Jeffrey May, September 2000

This chapter is going to be about two unabashed "mutual admiration societies"
—both of them between me and two protégés of mine, one of them forty years
younger than the other. Between 1959 and 1999, only four teens among the
thousands I had taught and/or coached were already *men* when I mentored
them. The *first* was Ken Burnley of Mumford, in 1959. The *second* was Arkles
Brooks of Southeastern, in 1961. The *third* was John Powell (now john powell)
also of Southeastern, in 1962. The *fourth* was Reggie Bradford of Pershing, in
1966. Now in 1999 at Southwestern—*forty years* after I had guided Burnley—
I had finally found for only the fifth time that extremely rare phenomenon,
a *teenager* who was already a *mature man.*

In September, Southwestern High School honor student Jeffrey May—
a colonel and the Commander of Cadets in Southwestern's Junior Reserve Officer
Training Corps (JROTC)—enrolled in my twenty-seven-student journalism class.
By October, I had already tapped him to be the editor of the school newspaper,
the *Prospector.* By January, this sixteen-year-old eleventh-grader was *teaching*
the journalism class, maintaining *order* in the class, writing *editorials*, and select-
ing and editing his classmates' pieces for publication in our monthly newspaper
and weekly newsletter!

On January 19, 1999, a man who undoubtedly had also been an honor student in high school—interim DPS superintendent David Adamany—submitted an eighty-four-page school improvement plan to the "reform" Board. In it, he pointed out that the Detroit school system was dysfunctional and cited several of the same suggestions for improvement that I had cited in my *Detroit Free Press* column the previous March. Shortly afterward, in an eleven-thousand-word treatise on reforming the schools via site-based management that I used as a teaching tool both in my Southwestern classes and, more fully, in a graduate-level night-school class I was teaching at Wayne State University, I posed this question: "How can we refashion Detroit Public Schools into a learning organization that would be expert in dealing with constructive change as a *normal part of its work?*" I continued:

> To answer this question, one must recognize that systemic change is full of components not always seen as going together. In addressing change in DPS, we must confront a conformist view that sees top-down reform as the only way. There is another seemingly irreconcilable perspective that favors bottom-up. Actually, both can work together.

I proposed the institution of site-based management, with *principals* and *teachers* deciding what's best for students without interference from "experts" far from the front line. I said that we needed to get most of those experts back into classrooms and decentralize decision-making in that sprawling system, which I said should ideally be divided into four autonomous districts that could then compete with each other for students. I went on, in a continued partial paraphrase of some of the progressive ideas of noted Kansas City change facilitator W. Patrick Dolan:

> The pursuit of positive change accepts both individualism and collectivism as essential to organizational learning. Individual-ism isn't always accepted by those in power, but constructive change can be effected by individual teachers. In the long run, the individual will leverage change more effectively than *the* institution. Organizations learn through individuals who learn.
>
> While individual learning doesn't guarantee organizational learn-ing, no organizational learning can happen without it. Growth and reformation occur as teachers and administrators deepen

their relationships by disregarding rank and egos and continually strengthening their interdependent connections.

I believed DPS needed site-based management then, and it's an even clearer and more obvious need today. Too bad for the kids that DPS honchos didn't listen to me then and have turned a deaf ear to me now.

JROTC Cadet Commander Jeffrey May's unquestioned command of the journalism class made it easier for me to run downstairs to the lavatory inside the English office to relieve my sixty-four-year-old bladder and enlarged prostate gland. I had asked my department head, Willie Wooten, to give me a classroom next to a bathroom, and he *had*—but it was in the anteroom of the office of a counselor in her late forties named Norma Grant who had an aversion to males using it and therefore had put a "Ladies Only" sign on its door. I told Ms. Grant that I needed to use "her" restroom because I had a bad prostate. She replied that *she* had a bad prostate, too. "Ma'am," I said, "with all due respect, unless there's some covert or unusual aspect of your physiognomy or gender that I'm unaware of, it is not physically *possible* for you to have a bad prostate or any *other* kind of prostate."

Department head Wooten and Principal Hines didn't want anything to do with this ridiculous tug-of-war, so Dr. Hines told Assistant Principal Patricia Benjamin to handle it. Dr. Benjamin wrote me a note advising me that counselors are special people entitled to have their own restrooms, and she summoned me to come to her office to discuss it. I wrote back that I was too busy *teaching* to come to her office to discuss it, and that *teachers* are special people, too— and moreover, that she should wear shorter heels so she could more easily walk up the stairs to come to my *classroom* if she wanted to discuss it.

Betty then sent assistant principal Jim Ellison to talk to me about it, to no avail. Finally, she had the stool in the restroom *removed* so Ms. Grant and I could no longer argue over it, and she assigned me another classroom nearer the bathroom downstairs. I told her I had all my materials in my room arranged just how I wanted them, and I would quit if she gave me another room—so she didn't. I tried not to take too long going to the bathroom downstairs, but sometimes I did have to leave my kids untended for a few minutes. My union representative, Tim Mihalik, said I should file a grievance regarding the matter to protect my male colleagues' rights. I told him that if *he* wrote it, I would sign it. He *did*, and *I* did—and Virginia Cantrell, who then was my union's vice president, got a big kick out of the ludicrousness of it all.

By April, Jeffrey May had been selected for a journalism internship at the *Detroit Free Press*, which published our monthly newspaper under the sponsorship of the Ford Motor Car Company. (The eleventh-grade Jeffrey had already garnered a full scholarship to study journalism at Eastern Michigan University in Ypsilanti!)

My journalism class at Southwestern wasn't stacked with honor students, either. Except for Jeffrey, and in the second semester, a senior named Mitchell Carroll who named me his "inspiration" in the *Free Press* when it published its All-City Academic Team, they had been kids with ordinary grades until they were randomly enrolled in this class, which semi-miraculously transformed them within a few short months into inspired and significantly accomplished writers. This served to improve their grades significantly in their regular English classes, as well.

I still have a copy of the *Prospector* that featured some of this large, multi-grade-level class's incisive satire that demonstrated a surprisingly sophisticated use of irony—most of it written by students *other* than the precocious Jeffrey himself. Examples:

> The Winners' Circle
>
> Assistant principal James Ellisong [*Jim Ellison*] has nominated sopho-mores Lament Smitten [*Lamont Smith*] Courting Duffel [*Courtney Duffy*], and Dark Mockery [*Mark Dockery*] for Best-Behaved Student. [*This trio was* always *raising hell—separately and together.*]
>
> Dr. Betty Chimes [*Hines*] has honored Ferdie Peashooter [*Freddie Peterson*], Warble Wheels [*Wardell Wheeler*], and Tyrannosaurus Ricketson [*Tyren Richardson*] as Students with the Fewest Tardi-nesses. Chimes tolled proudly, "These admirable students never bring electronic equipment, hats, coats, or food to class, laugh out loud in class, or address a teacher as 'Hey, man.' It was students like these three that helped me become Principal of the Year." [*Freddie, Wardell, and Tyren were three more* hell-raisers.]
>
> Former Southwesterner Lakita "Fisticuffs" Ballantyne [*Lakeisha Valentine*] recently defended her sophomore welterweight title with a TKO over former Southwesterner Sharlene Briar [*Charlene Bryant*], for the seventeenth time. [*This pair were always trading*

insults and fighting over one boy or another: One time I was pulling Charlene in one direction and Mr. Wooten was pulling Lakeisha in the other—and they were tugging to get at each other for all they were worth. While I had a tight hold on Charlene's wrist and was pulling her away from Lakeisha with some difficulty, I reinjured my right rotator cuff which I had initially hurt in 1995 separating two large residents at Wolverine Human Services who were trying to gouge out each others' eyes. Charlene and Lakeisha finally got themselves expelled. They both then enrolled in the nearby River Rouge schools, where I can only hope they didn't resume their feud.]

Anarchy Massing [*Anika Massey*] and Darnetta Missile [*Donetta Mitchell*] tied for the Principal's Award for Quietest Student. [*Although Anika was a good student, even her own* classmates *sometimes would try unsuccessfully to get her to shut her mouth.*]

On April 1, Christina K. Rillo [*Carillo—my student*] asked to go to the lavatory only 27 times! [*Truthfully, it was actually more like* six *or* seven *times.*]

Assistant principal Patricia Benedryl [*Benjamin*] awarded Certificates of Expertise to 87 of SW's 93 substitute teachers, who were also lauded by students for usually staying awake in classes.

[*Some subs that were sent to SW were less conscientious than others, and some SW teachers' attendance could have been better. I, incidentally, was the only teacher—and only one of two staff members—who got the Perfect Attendance Award at the end of the 1999–2000 school year. I thought that was kind of cute—a retired suburban assistant superintendent getting a perfect attendance award as an inner-city teacher at the advanced age of 64.*]

Airwick Memory [*Eric Henry*] was given the school's Creativity Award for demonstrating the most imaginatively natural method for washing teachers' cars. [*Eric, one of my runners, had been caught using that* extremely natural method for *"washing" the car of a certain teacher he didn't like.*]

Forecast, Dateline April 1, 2050
by A. Noni Mouse, [*anonymous*] Staff Writer
Dr. Teachford—114 years old and ponytail still uncombed—is finishing his 92nd year in education and is making his helpless

students analyze his ten-trillionth newspaper column [*guilty as charged*]. Dr. Chimes is completing her 65th year as SW Principal. The "swimming pool issue" is in its 51st year of litigation, and the pool still has no water in it. [*At this point, Betty had been SW's principal for nineteen years, and the new pool's opening had been delayed for what had seemed to the kids like* eons *by egregious construction blunders.*]

There was also a piece by "Lirpa Loof" ("April Fool" backwards)—a "visiting Transylvanian student" (aka Felicia Ray, who appeared with it grinning and wearing a babushka in an accompanying photo). It was headlined "SW a 'Wonderland,'" and it was "translated" by students with appropriately disguised Balkan-like names, in addition to crediting in the byline the administrators who had "hypnotized Ms. Loof."

It began:

> My April 1 visit to Detroit's wondrous Southwestern Castle amazed me! I loved SW's valet parking and Olympic-sized pool. Its restrooms have gold toilet seats, and mirrors so clear you can see your inner self! . . . Students love the hallway cameras that watch them around every corner, re-assuring them that their Big Brother is always guarding—er, I mean *guiding*—them. . . . When I return home, I will tell all Transylvania about SW's faraway splendor across the sea.

There was a well-drawn cartoon by "Cadmiel *Bananas*" (aka Cadmiel Banas) featuring a goon-like, shades-wearing guard with a shaved head and a shirt emblazoned with the words "Southwestern Security." The hulking figure brandished A-K-47 machine guns in each hand.

After the Detroit "reform" board had selected a superintendent from Oklahoma whose appointment as Detroit superintendent was blocked by the vote of Michigan Governor John Engler's representative on the board, Wayne County RESA superintendent Mike Flanagan and I resumed coaxing Colorado Springs District 11 superintendent Ken Burnley to apply for the DPS superintendency. Mike and I had tried to talk Ken into applying in the first search, but he had declined, saying that to fix DPS would be a Herculean task, and he was perfectly happy in Colorado. Mike and I had also been pushing Mayor Dennis Archer and Dennis' appointed "reform" school board president—former deputy mayor Freman Hendrix—to recruit Ken Burnley. (Months later, Freman would write to thank me for all I did for kids—and to thank me above all for helping bring former Mumford track star Burnley back home.)

Burnley finally applied for the superintendency and was interviewed along with a former board member, Detroit attorney Larry Patrick. The "reform" board appointed Burnley.

Here are pertinent excerpts regarding my long relationship with Ken Burnley and my teaching at Southwestern from a June 7, 2000, *Detroit News* article by reporter Brian Harmon. The article, accompanied by my picture wearing my blue-and-gold Southwestern coaching cap, was headlined, "John Telford is back teaching in Detroit":

> As a high school track coach in Detroit during the early 1960s, John Telford helped nurture the speed of a young Kenneth Burnley, the city's new school chief. Burnley never forgot Telford's mentoring. "He believed in me," Burnley said.
>
> Burnley isn't alone in his admiration. In 40 years as an educator across Metro Detroit, Telford, 64, has mentored thousands of students—and more than a few teachers and administrators. Lately, he's focused on students at Southwestern High. After 35 years of holding . . . high-ranking [*suburban*] positions . . ., Telford again is teaching high school English. Telford retired in 1991, but a new state law let him return to the classroom full-time without reducing his pension. . . .
>
> "He's not just here to get a paycheck. He's here to make sure you learn," said Tamara Canty, a senior in Telford's third-hour class.
>
> Classmate Denita Benson, 18, agreed: "He has so much energy—every day. I love coming to this class. I sprint through the hallway." [*Denita intentionally used the word "sprint" in that interview because it had special meaning: I had told her and her twin sister Kanita that they could be top sprinters, and both had kept promising to run track but never did.*]
>
> . . . Burnley said Tuesday he'll likely offer his ex-coach an administrative post.
>
> "I love working with these kids. It's like I'm going to recreation every day," said veteran educator Telford, who moved back to his native Detroit two years ago. "But as an administrator, I may be able to reach more children.". . .

> Burnley isn't surprised Telford went back to teaching in Detroit. "He's been a champion for the underdog his entire career," Burnley said.

Shortly after this article ran, I wrote a column in the *Detroit Free Press* hailing the impending return of Burnley to Detroit as practically that of the biblically prophesized Second Coming. History would prove that statement to be a bit hyperbolic, but I still assert that Ken Burnley was a far better DPS superintendent than he ever got credit for being.

That summer, Burnley snatched me out of my Southwestern classroom to become the executive director in charge of the secondary schools and principals in southwest Detroit. I was also assigned Mumford High School (Burnley's alma mater), the High School of Commerce, and Catherine Ferguson High—a school for pregnant girls that once had been the old Chaney Elementary School, where my gentle mama had tenderly taught her bedraggled and beloved little kindergarteners some sixty years before.

I told Betty it was a *relief* (no pun intended) that my five-tier promotion would probably nullify my grievance concerning her removal of the lavatory, and the less said about it, the better for both our sakes: Mine because I didn't want anyone downtown to know I was in imperfect health, hers because it wouldn't be good if Burnley heard about it and concluded that she was high-handed or even unbalanced. I had recommended her to him for an executive directorship.

Here are the final three sentences of what the one-day-to-become-great Jeffrey May wrote in the *Prospector* that fall after new superintendent Ken Burnley had stolen Southwestern's old, pony-tailed English teacher:

> Telford not only *taught* students—he *nourished* them. He allowed them to see their potential. Telford is a great teacher, and he will be truly missed.

I, in turn, would always truly miss my Southwestern kids.

CHAPTER FORTY-NINE

A DREAM COME TRUE—
ALMOST

"He calls Telford one of the most influential people in his life."

—Detroit News *reporter Brian Harmon,*
quoting new Detroit Public Schools CEO Kenneth Burnley

I first met Ken Burnley in 1958 when he was a fifteen-year-old budding sprint prodigy at Mumford High with the tapered body of a lighter-skinned Sugar Ray Robinson [five-time middleweight champ, and a Detroiter]. Burnley's coach had invited me and my Detroit Track Club teammate Pete Petross to help perfect the young speedster's *technique*—his *physique* was already perfect.

In January 1960 Ken was one of the first spectators to reach me and grab my hand when I won a close, comebacking 600-yard race against George Rhoden, Jamaica's former Olympic champion and world record holder, at Yost Fieldhouse in Ann Arbor. I remember Ken was wearing a stylish dark brown leather jacket.

That June, as a graduating high school senior, Ken Burnley ran a full 440 yards (not the shorter 400 meters) in a precocious 49.4 seconds, behind my 47 flat in a match race between me and Farmington's future Olympian Rex Cawley of the University of Southern California. In the long history of Michigan high school track, only the legendary Cliff Hatcher and Burnley nemesis Henry Carr had ever run faster than Burnley's 49.4. (Cawley edged me in 46.8 after I stumbled on a marble-sized loose cinder five yards from the finish—this was before they had fast rubberized tracks.)

Late that summer, Burnley got his revenge—nipping me at 100 yards on a muddy track after I had cruised to a 48.3 win in the 440. He attended the

University of Michigan on a track scholarship and competed with some success at 60, 100, 220, and 300 yards. However, his long, silky-smooth stride was *really* tailor-made for the grueling 440. *Track & Field News Press* had published its first (1965) edition of *The Longest Dash*, my now out-of-print book on the quarter-mile, and Ken asked me to train him for the quarter. I was administrating and coaching in Detroit and finishing my doctoral studies, and he was a busy grad student in Ann Arbor, so we had to communicate mainly by mail and telephone. Still, he managed to bring his time down to a very promising 48.2. Had he continued competing, I believe he could have attained national rank.

As fate would have it, Dr. Kenneth Stephen Burnley was to attain that national rank in an entirely *different* way. In the years after I coached him, Ken and I officiated at the annual NCAA indoor track meet in Detroit together and ascended K-12 education's administrative ladder *apart*—in districts that became increasingly distant. In 1993, Dr. Burnley was named Superintendent of the Year by the American Association of School Administrators (AASA). In a 1993 interview in the *Detroit Free Press*, he named me as one of his mentors. In 1990 he had sent me that letter telling me to hang tough when the bigots were trying to get me fired from the Rochester deputy superintendency. We had always kept in close touch, dreaming and fantasizing in frequent phone conversations about how we would come home some day and rescue the failing Detroit schools—with him as the superintendent and me as his deputy.

I felt that our fantastic dream had now actually come *true*! Ken Burnley, Mumford's once swift and mighty Mustang (the school's team name), was now Detroit's even mightier *CEO,* and I, the other old "Mustang" (as my high school coach had dubbed me so many years before), would be galloping by Ken's side. While I wouldn't be his direct deputy, I would at least be an executive director (ED) *reporting* directly to his deputy, Dr. Kay Royster. In that close capacity, I would still be able to afford them both the benefit of my long and rich experience at the executive level in cutting-edge suburban divisions of instruction such as Plymouth/Canton's and Rochester's.

Not only that—two highly-respected retired DPS high school principals, my old teammate Pete Petross and Dr. Walter Jenkins (whom I had recommended), would be part of Dr. Burnley's corps of ED's as well. Add to that mix Dr. Patricia Dignan, a former suburban superintendent who had supervised Burnley when he worked in the Ypsilanti schools, and he now had an impressive array of knowledgeable and honest leaders he could trust—a "kitchen cabinet" that could steer him around the rocks.

Except that it didn't turn out that way. The *Detroit News'* front page headline on Sunday, October 1, 2000, blared, "Detroit school hirings questioned" over pictures of Burnley, me, Burnley's U-M roommate John Harris, and a promoted principal whose school had low test scores. The article said, "John Telford, a successful school administrator for more than thirty years, coached Burnley in the quarter-mile...." It essentially accused him of cronyism for hiring us, which was unfair. The people he chose to be ED's were qualified, and I had more exalted credentials than any of them. (At least the article said I was "successful.")

Dr. Royster had her favorite executive directors, including a couple she had brought with her from Kalamazoo, where she had been superintendent. We four retread retiree Burnley loyalists—Petross, I, and Drs. Dignan and Jenkins— were close to Burnley and "had his back," so Dr. Royster made it fairly clear early on that she hoped to *re*-retire us as soon as she could. She had been an unsuccessful applicant for Burnley's job in an earlier series of interviews, and she was rumored to be favored by some of the ladies on the board to eventually replace him. There was also speculation in some quarters that she was still casting a covetous and *immediate* eye on the superintendency.

Dr. Royster wanted to raise the number of hours it would take for a high school student to graduate to a figure far above the twenty-two hours that even the suburbs required. Old-time Cooley High School principal Walt Jenkins— an old WSU Tartar, Detroit Lion, and Hamilton Tiger-Cat of the Canadian Football League—worried along with me that this would cause thousands of kids to drop out. Dr. Burnley, of course, hoped to accomplish precisely the reverse.

Executive director Jenkins and I tried to talk chief instructional officer Royster out of doing this, explaining that it would give kids who had failed to pass a class no opportunity to catch up even in summer school. When we weren't able to convince her of this, I went to Burnley and got him to reverse her on it—which understandably didn't exactly endear her to me.

Also, after fruitlessly recommending to Dr. Royster that she bring the knowledgeable Betty Hines downtown to join our executive director corps, I went to Burnley with *this* concern, too.

"John," he told me, "there's a *huge* personality clash between those two strong, dominant women. Kay refuses to even *consider* promoting Betty—*ever*.

We're simply going to have to leave it alone."

"Well, Ken," I replied, "then maybe you'd better put Juanita [former associate superintendent for instruction Juanita Clay Chambers] back in that job and give Dr. Royster some other job where she can't do any more damage. Folks are telling me they think Dr. Royster is after *your* job. Has it occurred to you that Betty Hines may be a threat to Dr. Royster because Betty is loyal to *you*—and to *me*?"

Ken didn't answer, but I knew the wheels were turning in his head.

Dr. Royster had also brought a test with her from Kalamazoo called ESAT —Essential Skills Attainment Test—which was really nothing more than a warmed-over MEAP (Michigan Education Assessment Program). Pete and Walt and I suggested to her— fruitlessly—that our kids were already being tested enough. What they desperately needed was more instructional time—not more *test* time. We already *knew* what those test results would be. I went to Burnley with this concern, too, but he didn't reverse her on this one until it was almost too late.

I had several other deeply serious concerns, because they directly involved thousands of kids I was specifically responsible for. I was concerned that the academic and social needs of the comparatively few white students who still remained in DPS—and I had thousands in my schools—were being ignored by the black leadership in our 175,000-student district. The district was 95 percent black and was becoming increasingly preoccupied with "Afro-centered" sloganeering, to the academic detriment of our few white students *and* of our many black students as well. I also noted the emergence of a form of classism— not racism, but *classism*—arising in the schools' central leadership. They were erecting a few palaces like the new Cass Technical High School and the new Renaissance High for the children of professionals—doctors, lawyers, politicians, school and municipal administrators, etc.—but neglecting hundreds of other schools whose parents weren't affluent or influential.

There also existed a particular and historic lack of sufficient support for the area's bilingual students in southwest Detroit, who were predominantly Latino but had a significant Arab percentage as well. When I had taught at Southwestern the previous year, I had often needed to have an Arabic or Latino student translate what I had taught them to another Arabic or Latino student who was less fluent in English.

I decided that I would write a memo to Dr. Royster and Dr. Burnley listing these handicapping problems under which the bilingual students in my schools were suffering in southwest Detroit. In this memo, I also offered an annotated list of solutions to the problems.

I entitled my memo, "Concerns and Recommendations Regarding Bi-lingual Education: A Blueprint for Betterment."

I was confident that once Drs. Burnley and Royster read this document, they would realize how crucial it was for them to take immediate action.

CHAPTER FIFTY

BAD BILINGUAL PROGRAMS IN THE SOUTHWEST CLUSTER

"Schools neglect Latinos, says DPS executive."

—*Headline in the weekly* Michigan Citizen *newspaper*

In addition to my six-page "Blueprint for Betterment" memo regarding bilingual education, I had already also given Dr. Burnley a copy of my eleven-thousand-word treatise on how to reform the Detroit Public Schools via site-based management that I had written and used in the night school graduate-level education class I had taught for Wayne State University during my previous year teaching at Southwestern. After skimming that treatise, Dr. Burnley had passed it down to Dr. Royster. I wasn't too surprised when I learned that she had simply consigned it to the "circular file," but I was almost certain that she wouldn't do the same with my memo citing my immediate concerns regarding bilingual education.

Also around this time, I dreamed that my daughter Katherine, now twenty-six, was having terrible marital trouble. My dream turned out to be real—Katherine filed for divorce and came to the River House and cried in my arms. Her mother had wanted to extend the PPO for a ridiculous *third* year and keep Katherine on it with her—and any Republican judge in overwhelmingly Republican Oakland County probably would have granted the extension—but Katherine had told her mother, "I need to be with my father again."

Having my daughter back helped me concentrate better on my job, because I was no longer worried about her emotionally abusive domestic situation and whether I might have to intervene, which I had been seriously considering.

Here are parts of that six-page "Blueprint for Betterment" memo regarding bilingual education that I wrote to Drs. Royster and Burnley:

> Our 10,000 bilingual students face daunting, debilitating, and discriminatory problems. Seventy percent of these students are eligible for bi-lingual education services, and nearly 5,000 are of "high need" (scoring below the 11th percentile in reading or being at an English-language proficiency-level of grade 1 or 2). Nearly all attend high-concentration schools . . . with some in schools where . . . a full 70% of the students are bilingual. While 12% of Detroit citizens are Hispanic, only 2% of DPS students are Hispanic; the other 10% that are of school age are either enrolled in parochial or charter schools or aren't attending school (thus we collect no monies for them).

I then cited my concerns with a) the abysmal bilingual dropout rate; b) the lack of bilingual teachers and support staff; c) the lack of access to new schools and vocational centers in my area of southwest Detroit; d) exclusions of bilingual students from state tests; e) inequitable distribution of resources; f) the lack of parental and bilingual community involvement; g) a lack of any bilingual person at the top executive level in the central office; h) the absence of any bilingual principal, and i) a dearth of bilingual assistant principals (especially in my southwest area, where I had helped arrange the promotion of Dr. Alex Shami, an Arab-American teacher at one of my high schools—Chadsey —to an assistant principalship. He was unfeelingly fired a year later when he had a heart attack).

After each concern I had cited, I wrote an extensive list of recommendations for addressing each one.

In my summation of this long "Blueprint for Betterment" memo, I referred to several events I have already listed in this book that involved risks which I and a small cadre of my white colleagues had taken to protect black students and athletes in Detroit during the racist days of the 1950s and 60s. Then I wrote:

> Last summer, I prevented a group of black street thugs from stomping a white man to death on Gratiot Avenue; ergo, the protective sword of social conscience must always cut both ways. . . . White citizens in Detroit and white children in Detroit Public Schools

have been a steadily diminishing minority for many years, and Hispanics have always been and still are a minority here (although their numbers are growing). Resultantly, white children—and even more damagingly, bi-lingual or non-English-speaking children —have suffered from long neglect at the hands of DPS. . . .

Interestingly, I am one of only 99,921 non-Hispanic white residents remaining in the city where I was born and raised. [*This represented 10 percent of Detroit's population, according to an April 1, 2001 Detroit News article.*] Unlike many whites, I am here because I want to be—not because I have to be—and I work because I want to—not because I have to. To me, educating the kids in the city where I was born and raised is a divine mandate and ongoing mission, as well as an absolute labor of love.

Our city is blessed with a Mayor [*the great Dennis Archer*] and our schools are blessed with a CEO who are both egalitarian to the bone. The Michigan Department of Public Instruction is similarly blessed in the person of Tom Watkins, its new superintendent.

When Superintendent Watkins, who was then a long-shot for the job, called me at home to request that I make some key phone calls to help him get it, I obliged immediately—and I also told him that DPS would need a lot of support from him, including particular support for its bilingual student population. [*Note: in my capacity as a former member of the Oakland County Democrats Executive Board, I had telephoned key Democrats on the Michigan Board of Education on Tom's behalf, and I also extracted a promise from Tom that he would serve on the DPS board himself, rather than assign one of his assistants—and he kept his promise. The language of the ill-advised state takeover had included a requirement that one board appointee be a state official.*]

As both of you know, I wrote a February 14, 2001 Oakland Press column calling upon the State Superintendent and Legis-lature to mount a mandate that Michigan's K-12 curriculum specifically include multiculturalism and that all of our teachers receive bilingual and multicultural teacher education as a part of their state certification requirement. [*To date, these things have not happened.*] . . .

The two of you and I sat in a meeting with representatives from LASED [*a powerful local Latino coalition*], where Dr. Burnley pledged to appoint Hispanic principals and more Hispanic assistant principals in the Southwest Corridor. He charged those who were present at that meeting to supply him with suitable names. He has already done some of that appointing, I have done some of that supplying, and he is acting on similar additional appointments. It now remains for you to address the remaining urgent concerns I have defined for you in this memo.

This memo from me to Drs. Burnley and Royster contained several more concluding paragraphs. Someone (not me) leaked it to the *Michigan Citizen*, a weekly local newspaper that had been ongoingly critical of the Detroit schools. A *Citizen* reporter named Ramona Curtis called me and interviewed me, but she *mis*read the memo—and *mis*quoted me personally—about the situation in an article *mis*leadingly headlined, "Schools neglect Latinos, says DPS executive." I was criticizing *past* school leaders, not the *present* ones—the verb in the headline should have been "neglect*ed*."

Ramona Curtis' article in the *Michigan Citizen* began:

> A Detroit Public School executive is saying that the school district has violated the civil rights of its Latino students by denying the schools in their community Spanish-speaking administrators, teachers, and support staff. Calling the 57 percent dropout rate of Latino students a "crisis of the first degree," DPS southwest cluster executive director John Telford alleges that the high dropout rate is a result of the school district's neglect. [Result *means in the past—Burnley was the new, present CEO.*]

Curtis quoted bi-lingual director Felix Valbuena: "Because of Dr. Telford's intervention and outspoken position regarding bilingual education, I think the central administration is moving quite fast and responding positively."

The article called me a "lifelong community activist." (At least Curtis got *that* right.) "The Hispanic kids *are not getting educated*, she quoted me as saying, but again, I had not used the *present* tense. It concluded with this quote (of me): "If those kids *aren't* [present tense, again] getting educated appropriately, it's *my* responsibility."

Ken told me that his wife Eileen was very upset when she read that article. I replied, "So was I! Show Eileen the memo—she'll see I was misquoted."

While Eileen Burnley was *upset* by the article, Dr. Royster was absolutely *incensed* by it—possibly because in it, DPS bilingual director Valbuena had indicated that it was *I*—not *she*—who was DPS' major champion of the city's Latino children.

Even though I was one of the few executive directors that followed Dr. Royster's order to write annual performance objectives (I wrote—and *fulfilled*—over a *hundred*) and evaluate our principals (I wrote evaluations of them *all*), she released me at the end of the school year without ever evaluating *me*. She also released the other Burnley loyalists—Pete Petross, Dr. Walter Jenkins, and Dr. Patricia Dignan—without evaluating *them*, either.

Dr. Burnley eventually brought Pete and Pat back, but not me or Walt—Dr. Royster had called our releases "budget cuts." I was too angry and proud to ask Ken to give me back my job, but I did tell a *Detroit News* reporter that I was willing to do that job for free—an offer I was later to make fruitlessly many times concerning various central-office positions in DPS. My Southwestern colleague Tim Mihalik, who was now an elected union official downtown, told me he was present when Dr. Royster boasted that she had got rid of my "wrinkled white ass." No way would I have ever given Dr. Royster an opportunity to get even a fleeting *glance* at my ass to learn whether it was wrinkled or not—but actually, at this writing my young wife will attest that my now seventy-three-year-old ass happens not to be wrinkled just yet! (However, I'm getting my unwrinkled ass ahead of my story.)

Dr. Valbuena was right when he said I had intervened for the bilingual children, and he was right when he said I was outspoken—and he was *so* right when he said that the "central administration" was moving fast. The "central administration"—in the singular person of CIO Kay Royster—was moving *fast*, all right, to fire *me*!

I was hurt, but Fate rescued me once again. With high and confident expectations, I accepted a serendipitous offer to become the executive deputy director of the celebrated and historic Detroit-based Team for Justice.

CHAPTER FIFTY-ONE

TEAM FOR JUSTICE BECKONS—THEN BACK WITH BURNLEY!

"Man's capacity for justice makes democracy possible, but man's capacity for injustice makes democracy necessary."

—*Dr. Reinhold Niebuhr (1892–1971)—world-renowned theologian and former pastor of Detroit's Bethal Evangelical and Reformed Lutheran Church*

I had high and confident expectations regarding the things I could accomplish democratically for Team for Justice, and that venerable egalitarian agency had those same high expectations of me. I had resumed writing weekly newspaper columns—this time for the *Michigan Citizen* and the *Michigan FrontPAGE* (a new youth-oriented sister paper of the prestigious *Michigan Chronicle*). In one *FrontPAGE Telford's Telescope* column headlined, "Hear that ticking time bomb? That's Detroit," I wrote about the grossly disproportionately high number of the two million men imprisoned who were black—"a sinister reminder," I called it, "of our country's failure to solve its race problem."

That article and a steady stream of others I wrote continued in the same vein, railing against the insufficient number of criminal justice advocates and the lack of training and rehab programs that made the problem of thousands of prematurely released prisoners returning to the streets even more explosive. I wrote a column on the same subject in the *Detroit Free Press* at that time. Indeed, Michigan was then and continues to be one of four states that spends more money on its prisons than on its universities. It has the highest incarceration rate of any of the Great Lakes states. Like other states in similar circumstances,

Michigan needs to contract out portions of the correction system and seek out other efficiencies while modifying its sentencing guidelines that do nothing to keep its citizens safe.

Team for Justice had my two newspapers' collaborative approval to feature my picture with their phone numbers on big billboards all over the city. The caption read, "Dr. John Telford crusades with Team for Justice, the *Michigan Citizen*, and the *Michigan FrontPAGE*." I didn't write for the *Citizen* for long, though—it discontinued my column when I refused to write anything bad about DPS CEO Burnley, who was coming under increasing grass-roots criticism for some of the excesses and missteps of his immediate subordinates.

Team for Justice (TFJ) is a venerable rights organization dating back to the bloody Detroit insurrection of 1967. When I went to work for Team for Justice in June of 2001, it was primarily an agency that advocated for prisoners who for the most part were incarcerated in the Wayne County Juvenile Detention Facility or the city and county jails. Its executive director was Sr. Janet Stankowski, a Catholic nun. I had served previously in a voluntary capacity on its board. Criminal defense attorney Robert Plumpe had brought me onto the TFJ board to serve with him in 1998 after having met me for the first time the previous summer by the outdoor swimming pool at the River House, where we both owned units.

When I introduced myself to Plumpe at the pool, he had mused, "Hmmm, John Telford . . . there was a great black sprinter by that name out of Wayne State back in the 1950s." I responded, "You're *talking* to him—but as you can see, I'm not *black*. I guess you never saw my picture. However, you're not the first person to make that assumption." I told him about how I'd nearly missed getting hired in Walled Lake.

Bob Plumpe quickly became one of my most trusted friends. He was with me later (in the summer of 2000) during the black-on-white beating incident I had briefly cited in my memo to Drs. Burnley and Royster that concerned the school district's neglect of its bi-lingual students.

On the day that beating incident occurred, Bob and I had been driving north on Gratiot Avenue when several rows of cars got halted in front of us by a violent altercation in the street. Seeing what was happening, I drove over the curb up onto the sidewalk to where four or five young black men were stomping a still-conscious white man lying on the pavement in a fetal position, his convulsively clutching hands covering his head. Instructing my nervous passenger to pretend he was talking on his cell phone, I jumped out, flashing a gold replica of a Detroit police lieutenant's badge with the words *Detroit SNAP* emblazoned on it that a precinct captain had given me when I was directing SNAP out of the police mini-station on Chene Street. Seeing the badge, the thugs scattered across Gratiot Avenue and kept running.

The man they would have killed didn't want to talk. Getting unsteadily to his feet, he staggered—trailing blood—to his nearby car, got in, and managed to drive away.

Bob was still shaken. "Johnny, that was pretty risky."

"No it wasn't—I figured they'd think we were cops, and I figured they'd think you were calling for backup."

"Damn good thing for us you figured *right*."

My selection as Wayne State University's Distinguished Alumnus of the Year that year also helped enhance our Team for Justice agency's historic prestige. Jeff Pope, the student editor of the *South End* newspaper, wrote under this December 12, 2001, headline, "WSU to honor track star, rights activist":

> For fifty years, John Telford has spent his life running and fight-
> ing. In honor of his life's work, the WSU Alumni Association
> will give Telford the Distinguished Alumni Award at Thursday's
> Commencement Ceremonies.

I was mightily surprised to be chosen. My most highly-publicized human-rights initiatives were at least a decade behind me. Also, I still suffered from my partially-deserved *leftist* reputation, and even though WSU is an urban university, it's still a *state* university. State universities, relying as they do on state funding, had to demonstrate that they were dutifully conservative in those days of a conservative legislature and a Republican governor who was well aware of my opinion of his mean-spirited social policies.

So, when the university's vice president for alumni affairs informed me that I had been chosen for this honor, I asked her why. She said she thought it was because I'd been a world-ranked athlete as well as a high-ranking educator—but she would send me the names of the selection committee.

When I got the list, I noted that rather than being all old-time black men from the city—as I had expected—they were mostly *young suburban white women*!

I called one and asked why *I* of all people had been chosen. She said she had voted for me because of my liberal newspaper columns and my advocacy for African-Americans. Coming from someone of her background, her words were an encouraging testament that my multicultural incursions and those of a few like-minded activist educators were finally having some impact. There was hope for the future after all. Within the decade, Barack H. Obama would be President—and Robert F. Kennedy's plan for an egalitarian revolution would be resurrected.

At a dinner in my honor before the graduation ceremony, where I was to speak, I was seated next to then-WSU president Irvin Reid. Some of my guests at the dinner included Dr. Kenneth Burnley, several other DPS colleagues, and Eva, my now-nearly-estranged longtime love, who sat next to me. Dr. Reid had announced to reporters months earlier that the university would restore its vaunted and historic track program, so I remarked to him hopefully, "I understand you're bringing back *track*."

He gave me a curious look. "Do you know something *I* don't?"

That rather flippant retort disappointed me, so I didn't say much to him during dinner after that. A university publicist photographed Dr. Reid and me together that night in our caps and gowns, and the photo appeared in a number of publications inside and outside WSU, including a calendar on the same page with the venerable Detroit labor leader Horace Sheffield and the late Mayor Coleman Young on the cover.

When I addressed the thousands of graduates at Cobo Hall, here is what I said:

> Dr. Reid, graduates, and guests: I'm grateful to the University for naming me its Distinguished Alumnus. I'm also grateful to see all you tenacious graduates graduating! And whatever your undergraduate major was, consider taking a graduate degree in education or getting certified as a teacher. Good teachers are social activists who can fix this country's crisis and Detroit's crisis....
>
> Also, continue to educate yourselves. The knowledge of the ages is but a droplet in the oceans compared to what is yet to be learned—and our technological learning has outrun our humanistic learning, as witness the [attack on the] World Trade Center, the Holocaust, ethnic discrimination.... We need you younger folks teaching in those classrooms! Please consider that, and Godspeed.

After I had returned to my seat next to President Reid, Board of Governors president emeritus and human-rights icon Mildred Jeffries left her seat on the dais to come over to me and say, "That was the best acceptance speech I have ever heard—and I have heard many." I asked her, "Probably because it was the *shortest?*" She just smiled. Later I wished I hadn't been so flip in my response. I sought her out after the ceremony to tell her how much I admired her, but she was already gone. She died a few weeks later.

I had begun to date a tall, slender, dark-haired former Detroit principal I had worked with who now was a principal in a suburban school—a job I had supported her in getting. She introduced me to her family and closest friends, and I brought her to meet mine, including my daughter and Bob Plumpe and Cliff and Barbara Hatcher. I took her to Minneapolis with me when I served as a consultant for the National Institute on Race and Poverty, and I also took her to spend part of Christmas week with me in Arkansas with my cousin Carl and his wife Ginny. She flew with me to Florida to visit my former Berkley colleague George Blaney and his wife Joyce at their winter place near Fort Myers. I found myself staying overnight at her condo more and more and becoming more and more emotionally involved with her—and she with me.

One day, old Harlem Globetrotter and WSU All-American Charlie Primas came down to the Team for Justice offices at 3000 Gratiot Avenue to tell me that the Miller Middle School in old Black Bottom had been designated a historic site. When it had been a high school, Miller had educated many prominent black Detroiters, including Mayor Coleman Young. Charlie had been one of old Miller High's premier athletes, and he was on the TFJ advisory board. He asked me if I could get Dr. Burnley to have Detroit Public Schools donate the money for a marker. I said I thought I could. I called Ken, and he made it happen.

Meanwhile, I had been able to get many thousands of dollars in grant money for Team for Justice, and even though we had several volunteers, I did a bit of the Team's advocating myself. One of our most dedicated volunteers, Parris McCloud, came to me with a case he said he needed me to help him with *fast*. A seventeen-year-old Denby High School student was sitting scared out of his wits with dangerous adult criminals in the Wayne County Jail, about to be sentenced for participating in a street robbery that had ended with the victim dead. His two much-older brothers had already been handed life sentences for the crime. The judge had told Parris that she was going to sentence the kid to

thirty years! The United States, although home to only 5% of the world's population, by then had become home to 25% of the world's prisoners—2.3 million
souls—most of whom are incarcerated for non-violent offenses. While his
offense involved not only violence but also murder, he was not the actual killer,
and I did not want to see him incarcerated for thirty years.

We obtained affidavits attesting to his potential for rehabilitation from
Denby principal Woodrow Miller, from his employer, from his mother, and from
his pregnant girlfriend—and we presented them to the judge. She relented
and sentenced him to the Maxey Training School as a juvenile. He was freed
at nineteen and hasn't strayed toward trouble since.

At Team for Justice's annual dinner at Sacred Heart Seminary, the Team had
previously had and again would have several prestigious honorees, including
ninety-year-old civil-rights icon Daisy Elliott, former City Council president
Erma Henderson, Judge Claudia House Morcom, future mayor Ken Cockrel, Jr.
(son of my radical friend from the 1960s), and Dr. John Kline (my fellow member
of the WSU Athletic Hall of Fame). Other more recent honorees were Council-
person Sheila Cockrel (widow of Ken Cockrel, Sr. and Ken Cockrel, Jr.'s
stepmother), Judge Rudy Serra, and Rev. Jim Holley, a former councilman.

This year, at the direction of TFJ board members, I used my past prestige
to gain access to then-Sheriff Robert Ficano of Wayne County and asked him
to be the speaker at our dinner. The Sheriff *accepted*—what a *coup* for TFJ! Then
our board president, Wayne County Sheriff's sergeant Janice Gilbert (now has
resumed her maiden name of McClellan) and a majority of other TFJ board
members belatedly decided that since Sheriff Ficano was a declared candidate
for County Executive, it would be better—for political reasons— not to have
him speak!

They then asked me to *un*-invite the sheriff. I angrily refused, so a board
member did it. (The sheriff did become the Wayne County Executive, and still
is, at this writing.)

In the meantime, Dr. Burnley had released Dr. Royster and helped her get
the superintendency in Peoria, Illinois—a job which she then kept for only
two years. Ken called and told me, "John, Dr. Royster is gone, and I've seen the
billboards. I've also been reading your columns. I saw the McClellan book,
too. I want you to come back home to DPS." (The McClellan book was Keith
McClellan's *The Hero Within Us*, a 700-page history of Michigan track and field

in which I was named one of the 100 best track and field athletes of the past 100 years.)

Ken Burnley's timing couldn't have been better for me, because I was upset with the members of my TFJ board who had embarrassed me in the Ficano debacle after all my work securing the popular sheriff to be our dinner speaker. Also, since the crash of the tech stocks in 2001, I had lost hundreds of thousands of dollars in a mutual fund called American Skandia—a plummeting enterprise where I had invested my entire six-figure salary during my first stint as a DPS executive director, in addition to much of my pension (which I could still collect, as I was working for DPS under a consultant contract). I had sunk nearly every other dime in that fund which I had earned during the previous five years, as well.

"Ken," I said, "Listen—I've got this really great job now. If I come back, you won't let anyone fire me *again*, will you?"

"Absolutely not—I want you to come back home to DPS and head up my Community Affairs Division!"

CHAPTER FIFTY-TWO

LUNCH WITH
EX-MAYOR ARCHER;
AN *INAMORATA* RETURNS

"This is Gina Morris. Do you remember me?"

—A soft, sexy voice from long ago

After hiring Dr. Emanuel Bailey—a local minister and a native Liberian—to take my place directing Team for Justice, I did indeed come back home to DPS and did indeed head up Dr. Burnley's Community Affairs Division, with little fanfare. I learned, too, that there had also been some nebulous plan to have me function concurrently as ombudsman, and I wrote and submitted a job description for that role, but it never got off the drawing board.

In Community Affairs, I supervised fourteen hard-working activists called parent/community liaisons. My new immediate superordinate was Dr. Lavonne Sheffield, Dr. Burnley's chief of Staff and the sister of Rev. Horace Sheffield III, a prominent local activist minister and the grandson of the great union leader. When Dr. Burnley gave Dr. Royster's old job to Dr. Sheffield, a lower-level aide of Dr. Sheffield's was provisionally promoted to be "acting" chief of staff, and *she* became my supervisor.

My office and staff were housed in the former Children's Museum, a multistoried nineteenth-century mansion across the street from and directly north of the Detroit Institute of Arts. The huge old home was said to be haunted. I often worked there into the late hours of the night, and sometimes I would hear strange noises, but I never saw the actual apparition. Others, however, told me they had seen it—the silent ghost of a young girl in period apparel.

I had continued to write my weekly *Telford's Telescope* newspaper columns for the *Michigan FrontPAGE*, and on September 27, 2002, I penned these prescient passages:

> President George W. Bush has complained . . . [that] he has little to say in how the nation's budget is prepared, and there are constraints in place regarding how he may and may not use the military. Thank God for the few constraints that have been provided for in the Constitution, where he has tried to find any loophole he can in order to be able to make a unilateral decision to attack Iraq. This is in spite of Iraq having now agreed to let United Nations inspectors in to see whether it is making weapons of mass destruction. Even if it is, we mustn't just barge in and kill innocent civilians and get our soldiers shot, as Bush wants to do, with no concrete evidence. (If he wants to act on something without final evidence, a far preferable area for action would be the global warming problem and preservation of the ozone.)
>
> The Chinese and the former Soviets had and still have enough hydrogen bombs to wipe us out a thousand times over, but thanks to a time-proven international policy called <u>détente</u>, they never launched them. <u>Détente</u> will work with Iraq, too as it does with North Korea, a probable [now actual] nuclear power. Our enemies know that if they attack us with nuclear weaponry, our immediate retaliation will blow them to smithereens.
>
> Bush reminds me of a small boy playing in his playpen with toy soldiers, pilots, and planes. But Bush's playpen is the Oval Office. His very real soldiers and pilots can bleed lots of very real blood.
>
> This entire brouhaha isn't about blood, though—it's about <u>oil</u>. And when Bush complains that he doesn't have more power over the budget and the military, what he is really saying is that he has no respect for the Constitution he swore to uphold.

The following March (March 17, 2003), President Bush warned United Nations weapons inspectors searching for weapons of mass destruction (WMDs) to leave Iraq within forty-eight hours. Hans Blix, the chief weapons inspector, and Mohamed El Baradei, head of the International Atomic Energy Agency, had found no WMDs, nor any evidence of a renewed Iraqi nuclear weapons program.

Despite increasing cooperation from Iraqi president Saddam Hussein in reaction to international pressure, Bush refused to allow the inspectors to complete their work. Shortly afterward, the United States attacked Iraq, and our country's long descent into its economic maelstrom began. I was to rerun the same column in the same newspaper on October 21, 2005, under the headline, "Didn't I warn you about Bush?"

I would also write a column on Hurricane Katrina and Bush's failure to launch a massive airlift to save the stranded black denizens of New Orleans. (He was on a *five-week* vacation when the hurricane hit.)

After I had been on the job as Detroit Public Schools' executive director of community affairs for nearly a year, and I had co-authored (with Steve Czapski) the action plan for the successful special education millage campaign (which my supervisor took full credit for), I received a phone call.

"This is Gina Morris," a soft, sexy voice said. "Do you remember me?"

"Do I *remember* you?! I still have *pictures* of you, and *poetry* you wrote me!"

Gina was the beautiful African-American girl with whom I had what she had described in a poem as our "red-hot" affair when I was the executive director of secondary education in Plymouth/Canton. Now thirty-nine, she had an autistic son, Michael Morris, who at twenty-two was the same age that his mother had been at the time she had ended our torrid two-year liaison because she saw it going nowhere—I was married at the time, with a young daughter. Gina had missed all my lavish publicity of the 1990s when I had been recruiting the black administrators in Rochester and the bigots had come after me. She had spent eleven years as an airline stewardess—several of those years based in Florida— but she was back in the "D" now. She had seen my picture on an old billboard and called the number, and my former secretary at Team for Justice told her how to reach me.

I invited her to my office that same day. It was the first time I had laid eyes on Gina in those eighteen years, but she was as gorgeous as ever. Spontaneously, I kissed her—and all the old feelings instantly returned. While I had ordinarily continued to limit most of my liaisons to women who were connubially attached (they were more appreciative, less hassle, and far more discreet), I nonetheless decided to date the unattached Gina again.

I continued to date the pretty principal as well, in occasional addition to others. Those others included a petite and very married sixty-five-year-old survivor of uterine cancer named JoAnna who—when an also-married colleague of mine with whom she was involved had introduced me to her twenty-five years earlier—decided she wanted to trade him in for me. They also very briefly included a married twenty-eight-year-old Detroit lady named Moniqua who became pregnant during our liaison and then vanished from my life— and a tall, long-haired, twenty-two-year-old Detroiter named Raven who was currently separated from her husband and whose younger siblings had attended Finney High. In addition, there was yet another *suburban* lady who—if she reads this book—will recognize herself in the following scenario. I had nearly come a-cropper with this particular lady in a droll incident wherein she insisted that we use a common means of male contraception—and the "means" slipped off after our mutual culmination, becoming lodged and in fact *lost* deep inside her. Panicking, this lady hysterically ordered me to insert a thumb and forefinger to find it and fish it out. I proudly performed that delicate operation with the deftness of a practiced gynecologist—thus circumventing the eventuality of her being obliged to go to an emergency room and having to try to conceal the incriminating reason for her presence there from her unsuspecting spouse.

In that same near-east-side neighborhood where the tall, twenty-two-year-old Raven lived, there also dwelled a voluptuous lady ten years Raven's senior named Tamika, whom I had successfully encouraged to complete her degree in psychology. When the affluent white businessman she was living with was out of town, Tamika liked to come and sit up on the flying bridge of my cruiser, the *High Life*—a 44-foot 1979 Burns Craft I docked at Kean's Marina on East Jefferson near the River House in the boat well second-closest to the river. She had done prison time for drugs in her "previous life." My daughter didn't warm up to her very much, nor did my son.

However, they *did* warm up to *Gina*—and given my advanced age and the attraction I felt for her, I had seriously begun to consider being with only *one woman* for the first time ever!

Part of my father's and grandfather's ancient, unwritten Code and credo that I described in the first chapter of this book is: *Honor* is a gift a man gives to himself. No other man can give it to him; no other man can take it away. As I mentioned earlier, another part of the Code is: Another man's woman is not to be touched, no matter the circumstances—and no matter how amorously eager she might be. Yet another part of the Code is: Once a man's oath is given, it is ironbound. Many years earlier, I had sworn an oath to Lynn before God to forsake all others when I married her, but at that time I hadn't the slightest intention of honoring that oath; thus, I dishonored my God, my ancestors, my father, my wife, and myself by breaking that oath countless times.

This juncture in my story, then, would seem to be as good a place as any for me to own up to the fact that by this point in my life I'd been involved with literally *hundreds* of females. If in the uncommon instance they were pleasing to my eye but still didn't get indulged, it was simply because I was on amatory overload during that particular period—and I therefore had to hope that they wouldn't be unduly offended by such a rare but necessary rejection. After all, I had to have enough time to practice my profession, too.

Some ladies—particularly the *married* ones—may be relieved that I don't fully name them here, or name them at all, or in some instances even specify the time periods during which I was seeing them. Others may feel left out. I don't go into relevant depth or detail because that's not what this book is about, and I also don't want to hurt anyone any more than I already have in this life. I'd rather not be shot by some incensed husband, either—even at this late stage.

The unvarnished truth is that despite my father's Code, I had remained a shameless and prolific womanizer for half a century and more. Amorous opportunities constantly "dropped in my *lap*," as it were, throughout my twenty-eight-year first marriage—as well as before and after it. Some of the ladies knew about each other, and some didn't. Those who *did* became determined to become the *only* one, but their relevant efforts were doomed to fail, because to have only one woman just wasn't in my nature for most of my years on this planet. My nearly lifelong situation in that regard was akin to that of a glutton working in a gourmet restaurant, or to that of an alcoholic employed in a distillery. The only comely females who tried but failed to breach my feeble defenses were my students or the wives of friends—or in infrequent instances, female co-workers or parents or community members with whom I functioned professionally. Right or wrong, that's the way it was.

A rare romantic *few*—married and unmarried—who didn't end up with this romantically dishonorable rogue nonetheless did him the great but un-deserved honor of not only longing to be with him *permanently* but also of genuinely *loving* him. He loved some of *them*, too—but no lone mortal could possibly divide his body into pieces and give away *permanent portions* of himself to even a *few* loving ladies (much as he might have wished to). Off and on over the years, I've been in intermittent and strictly *platonic* touch with yet a precious *fewer* of that rare romantic few of those old flames, with whom the *emotional* parts of the relationships were often as (or *more*) intemperate than were the *physical* parts. That precious *fewer* included Eva—and it includes Gerrie, who was the consummate intellectual avatar of my college and immediate post-college years and who now is a respected state-level official of the National Organization for Women.

Indeed, there is something deeply tragic about a man and woman having a visceral relationship and then becoming psychically estranged after their relationship has run its course. To end up thus disconnected, as so many millions of us do, is to eviscerate an intense part of our own past, leaving only memories— some fond, some inevitably *not* so fond.

So—for that rare romantic *few*, may at least this *permanent portion* of this *penitent page* serve as my humble blessing and thanks. May it serve, too, as my admittedly inadequate yet deeply heartfelt *apologia* to that even *rarer* romantic few who truly *merit* that *apologia*. (Also, let this even more *minute* portion of this page be my one inscribed plea to the Eternal Presence for absolution on their behalf and mine for the countless times we broke Its seventh commandment.)

Meanwhile, back at the ranch (now that I've indulged myself by inflicting on you that long, ultra-personal philosophic confessional)—a *Telford's Telescope* column that appeared on the front page of the *Michigan FrontPAGE* decrying what I called the "white noose surrounding Detroit" drew considerable commentary. So did another similar piece I wrote for the *Detroit Free Press*. Partially as a result of those two columns, I was invited to serve with Dr. Manning Marable of New York's Columbia University, Dr. Alvin Poussaint of Harvard University, activist film actor Danny Glover, and other national notables on a panel on racism that was to be televised across the country from the State Theater in Detroit. Dr. Burnley had been invited to serve on the panel, too.

Without his knowledge, I believe, one of his top lieutenants learned I was to be on the panel and leaned on sponsors from the Wayne County Community College District to remove me. This unnamed lieutenant of Burnley's told the sponsors, as it was confided to me, that this person didn't want me to "outshine Burnley" (which I wouldn't have—we would have been a good one-two punch on the panel). I couldn't go to Burnley with this information regarding what his lieutenant had done to me, since it had been shared with me in confidence. It could have gotten the organizer in trouble, so I simply participated from the audience. I was able to get my staff into the limited-seat audience, too, which chagrined the lower-level aide who had become my supervisor. To her further chagrin, I had also been contacted by a *Detroit News* reporter and quoted on the front page regarding the conference.

I was having lunch in the Detroit St. Regis Hotel a week or two later with my old Berkley administrative colleague Joe Haddad when former Detroit Pistons star Dave Bing, the president of Detroit-based Bing Steel, who was to become a mayor of Detroit six years later, walked by my table and said, "Telford, keep up the good work with your columns—I read them all the time. I particularly liked that one you did on Creative Insubordination."

Dr. Sheffield had told me that my supervisor *didn't* like that column, though —and this paranoid concern with my columns that gave me a public voice which my supervisor felt was some kind of a threat to her turned out to be a harbinger of very bad things to come.

In that specific column, I had written:

> Creative insubordination *[a term I had coined and given seminars on]* is "strategic rebellion against dehumanizingly undemocratic institutions or obstructive persons or programs within those institutions.". . . . Here is a seminal CIA (Creative Insubordinate's Axiom): "One's superordinate isn't necessarily one's superior. He or she may merely have been better-connected or just dumb-lucky." Here's another: "Position power isn't always the greatest power."

The next week, I had lunch at Mario's restaurant on Second Avenue in Detroit with former Detroit Mayor Dennis Archer. He had been the first politician I had ever really gotten excited about since Robert Kennedy.

Dennis had read the "Creative Insubordination" column, too. "John," he said, "that column said a mouthful. I'm hearing that Dr. Burnley has some people around him who aren't doing him a lot of good. I'm glad you have his back."

I decided that it was necessary for me to try to "have Burnley's back" even more. With my encouragement throughout the year that followed, my fourteen parent/community liaison officers began to sing Dr. Burnley's praises more and more and attend more and more community meetings and functions at night on their own time—and I was delighted to encounter them at all of these events.

My supervisor, however, wasn't. She wrote a memo to my staff directing them not to go to any more community meetings without her permission—and I blew my top.

Her memo got leaked to the *Detroit News* and the *Detroit Free Press*, and the two daily papers broke the story.

CHAPTER FIFTY-THREE

FIRED *AGAIN*!

"Dr. Burnley shrewdly put the Office of Community Affairs under
the leadership of Dr. John Telford, a skilled and seasoned administrator with a long history of human-rights activism."

—*From an editorial in the* Michigan Chronicle

Dr. Burnley was in the hospital having prostate surgery at the time my supervisor's gag memo got leaked to the newspapers. An editorial headline asking,
"Do the parental liaison restrictions stifle school reform?" then appeared in
the March 19–25, 2003, edition of the *Michigan Chronicle*.
    Here are excerpts:

> The internal memorandum recently written by the Detroit Public
> Schools' Acting Chief of Staff . . . to Parent/Community Liaisons as
> reported by local news sources, raises some legitimate concerns
> about our efforts to improve the district.
>   The memo, addressed to Executive Director John Telford's
> staff of 14 liaisons, appears, in effect, to be a gag order. It warned
> the Liaisons, "Effective immediately, you are not to schedule any
> meetings or phone calls with external stakeholders without prior
> discussion or approval from me." . . .
>   The memo comes at a time when Mayor Kwame Kilpatrick
> has just appointed four new school board members and charged
> them with helping the district continue to increase parent and
> community involvement with the schools.

It also comes at a time when the U.S. Department of Education is coming to Detroit to determine if the school district is following federal regulations for parental involvement and whether the district's Title I funds are being appropriately spent.

Shortly after Dr. Burnley became the district's CEO in May 2000, he created the Office of Community Affairs, and after a number of directors of the office had come and gone, he shrewdly put it under the leadership of Dr. Telford, a skilled and seasoned administrator with a long history of human-rights activism. We applauded the move because it recognized how important parental and community involvement is to the district's reform efforts.

Since then, the Office has diligently endeavored to fulfill the charge Dr. Burnley gave it to increase parental involvement in the schools, help resolve parental concerns, and provide an interactive bridge between the school district and its community. . . . We question whether the memo stifles the very people we need to be empowering to improve Detroit's failing school district. . . . The school district needs an open line of communication with the community, and the Parent/Community Liaisons help to foster those lines. . . .

While the administrative control the . . . memo implies is the last thing the district's parents, children, and community need, it is good that the memo has come to the attention of the new school board, Dr. Burnley, and the public. We are confident that the issue will be addressed.

The school district's parent/community liaisons need to have free and ongoing access to community leaders and all other external stakeholders. Perhaps the community would be better served if Dr. Telford reported directly to the CEO.

From everything we have seen and heard of Dr. Burnley, who has made swift and significant inroads in the right direction on multiple fronts, this memo does not appear to reflect his style. Burnley clearly realizes the importance of parental and community involvement, as we all should.

I doubt that the administrators closest to Dr. Burnley ever let him see that editorial.

During these persecutions that my staff and I were suffering from at the hands of my gag-memo-writing supervisor, I was getting closer and closer to sultry-sweet little Gina Morris. She was spending more and more time at my place, and I at hers.

One day when I was in my bed with the flu sipping copious amounts of straight Johnny Walker Red, a very upset Gina came back from shopping for juice, Tylenol, and more whiskey for me in the ghetto area due northeast of my place on East Jefferson and told me a man in a liquor store had tricked her out of her cell phone. Furious that someone would do this to the young lady who had once again become my number-one girl, I leaped out of bed and loaded my gun. Gina's seamy childhood and early teen years had made my Sixteenth Street origins resemble a country-club upbringing by comparison, and I was committed to making her adult life a much better one. Thus, I was doubly angry about what had just happened to her.

Sweating, feverish, and more than a little inebriated, I dragged Gina back to the store and then down rutted streets all over that neighborhood seeking the thief. The store owner and another man said he was a druggie everyone called "Party Time" who prowled those streets on a regular basis looking for easy marks. I think someone must have tipped Party Time that I was coming after him to pistol-whip him for that phone, because he was nowhere to be seen.

It was a good thing for him—and maybe for me—that I never found him.

While Dr. Burnley was in the hospital, my supervisor somehow convinced him that my release was a necessary "budget cut." She yanked me off my job and stashed me in an office high up in DPS' leased headquarters in the towering Fisher Building at Second Avenue and West Grand Boulevard for two and a half long months to ride out my contract, which ran through June. This fulfilled a prediction my Scottish grandma had made sixty years before that I'd have an office in that palatial building some day—but it wasn't quite in the way she'd envisioned. (The school district had ill-advisedly sold its huge, historic headquarters at 5057 Woodward.)

However, since I had three months left on my contract anyway, why not let me serve in my job? They said I was to be assigned topics for "press releases" to write instead of running my community affairs division, but they never gave me any.

Still, I dutifully reported to my office every day and wrote my newspaper columns there. The principals I had supervised in 2000–2001 also continued to call me for advice.

Neither my supervisor nor some other top officials around Dr. Burnley had ever been comfortable with my vintage closeness to him. One of those administrators, who was in charge of the Human Resources Department, was conducting kangaroo court-style "hearings" for people who wanted to protest and petition against losing their positions. The "hearings" could be public or private, at the petitioner's request.

I petitioned, and of course I chose that my "hearing" be public. I brought thirty or forty folks with me for moral support, including Gina, Rev. Arkles Brooks, Mrs. Louise Harris—the long-time LSCO president at Fleming Elementary School, and Andre Broadnax, my old city champion quarter-miler from Pershing. Monica Johnson, one of my parent/community liaisons, called me on my cell phone and told me she was walking over with a dozen of my liaisons to speak in my behalf, and they were *minutes* away.

I headed them off. "It's way too risky for you guys to do that for me, Monica," I said. "My supervisor might go after *you*, too—but thanks, anyway."

In the anteroom before my "hearing," DPS security officer Lamont Cochran—whose father, DPS Police lieutenant Maurice Cochran, was an old Detroit Chadsey High track star—came to me and said apologetically, "Dr. Telford, we've been told you've caused disruption at board meetings, and we've got orders to remove you forcibly from this hearing if you get disruptive again."

"Lamont, someone has just told you a slanderous lie. I never disrupted any board meeting, *ever*. May I ask who gave you that outrageous order?"

"Dr. Telford, I'm not at liberty to say."

"That's okay, Lamont—I know who it was, anyway." Rev. Brooks had seen my supervisor talking to Lamont in the hall.

My petition, of course, was rejected. Many colleagues and friends urged me to sue, and I did pay an attorney to ask for a copy of the tape of my "hearing." (The attorney was advised in writing that there *was* no tape, but I was tipped that publicity director Stan Childress had been seen taping the "hearing.") I decided not to sue, because I didn't want to get Ken Burnley caught in that kind of crossfire. Still, with my departure, his whole left flank was exposed—not to speak of his *right* one—but I don't think he realized that (at least, not *then*).

At this point, I was so disgusted with the top DPS administration's unjust treatment that I was ready to either *re*-retire or else seek a charter school principalship or suburban superintendency. I did interview and get chosen for the top job in Hamtramck, a small enclave of Detroit, but instead they decided to re-hire a former superintendent so he wouldn't sue them for breach of contract. It developed, however, that I was far from finished with DPS. Miraculously, it came to pass that I was about to embark upon five of the wildest, most wonderfully rewarding, and thoroughly *energizing* years of my long career.

CHAPTER FIFTY-FOUR

A SIGNAL HONOR;
BACK TO FINNEY;
MARRIED ONCE MORE!

"The time you won our town the race, we chaired you through
the marketplace. Man and boy stood cheering by, as home we
brought you, shoulder-high."

—*A. E. Housman*

A few weeks before the end of the 2002–03 school year, Finney High School
principal Alvin Ward and athletic director Andy Rio named the Finney track
for me because of my athletic accomplishments and my long history of human-
rights activism—and because I had been Finney's first track coach back in 1964.
They announced the naming of the track in the sports sections of the two
Detroit dailies, so a lot of my old athletes from Finney showed up, as well as
some from Southeastern, Pershing, King, and Southwestern, and one—former
Midwest Collegiate Conference high hurdles champion Ken Riley—from the
University of Detroit-Mercy. The young sportswriters were generous, with lavish
references to my long-ago glory and speed.

Some friends and colleagues showed up for the ceremony, too—along
with my son and daughter. My illustrious ex-student john powell drove all the
way up from Columbus. Two of my past girlfriends came—the brilliant Geraldine
Barclay from my college days, and my old/new flame, the beauteous Gina, who
was fast recapturing my heart.

Someone told me he'd seen Dr. Burnley circling the school with his driver,
DPS Police Sgt. Jerome Gray, but he never came in. The entrance to the auditorium
where the ceremony was held was out in back of the school, so maybe they

couldn't find it, or else Burnley was called away abruptly on school business.

Finney's state two-mile champion, Ken Howse, was the speaker. Kenny declared that the effect I had on him transformed his life. Hearing him, and hearing the touching things that other old athletes of mine said—plus the track-naming itself—meant more to me than any honor I had ever been given, including the WSU Alumnus of the Year award and my four national track medals, my WSU Athletic Hall of Fame induction, and even the medal that Pope Pius XII had put in my hand at the Vatican.

I had supervised Principal Alvin Ward in the 2000–2001 school year when he had been acting principal of Western High School, and I had collaborated with my fellow executive director Beverly Gray to get Mr. Ward the Finney principalship when Dr. Royster yielded to community pressure to put a Latino principal in his position at Western—where his performance had been exemplary, and he had cleaned up the gang problem. Dr. Gray owed me a chit, because I had talked Dr. Burnley into keeping her on as an executive director when a minor money contratemps that surfaced from her recent days as King's principal landed her photo in the newspaper next to other allegedly fiscally errant principals whom Dr. Burnley then removed as executive directors.

I had also been instrumental in ensuring that Becky Luna, Al's talented Latina assistant, got the Western job, even though I had a hard time initially talking her into taking it. Dr. Royster hadn't been Mr. Ward's greatest fan, because he'd been moonlighting as a security supervisor at a Detroit casino to help feed his family and put his children through college, and she didn't like the moonlighting. During that spring of 2001, I had realized then that if somebody was ever going to help Alvin Ward secure another principalship, that *somebody* would have to be *me*.

Now that my supervisor had arranged to have me fired again, Al Ward asked me if I would like to come and be his curriculum coordinator. Even though this would equate to a quadruple-level demotion from my previous job that my supervisor had snatched away from me, I didn't look at it from that perspective. The main thing to me was that I would be working with my good friend Alvin Ward, and I would get to work directly with kids again one last time. I warned Al that I didn't believe my influential supervisor would want me working in DPS again in *any* capacity. (I later learned that she was furious that I would remain in the district.) Al simply and courageously repeated his offer. I accepted it enthusiastically and gratefully.

When I reported to work at the school at the end of August 2003, Finney had no science or English department heads assigned yet to the school, so I set up my curriculum-coordinator office inside the science office to help the science teachers with their discipline and planning, and I taught the not-yet-assigned English department head's three ninth-grade English classes. (Ultimately, Finney would get an expert curriculum person for the science job in the person of Natalie Jacobson.)

A few months later, the Central Office sent us Gloria Cunningham to be our English department head, so I gave Gloria my three classes and began to concentrate on helping dean of students Alvin Sims and assistant principal David Pryor with school discipline. They needed all the help they could get, because Finney was a wild school with hundreds of kids who were in near-open rebellion.

Again, I was in my element—and I was exultant. I got a kick out of the amazed expression on the faces of misbehaving students who had run from me in the hall when I told them to stop and they kept right on running—and then this bearded old two-hundred-pound white guy with a ponytail chased and collared them within a few seconds. I had taken to wearing a pair of low-cut black gym shoes so I could accelerate more quickly on straightaways and get better traction around corners and up and down stairs.

Principal Ward worried, though, about the increasingly creaky old Mustang getting hurt. Once I was in full stride chasing a kid across the grass outside the principal's office window when he got on the public address system and blared an order at me to give up the chase. I did give up the chase then—but I gave it up reluctantly, because I had gained ground to within ten yards of my quarry and would certainly have collared him within the next couple of seconds.

Some of the most tension-filled times were when school let out at 3:30, and I would join other administrators and our male security guards on the sidewalk to monitor the dismissal and head off potential problems. Carloads of young dropouts or truants from other high schools nearby would slowly circle Finney looking for girls or for trouble—which often amounted to the same thing.

One carload shouted to me, "We gon' get your white ass!"

I made a beckoning gesture. "Come and get it—my white ass is right here waiting."

The departing Finney kids, of course, saw and heard this; I was actually saying it for their benefit. As I had at Southwestern, again I was deliberately establishing my rep.

That fall, Rev. Arkles Brooks, my old quarter-miler of 1961 (the year Gina was born!), performed my and Gina's simple marriage ceremony at Cliff and Barbara Hatcher's stately Sherwood Forest home, with Bob Plumpe as best man. Finney principal Al Ward and my old teammate Jerry Catalina and Gina's friend Sierra Smith were among the few wedding guests.

A week after my wedding, I met the dark-haired principal in a Grosse Pointe restaurant, broke the stunning news to her, and bade her what I intended to be a permanent goodbye. As we walked out of the restaurant together, she suddenly ran away crying across the street into the rainy November night, leaving me standing there with a feeling of sad emptiness unlike any I had felt since I had broken up with Gerrie Barclay more than thirty years before.

I moved Gina and her twenty-three-year-old autistic son Michael into a six-bedroom mansion I bought on Parkside in the historic University district on Detroit's northwest side, a few blocks from Cliff and Barb's. Due to some residual mutual misunderstandings that remained simmering between Gina and me, as well as the deep, unresolved feelings I still had for the principal I'd been dating, I moved out of the Parkside place six months later and into the principal's condo. (I owned two units in the River House, but I had signed over the larger one overlooking the river to my son Steve to give him a permanent home, and my now-deceased cousin Carl's younger brother Dick—a retired U.S. Army master sergeant and many-times decorated Vietnam War hero who had just separated from his native German wife in Washington State—was staying in the other.)

Five months after that, most of our marital issues got resolved with the help of my best friend Cliff, who had introduced Gina and me more than twenty years earlier. Gina—who at a hundred and six pounds and half-an-inch under five feet had already been somewhat smaller than petite—had pined away during our five-month separation to a pitifully emaciated weight of eighty-eight pounds, despite my having continued to give her twenty-five hundred dollars a month for her to buy groceries and other necessities for herself and her autistic son, Michael.

In the late summer of 2004, I sold the six-bedroom mansion (at a loss).

I had already bought a smaller house on Mackenzie Street for cash in the upscale Aviation Subdivision near Mackenzie High School on the west side. While dolefully realizing that this would devastate the lovely lady with whom I had been living, I made a final and ultimately irrevocable decision to move into the Mackenzie house with Gina and Michael, one small dog, one much *larger* dog, and one large, well-fed, and incredibly coddled cat.

I also sold the huge *High Life*—at a huge loss. For Gina, the big boat held too many unhappy mental images with regard to the things I'd been doing on it—and with whom—prior to our marriage.

CHAPTER FIFTY-FIVE

UNJUST REJECTIONS OF A "CIVIL-RIGHTS LEGEND"

"The incompetent and corrupt don't promote the competent
and incorruptible."

—From a Telford's Telescope *column
in the* Michigan Chronicle

Happy again now that I was back at Finney after nearly forty years—and
happy, too, that Gina and I were finally together again, I wrote an impassioned
poem I entitled *Novena for Gina*:

> *I am your <u>instrument</u>.*
> *<u>Play</u> me.*
> *Play me, baby, play me.*
> *I'm your old bagpipe beneath a blood moon,*
> *Your Hibernian chant and your dark, Druid rune.*
> *I'm your rare violin that's the best in the room!*
> *Play me, baby, play me.*
>
> *I'm your violincello that's always in tune,*
> *Your viola, accordion, trumpet, bassoon;*
> *And you are my <u>player</u>, my God-given boon—*
> *So play me, baby, play me.*
> *Tune me and croon me.*
> *Completely <u>bassoon</u> me.*
> *Play me, baby, play me.*

You're my sacramental firmament;
I'm your instrument for permanent—
So play me, baby, baby, baby,
Play me, baby.
<u>Play</u> me!

Thus inspired, Gina did *play* me—repeatedly—and she gradually regained her normal weight and health. She also wrote in-kind poetry to me again for the first time in twenty years. We began reading our poetry to each other and sharing it with artsy gatherings at the Friday night Picnap Poetry Series in the Java Café at 440 Burroughs in Detroit's New Center, where I often ran into young folks I knew, or who read my *Telford's Telescope* columns in the *Chronicle.*

I even mentioned the Java Café in a lead-in poem on vigilantism in a column about a young criminal who'd been videotaped beating up a helpless old man in a supermarket parking lot and stealing his car. My late papa, who was a virtual one-man vigilante posse himself in the old Sixteenth Street days, would have relished this poem:

<u>*The Mad Vigilante from the Java Café*</u>

I'm the Mad Vigilante from the Java Café,
And I just wrote this poem—I just wrote it today.
Now, vigilantism's part of my Creed.
Vigilantes have become what we need.
So proffer me a smoothie and an Uzi, my good fellow.
The smoothie's for my belly, and the Uzi's for the yellow
Four-syllable curse word who beat the old man.
He beat the old man.
He beat the old man!
He BEAT
The old man!

Yes, I just wrote this poem—I just wrote it today.
I'm the Mad Vigilante from the Java Café!

The smoothies at the Java Café are really *smoooth*, and I often made them even *smooother* with a wee dram of Scotch I sneakily slipped in mine when I was in the café bathroom. My late vigilante daddy would have disdained wasting good Scotch in a smoothie, though. That old Scot preferred his Scotch straight up and flowing *free*, like him.

In the meantime, my late vigilante daddy's granddaughter Katherine had gotten engaged again—to a man I actually approved of! Richard Garrett, her new fiancé, was a journeyman pipefitter, an ex-Marine, and a former state champion swimmer at Oscoda High School. When they got married, this time I was privileged to walk my daughter down the aisle.

My friend and colleague David Pryor, whom I had recommended to Al Ward for an assistant principalship at Finney, had been notified that he was going to be laid off from that job after having served in it for three years. I therefore "ghost-wrote" David's letter of application for him to my protégé, Superintendent Gary Faber, for a similar job in West Bloomfield and printed it for David on my office computer and had him sign it. David mailed the letter the same day—which was only a couple of days from the deadline. I then called Dr. Faber and alerted him to be on the lookout for the letter. One of my former African-American principals in Rochester, Gene Seaborn—who had been basketball coach Bob Samaras' team captain at WSU, and whom I had *also* recommended to Gary—was the high school principal in West Bloomfield. Gene hired David immediately.

Losing David definitely didn't make our jobs any easier at Finney, but I had done what he had needed me to do—and we would probably have lost him, anyway.

The Detroit NAACP's director, Heaster Wheeler, and its president, Wendell Anthony, recommended me for membership on the Governor's Task Force for Detroit Public School Reform. I was appointed to the committee that critiqued the DPS human resources department, which was in dire need of revamping. DPS' hiring, firing, promotion, and demotion practices had become ever more capricious, arbitrary, nepotistic, and discriminatory.

A good example of this was my own case: between 2003 and 2008, I applied and was interviewed and rejected for approximately twenty jobs, despite being by far the most qualified candidate for every one of them. They ranged from assistant superintendent-level jobs like the ones I had done successfully in the suburbs for years all the way down to principalships and even *assistant* principalships. I had been an assistant principal nearly forty years *earlier*!

Three principals who interviewed me for their assistant jobs called me a "legend," but I still didn't get any of those three jobs. One of the principals later nervously confided to me that she and other principals had been ordered not to choose me, but I mustn't tell anyone that it was she who told me.

Speaking of *legends*—I'm on the advisory board of the Wayne County Community College District's Institute for Social Progress along with Dr. Manning Marable of New York and two *true* human-rights legends—my acclaimed protégé john powell and the great Grace Boggs, a ninety-six-year-old Detroit activist. In a January 28, 2008, letter of recommendation for an out-of-state university fellowship for me (that I didn't get), Professor Joshua Bassett, the Institute's young director, would write effusively: "John Telford is no less than a living civil-rights *legend!*"

But what good is it to be a living civil-rights legend if the "legend" can't get the jobs he seeks, in order to able to share his knowledge, expertise, and experience with young teachers and administrators?

However, I was nothing if not tenacious; I stubbornly interviewed for my old job directing the Detroit Public Schools' parent liaison and community programs which had been unjustly taken from me.

Failing—again unjustly—to get selected, I then interviewed for a lower-level community liaison job within that same division. (I would have taken a $30,000 pay cut if I'd been chosen, but again discriminatorily, I *wasn't*.)

I even interviewed for a job writing press releases and was informed that I hadn't passed a ridiculously simple writing test they gave me. (I have authored more than a thousand newspaper columns, edited a number of *doctoral* dissertations, and done proofreading and editing for two large corporations.)

Insiders I knew at the board office told me their bosses were extremely afraid of my outspokenness and my penchant for poking my nose into dark, dishonest places where they didn't want it, so they were *never* going to bring me back downtown.

Still, again I was reluctant to sue, even though my wife wanted me to. DPS had been good to me in the old days, and despite this prevalent cronyism and corruption, I just couldn't bring myself to file suit against the district that had educated me.

Instead, between 2004 and 2008, I used my radio shows and my regular *Telford's Telescope* columns in the *Michigan FrontPAGE* and later in the *Michigan Chronicle* to fight back on my own behalf and on the behalf of others who had been unjustly passed over by the nepotistic ladies downtown.

One *Chronicle* column late in this plaintive process was headlined, "DPS job-seekers compete under handicap."

Here is part of that May 7–13, 2008, column:

> An editorial in this newspaper last August pronounced DPS a "cesspool of corruption." That it has been indeed—but not only for contract scandals. Its handicap-based promotion process is notorious. As a first-generation Scottish-American, I decided in 1959 to sojourn to Williamsburg, New York to compete in the 440-yard dash at the WNY Scottish Games, only to find that the race would be run on a handicap basis.
>
> Based on my fastest time, I was assigned to run from "scratch" (the full distance). Spread out ahead of me for 70 yards were a dozen runners. I caught the lead runner just before the tape. In my other 173 wins, my competitors ran the same distance I did. But in competing for jobs in DPS, I have had to run farther than the full 440 (metaphorically). In many such "competitions" predetermined "winners" who were given the jobs didn't really race at all.
>
> Public employees shouldn't have to compete for promotions on a handicap basis. Colleagues have said my handicaps are being too old and too white, but my true handicaps have been my skills and integrity. The incompetent and corrupt don't promote the competent and incorruptible.

I continued to drive every day—fall, winter, and spring—across town to Finney, where Principal Al Ward had now assigned me the additional responsibility of being his in-house community liaison officer. My duties relevant to that responsibility included attending Saturday meetings of the Finney LSCO (Local School Community Organization), keeping track of the outside entities that supported Finney, and attending night meetings (as Al's stand-in) of a charitable agency called Christ Community Development Center that was housed in the Finney building. I eventually even *chaired* that agency.

I used my community and athletic contacts to bring in distinguished guests to speak, including former Harlem Globetrotter "Jumping Johnny" Kline, my old compadre in several enterprises. I brought in my Pershing All-State and U-M All-American relayist, Reggie Bradford. I brought in Rev. Arkles Brooks, who was now delivering the spiritual messages on the *John Telford Show* on *NewsTalk 1200*.

Also, I brought in another of my old quarter-mile record breakers at Pershing, who had triumphed over his many hard years of rough and misguided experiences to become a certified social worker, and for whom I had recently stood up as best man at his wedding.

His name? Thomas Moses Jones—aka *Outlaw*!

Even though I had turned over my duties as president of the Detroit Track Old-Timers to my old WSU teammate Allan Tellis, I was a very active vice president, and at this time I wrote yet another of what had become my interminable gadfly columns in the African-American-owned-and-operated *Michigan Chronicle* urging the university to restore its vaunted and historic track program. Two years earlier, I had led a large delegation of principals, coaches, and athletes to a WSU Board of Governors meeting in an attempt to get the comparatively low-budget program restored. Our attempt was fruitless, despite strong support from Richard Bernstein—one of the WSU board members whom my DTOT had helped get elected. (Bernstein now is the board president, and the university has a receptive new president, too. Therefore, our soon-to-be renewed and redoubled efforts to restore the sport should surely be successful this time.)

I introduced this particular *Michigan Chronicle* column about the sad and troubling demise of WSU track with thirty long and un-lyrical lines of rhymed iambic pentameter which I had penned some years earlier but kept periodically updating. The poem was entitled *Lo and Billy and Buddy and I*:

> *We showed them our heels from Rangoon to Rome.*
> *In Portugal, we gave them all our gears.*
> *We won in London—and then back at home*
> *We dominated totally for years.*
> *Lo's held the long jump record fifty-six;*
> *For forty-nine, the quarter-mile's been mine—*
> *Twenty-six feet, and forty-six quick ticks*
> *Of a stopwatch, more or less. And that fine,*
> *Fleet Buddy Coleman (dead a long time past)*
> *Streaked his sweet sepia self to national fame*
> *Indoors at sixty yards! Our fireball-fast*

Low-hurdler, Billy Smith, high-stepped the same!
Now, bureaucrat "economists" have killed
The Wayne State University track team.
Long legacies of partially fulfilled
Commitments drift like fallen leaves downstream.
Our children join no more that native chain
Of champions who linked our school to fame
With headlines coast-to-coast and hill-to-plain,
And, graduated, came home with the aim
Of serving in the Motor City scheme
As teachers, coaches—<u>hundreds</u> of them—seers
Who toiled toward restoration of a dream
And spawned rebirth from Twelfth Street's after-years.
Yet hustled into halls of fame we go—
Lorenzo, Buddy, Bullet Bill, and I.
Officials name Wright Field after Lo,
But such enshrinements pale when programs die.
Our marks are bedded in a dried-up stream,
While Wayne State U. still sports a <u>tennis</u> team.

The late Lorenzo Wright has now held the long-jump record *for sixty years*, and I've held the quarter-mile mark for *fifty-three*. The "Twelfth Street" reference was to the bloody 1967 rebellion that started there, about a quarter-mile due north of my father's parents' house, which was in a predominately black neighborhood. I can still remember my devout old Scottish grannie belting out hymns in the old black church she attended down the street. That street has since been renamed Rosa Parks Boulevard. Also, old Miller High alum Buddy Coleman—who became a Detroit cop and was later shot to death by a girl-friend's angry husband—tied the world indoor record (seven seconds flat) for *seventy* yards. I used *sixty* in the poem because *seventy* had one syllable too many for the line to scan properly.

In addition to writing that column and all my other regular newspaper columns, as well as those many other duties of mine I have listed here—both assigned and assumed, at Finney and beyond Finney—I was now chairing the Team for Justice board, as well.

Thus, I was a pretty busy old boy.

CHAPTER FIFTY-SIX

SUPERINTENDENT JOHN TELFORD!??

"Mr. [*sic*] Telford is 70 years old. He doesn't <u>look</u> like it, but . . .
it may not <u>last</u>."

*—A legally naïve member of the Madison Board
of Education, quoted in the* Daily Tribune

In late 2005 or early 2006, then-Detroit Board of Education President William
Brooks had been under heavy community pressure from several quarters to
ask Dr. Kenneth Burnley to resign from his job as DPS CEO. Becoming aware
of this, I wrote a column in the *Detroit Free Press* in which I said that to dismiss
Dr. Burnley would be detrimental to the students.

I then went before the Board of Education and told the board members,
in Dr. Burnley's presence, "Dr. Burnley doesn't deserve to be dismissed—and
I say this to you as a man *whom he twice allowed to be fired*. He has built new
schools, he has initiated a full-day kindergarten, he has instituted a language
arts program at the elementary level that has begun to produce positive results,
and he has done other things that were necessary to bring about the gradual
recovery of this beleaguered district he inherited that was closely approaching
total chaos." My defense of Dr. Burnley was roundly booed by a large audience
of parents and community members who were after his scalp, as the raucous
Rochester bigots had been after mine at another board meeting thirty miles
north and sixteen years earlier, for different reasons.

Reading the fateful handwriting on the wall, Dr. Burnley ultimately expressed
no further interest in remaining in the job. I asked him if he indeed meant this.

He said he did—he was weighing other options, including a chair he had been offered at the University of Michigan—so I told President Brooks I was willing to do the job on an interim basis for a year without salary to demonstrate what I could do. This wasn't the first and it wouldn't be the last time that I would offer to do a DPS job without pay, but every time I proposed such an offer, the Board and administration made me feel like a ping-pong ball by bouncing me back so many times. These offers, incidentally, have been my way of consciously trying to give something back to those long-dead PSL coaches who quite possibly saved my very *life* so many years ago when they never gave up on me.

President Brooks said he would submit my offer to the board. I don't know whether he ever did, but the board interviewed only William Coleman, Burnley's Chief Operating Officer, and they voted to hire Mr. Coleman for the interim position on the spot that same night in a flagrant example of "insider trading"— despite others in and out of DPS being interested in and qualified for the job.

A large Superintendent Search Committee of community members under the chairmanship of new board of education member Carla Scott, a physician, was appointed to draw up specifications for the new job of superintendent. I was named to the committee. The board posted the permanent job, and I applied along with approximately fifty others and then withdrew from the large community committee. A board screening committee narrowed the number of superintendent candidates to thirteen, and I made the cut.

Concurrently, I had been recruited by professional "headhunter" Tom McLennan, a former Dearborn, Michigan, superintendent, to apply for the super-intendency of the Madison District in Madison Heights, Michigan—a blue-collar, predominately white suburb of Detroit which I knew was going perforce to have a huge influx of black students from Detroit, due to its need to become an "open enrollment" district to shore up its flagging student population. Once that policy gained momentum, my multicultural skills and experience would be sorely needed, not to speak of my background as a champion athlete, coach, and athletic director. When non-resident black kids converge on a white district, they almost inevitably absorb the top spots on track, football, basketball, and wrestling teams, which can generate resentment among white booster club parents when their resident offspring are no longer starters on varsity squads. Also, cultural differences—if they're not fully understood or accepted—can pose problems for teachers, administrators, the local police, and the surrounding business and residential community. Those differences can in turn pose a variety of problems for the incoming students and the ones who are already in residence there.

I had two good interviews and became one of three finalists. I took my wife to both interviews and introduced her to the selectors so they could note Gina's beautiful brown countenance and thus have no difficulty divining my activist social views. I was told by an inside source that I was on the verge of being chosen when a local female judge informed Dr. Keith McClellan—who in turn informed me—that a Madison board member had told the other members she had "inside information" that I'd been fired in Rochester! I immediately asked retired Rochester superintendent John Schultz to write to counter this slanderous lie, and to call the board president. John did both—but it was too late. The president was unreachable, and the board chose the man whom I had been tipped was the number-two candidate.

This same female board member had been quoted in the December 1, 2006, edition of the *Daily Tribune*, to wit: "Mr. [sic] Telford is 70 years old. He doesn't look like it, but . . . it may not last." I was too exasperated, too bemused, too busy, and just too plain *tired* to sue—which of course I could have, and I would have won substantial damages if I had. However, the main reason I didn't sue over the board member's illegal comment in the newspaper was the Madison district's dire financial plight. To take money from them would be to take money from needy kids, even though the district was insured against suit. Also, I never had been able to bring myself to sue a school district. God knows that over the years I have had ample grounds to sue DPS—but to me, suing a school district is tantamount to suing my own mother.

This wasn't the first time I'd been called "too old" for an administrative job. An associate superintendent in Detroit did it, too—and I had a formidable and willing witness in Northwest Homeowners Association president and former WSU basketball great Charlie Primas—but I didn't sue then, either. The most ironic part of school officials saying I'm too old to administrate is that I was frequently outrunning and collaring ordinary young male "civilians" at Finney who had misbehaved—even if I *was* in my seventies. (When I was a young athlete coming up, we used to call non-athletes "civilians.") Also, I was away from home at Finney or at various meetings fifty to sixty hours a week, including evenings and weekends—and those long hours would certainly have taxed the energies of many far younger men.

The Detroit Board of Education voted to allow the interim CEO, William Coleman, to throw his hat in the ring—so now there were fourteen of us semifinalists for the DPS job. Mr. Coleman had released my former supervisor because of some well-publicized allegations of malfeasance involving more than half a million dollars in contracts given to her brother and a now-deceased ex-convict named Larry Nelson (who happened to be a good friend of mine). At some point in this continuum, Mr. Coleman came under fire himself for some even more lavishly publicized alleged improprieties regarding contracts. He also got indicted on sixteen counts of various forms of malfeasance in a large school district in Texas where he had previously served. Consequently, he was out of the running to become the Detroit superintendent, so we were back down to thirteen—an *unlucky number*?

We thirteen semifinalists were asked to write our answers to ten questions. I did, at *length*—but my answers were withheld from the large committee of community members, so I wasn't one of those chosen for a public interview. Had the large committee seen my answers, I'm certain I'd have been interviewed— and in a fair public interview, I'd have been off to the races. One of the promises I made in my document of answers that the full committee never saw was to use my own car—not the district's—and to have no district-paid chauffeur. I promised to serve without pay for one year, too. My wife Gina calls me a WHOM—white, honest, old, and male—all apparent handicaps in DPS for promotions of any kind. This has obviously been so—at least in my case— in terms of the "honest" part of that acronym.

Here is my e-mailed response to search committee chairperson Carla Scott's e-mailed admonishment to me that my having contacted those who were involved in the search, including her, was "inappropriate and out of order":

> Let me begin by saying that I absolutely couldn't DISAGREE MORE with your statement that my having . . . contacted you . . . was "INAPPROPRIATE and OUT OF ORDER." Not only do I hold that my contacting you in this regard was fully APPROPRIATE and IN order—I respectfully submit that it was LONG OVERDUE. In a constitutional democracy (which at this writing I tend to believe the United States still is), any applicant for a public school superintendency should be free to communicate at any time in any

way with whomever (s)he chooses in order to explicate his/her platform for reform that (s)he would advance if (s)he were to be chosen by an elected board of education to do the job.

I would therefore suggest that any single one of us thirteen semi-final candidates for the DPS superintendency has the right to communicate via e-mail, media ad, public forum, telephone, facsimile machine, supermarket or barber shop or beauty parlor bulletin board posting, or indeed, CARRIER PIGEON to make known his/her platform to anyone and everyone who will heed it—prominently including, in this instance, DPS Superintendent Search Committee members and DPS board members. This is especially so since those governing the DPS superintendent-selection process—most particularly and specifically YOU—have thus far neglected to share not just MINE but ALL of our written responses to your ten questions with the full Search Committee!

Unless you do that and do it IMMEDIATELY, your entire selection procedure becomes utterly suspect—and I use the adjective "suspect" KINDLY. I did not communicate to you solely on my behalf, but also on behalf of ALL the candidates. To with-hold our responses to the ten questions from the entire Search Committee does a grave disservice to us all, and to the district and the Detroit community.

Once I had exchanged these e-mailed communications with Dr. Scott, I knew for sure that I wouldn't get a public interview for the DPS superintendency, even though—given the importance of the job—they probably should have interviewed all thirteen of us (they interviewed only *four*).

My newspaper column, *Telford's Telescope*, was appearing regularly now in the *Michigan Chronicle*, the city and state's largest and oldest black-owned newspaper, with a circulation exceeding one hundred thousand. I was using my column to lambaste the DPS leadership for all their classist, unjust, reverse-racist, incompetent, corrupt transgressions—including *this* one concerning my candidacy for the superintendency.

I was also relentlessly attacking them on the *John Telford Show*, my weekly half-hour show that ran live on a popular local talk-radio station. My wife Gina did the commercials for my sponsors—Rumors on the River lounge (owned by Jack Ostoin and John Travis) and the law firm of Thomas Randolph III, my unjustly-imprisoned Detroit Track Old-Timer colleague's son and my fellow Team for Justice board member.

At the beginning of every show, Gina and I would recite alternate lines of my poem *Blue Salt*—the poem which I had shared with my Butzel kids thirty years earlier—which begins:

> My name is Detroit.
> I'm a blue-collar town.
> Blue salt melts my mid-March snow . . .

and ends:

> No complex chemistry here—
> Only the old color of a new sky.

Indeed, I was trying my utmost to give Detroit a new and better sky—or at least a new and better *school district*. I had Michigan Governor Jennifer Granholm on my show, and Detroit interim Mayor Ken Cockrel, Jr. (who then was the City Council President), State Senator Hansen Clarke, National Conference for Community and Justice director Dan Krichbaum, Children's Hospital of Detroit president Herman Gray and former city councilman Clyde Cleveland (now deceased)—plus NAACP and other rights-organization officials and an assortment of more than forty celebrities who included several old-time track and basketball luminaries.

When State Rep. Lamarr Lemmons III came on the show, Lamarr and I discussed my columns that had expressed our mutual plea to the state legislature to forgive the $250 million debt the Detroit "reform board" had accrued, since the state takeover of the Detroit Public Schools was the legislature's doing, not the thus-disenfranchised Detroit voters'. We felt that the legislature should assume the responsibility for cleaning up its own mess, and several listeners who called in agreed with us.

My friend Hilmer Kenty, a former world champion boxer, appeared on my show. A probated twenty-one-year-old named Nathaniel Abraham, who had been incarcerated since the age of eleven for murder, came on the show, too. Sadly, at this writing Nathaniel has been sentenced to four to twenty years in prison on drug charges.

I also had executive director Luther Keith on my show to talk about his agency—ARISE!Detroit—which was a clearing house for the many charitable organizations in the city. The week after that, Dr. David Snead came on the show. Snead is the superintendent of the Waterbury, Connecticut schools. He was a finalist to return to the Detroit superintendency he had once held, and I had mentioned over the air to another talk show host on my station during her show that Dr. Snead just might be the superintendent DPS needed. This talk show host responded to me that if the board brought Snead back, she would do everything she could to get whoever had voted for him *recalled*.

When I told Dr. Snead about this, he said on my show that he had turned the talk show host down for a job making motivational speeches in the Detroit schools, and he presumed that this was why she wouldn't support his candidacy. I repeated his statement on one of my later shows, and she replayed that portion of my show on her show and called *me* a liar. The station manager got into the act, telling me that I needed to apologize to her.

I countered that she needed to apologize to *me*, because she had called me a liar and I hadn't lied. As a matter of fact, Dr. Snead told me that he had a very credible witness in the person of a highly regarded elected state official who he said had been present when the talk show host made her job request. (The state official had been a member of the Detroit school board at the time.) We ended up agreeing not to comment on it further over the air on our shows, because our little feud wasn't doing either her or me any good.

On every single one of my shows, my persistent topic was the failing Detroit public school district—and my constant target was its *failing leadership*.

CHAPTER FIFTY-SEVEN

A PRINCIPAL'S JAW BROKEN BY GANG-BANGERS

". . . gang fight on corner going to happen between . . . Chili Boys and G.M.I.'s ('Get Money Immediately'). . . ."

—*Cautionary reminder note on a daily disciplinary list on the author's school computer*

At the moment that Finney principal Alvin Ward got his jaw broken breaking up yet another gang fight, I was helping assistant principal Julie Buchanan delve through a seemingly endless paper blizzard of MEAP materials, so when it happened, I felt *horrible*—and somehow *guilty*. I had *put* Al at Finney, and he was like a son to me. I was sure that if I had been there backing him instead of working on those MEAP materials, I could have prevented him from getting hurt.

Finney had earned the dubious reputation of being the most dangerous school in the most dangerous city in the country—but if that was so, it was only by a matter of a *very* few degrees. Except for a couple of elite schools that got all of the money and attention from downtown, most of the twenty other Detroit high schools were nearly as tough. Most substitute teachers refused to come to Finney because of the almost hourly violence, so sometimes when we had fifteen or twenty teachers out, we had to put hundreds of students in the media center with only one or two staff members to monitor them.

While Mr. Ward was out for almost two months recovering from his broken jaw, the situation at Finney got even more dangerous—if that was possible. A few days after he was injured, I nearly got hurt myself in a similar situation. I was breaking up a fight in the media center when two new AT's (*administratively transferred* misbehavers) from Denby were about to jump me from behind to prevent me from breaking up the fight. A tall, rangy kid named Dexter House, who was still in pain from half-healed *bullet wounds* (!) in his abdomen, saved me by leveling one of the AT's and holding on to the other until I could get him.

I wrote Dexter a commendation for rescuing me. He had been in my office for discipline earlier in the week for threatening a teacher who had grabbed him by what he called his "sore" (!) in an attempt to get him to come into class. Instead of suspending Dexter, I had *counseled* him—and luckily for me, he hadn't forgotten it.

During my first three years back at Finney, I recorded the names of well over one thousand students I had disciplined/counseled—some many times and with indifferent success or with (I hate to admit it) *no* success, and many others whom I felt I had virtually *transformed*. I remained (and remain) in close touch with many of them even after they had left school. Every day, teachers would send me (or I would grab from the halls) as many as fifteen or twenty misbehaving students—singly or together—and I made an initial entry in my computer regarding each of them, listing them in order of contact rather than alphabetically.

I recorded these initial entries so hurriedly that I didn't bother with capitalization, punctuation, or paragraphing—usually separating each incident with only a semicolon—since the notes were for my eyes only and were a form of shorthand written to remind me of the situation or incident which I would write up later more fully and formally, as needed, and deal with further, as needed. Before long, in any given month I would usually have as many as three hundred students notated, many of them repeatedly. Here are sample entries to that document, and—except for some name changes or name omissions—exactly as they were written:

> Norman Butts [not his real name] cursed me and said he was going home I followed him out of school onto sidewalk and challenged him to fight gave my glasses to female security guard she said don't do it dr. telford it's not worth it; I spoke with Normans grandfather mr byers [*I spoke again with Mr. Byers most recently on the day before Thanksgiving, 2008 and found out that Norman is in prison: I have written to him*]; AT from SE [*Southeastern; Finney got hordes of ATs from their former schools routinely*] Antwaun

Asbury snatched his I.D. card back out of my hand and ran from me I chased caught and grabbed the AT [*Antwaun*] and slammed him against locker he said he would press charges—i got his I.D. card; lost my temper with Ralph gaston II (threatened to beat up Mr. Hamid and mis-behaving in his class and bragging how tough he is), I yanked him out of class and slapped him all the way down the hall saying so you think you're tough, huh? Are you tough enough to mess with me? to get him to try to hit me.

George Andres grade 10 hollering motherfucker in hall I grabbed him; Anthony freeman threw water on mr. nowicke; james long saw my wife Gina's picture on office wall said you like black pussy, huh? in front of five other boys I said you're damn lucky I didn't coldcock you I can't believe you said that; dionte white got F's in ms. Yan's and mr. Lazeru's classes (stole books?); I went nose-to-nose with bryan dye grade eleven told him I would make him very unhappy if he didnt start going to classes and behave; cortez freeman (said hello to me at Rev. Brooks' church [*Gospel Chapel of Detroit*]) Cortez always in the hall I spoke to his grandmother will speak to Arkles [*Rev. Arkles Brooks, my Southeastern quarter-miler and old friend*]; Melissa mcvey and devone driscoll want to go on my radio show; Trav wms ran from me I chased and caught and threw him on floor Nov. 2.

Bryan Dye in hall again; Darius Lloyd took off shirt to fight me I grabbed his arms and slammed him against locker til his teeth rattled he decided not to fight; cheerleader lakita mills out of class again; d'angelo reed says he didn't call me a white mother-fucker; matthew king was going to fight Coach E. [*Coach Tony Elliott, the football coach—Matthew was an amateur cruiserweight*] Victoria Dana [*Matthew's girl, an "A" student*] trying help keep him out of trouble but going to be hard; I suspended donzell Jackson and tyrell wells for fighting; Brandon Stinson grade 9 called me a white bitch and a few days later a white mother-fucker; Darlene sweeney's mother won't let her run track she [*Darlene*] says coach propositioned her; walter Johnson needs attitude change; Rodney taylor loud cursing outside room 123; emmanuel ivey said I am one of 3 staff he trusts; my student Kenny edwards is back [*I had taught Kenny in 9th Grade—he became a high-ranking JROTC officer*]; Jerrod hutchins called girl bitch—she liked it; Darius morris good boxer but hotheaded—wants to fight in school— going to be hard keeping him straight.

Raymond M. ran from me I caught him he was surprised; lee moorer ran from me i caught him, in hall again 10/14; demario white going to college but won't take off his do-rag—I grabbed it off his head now it's mine; Ja Ja Fitzpatrick cursed me got me mad I was going to fight him police arrested him; Chauncey (his girl Mia trying to help me keep him out of trouble) suspected of shooting up house Enis beat up [*I don't remember who "Enis" was or what "Enis beat up" means, but it somehow involved Chauncey: after Chauncey graduated I went to court on his behalf as a Team for Justice officer when he was a second-time offender suspected of selling illegal firearms and helped get him probation*] ronald tipped me gang fight on corner going to happen between Chauncey's and Keith R.'s feuding gangs Chili Boys and G.M.I.'s (Get Money Immediately) already shot Fred J. four or five times in back gats AK 47s; I will take Alwarithun Maqaribu to Optimists club luncheon; . . .

Some of the preceding hastily notated, unrelated incidents are nearly *indecipherable*—now, in retrospect more than a year later, even to *me*. (Principal Ward may be able to interpret some of them.) I share them merely to project an understanding of what we were dealing with at Finney on virtually a *minute-to-minute basis*.

Most incidents, of course, didn't get recorded in my computer. I often broke up groups of boys gambling with dice on stairwells or smoking marijuana in the lavatories. To this day, I have nearly enough confiscated dice to open my own casino, and as for the ubiquitous but *comparatively* harmless weed-smoking—well, I'll say again what I said in the original *Telford's Telescope*: were the government to legalize marijuana, tax it, and spend some of the new tax revenue on preventive health education, think of the billions of dollars it could save!

We averaged several fights per day in and around the school, with the fights often occurring simultaneously in different parts of the building, sometimes involving a group of students beating up one person. These included fights between male students, students and outsiders, staff and outsiders, parents and students, parents and other parents, parents and staff, students and administrators or teachers or security staff, and fights between *girls*—which often could be the worst.

On one occasion, I helped carry a large, semi-conscious girl into the office, beaten bloody by another equally large girl who had bashed her with a heavy combination lock. On another occasion, athletic director Andy Rio and I had hold of two students (impregnated concurrently by the same boy) who were clutching tight onto each other's hair. One girl was pulling so hard that the other girl's scalp was bleeding. We told them to let go of each other *at the count of three*, and they *did* (shades of the incident with Mickey and Ken in the Butzel Junior High boys' lavatory in 1967. For some as-yet uncharted neurological/psychological reason, having antagonists drop their blades or let go of each other's hair *at the count of three* often seems to work in such situations).

In January 2006 my baby-wife Gina threw a seventieth birthday bash for me at Sindbad's restaurant overlooking the Detroit River. (I didn't like the number "70," and at first I didn't want the party—but Gina insisted, and later I was glad she had.) Gina demonstrated the incredible classiness to invite my ex-girlfriend Eva and my ex-wife Lynn, and they both came. Gina also invited Gerrie Barclay, the premier girlfriend of my college days, and her elder sister, Greta Barclay Lipson, Ed.D. Ger and her sister Greta couldn't come—but her brilliant brother, Mel Barclay, M.D., and his brilliant wife Roslyn Barclay, Ph.D., drove in from Ann Arbor.

Wolverine Human Services chief executive officer R. E. Wollack came with his former right-hand man, Jeff Ferguson. Senator Hansen Clarke came, as did City Council President Ken Cockrel—plus some other politicians, as well as many of my Finney colleagues.

My friend and protégé john powell, who now had become the Executive Director of the Kirwan Institute for the Study of Race and Ethnicity at The Ohio State University, came up from Columbus and spoke.

My son, daughter and son-in-law, godson, stepson, infant grandson, and cousins were there. So was Rev. Nicholas Hood III, my wife's pastor at Plymouth Congregational Church of Detroit and a former councilman. So were Cliff and Barb Hatcher, and many of my other old college and high school teammates, including my best friend in high school, Hiram Badia. My U.S. teammate, the great hurdler Hayes Jones, came. So did Stan Childress, now a Downriver suburban high school principal. So did many of the old athletes I had coached and old students I had taught and counseled. So did my entire Team for Justice board, and most of the board members of the Detroit Track Old-Timers—the organization Col. Aaron Gordon and I had founded fourteen years earlier.

My old bosses John Schultz and Bill Keane came, and my Rochester administrative colleagues Greg Owens, Duane Hull, and Marv Rubin.

The courageous Craig Bryson—the former crusading *Rochester Clarion* editor—also came. Craig is now the spokesman for the Oakland County Road Commission.

My old friend and protégé Wayne Dyer couldn't make it, but he did call with his good wishes. At his request, I had recently written *Detroit Free Press* and *Michigan FrontPAGE* columns announcing the one million dollar grant Dr. Dyer had just given to Wayne State, which had publicized it hardly at all.

Students from Finney and several former students from other schools where I had taught and coached came, including Southwestern's Lamont Smith, who had matured significantly since the day in 1999 when he had jauntily announced to his classmates in a future-life-plans oral report that his fondest ambition was to become a pimp.

Gina and I talked to as many folks as we could, and neither of us got to eat any of the exotic fare we had paid for, including the tempting oysters on the half shell. Later, we counted 411 signed-in guests—most of them invited.

The lawful capacity in that upstairs room was two hundred, so it was a good thing no one called the fire marshal.

CHAPTER FIFTY-EIGHT

AN ALL-TIME GREAT MAKES HIS TRANSITION

"Quick quarter-horse Cliff will chomp at the bit and shout 'Showtime!'—and the stadium will resound! . . . Again! Again!

The 2006–07 school year marked my fourth consecutive year back at Finney after a hard but hardy hiatus of forty years. Our administrative team (Principal Al Ward called us his "A" Team) got two new and badly-needed assistant principals that year.

Kenyetta Wilbourn-Snapp was only twenty-nine years old and significantly shorter than five feet tall. When she patrolled our wild halls, she could sometimes get lost in the crowd—she looked like she was maybe one of our smaller freshman students—but she was *tough*.

Tracey Thomas, a former champion kick-boxer, was more than a foot-and-a-half taller than the tiny Kenyetta and nearly two hundred pounds heavier. One time in the hall in front of the main office, I grabbed a kid who was fighting—and Tracey collared the other one. My kid wrenched free and ran back to resume battle with his antagonist that Tracey had hold of. Tracey lifted one big leg and gave my kid a kick that sent him flying. It was a sight wondrous to behold—for a second or two, it looked like the young man had sprouted wings. He was absolutely *airborne*! When he landed in a heap with a loud *thump*, he didn't feel like fighting anymore.

Tracey moonlighted as a Detroit fireman, and my then twenty-six-year-old autistic stepson Michael just happened to be fascinated with anything having to do with firefighting. Michael has several toy fire trucks he plays with—so

I asked Tracey if Gina and I could bring Michael to the firehouse, sit him in the fire truck, and let him don a fireman's hat. Tracey kindly agreed. We also took Michael to visit my friend Hugh Gersch, a retired Detroit fire chief, and Hugh showed the appreciative Michael his badges and other artifacts from his days as a firefighter.

I was thriving in my exciting environment at Finney until one tragic day in late November when the legendary Clifford Alsworth Hatcher slumped over the wheel of his car in his driveway and died, one year—almost to the day— after his beloved thirty-five-year-old son, Martin "Marty" Hatcher, had died of a stroke. In high school, Marty had taken after his father, running a 50-second quarter-mile at Lutheran West.

Cliff Hatcher would have been in my house the next day having dinner and sipping his favorite rum and Coke and reminiscing on our many escapades again. This once-great athlete had been my mentor, teammate, friend, confidante, fellow member of various philanthropic boards, and constant companion *for fifty-two years*. I was godfather to his daughter Joy, and he had been the best man in my wedding to my first wife and had introduced me to the lovely lady who became my second and final one. When I got the call that Cliff was dead, *I* felt like dying—and a vital part of me *did* die that day.

I want to share a poem with you that Cliff liked tremendously and often asked me to read to him. I wrote it on my seventieth birthday. The poem is entitled *Again*:

> *Someday the souls of great Johnson and Jeffries will <u>war</u> again—*
> *And the Black Hope's soul will <u>soar</u> again.*
> *The souls of Jackie Britt and Scotty Telf will war—*
> *And my daddy Scotty's soul will soar.*
> *(After all, Jack the Britt was a welterweight over the hill.)*
> *Running in the outside lane,*
> *I'll race the churning, charging champion Charley Jenkins again.*
> *Quick quarter-horse Cliff will chomp at the bit and shout "<u>Showtime!</u>"—*
> *And the stadium will resound!*
> *It will <u>resound</u>!*
> *<u>Again</u>! <u>Again</u>!*
> *But my baby-wife Gina must promise*
> *That no indulged white boys*

Will sit in the front row.
Only black kids should sit there—
For they were my truest children.

The first line of the poem was a reference to the heavyweight champion-ship fight in the first decade of the twentieth century when Jack Johnson beat James J. Jeffries, the "Great White Hope." "Jackie Britt" was Jack Britton, the old ex-champ my dad knocked out in 1921 in Toledo.

Cliff and I had often daydreamed together about us racing national champion Charley Jenkins of Villanova University, who was then the world's foremost participant in the track race I have dubbed "the longest dash" (the title of my 1965 and 1971 book on the event). I did race and beat Jenkins three times in the spring and summer of 1957. However, by the fall of 1956, when the celebrated Villanova quarter-miler won the Olympic 400 in Melbourne in a scintillating 46.7 seconds, Cliff had dropped out of school after three years of winning relay races with me and our intrepid teammates all over the East and Midwest.

Sadly, the great Cliff Hatcher and I weren't teammates anymore.

The next summer, at the very moment the newspapers were headlining my European victories, Cliff's first wife, Jean—back home in Detroit—told him she was leaving him. The man whose 48.8-second quarter-mile in 1951 still stood as the fastest in Michigan high school history was trying without success to deal with depressing economic and personal problems.

Cliff slashed his wrists and was hospitalized. It was a terrible time in his life—a time I was painfully well aware of but glossed over when I did a biographical piece on him in 1994 during one of my Detroit radio broadcasts.

After he heard the program, Cliff said, "John, to tell my whole story, you needed to include the *bad, sad* stuff, too."

Well, Cliff, this time I've included the "*bad, sad* stuff"—but no one was remembering any of that bad, sad stuff when we eulogized you at your funeral, which was attended by hundreds of grieving mourners.

Regarding the reference in the poem to black kids belonging in the front row: My big, strong, handsome, blue-eyed son Steve, in whom I still take great pride, had recently sold my River House place with a water view after I had indulgingly deeded it to him so he could have a splendid permanent home free and clear. With the money he got—which was many thousands of dollars less than my former home was worth—he had paid off credit card debts he never should have acquired. At the time I wrote that poem, I was still very hurt and angry about this.

Indeed, I had written a poem for *Steve*, as well—which I had aptly entitled *For Steve*—and which I had *also* shared with Cliff (I always shared everything with Cliff):

> *I sired a son with another man's wife.*
> *The other man had him for half of his life.*
> *Now I and my son suffer conflict and strife*
> *That cuts and can stun and stab deep as a knife,*
> *But I gave him my <u>home</u> to live in, because he is my son.*
>
> *Our bonding may wane and our pain remain rife,*
> *With ongoing strain and great struggle and strife*
> *That cuts and can stun and stab deep as a knife;*
> *Yet <u>love</u> will remain for the rest of my life—*
> *So I give him my <u>heart</u> to live in, because he is my son.*

The incontrovertible fact remains, however, that my *black* kids—old and new, young and no longer young—have basically been the ones I've remained closest to and identified with the most throughout my life. They're in my spiritual *blood*—and for as long as I live, they'll be just as much in my *real physical blood* that courses through my veins.

Cliff's abrupt and shocking death caused me to contemplate my own legacy. I decided to donate my prized Jesse Owens autograph to the Charles A. Wright Museum of African-American History in Detroit. The legendary Olympian had signed a meet program for me when I was officiating at the 1967 NCAA Track Championships in Cobo Hall with my old compadres Ken Burnley, Hayes Jones, Lorenzo Wright, and Col. Aaron Z. Gordon, Ph.D., for meet promoter Don Canham —who at the time was the enterprising head track coach at the University of Michigan. I had signed a few autographs myself in my time, but Jesse's is the only autograph I ever *sought*. Earlier, when newspaper photographers had snapped me and old Detroit Lions cornerback Lem Barney cutting the ribbon for a sports exhibit at the Detroit Historical Museum on Woodward Avenue,

I had generously (and admittedly somewhat *reluctantly*) donated my All-America certificate, my United States team uniform, three of my trophies, and one of my four cases of medals to that exhibit—and permanently to the museum.

Long ago, Cliff had lost his individual trophy that he and "Bullet Billy" Smith and Jerry Catalina and I had each also won as a sprint team at the popular Livingston Relays in the field house at Denison University in Granville, Ohio, in 1956. (I'll never forget that race, because world 100-meter record holder Ira Murchison had led off against Billy and grabbed a good-sized lead for Western Michigan, and we were still fifteen yards back in second place with Ohio State in hot pursuit when Cliff got the baton on the third leg. I saw him speed behind the long spectator stands on the other side of the track—and when that tall, tawny phantasm of long-striding lightning *emerged*, he miraculously had the *lead*! He proudly handed me the baton for the anchor leg with a broad grin I'll never forget—and I sped off happily to win going away.)

Cliff had also lost his individual Penn Relays plaque that he and Ralph Williams and Ralph Carter and I had each also won that same year. When the Wayne State athletic department threw away the big bronze team plaque depicting a seated Benjamin Franklin in bas-relief with a relay team at his feet and our four names and winning time engraved on it, an old athletic equipment manager named Stan had rescued it from the trash and thoughtfully phoned me to come and get it. (The university had already thrown away near life-sized, full-length framed photos of me, "Bullet Billy," and Lorenzo Wright in our track suits with our records and titles penned in little cards at the bottom in Coach Holmes' personal hand—photos that had been on display for decades.)

I had just recently given Cliff my own individual trophy from the Livingston Relays and that bronze Penn Relays plaque mounted on varnished wood. I had also given him a framed pastel portrait he had admired that I had done of John Smith, UCLA's world-record quarter-miler of the 1970s, wearing his United States team uniform. Now with Cliff gone, I was extremely glad that I had given these things to him before he passed away. I still plan to make a copy of a beautiful meet-program picture I have of him in the starting blocks and give it to his still-grieving widow. [Note: that picture is one of the photos in this book.]

When Cliff died, the Detroit Track Old-Timers redoubled their efforts to get the new track named for him at Central High School, where he had been an All-American quarter-miler. Cliff's widow, Barbara, and their daughter,

Joy—my goddaughter—and some parishioners of their Berea Lutheran Church also tried to get that track named for him. Four high school tracks in Detroit are named for trackmen—King's for Lorenzo Wright, Mumford's for Pete Petross, Finney's for me, and Northwestern's for Henry Carr. At this writing, the fifth track hasn't been named for Cliff yet—despite Central principal Anthony Womack's promise at our 2007 DTOT dinner that he would try to make it happen. We're far from done with those efforts, though.

Also, how I wish that Cliff could have lived at least two years longer to see Barack Obama elected president!

CHAPTER FIFTY-NINE

PERTINENT, PENITENT POETRY: A KID KILLED IN SCHOOL

"James Scott entered our school alive. / James departed it un-alive."

—First two lines of a four-line memorial poem for
a young man murdered in a Finney High hallway

By January of 2007, the Finney staff's battle fatigue had become epidemic due to the students' pervasive violence and misbehavior, and due also to the frequent invasions from outsiders. Our teachers were calling in sick in *droves*, and our dedicated dean of students, Alvin Sims, was on the verge of a breakdown and had sought medical help. Since we couldn't get substitute teachers, I volunteered to sub for three hours almost every day even though I was still reeling from Cliff's death—and resultantly, I was in a dangerous mood on an almost daily basis. My contract as a curriculum coordinator precluded my ever having to sub, but our school was in crisis, and I felt a deep loyalty to Principal Alvin Ward. I was profoundly proud of the job this indomitable man was doing against daunting odds. I would have done anything for him.

I didn't just sub in English or social studies classes, either. I also subbed in science, math, physical education, business, art, and music (until the central office cut Finney's music classes).

I shared some of my poetry in the English classes. One pert poem the kids particularly liked was this one—about a long-ago race in which I was runner-up, and the reigning Olympic champion finished in third place—marking the third consecutive time that I had outrun him. The poem was entitled *The 1957 National AAU 440-yard Final—a Fifty-Year Perspective*:

> *We hadn't enough space*
> *To run a reasoned race.*
> *Eight headlong quarter-horses humored*
> *No such thing as pace.*
> *If that race could be erased*
> *And galloped once again,*
> *I'd start my homestretch run*
> *When the starter shot the gun!*

I also shared my long-ago-published poem *The Pushbutton Prayer* with them:

> *O Great God Computer,*
> *Compute me some stars.*
> *Construct me a meadow of green isobars.*
> *Present me a poem. Produce me a brother.*
> *Research me a methodological lover.*
> *Compute me a silver, moon-shimmering sea,*
> *But great God Computer, pray <u>don't</u> compute <u>me</u>.*

I told them that computers were only soulless machines, and that we mustn't become too dependent on them, for fear they might render us robot-like automatons.

I quoted a piece to them from *Julius Caesar* that I had made my Southeastern kids memorize more than forty years earlier:

> *There is a tide in the affairs of men,*
> *Which taken at the flood, leads on to fortunes;*
> *Omitted, all the voyage of their life*
> *Is bound in shallows and miseries.*

I told them that they were riding that high tide now *in their English class right here at Finney High School*, and that they had to master the language in order to *keep* riding it. "The limits of your *language*," I told them, as I had told so many students before and would tell yet many more again, "are the limits of your *world*."

I had them write short verses like these that I had shared with them, and awarded little prizes and sometimes certificates my wife Gina had waxed and sealed with the Telford "T" for being FPPP's (Finney's Potential Prize Poets).

I also taught them grammar, including how to diagram sentences on the blackboard, as I had done in so many previous classrooms.

A few students in the English classes sometimes slipped and got a little free with throwing around the common four-syllable curse word that began with "m" and ended with "r," so I told them flat-out, "That word is disrespectful to your mothers. I want you to stop that *motherfuckering* right *now!*"

"Oooo, did you hear that? Dr. Telford said 'motherfucker'!"

"You heard wrong. I didn't say 'motherfucker'—that's a *noun*—a compound noun, and also a *common* noun. As a matter of fact, it has become *so* common a noun that it's no longer even *hyphenated*. No, what I said was '*motherfuckering*.'"

I wrote the five-syllable word on the board and pointed to it.

"'Motherfuckering' is a *gerund*—which is a noun made from a *verb!*"

In my voluntary sojourns to substitute-teach, the science classes in that wing of the building were causing me particularly constant trouble. Some of the seating charts were useless or nonexistent, and students who didn't belong in certain classes would come in there to hang out with their buddies and try to cause general chaos. Being of the "old-school" mode in my disciplinary procedures and harboring a hair-trigger temper again at this low point in my life—having just lost my lifelong friend—I got into quite a few physical encounters in that wing with kids unfamiliar to me.

These kids' bad behavior, however, wasn't all their fault, because the schools hadn't taught them to *read*. Kids like this must be isolated from their better-behaved peers and placed in small, alternative, uni-sex settings with small classes, because if they're left in the traditional setting, *no one* gets taught well. Then these misbehaving kids must be afforded wraparound support—social workers trained in drug prevention and ethics-education (including sexual ethics and contraception), teachers trained in remedial reading and specifically Ebonics-antidotal traditional-grammar methodology, truant officers, and strict but caring principals who have been thoroughly battle-tested.

As I've said many times on the air and in my newspaper columns, in order to make this happen, the financial balloon must be squeezed in these troubled kids' favor. The classes of the better-behaved students left behind must then obligatorily become larger. There are additional ways to finance this plan, too: get rid of the non-mandated student testing, stop passing out free books to students, build all schools with hardier materials so they can't be easily torn apart, and decrease the administrative staff in the central office and in the schools. As my retired DPS colleague Perry Munson suggested in his excellent book *Lights Out at Northern* (Xlibris Corporation, 2008), DPS should hire one skilled community person per high school at $40,000 per annum to hand out the bus passes, etc., that are now being handed out by assistant principals making twice that salary.

As early as the 1990s, I had written that dividing DPS into four districts and making them compete against each other for students might be an additional wise move, or else banish open enrollment entirely and foster neighborhood schools again, with an emphasis on site-based management. However, when I first proposed dividing DPS into four districts, the schools still housed nearly two hundred thousand students. It now has well under one hundred thousand—and it is losing many more of them fast to charter schools, the suburbs, other states, and the streets.

Also, in the *ethics* portion of this wraparound support that I have proposed for these misbehaving kids as it relates to the curricula, it is crucial to teach these students (and *all* students) to attend to every kind of life around them—whether human or animal, old or young—with loving, open, connected hearts. This is what I tried to teach the gangs I counseled when I directed Detroit SNAP—that to beat and rob old people was wrong, and to help them was right.

Years earlier, in December 1990, when I was still the deputy superintendent in Rochester, Dr. Wayne Dyer sent me a Christmas present—a book of essays entitled *The Love of God*—in which he is anthologized along with others, including the Native American author Brooke Medicine Eagle of the Lakota tribe. Ms. Medicine Eagle writes, on page 74:

> The primary job of the native Lakota mother was to teach the child that he or she is connected with everything in the circle of life. She would take the child walking and say, "See the squirrel? That's your brother. See the tree? We are related. This is your family; these are all your family."

I tried several times to teach this Lakota concept to the Finney kids in the classes where I was substituting.

Another thing I have found to be the case in all of my urban teaching experiences is that the *girls* who tend to misbehave are far more advanced—if not *advancing*—in their sexual maneuvering than are their male counterparts. At Finney, the female students were almost always the ones making the more sophisticated sexual overtures, including a disconcertingly surprising number of earnest, albeit unsuccessful, attempts to seduce a certain septuagenarian teacher/administrator from the monogamy he was practicing faithfully for the first time in his long life. Some of their mothers made similar overtures to that same septuagenarian educator, thus clearly illustrating why their daughters were the way they were in that regard. Until the pervasive cycle of open promiscuity, teen pregnancy, and illegitimate parentage is broken in Detroit and our other great cities, urban America will continue to wallow in moral maggotry, violence, illiteracy, rampant criminality, and economic decay. One of the most immediate and productive ways to break that pervasive cycle is to isolate misbehaving teens by age and gender through the intervention process I propose here (and take away their cell phones so they can't text each other about impending fights). Only when these isolated teenagers' scholarship improves markedly and all of their tendencies to misbehave are entirely eradicated should they be allowed to return to the regular setting. There are between fifteen and twenty thousand teenagers in Detroit right now who need these kinds of corrective interventions. Thus far, despite my repeated urgings in print and on the air, the present and past Detroit Public Schools "leadership" hasn't done that and isn't doing it.

I hope, too, that President Barack H. Obama will institute a contemporary version of President Franklin D. Roosevelt's Civilian Conservation Corps of the 1930s to put people to work building their communities. [Incidental note to President Obama: President Obama, please ask your Secretary of Education to consult the *teachers in the trenches* rather than just the college professors, the central-office administrators, or the corporate purveyors of esoteric textual materials when you're trying to find the best ways to improve America's urban public schools.]

As I later wrote in a December 10–16, 2008, *Telford's Telescope* column in the *Michigan Chronicle* headlined "How to stop youth violence":

> Here in Michigan, we must offer innovative educational options
> to kids older than fifteen. By legislative decree, give every Detroit

(and Michigan) youngster age 16–18 a variety of alternative choices: work, training in skilled trades and other specialty areas, community or national service, and college. The Legislature must also adjust statewide school funding for full equitability for all districts. Re-open most of the city's closed recreation centers during afternoons, evenings, and weekends and staff them partially with volunteers. [*The city's Cannon Recreation Center attached to the Finney building is closed, and we had been trying for two years to get the schools and the city to let us use it for classes.*] The schools must ensure that all of Detroit's children know how to read and write literately. <u>Grammar-based, culture-specific instruction must be reinstituted for students with "non-standard" speaking and writing patterns.</u>

"*Grammar*-based, *culture-specific* instruction"—sound familiar? Yes? Good —now I know for sure that you've been studiously reading the academically pertinent parts of this book.

Toward the end of that column, I also outlined some processes that can cause the eventual eradication of racial segregation and the drug trade.

However, while we teachers in Detroit and other great urban centers across the country wait for all of these wonderful things hopefully to happen, we still must survive and sustain student discipline in still-savage surroundings.

Case in point: one time in the science wing, I grabbed a repeatedly insubordinate young man by his belt and collar and threw him bodily out of the classroom. He had refused to leave when I told him to get out. That same day, he called his father on his cell phone, and his father came immediately to school, examined his son, and reported that I had left choking marks on his son's throat. He said he was going to have me arrested for assaulting his son. I was summoned out of a class to the front office, where some school-district and Detroit city policemen I knew, including a DPS police officer named Robinson and my deceased elementary school buddy Earl Couch's son, Detroit Police officer Earl Couch, Jr., tried to protect me from lawsuit or arrest by practically *begging* me, in the father's presence, to apologize to him.

I said to the policemen, for the listening father's ears, "Hell *no*, I won't apologize to him—what I did to his son is what he *should* have been doing to him ten years ago. *He* should apologize to *me* and his son's *classmates* for his son's behavior—and he should apologize to *his son* for not disciplining him the way he should have when he was little. It's not too late for him to start whipping his son's behind, though—and I suggest that he start doing it *right now*."

I got away with this brand of impertinence that younger teachers couldn't have, because both the kids and the cops thought I was a little bit crazy—which maybe I was. The father never did sue me. Maybe he realized I was giving him some good advice.

Drive-by shootings are other commonplace events in Detroit, and one took the life of a young special education student who was about to graduate from Finney. The bullet that killed him had been meant for his brother. I had worked with that kid for the past two years to help him to modify his behavior, and the "vaccination" had taken. I cried when I heard he had died.

A second shooting took the life of another special education kid—an "Administrative Transfer" named Jamaal whom I had tried to salvage, but he dropped out of school. His death was an eerie replay of this prescient poem:

> *Jamaal, Grade 10, Detroit Finney High School*
>
> *Once when Jamaal got sent to me I said,*
> *"Write that you won't throw pens in class."*
> *He wrote, "I wont thow pent in class.*
> *I wont thow pent in class no moe."*
>
> *Jamaal doesn't come to school much.*
> *"It's 'cause I lost my bus card," he told me.*
>
> *"Get your butt up at six a.m. and walk the two miles.*
> *I did it—so can you."*
>
> *"You like a father to me," he said.*
>
> *"Oh, no, I'm not—if I were your father,*
> *You can bet I'd be beating your behind."*
>
> *I don't want to be his father.*
> *I don't want to have to go one dark day*
> *To a family hour for a miseducated manchild*
> *Who wont thow pent in class*
> *Ever, ever again*
> *No moe.*

From 2003 to 2007, I attended seven funerals for Finney kids, plus one for an outsider—a young man named James Scott—and it's a wonder there weren't more. James had invaded the school with some of his homies to avenge a verbal slight to his sister, who was a Finney student, and our kids had beaten and chased his friends back out the door—but James had run alone down a dead-end hall leading to the auditorium and got cornered.

Our students stomped James to death a few feet from my office on the first floor when I was up on the second floor breaking up *another* fight. They had been kicking James in the ribs and jumping on his head. Even some *girls* had kicked him. We had the whole incident on videotape. If I had been down near my office where I ought to have been when my kids started to leap up and jump down on James' head, I could have saved his life.

It took the EMS forty-five minutes to get to Finney from the other side of town due to a budgetary cutback in the number of units on the road—but for the poor kid lying on the floor, it didn't really matter any more how long it took them. One look at that kid told me he wasn't ever going to wake up. His head was crooked, his eyes were rolling back, and he was bleeding from his nose, mouth, and ears.

I spoke at James Scott's funeral, standing in for Principal Ward, who had been summoned downtown. Trying to console James' mother afterward was one of the hardest things I ever had to do.

A few weeks after James' death, I penned this poem, which I made my social studies students memorize the next year:

> *James Scott: In Memoriam*
> *James Scott entered our school alive.*
> *James departed it un-alive.*
> *Now we remember James Scott's name*
> *With deep regret and lasting shame.*

CHAPTER SIXTY

A ONE-DOLLAR OMBUDSMAN OFFER— *SPURNED*!

"Dr. Telford is a great teacher."

—*Dominick Countryman, Detroit Finney High School eleventh-grader, in a written evaluation, Winter 2007*

Two weeks before the end of the turbulent 2006–07 school year at Finney, I became afflicted with kidney stones. Not wanting to deprive my colleagues of my necessary presence in the school during those last days with the students, I gulped painkillers like candy, which was a bad mistake—my kidneys almost stopped functioning. At noon on the last day of school, I drove myself straight to the emergency entrance at St. John Riverview Hospital on East Jefferson in excruciating pain. The doctors took one look at me and sent me in an ambulance to the main hospital on Seven Mile Road, where they performed some agonizing procedures on me I won't describe. I'll just say that my wife Gina was a superb nurse, in and out of the hospital. She slept by my hospital bed for four nights.

They had left a shunt in one of my kidneys, so a few weeks later they had to repeat the procedures and remove yet another kidney stone. This time they sent me home with a catheter stuck in me that felt like a broomstick.

I had been required to take some coursework by the following June if I wanted to keep my administrative job. Being a Doctor of Education with half a century's worth of eclectic administrative and teaching experience, I resented having to *take* courses I could have just as easily *taught*, but I had planned to complete them that summer anyway. My kidneys abruptly changed those plans.

In the fall, Principal Alvin Ward advised me that he was under escalating pressure from downtown and within our own building to rotate my job to one of the other curriculum leaders, as was required by contract, so we decided that I would trade jobs with Mrs. Penny Adams, the social studies curriculum leader, and teach *her* three classes. Thus, not only had I become America's only retired assistant school superintendent *ever to return to an inner-city high school classroom* when I taught at Southwestern—now at Finney I was the *oldest teacher* in the state's *largest school district* as well!

DPS had a new superintendent now. Just before Dr. Connie Calloway was chosen by the board in a search process that had been badly botched and compromised, I had spoken with her, and when I learned she had once worked in the big-city Cleveland schools, I endorsed her on my radio show, thus: "Calloway's Cavalry is coming! Calloway's Cavalry is coming!"

Very soon after Dr. Calloway and her "Cavalry" came, she invited me to meet with her and two of her top "Cavalry officers" she had brought with her from her little Normandy (Missouri) school district. When one of her two lieutenants asked me how we determined which schools were "east-side schools" and which ones were "west-side," I knew that we were in trouble. I told them, "Well, there's this big street in the center of town called *Woodward Avenue*. . . ."

I offered Dr. Calloway my supervisory sword in her service, but my inside sources presently told me that some of the same corrupt, incompetent holdovers who had plenty of reason to fear that razor-sharp sword and had done their dirty number on me so many times before had wormed their way into her confidence and done the number on me yet *again*. Upon belatedly concluding that it had made a "mistake" hiring Dr. Calloway, the board would vote to release her on December 15, 2008, a scant year and a half after her hire. She was in the process of exposing improprieties she had begun to uncover that apparently might have compromised some board members. Had she brought me downtown, I might at least have been able to prolong her days on her job, if not save it.

Throughout the Calloway superintendency, I stubbornly continued to try to get back downtown. I interviewed for posted jobs as alumni relations coordinator and ombudsman and was advised that I had been placed on an "approved list" for both jobs. Presently, they announced that they were putting the two jobs on hold due to "budgetary concerns." This prompted me to go to a 2008 board meeting and offer to do the ombudsman job for an annual salary of one dollar, in an unsuccessful attempt to force their hand.

After all, I was setting a reasonable precedent: Dave Bing, the CEO of Detroit-based Bing Steel, would later serve as Mayor of Detroit for one dollar. Still later, the Ford Motor Car Company's Alan Mulally would vow to toil as the troubled company's CEO for that same munificent sum. (Mulally's offer to Congress incidentally came on December 4, 2008—one day after what would have been my late, great coal miner/autoworker/fighter father's 106th birthday.)

As the last living head coach to serve in the same athletic department with the legendary Will Robinson, I also asked the board to name a school for my old Pershing coaching colleague (at this writing, they haven't). *Time* magazine had just announced Will's passing at ninety-six, and I held up a copy of the magazine to show the board how universally celebrated he had been.

Further, I suggested to the board that perhaps they must think that my Finney students weren't public-school students at all, since the swimming pool at the palatial new Detroit Cass Technical High School and those Olympic-sized ones in suburban Birmingham and Grosse Pointe were functioning quite *well*, thank you—but Finney's hadn't functioned for *eight years*. I further suggested to them that if as deputy superintendent I had let that happen in any school in Rochester, they'd have called out the National Guard, the Marines, and the Royal Canadian Mounted Police—and I'd have been fired fast.

When I returned to DPS from my suburban executive jobs where it was well-known throughout the tri-county area and beyond that I had put those jobs on the line many times for the cause of racial and social justice, I had naïvely presumed that I'd be welcomed with open arms by the powers that be. After all, the Detroit powers that be were *black*—and I had been fighting for the rights of blacks all my life.

How wrong I was! I found myself dealing not with racism but *classism*—and a classism of the most virulent and elitist sort. Some classist members of this DPS board and past DPS boards and some classist members of this DPS administration and past DPS administrations were guilty of lying to my Finney public school students and their parents by trying to make them believe that they held them in as high regard as they held students at the elite Cass Tech or Renaissance high schools.

However, my kids knew better. They may have been less than literate, but this didn't mean they were stupid. When I took some Finney kids on a student exchange visit to so-near-and-yet-so-far Grosse Pointe North High School three miles away and they saw the beautiful pool there and the many other lavish accoutrements they could only dream of, you could see the hurt in their eyes. Also, the Finney football scoreboard was a hand-me-down from Grosse Pointe South High School.

Those guilty board members needed to take note of renowned Russian poet Yevgeny Aleksandrovich Yevtushenko's cautionary words:

> Telling lies to the young is wrong. . . . Forgive no error you recognize. It will repeat itself; increase. And afterwards, our pupils will not forgive in us what we forgave.

Now that I once again had my own classes to teach at Finney and my single department to lead there, I decided to concentrate on them and not take the required coursework at night that I had planned to take during the previous summer. I realized that this decision would cost me my administrative position at the end of the 2007–08 school year. Still, I had teacher tenure in DPS, I held a Michigan Secondary Permanent Teaching Certificate, and my administrators' union president—Diann Woodard—had assured me that my administrative contract guaranteed me an immediate teaching job were I to step down from my administrative post at Finney. Mark Cousins, my attorney for OSAS (Organization of School Administrators and Supervisors), corroborated this.

When teachers kept interrupting me in my classroom to help them discipline their unruly students throughout that 2007–08 school year, I knew that my decision not to take the required coursework I needed to retain my administrative rank had been the right decision. At my then-age of seventy-two (or at any age, for that matter), to teach three classes and still try to administrate in such a disruption-filled building would have been a disservice to my students. I decided that in the 2008–09 school year to come, I would only *teach*—I would administrate no longer.

In the meantime, I set about giving my students in my three social studies classes an instructional experience for them to remember long after their radical old teacher was gone to glory. Starting with the questions that my students brought with them instead of only teaching from the textbook, I revived the Inquiry Process that I had first used at Southeastern in the early 1960s. As I had done there and done in other inner-city schools, I practiced my unorthodox, humanist approach to teaching and learning, showing compassion for my students' many personal problems—and preparing them, meanwhile, to become activists in the community. I taught them about geography and global issues, and how the global issues affect local issues—and how local issues revolve in turn to impact global issues. I showed them the relationship between these subjects and my 1968 dissertation containing the original literature I had designed for black kids and my 1962 prescriptive, antidotal treatise concerning what is now called "Ebonics."

I forbade them from calling each other the "n"-word even playfully or affectionately, emphasizing to them that I wasn't about to let them call themselves something I had *fought all my life to protect blacks from being called by white bigots.* I taught them the racist etymology of that word.

Also, I stressed to them again and again that the *limits* of their *language* are the *limits* of their *world.* Even though these were social studies classes, one day per week I force-fed them a healthy and necessary dose of traditional grammar instruction, and I made them write, write, and write some more.

I bought them a classroom set of dictionaries and a set of encyclopedias and a big globe for them to have in my classroom. I wrote "Telford's Activist Army" on the inside page of all the dictionaries and encyclopedias.

I also asked them to write evaluations of my teaching for my own information—evaluations which I told them could remain anonymous if they didn't want to sign their names. Their evaluations were gratifyingly glowing (even though many of them made it very clear that they definitely didn't like being taught the grammar).

The poet Langston Hughes once wrote, "No one loves a *genius* child. / *Kill* him—and let his *soul* run wild!"

As Jonathon Kozol, the caring former elementary school teacher who wrote *Death at an Early Age*—and whom my old colleague Greg Owens called my *elementary counterpart*—said, in commenting on those lines about the "genius child" from the Hughes poem:

All these little [*at Finney, big*] rebels who begin by flaunting their distrust and adversarial abilities in front of teachers in the first month of the school year are not "genius children." But many of these children do have gifts to bring to the table if we open our ears and our hearts to them sincerely and caringly, listen to them carefully and intuitively, and grant them time to forge the subtle bond that will permit them to reveal themselves to us, and us to them.

My three classes at Finney had gifts in abundance to bring to the table, and at least *one* of them *was* a borderline genius. Now, by 2008, every single one of the students in the school was African-American, so when Barack Obama announced his presidential candidacy, I put a big picture of him on a bulletin board in my classroom and told my kids, "Barack Obama can soon be president —and now one day, so can any of *you*! Instead of planning to become Maserati Ricks or Fifty Cents or Li'l Waynes, you can aspire to become *Obamas*!"

During the Father's Day week of 2008, I wrote a *Telford's Telescope* column in the *Michigan Chronicle* headlined, "On courageous fathers, and honor-bound Obama." In it, I wrote that Americans have finally found another young leader in that rare, honor-bound Rob Roy/Sir William Wallace mode of my fighter father and grandfather in the populist, Kennedyesque person of Barack Obama.

"Let us pray," I wrote, "that Obama will become our next president. We must do everything in our power to make it happen."

I taught my kids Langston Hughes' more famous poem about the "dream deferred." I told them that Langston Hughes' dream was also Malcolm X's and Robert F. Kennedy's and Martin Luther King's and Barack H. Obama's dream— and *my* dream.

I reminded them, "This dream is *your* dream, too—and your dream will be 'deferred' now no longer!"

CHAPTER SIXTY-ONE

DR. JOHN TELFORD'S LAST ALL-AMERICAN ACTIVIST ARMY

"Your 'Activism' Army will be carried on!"

—*Dominique Harris, Social Studies student*

I enlisted the eighty-six members of my three social studies classes as soldiers now in what I knew could possibly be my *final* All-American Activist Army (AAAA). I also enlisted the kids in two English classes I taught intermittently. I put all their names on my bulletin board under the heading "Dr. Telford's All-American Activist Army"—and I sprinkled the heading with stars, as I first had done at Southeastern five decades before. I told them proudly that I had named every one of my past armies my *"All-American* Army" because their wise, wonderful old teacher had been an All-American athlete. I added that our army here at Finney—as at my previous schools in previous years—also had to be an *Activist* Army, because their sagacious septuagenarian teacher also was a *lifelong social activist*. I emphasized to them that I intended that *they* become lifelong social activists, as well.

When Dominick Countryman, Elijah Coleman, Rhonda Weaver, Janae Allen, and Tyren Johnson all asked me in total seriousness who the *general* of their All-American Activist Army was going to be, I told them, and all of my classes: "Right now, *I* am your general—but ultimately you *all* are going to become generals out in the world and form your *own* All-American Activist Armies."

They *believed* me—and I had them hanging on my every word. These were rough, rambunctious kids who were a real handful for their other teachers, but when they came into my classroom and I began to speak, they always quieted down immediately and listened raptly, as if they were awaiting <u>The Word</u>. In my room, they miraculously transformed into true students—and many, into *actual budding activists*. It was like I was back with my AAAA kids in the 1960s. My colleague Tim Gore, who often witnessed this transformation, told me that their rapt attention to every syllable I uttered sometimes seemed almost *eerie*. For me, it felt as if those four decades had just melted away and I had been transported in time back to Southeastern and Pershing and Butzel and King doing my *main thing* again.

Maybe my Finney kids paid me such close and respectful attention because they knew my age and my story—and that their track was named for me. Maybe, too, it was because throughout their past three years in the school, they had seen me pursue recalcitrant individuals with every still-swift ounce of my two hundred still-sturdy pounds and *collar* them, and they knew I had no compunction whatever about doing this to *anyone* who merited such measures.

Most of all, though, they knew that I spoke plain truth—*and that I <u>loved</u> them*.

Arlandis Lawrence, Genaro Washington, Sironte Williams, and Danjetta Driver didn't *have* to ask who their general was. They already *knew* I was going to be their general for now, and they were also already certain that *they* were going to be generals, too, very soon. Arlandis and Danjetta were my two brightest kids.

Actually, Arlandis isn't really a *kid*. For only the sixth time in my fifty-year career, I had again encountered a sixteen-year-old who was already a *man*. (Fittingly, Arlandis Lawrence looks a bit like Barack Obama.) I gave Arlandis assignments to write and books to read that I didn't give the others. I hope one day to give him a copy of *this* book, as well—or better yet, to *sell* him one!

I made my classes memorize a David Icke poem I had revised for them and had changed the personal pronoun in the poem from *You* to *I*: "*I* am the power in everyone. / *I* am the seed of the earth and sun. / *I* am the hope that won't subside. / *I* am the *turning of the tide*." I often made them recite that poem in unison, and I made them write it from memory *repeatedly* on exams.

I told them that with Barack Obama supporting them and *them* supporting *him*, the *tide of opportunity and justice for <u>all</u>* is turning now in their direction, and their activism will speed up the process.

One day a prize-winning young Detroit filmmaker named Oren Goldenberg came to my classroom. Staff at the *Michigan Citizen* newspaper had tipped him about me and Grace Boggs as being two old-time radicals he should do a piece on. He had obtained permission from downtown to enter Finney and a couple of other high schools to film a documentary, but when they learned he was interviewing *me*, they canceled their permission in a hurry. Still, during the brief time he spent with my classes, he was able to share some intriguing and educational information with them about the filmmaking process.

Sometimes at the beginning or end of a class period, before I began the day's lesson or after I had completed it, we would veer from social studies into sports, philosophy, and even quantum physics. One day I told three chronically tardy students that they should try to make time run backward so they wouldn't be late to class so often.

"*Right*, Dr. T.—too bad that's impossible."

"Actually, it's *not*," I said. "Both space and time become distorted when moving objects approach or attain the speed of light. It's possible for two light rays from a single star to travel by two different paths of different lengths and end up at the same place simultaneously—even though one of the light rays would take longer to get there."

"*Right*, Dr. T."

Some of them had already frankly told me that they wondered sometimes whether I was a bit insane, and this way-out statement of mine simply made them wonder more. The hypothetical notion of some ultra-virile cosmonaut being able to make a return trip to Earth from the far side of the cosmos to encounter some nubile great-to-the-nth-power grandmother of his and engage with her in the procreation of his own ancestor and thus fuck himself into an endless circle of existence and non-existence and existence and non-existence by cosmic remote control was too far a psychic bridge for them (and for *most* people) to cross.

However, some of them believed me; and Charlie Hudgins—who never ever said much in (or out of) class—said something that day which I'll never forget: "When I travel back in time, I'm going to go back to 1967 and kill James Earl Ray."

He said it softly and flatly, with no discernible emotion. He was looking at a picture of Martin Luther King, Jr. that I had on a front bulletin board.

Charlie had convincingly proved his activist (or anarchist) potential with this one statement, and it earned him an "A" for the day: James Earl Ray, of course, is the man who murdered the great civil-rights leader in 1968.

Varsity running back/sprinter Clay Brewer and two other soldiers in my newly-formed Finney division of my historic All-American Activist Armies performed their first actual AAAA (All-American Activist Act) when they grabbed Charlie—who had been about to put an officious school social worker in the hospital—and pulled him off the social worker. I pointed out to them that their activist act had indeed been a certifiably bonafide AAAA, and I commended them for it. The social worker had put his hands on Charlie after Charlie and the social worker had had angry words in the hall as the tardy bell rang.

After those three strapping soldiers in my eighty-six-student-plus army had forcibly pulled Charlie off the social worker, they tugged their resistant classmate through the door into my classroom, and then—with considerable difficulty—kept him away from the social worker. I came out of the lavatory next to my classroom just in time to help them (my pesky prostate had made me a few seconds late), because Charlie was vigorously trying to get loose from us so he could still go after the social worker.

The social worker wanted me or Mr. Ward to expel Charlie, but I asked him to let me resolve the problem in a different way. I promised the social worker that my way would guarantee that he would have no more trouble from Charlie. I closed my classroom door and postponed the day's lesson on the economic and societal repercussions of a drought in Kenya for a few minutes to discuss the situation between Charlie and the social worker, because this incident had provided me with a Teachable Moment.

First, I pointed out to the class that their three fellow AAAA soldiers had demonstrated the very sort of social activism I was expecting from them by preventing Charlie from maiming the social worker and saving their fellow soldier from getting expelled from school, or worse. I asked Charlie to thank them, and he did.

Then I led a discussion regarding ways in which Charlie could learn to manage his anger better in order to prevent his recurrent engagement in this kind of incident. I shared with them a few experiences that *I* had had with my *own* anger *mis*management when I was their age, and I told them that in those days I had had no fellow soldiers in an All-American Activist Army like ours to help me.

"Soldiers in our All-American Activist Army," I said to the class (mostly for Charlie's benefit), "must be able to manage their anger—and Charlie has a serious anger-management problem he needs to work on—and which *we* need to continue to *help* him work on."

Indeed, Charlie was by disposition a silent, ticking time bomb with a short fuse. He was also one of the few seniors in that eleventh-grade class, and he was slated for graduation in June. He *did* graduate—but without his classmates' *activist intervention* in that one incident, he wouldn't have.

At his prom on the *Detroit Princess* riverboat on the Detroit River, Charlie came in his elegant powder-blue tux to the table where Gina and I were sitting and spoke with us for a few minutes. It was the longest conversation I had ever had with him. I pray that now that he is out in the unforgiving world, he will be able to manage his seething rage—because despite the ascension of Barack Obama to the presidency of the United States, there remains a multiplicity of injustices out there that can still make Charlie and young black men like him very angry.

Among those injustices is the chronic, pervasive, and escalating blight in urban neighborhoods. Mackenzie High—the magnificent old school a stone's throw from our west side house—had been closed and boarded up due to a multifarious loss of DPS students. The neighborhood even in its more affluent areas like our Aviation Subdivision was deteriorating fast.

In March 2008 I had therefore hastily sold the house (already at a 60 percent loss!) and used the money as an $83,000 down payment on our big Tudor-style three-story mansion that backs up to a peaceful little no-motorboats lake in suburban Shelby Township. It was a good time to buy a home, because the housing market had absolutely nosedived. Attractive features are a three-car garage and a beautifully finished lower level with a wet bar, shower, bedroom, ample storage, and even a sauna. The lower level provides an entire suite for my stepson Michael and our frenetic little dog Bee Bee (Mindy—our big, spoiled cat—stays upstairs). The house has a lower-level rear entrance leading out onto a pillared terrace under a huge deck, right down to the lake. Some weekend mornings when I didn't have to get up at 5:30 a.m. and go to Finney, I would look out my windows and see sleek, delicate *deer* nibbling the beautifully land-scaped flora and fauna by my circular driveway or drinking from the fresh, spring-fed lake—a far cry from my Sixteenth Street beginnings where the main flora and fauna were *weeds* and the only wildlife slithering through them were *rats*.

For the remainder of the school year, I made the forty-minute drive from

Shelby Township to Finney when we weren't staying at my one remaining River House place in Detroit, where I still vote—because at this writing I still am contemplating a run for the Detroit school board someday.

Once, when driving home to Shelby Township somewhat late after work, my 2000 midnight-blue Sedan DeVille with 118,000 miles on it stalled again after having already stalled and been given a battery charge once at the school. Still in Detroit, I pulled off the freeway and managed to maintain enough momentum to ease up the exit ramp and coast to a stop in the parking lot of an abandoned office building. I called on my cell phone for a tow truck to haul my car the twenty-plus miles to Two Brothers Auto Clinic in Shelby Township.

After I had been sitting on a curb by the car for maybe forty-five minutes waiting for the truck, two young hoods in do-rags approached, baggy pants slung low. One asked, "You got any spare change?"

I sprang to my feet. "No, I don't—*you* got any?"

I mentally prepared myself to go ballistic on them when they jumped me, when the second one said, "Hey, don't you work at Finney?"

"Yes, I teach and administrate there." The second young man tugged his companion's sleeve. "Come on, let's go—this guy helped my brother." I never found out which brother it was that I'd helped, but at that moment I was mighty glad I had.

I had broken a finger in a November fight, and in May an outsider cracked two of my ribs. When Gina saw the discolored ribs, she was afraid for me to go back to Finney in the fall. My wife's persistence in prodding me not to return was much of the reason I hadn't taken the required coursework to keep my administrative job, even though I kept assuring her that I was in absolutely no danger from *in*siders.

As a matter of fact, my All-American Activist Army was literally *that*—my *army*. Indeed, I had always had my internal AAAA anywhere I had taught. Tim Gore, the six foot four teacher in my department, had played basketball at Michigan State and was moonlighting full-time as a Detroit cop. Tim confided when he visited my house in Shelby Township with his family one day in May of 2008 that Elijah Coleman, Tyren Johnson, Clay Brewer, Sironte Williams, and others among my young soldiers—some of whom he had also taught—had told him in dead seriousness that if *anyone*, outsiders or insiders, ever tried to mess with Doc, they would *kill them*.

I told Tim, "Actually, you didn't *need* to tell me that, because I already know it—I guess I'll have to avoid folks who want to mess with me in order to keep my kids out of jail!"

At the end of the 2007–08 school year, I broke the news to my students that I probably wouldn't be coming back to Finney unless I returned as a full-time teacher. I had fought my fights and run my races, I told them, and now I was passing the baton to them. Some of the girls cried, but I assured them that if I didn't get a teaching assignment there, I'd still be back to see them every two weeks *for sure* when I brought the newspapers. (I had always brought a big packet of *Michigan Chronicles* every two weeks when my column was in the papers.)

My kids—young men and women now—promised me that they would call me—and that they will never forget me.

In my Finney yearbook, *The Highlander*, Dominique Harris wrote, "Your 'Activism Army' will be carried on!"

Robert Henderson signed himself, "a future Activist."

Most momentous of all, several of them wrote in my yearbook that they are going to continue to be good AAAA soldiers forever—and all of them solemnly vowed to fulfill the mission of what may indeed perforce prove to be Dr. John Telford's last-*ever* All-American Activist Army.

CHAPTER SIXTY-TWO

FINALLY,
A *SUPERINTENDENCY*!

"Yesterday Is <u>Today</u>!"

—*More currently relevant title of the*
1966 prize poem "Yesterday Is Tomorrow"

I had intended that the preceding chapter be this book's final one, because I'd sadly surmised that my reluctant second departure from Finney High School could likely mark the close of my half-century career. In June 2008 I had been duly advised in writing that I'd been terminated for neglecting to take the required coursework to retain my administrative post at Finney but that I could submit a request to be assigned to teach that coming fall. Since my administrators' union president had told me that I was contractually entitled to first-dibs on a teaching assignment, I submitted the request and waited for my fall placement, hoping it would be at Finney. However, no assignment ever came—for Finney or for any other Detroit school.

Quixotically, in January 2009 I again offered myself as a candidate for the Detroit board to appoint as interim superintendent until it could find a permanent superintendent. Again I volunteered to serve *pro bono*, but I wasn't exactly holding my breath until I got appointed, because a majority of that board had made it frequently and abundantly clear that it wanted no part of me, for reasons I've already stated. Indeed, I remained as pessimistic as ever regarding any chance that the Detroit Public Schools' bumbling board and fearful administration would ever dare to bring me back home—as either a fellow board member to fill the slot of a member who had resigned, as the interim superintendent with or *without* salary, or in any other capacity.

Then serendipitously, fate once again intervened to give my flagging old career a new lease on life. Steve Rhoads, my now-retired Berkley compadre of the 1970's, had been coaching basketball part-time in the Madison District Public Schools with his son Craig, and he called to alert me that the Madison Board of Education had fired several recent superintendents and the job was open again. I found myself unexpectedly and excitedly accepting the board's interim offer to become the superintendent of that school district in over-whelmingly white Madison Heights, Michigan, in order to help the district shore up its sharply declining student enrollment so it could replenish its heavily debt-debilitated finances. Desperate to accrue sorely needed additional state-aid monies, this small suburban Oakland County district had opened its doors to a large influx of hundreds of African-American "open enrollment" refugees fleeing the failing Detroit Public Schools. As a result, the district's high school student population had become 40 percent African-American! I tackled my new superintendent duties quickly, excitedly, and hard.

Also, in the last week of February 2009, I briefly left my office in Madison Heights to attend yet another Finney funeral—that of a fifteen-year-old student named De'Erion Sherrors, who was tragically shot and killed by a retired Detroit police officer whom De'Erion had allegedly made the fatal mistake of attempt-ing to rob. I know that within the past several years, my mentoring hundreds of at-risk teenagers helped circumvent many similar incidents from happening in Detroit.

As the new Madison superintendent, I interceded with a judge for a Madison student from Detroit who had shot out a thousand dollars' worth of car windows in nearby Ferndale. It was my intent to continue to foster and perform those same kinds of preventive interventions for *Madison* students (if I could avoid being fired for my infinite multicultural forays which have consistently con-tinued to render me so "*controversial*"!). I also held a persuasive conversation with a very fine Madison football coach named Drake Wilkins, a black man who had nearly been fired from Madison for waiting throughout a long weekend to report a gun he had confiscated from a Detroit open-enrollment student because he hadn't been able to locate an administrator (which would have been standard procedure at Detroit Denby, where he had coached and taught previously). I persuaded him to coach the track team, too—and to bring his football players onto that team.

Several times throughout the month of March 2009, I was on TV channels 2, 4, and 7 and radio stations WWJ, WJR, etc., and in the *Detroit News* and *Detroit Free Press*, etc., pronouncing DPS' non-elite schools a vast "wasteland" and inviting many more students from those dozens of neglected schools to sojourn north to Madison Heights for a better education than they could hope to attain in their mismanaged district of residence, with its abysmal 79 percent dropout rate. It was my deliberate intention that my remarks to the media trashing DPS' inept leadership would cause a firestorm—and as I expected, my remarks did *indeed* cause a firestorm—but as I also intended, they got Madison some extensive free publicity that trumpeted the debt-ridden little district's budgetary need to attract nonresidential students. The day after my first appearance on television, more than fifty student applications from Detroit poured into Madison, representing nearly half a million dollars in potential new revenue.

In a March 18, 2009, quote in the *Detroit News*, a DPS board member stated that my "wasteland" comment was "*tasteless*." In rebuttal, I suggested that perhaps this individual's *taste* buds were housed not in his *mouth* but instead in a lower, *posterior* part of his anatomy. He has been one of the many inept officials who have presided over a once-magnificent school district that within the past five years went into its near-hopeless tailspin due to their bungling and corruption.

One Detroit high school administrator remarked in a March 20, 2009, e-mail to me, "You know that your name has been the buzz for some days now, all over the city. I'm laughing because it's funny how this board and administration don't like smelling their own mess." Ironically, former DPS board president Jimmy Womack called to tell me I had treated his ex-colleagues *too kindly* in my comments. Even more ironically, ousted DPS superintendent Connie Calloway called me at home that same day to commend me for my "courageous public comments." Also, when Dr. Calloway visited Gina and me at our little lake in May, she confided to us that practically the minute she had walked in the door at DPS she had been warned against me by administrators and board members who were fearful of my ability, and even more—of my honest outspokenness. I told her, "those administrators were the ones you should have *immediately* fired."

On the *Detroit Free Press'* website, a DPS spokesman was quoted as saying, "DPS officials are busy educating students and aren't interested in responding to Dr. Telford's 'wasteland' remark." I'm unsure which *officials* he meant— but those in the offices downtown aren't educating *anybody*. The beleaguered DPS *teachers* are still intrepidly trying to do so, though—with no meaningful support from dozens of downtown *officials* who are making six-figure salaries. Small wonder that those *officials* weren't interested in responding to my "wasteland" remark.

In my first six weeks as Madison's new superintendent, I repeatedly expressed my intent to institute measures to recruit many *more* DPS students to come to Madison Heights, in order to offer them a far better education than they were getting in Detroit, and also in order to enable me to avoid closing schools and laying off staff. Somewhat to my surprise, my widely publicized comments in that regard caused some consternation in *Madison Heights*, as well. In fact, one backward-thinking local lady told me she didn't want her daughter to have any more black schoolmates! I asked her if she'd ever want to have her daughter work for the president of the United States—a query which took her aback somewhat.

At an April 1, 2009, town hall meeting attended by hundreds of Madison Heights residents in the Madison High School auditorium, I outlined my plans to bring in more Detroit kids. I endured sustained (and expected) abuse from several attending citizens who shouted at me into whirring television cameras that they didn't want any more Detroit enrollees, and they definitely didn't want *me*.

The day after that town hall meeting, former boxing commissioner Stuart Kirschenbaum e-mailed me this message:

> John, way to kick ass and tell it like it is. Been reading and watching your coverage in Madison Whites—oops, I mean Heights. I know you'll never back down from what you believe in. That's what makes you the leader you are. Amazing (or I guess not amazing but just sad) how ignorance and emotion rule the masses. I'm proud of you.

I remained confident that I could convince the skittish president of the all-white Madison school board, some of its equally skittish membership, and those even more nervous members of the still-overwhelmingly white-resident Madison District Schools community that as old WSU shot putter Gene Pash once said, I am on the *right track*, and as the eloquent john powell has written in his *Introduction* to this book, I am on the *righteous* track.

As I had assured the residents of Rochester within the final two decades of the twentieth century, *the graduates of those predominantly white Rochester Community Schools will need to be able to function cooperatively and successfully in an increasingly non-white world in the century to come.* Now, near the end of the first decade of this twenty-first century, the graduates of the Madison District Schools are going to have to be able to do that, as well. The best way to prepare them for this cooperative functioning is to provide them with many more school-mates of diverse backgrounds.

At the ripe young age of seventy-three, I was now convinced that I had found my next educative *encore.*

CHAPTER SIXTY-THREE

ETHNOCENTRIC ECHOES FROM THE PAST

Déjà vu all over again!

Diana Dillaber Murray's first feature on me appeared in the *Oakland Press* in 1984 when I became the assistant superintendent for instruction in the Rochester Community Schools. Now—a quarter of a century later—in a March 22, 2009, article in that same newspaper that was headlined, "New Madison Heights superintendent already in hot water," Diana Dillaber Murray wrote:

> When John Telford was the assistant superintendent in the Rochester school district, his egalitarian initiatives nearly got him fired and some board members recalled, and his maverick manner hasn't changed in the eighteen years since he retired from Rochester. Only a few weeks into his Madison superintendency, his outspokenness has gotten him deep into controversy again. Telford has become the focus of Detroit print, television, and radio media since he called Detroit's educational system a "wasteland." Despite the controversy—or maybe because of it—Detroit parents are heeding his call to come to Madison schools.
>
> "They are flooding us with applications since they heard," Telford said. "I'd like to get several hundred more Detroit kids in here and hire additional staff instead of lay off staff."

Then on April 16, I authored a follow-up column in the *Detroit Free Press* that contained these excerpts:

Detroit Public School students—especially teens—need an alternative to what DPS has offered them for the past decade. Except for the "elite" schools such as Cass and Renaissance, recent DPS "leaders" haven't given high school students the good educational environment they deserve. . . .

I was a DPS student from kindergarten through twelfth grade when the district was one of America's best. Intermittently during the past half-century, I've served in DPS as a teacher and track coach in four schools, as a counselor in one, as a building administrator in three, and in two assignments as an executive director—where I clashed with top officials. From 2003 until 2008, I was a teacher and curriculum coordinator. I would love to see DPS succeed, but I don't believe that Detroit's public-school students should have to wait for that far-off day. As the new superintendent of Madison District Public Schools and a native Detroiter, I want to enroll more Motown youths in Madison, which has an open enrollment policy. We can offer them a safer and better educational experience.

Like DPS, the Madison district has a devastating budget deficit. But <u>unlike</u> DPS, (until now, with the arrival of [*gubernatorially appointed*] financial manager Robert Bobb), Madison has leaders with a coherent plan to erase our deficit and amass a surplus. Madison's teachers and administrators and the mayor of Madison Heights want our board to lift the enrollment cap [*then at 500 students*] so we can bring in more non-resident students, along with their state foundation grant money.

Several Madison Heights residents have indicated that they are upset by my statements to the media about DPS mismanagement and my wish to lift Madison's cap. A few residents are protesting that Detroit recruits would dominate Madison athletic teams, and some <u>have</u>—along with filling top academic and student leadership slots.

Incidentally, Madison's board president was one of the protesters. His nephew was probably going to lose his starting quarterback job to a more-talented "open enrollment" athlete. Another "open enrollment" student, a young superstar named Ryan Aaron, would win three events on May 19 under Coach Wilkins to lead the Madison track team to the conference title with a scintillating state-best high jump of six-foot, ten-inches after having qualified earlier for the state meet, along with *eight* of his teammates! Ryan would then follow up those victories by winning the state high jump title.

My *Free Press* column concluded:

> Sadly, lifting the cap may be the only way to save the Madison District Schools and also ensure that hundreds more DPS teens will get the good, safe education their home district should have been giving them in the first place.

At the next board meeting, the Madison board—rattled by that same persistent bunch of raucous residents—opted not to grant my request to lift the cap and enable me to bring in more Detroit students, even though I was backed by all ninety-six of the district's teachers and principals, by my central administrators, by the regional executive director of the Michigan Education Association, and even by the mayor of Madison Heights. Thus somewhat inexplicably, the board undermined my efforts to return the little district to solvency and amass a fund *surplus* as well.

By that point, my televised and broadcasted remarks regarding the lack of leadership in DPS and my intent to bring a thousand more DPS students to Madison had attracted well over a hundred new Detroit applicants, representing nearly a million dollars in potential revenue. (We still needed another $1.5 million.) At that April 20 board meeting dominated by angry residents seeking my dismissal, the board took me by surprise, declaring its intent to post my job immediately and lower the requirements for it to a master's degree with their own "favorite-son" candidate already in mind. Having thus appeased the ravening racist residents, it appeared that the board had made short shrift of my latest egalitarian *encore*.

Then it suddenly appeared that it still might *not* have. On a local television show called *Let It Rip* whereupon I appeared on April 23 against the board president's orders (and where I would again appear in May with DPS financial manager Robert Bobb and Detroit Federation of Teachers President Keith Johnson, my former Finney colleague), I told host Huel Perkins that I was considering asking state superintendent Mike Flanagan in Lansing to set the stage for a financial manager to be appointed for Madison—which had been operating in the red for *fifteen consecutive years*—if my board didn't reconsider their *non*-decision to lift the cap. Were I to have been successful in this endeavor, the board would have been disempowered like Detroit's woeful board now has been similarly neutered by a similar edict from Lansing, and I'd immediately have asked the financial manager to order me, as superintendent, to lift the cap! I would have then *un*-laid off all the teachers and principals that the board's indecision regarding lifting the cap had forced me to lay off.

The day after the show aired, my board president telephoned me at my office as I was meeting with my business manager, Scott Johnson, and asked me to "call off" my "media dogs." He said that he was tired of fighting, and he couldn't take the pressure from either me or my noisy detractors any more. He told me to just go ahead and do anything I want! Scott, who was listening raptly, looked at me with widening eyes. We almost couldn't believe what I was hearing—it seemed to be too good to be true.

On that same day, I had sent this cover letter to the board president in reference to—and along with—a letter I had drafted to send to the state superintendent:

> I feel compelled to share with you and our board the first draft of a letter from me to state superintendent Mike Flanagan asking that Lansing appoint a fiscal manager for the Madison District Public schools, due to our already dire financial condition having been exacerbated severely as a result of your failure to lift the [*open enrollment*] cap, K-12. Along with this drafted letter, I am submitting to the Madison board my request that the board a) endorse this letter prior to my signing it and sending it, <u>or</u> b) the board reconsider its non-decision regarding the cap and call an emergency meeting to authorize me to lift it so the letter needn't be sent.
>
> In order not to blindside you the way you blindsided <u>me</u> with your last-minute April 20 board agenda addition calling for a motion to post my job (with a <u>clearly</u> <u>transparent</u> reduction in qualifications to eliminate the doctoral requirement, which the board promptly passed to appease those attending residents who were screaming for my scalp), I share this drafted letter to Dr. Flanagan with you now not only for the board to consider action on "a" or "b" above, but also as a professional courtesy to advise the board that I am going to have to do this with or

without board endorsement, should the board decide again not
to act on "b," above.

Thus, things were starting to get interesting again. However, given the strength, numbers, and vehemence of the fear-fueled forces of racism that I was fighting in the Madison Heights community, I was reluctantly obliged to recognize that my superintendency there still might not become anything more than a very *brief* encore.

CHAPTER SIXTY-FOUR

AN ACCOUNT TALLIED—
A RECKONING RENDERED

"You've done yourself proud."

—Mark Twain

My reluctant realization that my Madison superintendency might become but a very *brief* administrative *encore* for me turned out to be exactly the case: On April 27, I was tipped that the board was going to dismiss me at a special meeting that night, so as my final act as superintendent, I mailed my letter to the state superintendent asking him to put the machinery in motion to get an emergency financial manager assigned to the debt-ridden school district. That night, the craven board—with but *one* courageously dissenting vote—relieved me of my superintendent powers and advised me that my services were no longer welcome in any capacity. This old racehorse was again being consigned to the stable.

I was at peace with that, because my goal as an educator has never been simply to retain a job, but rather to do what's best for the students—*all* of the students. I could have sat back and collected my six-figure salary and deprived a thousand Detroit kids of a wonderful opportunity while simultaneously allowing the Madison district to founder further financially, but that of course wouldn't have been *me*. Had I opted merely to try to survive in the Madison superintendency and neglected to do the difficult but *right* thing swiftly and boldly, it would have been a mark of professional dishonor and a grievous abrogation of my responsibility to do what was best for the district's students and staff. Conversely, under the racist circumstances facing me, it was a job wherefrom

I can take great and lasting pride in once again having gotten myself fired.

The following day, under the headline "School chief blames racism as he resigns," *Detroit Free Press* reporter Bill Laitner wrote:

> With the school board looking on and its president asking him
> to leave, Madison superintendent John Telford resigned Monday
> and blamed racism. "This board buckled to the racists in town,"
> Telford said as he left the meeting.

Had that paralyzed board permitted me to bring in a thousand more Detroit kids, re-open a closed school, and give those students a safer, better education than they were getting in their failed home district, this might perhaps have marked my *crowning professional masterpiece*. If they had empowered me to open the doors of the Madison district to those additional Detroiters, there is absolutely no doubt in my mind that I would have returned the Madison district to solvency and ultimately restored its former flowering glory.

Tragically now, if someone were to ask me today to name my life's *one greatest achievement*—my *one most memorable masterpiece*—my answer sadly and certainly couldn't be, "I gave a thousand more Detroit kids a better, safer education in Madison."

Instead, my final answer to that schematically microcosmic yet nonetheless personally *macrocosmic* question *could* (but *wouldn't*) be, "Ever since my boyhood, I battled bullies and bigotry bravely—and, as the perspicacious former Detroit mayor Dennis Archer said of me, I always defended the underdog."

Or—a *summative aggregate* of my answers—in non-chronological order— also *could* (but *wouldn't*) be:

I finally became a faithful husband at the age of sixty-eight.

In 1947, I played a technically intricate violin solo that brought down the house at a concert in the Estabrook auditorium.

In 1952, I won (and in turn, *lost*) the concertmaster chair in the Detroit Denby High School orchestra, in competition with two persistent and consistent virtuosi who later played in the Detroit Symphony Orchestra.

In 1963, I saved a woman from getting badly beaten on Belle Isle.

In 1964, I saved a fleeing teenaged car thief from getting shot and perhaps killed by an off-duty policeman.

In 1966, I penned *one perfect poem.*

In 1957, I was named to the NCAA All-America team and went undefeated at 400 meters representing America on the United States team in Europe.

Between 1953 and 2009, a *minute* handful of rare, high-quality women truly loved me, and it was my rare privilege to love each of them (singly— and confessedly, sometimes *collectively*) in return.

In 1971, I sold several of my paintings (on consignment) to the Generous Critic art gallery in Grosse Pointe, Michigan—including one near-perfect acrylic rendering of a reclining, unclothed, brown-skinned girl with dark, rich auburn hair which I wish I still *had* (the *painting*—not her *hair*).

In 1966, I was blessed to sire a sound-bodied baby boy—and seven years later, a beautiful baby girl.

In 1973, I spearheaded a successful campaign to get a badly-needed $2.7 million athletic complex built in the Berkley, Michigan schools.

In 1978, my triple alma mater (1958, 1961, and 1968) inducted me into its Athletic Hall of Fame.

Between 1977 and 1991, I helped to build dozens of exemplary education programs.

In 1977, I pulled a bleeding girl from a burning car that exploded minutes later.

In 1980, I wrote a 600-page gothic novel set in fourteenth-century Scotland entitled *The Eye in the Emerald* that I never sold but may yet market one day.

In 1991, Congregation *Shir Tikvah* of Troy, Michigan, honored me for "stamping out prejudice and bigotry."

Between 1959 and 2009, I mentored hundreds of promising students and young professionals, many who became school principals and super-intendents, attorneys, physicians, and all-star athletes—plus one Rose

Bowl-winning coach, one world-renowned activist, one world-famous writer, and at least four more former students who will one day become world-famous.

Between 1937 and 2009, I have been a loyal friend to many—and within that span of time, I gained, in turn, the friendship of scores of loyal comrades and a few truly close ones.

In 2009, the JAMM (Just Aim, Motivate, and Move) Youth Program in Pontiac and Detroit named its Celebrity Basketball Game's Most Valuable Player (MVP) Trophy for me.

In the early 1950s, I was elusive enough to outpoint three amateur boxers who later became successful professionals (and lose one very *close, hard-fought* fight to a fourth one).

Between 1952 and 2003, I was also elusive enough (and *lucky* enough) to avoid perishing at the hands of some outraged husband.

In 1965 and then in 1971, I wrote and then updated an anecdotal techniques book on the quarter-mile that was published by *Track & Field News* Press of Los Altos, California and sold out in both editions.

In 2007, I authored a "definitive dictionary" and "almanac of advice" entitled *What OLD MEN Know*, which I intend to update and sell some day.

In 1998, my direct interventions prevented two gang killings.

In the summer of 2000, I saved a man from getting beaten to death by a bunch of street thugs on Gratiot Avenue.

In December 2001, my triple alma mater named me its Distinguished Alumnus of the Year.

While serving as the Detroit Public Schools' executive director of Community Affairs, I co-authored (with the intrepid Steve Czapski) the action plan that won DPS' special education millage in 2002 (although my supervisor took credit for it).

In the spring of 2003, my much-earlier athletic and coaching accomplishments caused the Detroit Finney High School track to be named for me.

In the fall of 2003, I returned to a ravaged Finney after nearly forty years away, and I spent a fruitful five additional years there teaching, administrating, and helping to keep the place in one piece.

In 2009, I was blessed to have the venerable Harmonie Park Press—late of Detroit and now of Sterling Heights, Michigan—believe enough in my writing ability and in the marketability of this autobiography to publish and market it at its expense.

In the 1960s, I coached state high school track champions.

In the 1990s, I coached college track champions.

In the 1950s, I outran *Olympic* champions.

Nor would my answer to such a question simply be:

In 2003, this lucky old rogue married the most beautiful girl in the world.

Nor even:

Within the historic span of half a century, I taught, coached, and counseled thousands of troubled youngsters and turned many in the right direction.

No—*one* of those thirty-five answers *couldn't* and *none* of the *other thirty-four* answers *wouldn't* have been my ultimate answer to this infinitely cosmic question. Indeed, were someone to ask me today to name my life's *all-time greatest and most memorable masterpiece*, my only *possible* answer—in the more modest mode of the then-*ninety*-year-old preeminent architect Frank Lloyd Wright—would absolutely and finally have to be (*drum roll*, please). . . .
MY *NEXT* ONE!

A DREAM TO FULFILL;
A BATON TO PASS

"I have a <u>dream</u> today. . . ."

—*Rev. Martin Luther King, Jr.*

If you are a *righteous American*—and even beyond that, if you are a *conscientious steward* of our *socially and environmentally endangered planet*—this *Epilogue* is as much *for you* as it is *about* me. Dr. King's famous and familiar dream has long been the dream of all righteous Americans. With the miraculous ascension of Barack Obama to the presidency of the United States, King's glittering egalitarian dream is now on the threshold of fulfillment. Thus, this *Epilogue* really is more a second *Prologue*, because much work remains to be done if that bright dream is to be fulfilled. One thing President Obama must do immediately is get an education bill passed that will include significant money, attached to *real reform*, for inner-city schools—longer school days and years, mandated tests for prospective administrators and teachers to pass, strict anti-nepotism regulations, annual evaluations for all administrative and instructional staff, and *perhaps* even the abolition of teacher tenure.

There are youngsters in ghettos all across America who still *burn* to *learn* and realize they haven't been fully taught—kids like my Finney student Genaro Washington, who told me he longs to know as much as *I* know, which he ultimately *can*! In June 2008 Genaro asked me if he could have one of the grammar books I had used to teach him. In July, I found him a good one I had in a box at the house—and when Principal Al Ward came out to Shelby Township in

September to fish in my little lake, I gave him this grammar book to give to Genaro. (Al had brought out all of his fancy fishing gear, while my wife Gina had only a puny old pole with a little worm at the end of a hook. Gina caught a delicious twenty-two-inch bass—which I ate—and Al caught a forlorn little four-inch fishy he threw back. So much for fancy fishing gear.)

Al told me that when he gave Genaro the book, the knowledge-hungry twelfth-grader smiled a wonderful smile. He later told me that Genaro had made the honor roll for his first time ever.

Big-city urban boards and central administrations like the incompetent ones in Detroit Public Schools—where four out of five kids aren't graduating— need to stop fudging graduation figures, as DPS did by falsely asserting that one in *two* aren't graduating (which in itself would still be a disgrace). Small-city suburban boards with open enrollment programs like the one I tried to accelerate in predominantly white Madison by bringing in a thousand more black kids need to face down their resident racists and loosen up and let in more of those needy and deserving urban students. (Late in July 2009, the state superintendent advised the Madison board that he would fine them $1,500 apiece and move to have them jailed if they didn't enact my proposed reforms or submit an alternative deficit-elimination plan before August 20.)

Some of these reforms that I propound here and elsewhere throughout the book will be tough battles, often even against Democratic interest groups— and I say this as a former teachers' union representative and a staunch Democrat. Yet by the time you have read this, I believe our dynamic young president will already have set the wheels in motion for many of these things to happen. I am also confident that those responsible for managing and carrying out President Obama's education policies will have wisely scrapped the Bush administration's ridiculous, ruinous, and draconically punitive *No* [rich] *Child Left Behind* mandates, stopped all the related extraneous testing of students, and freed teachers to *teach*.

A few still-practicing politicians and school executives who were offered the opportunity to write testimonials for *A Life on the RUN* took a rain check, saying that parts of my book—and *I, personally*—are "too *controversial*" for them to comment on comfortably for the record. Such reticence renders me all the more grateful to those many intrepid souls who *did* go on record with their testaments at the beginning of this book. That reticence also serves as mute testimony supporting one of the many reasons why the book so badly needed to be written and so badly needs to be *read*—and read *widely*.

Regarding the broad extent to which *A Life on the RUN* relates solely to my activities as an *activist educator*, I can look in the mirror without flinching when I get up in the morning—and this is more than some educators who have served at or near my executive level can honestly say. In efforts to advance administratively or to keep their jobs, too many of them hide in the weeds when confronted by controversial issues, as the "*good* Germans" did during the Nazi era.

Regarding the far narrower extent to which *A Life on the RUN* relates to my half-century of engagements in often illicit and occasionally indiscriminate amorous liaisons, I have only *this* to say: Like some alcoholics painfully learn that they would be wiser and healthier to swear off alcohol, I have painfully learned that a womanizer, whether married or unmarried, would be wiser and healthier to swear off womanizing—as *I* have for the past four years. The sexologist and addiction-expert Drew Pinsky asserts that men have certain biological commonalities—that we all crave sexual diversity and are therefore impelled by that genetic impulse to endeavor to spread our seed widely and indiscriminately. Regardless of Dr. Pinsky's (incidentally *correct*) assertion, I can finally and truthfully say for the first time in my life that I adhere 100 percent to *all* of the edicts within my father's and grandfather's ancient familial Code, rather than all of them but *one*. (As the saying goes, *better late than never*.)

Now that you've run all the way with me down the long, hard, exhilarating road I set forth for you between the covers of this book, you know that throughout the course of my seven-plus tumultuous decades on the planet, I've dedicated my life and career to help bring our dream closer to reality. *Who* and *what* I have been, foremost in my life and for *most* of my life—and *why*—is perhaps best defined by a poem entitled *Salvaging My Soul*:

> *I shook the tallest tree,*
> *Pierced every secret door;*
> *Then searched the deepest sea*
> *For what I'd sought on shore.*
>
> *My task was unachieved—*
> *I searched and sought in vain,*
> *Nor pondered why I gave.*

> *But now my soul is free;*
> *No more need I explore—*
> *At last it's clear to me:*
> *To give is to restore.*
>
> *To give is to receive;*
> *To give is to regain;*
> *To give is to be saved.*

My *lifelong commitment* of *giving* myself completely to *righteous causes* and fighting fiercely for what's *right* remains a flame burning in my heart. Oakland County Intermediate School District associate superintendent Tresa Zumsteg once said of me when she was one of my Rochester principals and my egalitarian battles were burning there at their hottest, "Some ships just weren't made to remain in the harbor."

My *lifelong commitment* includes my and Gina's having hosted two "Elect-Obama" telephoning parties in Michigan's initially anti-Obama Macomb County—which county we then miraculously carried!

My *lifelong commitment* also includes ongoing involvement with my Detroit Track Old-Timers organization, and an invitation I have accepted from former boxing commissioner Stuart Kirschenbaum to serve on a committee to select membership in the nascent Michigan Boxing Hall of Fame. (I'll be sorely tempted to nominate an old pug named "Scotty" Telford and my old Denby schoolmate Robert "Ducky" Dietz, a hard-hitting 1950s middleweight. However, I *won't* nominate them—at least, not until Joe Louis, Sugar Ray Robinson, Thomas Hearns, Hilmer Kenty, Milton McCrory, Stanley Ketchell, Ad Wolgast, and other old champs get in.)

My *lifelong commitment* includes, too, my having continued to chair Team for Justice (TFJ), with Rev. Arkles Brooks—my old athlete of half a century ago—as vice-chair. In the summer of 2008, Detroit hydroplane racer Jerry Bell—an African-American—appealed to Team for Justice to help him get in the races on the river. The big-time white promoters had rejected him (ostensibly for reasons having nothing to do with his *blackness*, of course). I donned my well-worn blue-and-silver TFJ shirt, coat, and hat which were emblazoned with the silver TFJ scale-of-justice logo and took him before the City Council and then to council president Kenneth Cockrel, Jr. for help.

Cockrel made a call—and Bell and his boat were in the program.

Ken Cockrel, who as interim mayor of Detroit kindly wrote an endorsement of this book, became interim mayor when his predecessor, Kwame Kilpatrick, went to jail—so I, in turn, helped Ken by recommending my knowledgeable friend Anthony Neely to him as his speechwriter. Ken hired Anthony, who had been the magnificent Mayor Archer's press secretary and trusty spokesman (and who incidentally has pronounced this book the best memoir on Detroit he has ever read).

In addition, that *lifelong commitment* includes my continuing to write my *Telford's Telescope* column *pro bono* for the *Michigan Chronicle*, the state's largest black-owned newspaper.

"To save Dr. Truvillion is to save the children" was the headline in my column in the January 7–13, 2009, edition of the *Chronicle*.

Dr. Terry Truvillion, the charismatic principal of Henry Ford High School—a benefactress of countless troubled teens through her ministrations to them in schools and also through her philanthropic Terry L. Truvillion Foundation—had been unjustly and summarily fired. This dedicated principal appealed to me for help; I, in turn, went before the DPS board twice and appealed to them on her behalf—but my appeals were fruitless. Then I wrote two columns supporting her. This January column was my second attempt via a column to get her job back. One board member who had become more sympathetic to Terry Truvillion after reading my second column informed me that the second column had its intended effect downtown—Dr. Truvillion was rehired. (Ah, the power of the pen!)

Also in January, Keith Johnson—my esteemed former social studies teaching colleague at Finney—called me a "great man" in an e-mail to me. This touched me deeply and indeed actually humbled me for a moment—and as those who have endured my palpitating prose and poetry long enough to read this entire book have undoubtedly divined by now, I am far from being an easily-humbled man. Keith was recently elected to the presidency of the Detroit Federation of Teachers, and I, in turn, do definitely anticipate seeing *great* accomplishments from him on behalf of students and instructional staff. (Keith has also been kind enough to pronounce me a "visionary civil-rights crusader" in his endorsement of this book.)

It was also in January that I had volunteered to serve out that unfilled term of Dr. Jimmy Womack, the Detroit school board member who had resigned (to take a seat in the State Legislature), but the board predictably appointed someone else.

Encouragingly, though, my Detroit readers have often e-mailed me to tell me I should be the superintendent or be the president of the school board. On March 27, 2007, Bruce Feaster—then a top aide to State Senator Hansen Clarke—had e-mailed me, "We need Telford for Superintendent!!!!" (Yes, he actually did use four exclamation marks.) On January 5, 2009, reader Tony Wilkes e-mailed, "Dr. Telford, I have been reading your columns for several years now. I have come to the conclusion that you are the best guy in the state to lead DPS out of the muck and mud."

Despite these and similar encouragements and involvements, now that I no longer teach my Finney students or my university students or superintend in Madison, I find myself suffering from an emerging case of *encore anxiety*— which is *a sense of irrelevance often suffered by high achievers who retired from or lost prominent positions*. I do grant that I've had more than my share of *prominent positions* throughout my career. I also concede that I've had more than my share of *encores* in my life. Therefore, I realize that now in the twilight of my days I should welcome the chance to enjoy more time with my wife and family and my many friends, old, new, and newest—and I *have* spent quality time with hundreds of them throughout the past several months out here at our little lake. My visitors included Richard "Dickie" Otten, the buddy I began hanging out with on Sixteenth Street as early as 1937. They also included Ken Burnley, my colleague of four decades and my compadre of five—and our mutual mentor, the now eighty-three-year-old Pete Petross, who despite recent knee surgery, looks like he could still run his consistent old 9.6 for 100 yards. They also included George Blaney, who resumed drinking Chardonnay with me and slept over for several nights in one of our lavish guest rooms, rather than on a couch with my doggy-smelly little pooch, Bee Bee—as I did so long ago with his good old pungent Peaches. Remember the memorable Peaches, from Chapter Twenty-nine? You'll perhaps recall that Peaches was the Blaneys' *golden retriever*—my snuggly couch-mate on that snowy night when a dozen vodka-and-Kahlua-spiked Black Russians were rumbling in my resistant belly and doing the sword-dance on my hurting head.

Still, with too much *rest*, I *rust*. I'm eminently ready for yet another *encore*, because I'm not ready to "rust" just yet! I'm not talking about an encore with my *violin*, either—although my violin and I did serve as the one-fiddle, one-fiddler musical chorus last year in an adaptation of Charles Dickens' *A Christmas Carol* that was dramatized by members of the Detroit Fine Arts Society, whereto my dramatic young wife belongs.

It was the renowned architect Frank Lloyd Wright who first answered, "My *next* one!" when asked at the age of *ninety* what his greatest masterpiece was, so my same three-word response to that same hypothetical question posed in Chapter Sixty-Four—the final chapter of this book—didn't originate with me. However, my response was no less heartfelt. Even though I'm still just a growing boy of seventy-three, I must say again that I'm with old Frank on that. If you keep in contact with me through my website, www.alifeontheRUN.com, I'll try to keep you posted regarding any impending masterpiece I'm about to fashion in the near future. As for the *far* future—well, let's face it: I *am* a septuagenarian, like it or not—so perhaps you'll let me know what *you* plan to do in both the near *and* the far future to save the world for our children.

Arlandis Lawrence, my smartest Finney student—the young man who looks like Barack Obama—called me at home on January 26, 2009, to tell me he's been awarded $12,000 in scholarship money to attend the University of Michigan at Dearborn, the institution where I had first accepted and then rejected that assistant professorship in 1970 to accept the divisional directorship at MCCC. This was a wonderful but unsurprising news flash. Rhonda Weaver and Roland Brown—two more of my smartest Finney students—contacted me in May to share similar news.

Also in May, Gina and I attended Jeffrey May's wedding reception on the *Detroit Princess* river boat. Jeffrey—my brilliant journalism student at Southwestern in 1999–2000—is now a rising motivational speaker. I told him and his bride, Melissa, to come to the lake again and we'll celebrate their marriage with a fish dinner. (We have several large-mouthed bass from the lake in the freezer.) I told the Finney kids to come out and eat, too.

Another much older protégé of mine, Frank Carissimi (*fifty years* older than my recent Finney kids!), whom I had helped guide to a PSL and state of Michigan one-mile mark of 4:17.7 when I was assisting my old coach Ralph Green at Denby, also called to talk about old times. We reminisced about our sojourn of half a century ago when he just about drove me crazy reading every roadside sign from Detroit to London out loud while I was taking him with me to the Ontario championships, where I was scheduled to compete in the 400-meter dash. (This time, I was a smart enough *Samson* not to take a seductive *Delilah* with me again.) Once we were in London, Frank made all my aggravation well worth it by running the fastest 1,500-meters any teen—Canadian or American— had run all year, with a 3:55.6 (the metric equivalent of a 4:12 mile). He finished an impressive fourth in that fast international field of veteran collegiate and post-collegiate runners and earned high school All-American status. I then confronted an even more star-studded field in the eight-man 400-meter final, which included that dangerous Celtic Doppelgänger of mine—twenty-year-old Bill Crothers, my long-striding nemesis from Toronto's East York Track Club— who like me was of Scottish descent and had defeated me at 440 yards in the North American Championships in that big upset the previous year which I recounted in Chapter Seven. Crothers had now blossomed into a forty-seven-second 440 man.

The art of the quarter-mile is to encounter the tape at the threshold of unconsciousness, and I came close to *crossing* this threshold when I barely won that 400-meter title in a meet record 47.3 on the dusty London track, narrowly holding off Crothers' vaunted finishing kick to claim the coveted McGill Cup. Not surprisingly, meet officials refused at first to let the huge sterling silver cup leave Canada, but the vociferous Carissimi raised such a ruckus for the benefit of the sympathetically listening crowd that the officials hastily gave me the cup just to shut him up. I had my name, time, and the year engraved on the cup below the names of previous champions, and I sent it back the next spring all polished and shiny (and yes, young Carissimi *again* read every street sign from London to Detroit out loud on the way home).

While the races I ran in my youth against Olympians—including that record race in London—were gut-wrenchingly grueling, the many races I have run every day and night of my life to *seek and safeguard social justice* have been every bit as hard. I'm not sure how many more of those egalitarian races remain for this old racehorse to run beside all of you egalitarian readers and runners out there on the fast track. When my wife Gina took one look at my black-and-blue ribs after my altercation with the outsider at Finney in May 2008, she insisted it was time for me to pass you the baton. (Still, I had retaliated reflexively with a perfectly placed right-hand punch and then reached down to where the dazed young fellow was lying on the floor and snatched his black do-rag off his head and put it in my pocket. I wear it sometimes—it's my trophy.) Eventually, though, the old Mustang may actually have to concede that his worried young wife may be right.

Be that as it may, *plenty* of those races remain for *you* to run, with or without me. My old foes—classism, racism, and segregation—still strangle the Detroit metropolitan area and persist throughout America. A Medicare program that already was headed toward bankruptcy suffers under an even worse burden imposed on it by the recent Republican Congress, which had managed to turn a $155 billion federal surplus amassed by the Clinton administration into an astronomical federal debt by the end of the ruinous George W. Bush era.

The income gap between America's haves and have-nots—black or white—is a widening chasm. Poverty and illiteracy still poison our inner cities throughout the United States. Michigan, for example, faces a nearly insurmountable deficit and has no way now to upgrade, maintain, or even *sustain* education and social services for Detroit—its largest, poorest city—let alone its other cities. Hopefully, the debt-ridden Detroit Public Schools *and* the equally (proportionately) debt-ridden Madison Public Schools can get some of the newly-budgeted stimulus money from Washington. My state ranks last in employment and first in population loss. My hometown where I was born, raised, still vote, and still own a place on the great river—with the teeming ghetto no farther away than across the street—has (again) been named America's most dangerous city.

The nationwide drug trade proliferates. International and domestic terrorism are growing threats, as is the possibility of biochemical and nuclear war. After a generation of speculative corporate self-seekers on their obsessive chase of evanescent profiteering disproved once and for all the existence of a benignly self-corrective business cycle, the stock market is now in free fall *internationally*. Wall Street's malady is the *whole world's* sickness. We need to recognize that we are in a world without borders, with all its global implications for climate change, food, energy, health, water, land, and biodiversity.

America remains mired in two wars—one which has been a graceless war of aggression over *oil* undertaken on a deceptive premise involving non-existent "weapons of mass destruction." Thus far, that Iraq war has cost the lives of more than four thousand U.S. soldiers (including those of a disproportionate number of *black* soldiers)—plus those of more than one hundred thousand Iraqi civilians. It has also cost unthinkable amounts of your and my tax dollars, and it continues to propel our soaring national debt ever-farther into the stratosphere.

In January 2009 a black American killed his wife and five children because he had lost his job and couldn't feed them; yet some of the rapacious, mendaciously treasonous leaders of the recent Cheney/Bush administration—including the corporate-collusive Dick Cheney himself—have launched themselves upon the lucrative lecture circuit instead of being treated as unpatriotic pariahs or condemned to languish in federal prisons or on death row. Doesn't anyone else see anything terribly wrong with this picture? I understand that President Obama wants to move forward and avoid casting blame, but the *swimming pool* in the inner-city high school where I taught and administrated for the past five years hasn't worked for the past *nine*. Connect the dots! Connect the dots!

Racial segregation has been my *own* paramount and lifelong foe. My old-time Southeastern High School student john powell and I have long attacked segregation as one of the last enemies—a penultimate un-cleared hurdle—of the American civil-rights movement. This is the hurdle that most of the liberals shied away from in the 1970s and 1980s. Along with re-emergent classism and still-pervasive racism, racial segregation remains America's huge, embarrassing "elephant in the room." As a matter of fact, it's an absolute, elephantine, wooly-mammoth *mastodon*—and it's far past time for it to become just as *extinct*.

Barack Obama will most assuredly reach out to visionaries like john powell at The Ohio State University's Kirwan Institute for the Study of Race and Ethnicity and propound the great powell's proposed prototype for a form of Federated Regionalism that can ultimately eradicate that "wooly-mammoth *mastodon*" of racial segregation in our cities and suburbs. Federated Regionalism is a metropolitan model wherein the large regional authority controls access to opportunities while the smaller local authorities control issues of local identity and governmental responsiveness. Powell's visionary version is an effective way to promote racial justice. It is representative of people of color in municipalities where they are the majority, and it adds provisions for their full regional participation.

In powell's version, Federated Regionalism's prime target-projects become the majority-white suburban communities that are basically driven by majoritarian motives and therefore often behave with abject self-interest. Self-interested local control too frequently becomes *exclusionary* local control. In powell's version, more attention and funding are applied to improve urban infrastructure rather than to provide new capacity for suburban growth. Powell's is a landmark prototype that demands adoption or adaptation by every far-seeing suburban, state, and nationwide legislative leader. I pray they will have the courage to resist any majoritarian impulse and heed powell's wise counsel before schools like Detroit's continue to deteriorate and 1960s-style conflagrations explode again to ignite a real revolution in this country. In a war-burdened, economically depressed America where ill-educated millions of urban youth are increasingly volatile social dynamite, john powell's and Barack Obama's powerful egalitarian voices rise in a clarion call for social justice.

Further, we must all support President Obama's mission to develop new technologies to clean and cool our planet and reduce our dependence on foreign oil, get us out and *keep* us out of trillion-dollar wars of aggression, reform health care, and restore the Constitution and the Bill of Rights—which the recent Bush administration did its utmost to trash. We must also support President Obama in his most *sacred* mission—the mission to turn the tide of bigotry and *egalitize* America, and thus eventually the *world*.

In the meantime, always remember:

> *You* are the power in everyone;
> *You* are the seed of the earth and sun;
> *You* are the force than won't subside . . .
>
> *YOU* ARE THE *TURNING* OF THE *TIDE*!!

ACKNOWLEDGMENTS

I wish to acknowledge distinguished school reformers J. Patrick Dolan of Kansas City, Canadian guru Michael Fullan, the late Professor Ronald Edmonds of Michigan State University, and the late professor Earl Kelley of Wayne State University. Their revolutionary ideas for the progressive transformation of schools—particularly *urban* schools—significantly influenced some of the transformative thoughts I have expressed in this book. I also wish to acknowledge *Time* and *Newsweek* magazines for their many insightful and cautionary articles on educational and economic reform in the United States. I would be *personally* remiss, too, were I not to acknowledge Dr. Drew Pinsky, the celebrated addiction-expert and sexologist, for his informed and influencing views regarding relevant male behavioral (and often *counter-societal*) sexual norms and their causations.

I am deeply and eternally indebted, as well, to the late syndicated columnist Sydney Harris for inspiring a verse that is representative of his rationalist viewpoint as it impacts the frightening but also viscerally *exciting* twenty-first century voyage whereupon our species has now embarked. This verse—which I entitle *Sonnet for a Safer Sea*—takes the philosophic form of a "sonnet for *sanity*," whose rational philosophy all of you righteous reformers must urgently embrace for the sake of *homo sapiens'* very <u>survival</u>:

> *This voyage of historic humankind*
> *Is one whereon we're fated to decide*
> *If cold creations of the corporate mind*
> *Shall specify the way we'll live, or die.*

> *We cruise now with mere nautical controls*
> *Which navigate us up no harbor path:*
> *We try to steer through anti-social shoals*
> *With sextants, when we need a sociograph!*
> *We automate our elemental selves—*
> *Computerized, transistorized, yet blind . . .*
> *And thus meander toward unfathomed hells*
> *Whence it will prove impossible to find*
> *The sort of social innovations we*
> *Must seek, to sail upon a safer sea.*

In another and darker vein, I must grudgingly acknowledge the hundreds of reactionary racists and other assorted bigots and bullies whom I battled in various jobs and venues. In many of those situations I defended only *myself*. In many more, I also was morally obligated to defend *others* who were being exploited and/or unjustly persecuted. Less happily yet, I must likewise acknowledge the several Detroit Public Schools executives and board members—present and recent past—whose cronyism, incompetence, and corruption discriminatorily deposed me from or prevented my assuming or *re*-assuming numerous key administrative posts in DPS. For the most part, these were jobs for which I was, if anything, eminently *over*qualified. Those hundreds of racists and various other misanthropic miscreants caused me much mischief, and the several self-aggrandizing and paranoid DPS central office administrators and board members who rejected my services thereby tragically helped drive what could well prove to be the final nail in the coffin of a once-predominant American school district. Still, the richly ironic fact remains that *all* of them *also* helped to ignite the reformative and educative authoring of some of the fieriest chapters of this memoir.

In a far *happier* vein, I need to cite additional individuals who merit my *particular* acknowledgement. The illustrious professor john a. powell, executive director of The Ohio State University's Kirwan Institute for the Study of Race and Ethnicity, took the time from his interminable coast-to-coast schedule not only to write a testimonial for this book but also to agree to write its *Introduction*, for which I am forever beholden to him. Dr. James Jacobs, my former divisional colleague at Macomb County College (Michigan) who is the new president of that college, and Albert Lorenzo, the college's recently retired president, critiqued the first draft of the manuscript and shared their incisive insights concerning the history of the Division of Basic Education at the school—which formerly was called Macomb County *Community* College (MCCC). President Jacobs' constructive critique specifically saved me from possible lawsuits regarding this book and from perhaps unfairly offending some still-sentient folks in it, as well as helping to keep tactfully grounded what would have otherwise become several fanciful flights of a (far more) frequently high-soaring eagle—er, I mean *ego*. Dr. William G. Keane, a retired superintendent of the Intermediate School District in Oakland County, Michigan and currently the interim Dean of Oakland University's College of Education, also proofread an early draft of the manuscript and offered similarly incisive and constructive advice.

I want to express my appreciation for the painstaking proofreading of Karen Simmons and Colleen McRorie of Harmonie Park Press and my gratitude to its vice president, David Gorzelski, for suggesting several enhancements that rendered the finished product a much better and more polished book.

Also, I must specifically acknowledge *three track coaches long-gone*—Jack Rice and Ralph Green of Detroit Denby High School and the great David L. Holmes of Wayne State University, plus my late *boxing trainer*, Tom Briscoe— who all, along with my father, helped shape my life and imbued me with their indomitable spirits.

I owe immeasurable thanks, as well, to my many Detroit Public School teachers and Wayne State University professors who over the years patiently taught me to think *strategically* (sometimes) as well as *poetically* (always).

In addition, I acknowledge my deep indebtedness to the staunch friends— male and female, alive and dead—who stood by me with courage and love during the many times the bigots attacked and it appeared I would surely go down.

Further, I need to thank all the caring parents, grandparents, and guardians who entrusted their precious young charges to me in my multiple roles as teacher and administrator for lo this past fifty-one years.

Finally, I wish to express my eternal gratitude to my thousands of wonderful students from junior high through graduate school who afforded me the divine privilege of teaching, counseling, nurturing, and befriending them. There were myriad times when they taught, counseled, nurtured, and befriended their *teacher* in turn. The reader has no doubt noted that many of their pithy quotes have been interspersed lavishly at the midpoint and in the final chapters of their grateful teacher's *long*, *lurid*, sometimes *torrid*, but hopefully *illuminating* and *unforgettable* life story.

JOHN TELFORD
Doctor of Education

Detroit, Michigan
July 31, 2009

INDEX

All listed public schools (K-12) and churches are in Detroit; cities, colleges, and newspapers are in Michigan unless otherwise indicated. In deference to space, some persons mentioned in the book are not included in the Index.

ABOUT THE AUTHOR

Dr. John Telford has been called a *lightning-rod for controversy*. He retired in 1991 as the Deputy Superintendent of Schools in 98 percent white Rochester, Michigan, where Skinheads riddled his house with midnight gunfire for hiring black administrators. After retiring, he became an executive director in the Detroit Public Schools, where he clashed with inept top administrators. He served most recently as the superintendent of the Madison District Schools and was fired for recruiting hundreds of Detroit students against the wishes of white residents.

Undefeated at 400 meters in Europe as a world-ranked sprinter, Dr. Telford coached champions and authored a noted book on the quarter-mile—*The Longest Dash*. In 1978, he was inducted into the Wayne State University Athletic Hall of Fame. He has written more than a thousand newspaper columns, hosted radio shows, appeared on television, and directed human-rights agencies. A former director of the innovative and controversial Division of Basic Education at Macomb Community College and a published poet, he also taught at Wayne State and Oakland Universities.

Wayne State University named Dr. Telford its Distinguished Alumnus of the Year in 2001 for his civil rights activism. A Detroit track is named for him. Throughout the years, his students have consistently pronounced him a great teacher. Their accolades are the ones the seventy-three-year-old activist values most.

Dr. Telford lives beside the Detroit River and on a little lake in Shelby Township with his lovely wife, Gina; autistic twenty-nine-year-old stepson, Michael Morris; enthusiastic dog, Bee Bee; and pampered cat, Mindy. He has a son, Steven, forty-three; a daughter, Katherine Garrett; a son-in-law, Richard; a grandson, RJ, $3^{1}/_{2}$; and an infant granddaughter, Torrie.